ABOUT THE AUTHOR

Seymour M. Hersh has been a staff writer for *The New Yorker* and *The New York Times*. He established himself at the forefront of investigative journalism in 1970 when he was awarded a Pulitzer Prize for his exposé of the massacre in My Lai, Vietnam. Since then he has received the George Polk Award five times, the National Magazine Award for Public Interest twice, the *Los Angeles Times* Book Prize, the National Book Critics Circle Award, the George Orwell Award, and dozens of other awards.

Reporter

A Memoir

SEYMOUR M. HERSH

PENGUIN BOOKS

PENGUIN BOOKS

UK | USA | Canada | Ireland | Australia
India | New Zealand | South Africa

Penguin Books is part of the Penguin Random House group of companies
whose addresses can be found at global.penguinrandomhouse.com.

First published in the United States of America by Alfred A. Knopf,
a division of Random House LLC 2018
First published in Great Britain by Allen Lane 2018
Published in Penguin Books 2019
001

Printed and bound in Great Britain by Clays Ltd, Elcograf S.p.A.

A CIP catalogue record for this book is available from the British Library

ISBN: 978-0-141-98909-9

www.greenpenguin.co.uk

MIX
Paper from
responsible sources
FSC® C018179

Penguin Random House is committed to a
sustainable future for our business, our readers
and our planet. This book is made from Forest
Stewardship Council® certified paper.

For Elizabeth

Contents

Reporter

Introduction

I am a survivor from the golden age of journalism, when reporters for daily newspapers did not have to compete with the twenty-four-hour cable news cycle, when newspapers were flush with cash from display advertisements and want ads, and when I was free to travel anywhere, anytime, for any reason, with company credit cards. There was sufficient time for reporting on a breaking news story without having to constantly relay what was being learned on the newspaper's web page.

There were no televised panels of "experts" and journalists on cable TV who began every answer to every question with the two deadliest words in the media world—"I think." We are sodden with fake news, hyped-up and incomplete information, and false assertions delivered nonstop by our daily newspapers, our televisions, our online news agencies, our social media, and our President.

Yes, it's a mess. And there is no magic bullet, no savior in sight for the serious media. The mainstream newspapers, magazines, and television networks will continue to lay off reporters, reduce staff, and squeeze the funds available for good reporting, and especially for investigative reporting, with its high cost, unpredictable results, and its capacity for angering readers and attracting expensive lawsuits. The newspapers of today far too often rush into print with stories that are essentially little more than tips, or hints of something toxic or criminal. For lack of time, money, or skilled staff, we are besieged with "he said, she said" stories in which the reporter is little more than a parrot. I always thought it was a newspaper's mission to search out the truth and not merely to report on the dispute. Was there a war crime? The newspapers now rely on a negotiated United Nations report that comes, at best, months later to tell us. And have the media made any significant effort to explain why a UN report is not considered to be the last word by many throughout the world? Is there much critical reporting at all about the UN? Do I dare ask about the war in Yemen? Or why Donald Trump took Sudan off his travel ban list? (The leadership in Khartoum sent troops to fight in Yemen on behalf of Saudi Arabia.)

My career has been all about the importance of telling important and unwanted truths and making America a more knowledgeable place. I was not alone in making a difference; think of David Halberstam, Charley Mohr, Ward Just, Neil Sheehan, Morley Safer, and dozens of other first-rate journalists who did so much to enlighten us about the seamy side of the Vietnam War. I know it would not be possible for me to be as freewheeling in today's newspaper world as it was until a decade ago, when the money crunch began. I vividly remember the day when David Remnick, the editor of *The New Yorker*, called in 2011 to ask if I could do an interview with an important source by telephone rather than fly three thousand miles to do one in person. David, who did everything possible to support my reporting on the Abu Ghraib prison horror in 2004—he paid dearly to enable me to publish reporting pieces in three consecutive issues—made his plea to me in what I thought was a pained, embarrassed voice, almost a whisper.

Where are the tough stories today about America's continuing Special Forces operations and the never-ending political divide in the Middle East, Central America, and Africa? Abuses surely continue—war is always hell—but today's newspapers and networks simply cannot afford to keep correspondents in the field, and those that do—essentially *The New York Times*, where I worked happily for eight years in the 1970s, constantly making trouble—are not able to finance the long-term reporting that is needed to get deeply into the corruption of the military or intelligence world. As you will read herein, I spent two years before I was able to learn what I needed to report on the CIA's illegal domestic spying in the 1960s and 1970s.

I do not pretend to have an answer to the problems of our media today. Should the federal government underwrite the media, as England does with the BBC? Ask Donald Trump about that. Should there be a few national newspapers financed by the public? If so, who would be eligible to buy shares in the venture? This is clearly the time to renew the debate on how to go forward. I had believed for years that all would work out, that the failing American newspapers would be supplanted by blogs, online news collectives, and weekly newspapers that would fill in the blanks on local reporting as well as on international and national news, but, despite a few successes—VICE, BuzzFeed, Politico, and Truthout come to mind—it isn't happening; as a result, the media, like the nation, are more partisan and strident.

So, consider this memoir for what it is: an account of a guy who came from the Midwest, began his career as a copyboy for a small agency that covered crime, fires, and the courts there, and eleven years later, as a freelance reporter in Washington working for a small antiwar news agency, was sticking two fingers in the eye of a sitting president by telling about a horrific American massacre, and being rewarded for it. You do not have to tell me about the wonder, and the potential, of America. Perhaps that's why it's very painful to think I might not have accomplished what I did if I were at work in the chaotic and unstructured journalism world of today.

Of course I'm still trying.

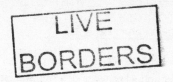

· ONE ·

Getting Started

I grew up on the South Side of Chicago knowing not a soul in the newspaper business and having little interest in the world beyond that of the nearest ballpark and playground. But I did read sports pages and, on Sunday, the comics. My parents were Jewish immigrants—my father, Isadore, from Lithuania; my mother, Dorothy, from Poland. They arrived at Ellis Island in the years immediately after World War I and somehow found their way to Chicago, where they met and married. I do not think either one, once in America, managed to get through high school—there was always a living to be made and a family to feed. Four children, two sets of twins, came: My sisters, Phyllis and Marcia, were born in 1932, five years before me and my brother, Alan. None of us fully understood what compelled our parents to leave their family and birthplace for the long boat ride to America. It was a conversation we never had, just as we never talked about my parents' lack of formal education.

We were lower-middle-class. My father owned a dry cleaning store at 4507 Indiana Avenue, in the center of what was then, and still is, a black ghetto on Chicago's South Side. It was a 7:00 a.m.–7:00 p.m. job, with deliveries often keeping him out for another hour or so. By the time Al and I were barely into our teens, we were expected to work at the store, when asked, on weekends and busy evenings during the week. My brother and I lived in fear of our dad, who had a quick temper and whose idea of a fun Sunday was to rise early, grab the two of us, drive to the store, mop the floor, and then take us to a Russian bathhouse, long gone now, on Chicago's West Side, where we would be sweated and then scrubbed down with rough birch branches. Our pleasure came afterward; there was a small pool to jump into, and fresh herring and root beer for lunch. Daddy was a man of mystery. I learned only six decades after his death that his hometown was Seduva, a farming village with a large community of Jews one hundred or so miles northwest of the capital of Vilnius. In August 1941, Seduva's Jewish population of 664, including 159 children, was marched outside the village and executed, one by one, by a German commando unit aided by Lithuanian collaborators. My father never discussed Nazi Germany or World War II. In his own way, Isadore Hersh was a Holocaust survivor as well as a Holocaust denier.

My father did tell me, however, that he had earned a few precious dollars after landing in America in the early 1920s by playing birdsongs on a violin. It was just a story until, under much duress, my brother and I began taking violin lessons on Sunday afternoons with David Moll, who was then, at the end of the war, a violinist with the Chicago Symphony. Al and I would pathetically scratch around for an hour or so, and then Moll and our father would play duets, on and on. Our father really could play but never did so outside the odd hour or so with Moll. I remember only one other of his pleasures—monthly Saturday night card games with his landsmen, fellow refugees from Seduva who, like him, were small-business men who somehow ended up in Chicago.

My father never figured out America. When Al and I were sophomores in high school, we moved from our bare apartment in what we thought was a largely Jewish community on East Forty-Seventh Street to a new housing development miles away on the far South Side. It had to have been our mother's idea. Our new home was a corner unit in a townhouse complex, replete with some new furniture inside, covered in plastic, and a small patch of grass outside. We hated it, even if it did have two bathrooms, because we were far removed from our friends and the playing fields we knew so well. Within a few days of moving in, I stood with my father as he dutifully, and very quietly—he was always quiet, until his temper flared—watered our lawn. At some point one of our new neighbors came toward us with a big smile. He was as Irish as could be, with a strong brogue. He said his name was McCarthy and welcomed us into the neighborhood. My father shook his hand and asked, very plaintively, "Do you happen to be of the Jewish faith, Mr. McCarthy?" I can still feel the mortification as I stormed into the house in utter shame. My mother must have struggled to adapt to America, too, but she found refuge, happily, I guess, in an obsession with cooking and baking. Food became her essential means of communication. Mom was, to be fair, a marvelous baker of cookies and pastry; I can still taste her apple strudel, even if I cannot remember sharing any private thoughts with her.

Dad smoked three packs of Lucky Strikes a day—I dreaded his constant coughing at night—and was diagnosed with acute lung cancer when I was barely sixteen. That kept me from smoking more than an occasional joint throughout my life. There was an unsuccessful operation, and the disease crawled along for more than a year, eventually metastasizing into brain cancer. I was the designated caretaker because I was less afraid of displeasing him and being whacked, as occasionally happened, by the leather strop he used to sharpen the straight razor with which he shaved every morning. One of my early memories is watching in awe as he sharpened and carefully shaved with the scary razor. My father remained incommunicative but was often inwardly enraged at his fate. And ours. You could sense it. He would pass away, at age forty-nine, in late July 1954, a month after my brother and I graduated from high school.

I barely made it, having slipped, along with my dad, into a funk. I had always been an aggressive learner, a self-starter who at the age of thirteen or so joined the Book-of-the-Month Club and dutifully mailed one dollar for the monthly nonfiction selection—more often than not an anticommunist diatribe written by J. Edgar Hoover or people who shared his views. But there were also delights—long histories of the Hapsburg monarchy and studies of the Roman Catholic Church and the Christian Crusades of the Middle Ages. High school, though, had become increasingly irrelevant for me as my father slowly faded away. I cut classes, ignored homework, smarted off to teachers, and in all sorts of other antisocial ways displayed acute distress that no one picked up, in school or at home.

I made a deal with Alan, who had been fascinated for years by the new science of cybernetics, led by Norbert Wiener of MIT, its guru, that he could flee Chicago for the downstate campus at the University of Illinois in Urbana-Champaign, two hours away by car. It was understood that in return he would take care of our mother after graduation. Al studied electrical engineering and made all in the family proud by going on to earn a doctorate in fluid dynamics at the University of California at Los Angeles.

I did not sulk because all along I had been much more engaged than Al in my father's cleaning store, with its constant sweatshop smell from the steam generated by a pressing machine as it pounded away on suits and coats. I wanted to make sure the struggling business survived and would keep my mother in pots and pans and flour. Talk about dislocation. It did not matter that I and two others in my high school class had scored the same highest grade on a standardized IQ test in our senior year; the other two went off to Harvard, and I had no idea what I would do, other than continuing to run a family business. My sisters had fled the family much earlier, and so it was just me, my mom, a new home I hated, and the store. Being smart was, at that moment, irrelevant. But I was my own man and made the choices I thought had to be made, even if they kept me on Indiana Avenue.

I got an early lesson in business ethics a few weeks after my father's death from Benny Rubenstein, the patriarch of the local temple in our old neighborhood—which none in our agnostic family went near, although Al and I had gone to Hebrew school there, essentially because it was adjacent to a great softball field. Benny, who survived the Holocaust, was a thin little guy in his late eighties or so with a big nose and huge tufts of white hair coming out of his ears. It was hot, a midsummer heat, and his apartment, like all others in our old neighborhood, had no air-conditioning. I was more than a little rattled about being summoned by Benny, and as I walked in, the old man flicked out his hand and caught a fly, squeezed it, and let it fall. Try it sometime. There is no way I could forget his words, said in the most Yiddish of Yiddish accents: "Seymour. You are now the man of the house, and you must take care of your mother. So let me give you some advice as a businessman. Fuck them before they fuck you!" I was nonplussed. Did he really say "fuck" two times? Was he talking about Nazis or a would-be business partner? I got out of that apartment as fast as I could.

A month later I followed the only path I had: I, a generalist who hated science but was consumed by novels and history, would go to a two-year junior college at the edge of downtown Chicago that had no admission requirement other than the ability to pay a forty-five-dollar semester fee for a locker. The school, known as Navy Pier, was opened by the University of Illinois immediately after the war in a former navy training base that jutted more than half a mile into Lake Michigan. It was meant to accommodate returning veterans with little money who were desperate for education. After two years, students had to transfer to the main campus at Urbana-Champaign to get their degree.

My weekday schedule called for me to open the store at seven o'clock and then, when help arrived, to drive a few miles north to the school to attend classes. I remember walking along a dim central corridor linked to dank wooden classrooms that had initially been used for teaching navigation and other skills to men going off to war. I especially hated the compulsory gym classes, which required all male students to run, or try to run, a quarter mile daily under one minute. I knew no one at the school and made no friends there. It was just driving, going to classes, running around a track, and driving back to the store.

And yet my life was changed there—perhaps salvaged—by an intervention that I managed to repress for three decades. Flash forward to 1983, in the months after I published *The Price of Power*, a very critical look at the White House career of Henry Kissinger. I was working in Washington, D.C., happily married with three children, and my days at Navy Pier had evaporated from my memory bank. The book made waves, lots of them, pro and con, and generated a flood of letters. One, carefully typed, was from a University of Illinois professor named Bernard Kogan who introduced himself by saying that he had been a recently frocked Ph.D. in English from the University of Chicago who, in the fall of 1954, was teaching a modern literature course at Navy Pier. "Dear Mr. Hersh," his letter began. "I am sure you do not remember me." I did not, even after he explained his reason for writing. "I intervened with you in a way I have only done two times in my career. In one case it was on behalf of a young man who became a surgeon and has saved many lives. The other intervention was with you. I am proud of both of you." I had no idea what the guy was talking about. And then, as I reread the letter, memory flooded back with a jolt, as did tears. It was three decades earlier and class had just ended. I was trying to hide in a back row, as always, and scrambling toward the door when Kogan called out my name and asked me to come talk to him. Total anxiety. Had I fucked up? I walked up and the first thing he said was "What are you doing here?"

"What are you doing here?" I remembered understanding exactly what he meant. It was a question I'd been asking myself for weeks. In response I mumbled something about my father dying and being left with no choice but to run the family business. I did not remember more until the editing of this memoir: Then I recalled that a week earlier I had turned in an essay comparing a novel by the British writer Somerset Maugham with a contemporary American work, perhaps an F. Scott Fitzgerald novel, and Kogan returned the paper to me marked A with a lot of kind comments scribbled on it. Kogan stunned me by asking if I would meet him at the University of Chicago admissions office as soon as possible. I did, took the entrance test given to all candidates that day, or soon after, was accepted, and immediately transferred, as the fall semester had just begun.

I was at home there, with its focus on critical thinking and its core curriculum that relied not on textbooks but on original works of scholars and theoreticians. Most important, the final grade for many of the courses was based solely on a four- to six-hour written test. I could always write—say exactly what I wanted to say in one take—and that ability got me through college with better grades than I perhaps deserved.

As for the wonderful Dr. Kogan, within a few weeks or so of receiving his letter, I flew to Chicago to meet with him and give a talk, at his request, before the Chicago chapter of the Phi Beta Kappa academic honors society, which he had founded in the late 1970s. I also made it a point from then on to be as available as possible for lectures or classroom discussions for those teachers in the Washington area who had questions about America's foreign policy, whether in college or high school. Bernard Kogan and I had our last exchange of letters in 1998, when he told me he was ill. In late 1997, he had written, with an obvious sense of satisfaction, "One thing is crystal clear, Seymour, that you're not now the fairly quiet young man whom I took aside and counseled outside the classroom one afternoon in the '50s." Thank you, Dr. Kogan.

My college days at the University of Chicago were exciting and fun. The university had more than its share of oddballs, many of them brilliant and iconoclastic, to be sure. I was not a Maoist, or a Platonist, or a Socratic, but I obviously was a fellow oddball, because I mixed education with continuing to run the family cleaning store and still sharing the townhouse with my mother. Nonetheless, I found time to study, play a year or two of varsity baseball, join a fraternity, try to figure out girls, and grow up. My mother, to her credit, had become more involved in the day-to-day running of the store, which was on a glide path steadily going down but still producing enough income to keep us afloat. I had nothing to do with journalism, other than learning to do the daily *New York Times* crossword, looking at headlines, and worrying about Ike and Nikita and the bomb. By 1958, with graduation for me and Alan approaching, freedom beckoned. Al, faithfully living up to the commitment he had made, took an engineering job in San Diego, moved there with his wife, and arranged a nearby apartment for our mother. The cleaning store was sold, for little money, to an employee. I moved into a twelve-dollar-a-week basement room in Hyde Park, the South Side neighborhood of the university, with a bathroom down the hall. It was glorious.

With my degree in English, but with no honors, for the next few months I couldn't find a decent job. I was most interested in the Xerox Corporation, which was then a year away from marketing the first commercial copying machine. I don't remember who gave me the heads-up about the company, but by the end of summer it was clear the company was not interested. One of my good friends in college was David Currie, a fellow baseball player whose father, Brainerd, was a leading legal scholar and professor at the University of Chicago Law School. He also loved baseball and spent hours hitting fly balls to his son and me.

David had gone off to Harvard Law School the year before; he clerked for Supreme Court justice Felix Frankfurter and went on to spend more than four decades teaching at the Chicago Law School. When I went to see his father and explained that, late in the summer as it was, I wanted to be admitted to the U of C Law School, Professor Currie got it done within a few days. He, like Bernard Kogan, saw more in me at that time than I saw in myself.

I got through a few quarters with reasonable grades, but found the law boring, and felt the same way about law school, with its emphasis on reading cases and memorizing them. I had pretty much disappeared by the end of the year and was kicked out of school by the dean, Edward Levi (who would reenter my life a decade later). I was far from troubled, because I knew the dean had done the right thing. My only regret was that Brainerd died in 1965 and did not live to see me make my mark in another field.

The next few months remain a blur. I thought about business school and went to a few classes. Nope. I had worked part-time while in law school selling beer and whiskey at a Walgreens drugstore in suburban Evergreen Park, in the far reaches of southeast Chicago, and began doing the same full-time at a Walgreens in Hyde Park. One evening two Chicago writers I admired greatly, Saul Bellow and Richard Stern, came in to buy some booze. Stern, whose seminar on writing fiction I had taken while in college—he personally picked the students— shamed me by essentially asking, as had Kogan, what are you doing here?

It was in a what-to-do? mood that, while having a beer at a neighborhood bar, I ran into a guy whom I had met but could not place. His name was Peter Lacey, and he reminded me that he had tried to pick up my date a year or so earlier at a party. (Such thievery was known in Hyde Park as bird-dogging.) We shared a laugh and began talking over a few beers. What was I doing? Selling whiskey. Peter, in turn, told me he was now working for *Time* magazine, or wanted to work there, but had begun his career in journalism as a cub reporter for the City News Bureau (CNB) of Chicago. City News, as I subsequently learned, had been set up at the turn of the century by the Chicago newspapers to field reporters who would cover the city's courts and police headquarters, sparing money and staff for the big boys. The bureau's focus was on street crime—of which there was plenty in Chicago—and its reporting served as a tip sheet for the big dailies; the bureau was also a source of young, ambitious reporters. City News had been made famous, briefly, by *The Front Page*, the perennial hit play—later a movie—written by Ben Hecht and Charles MacArthur.

It sounded like fun, especially because Lacey had also told me that City News had two recruiting vehicles for its constantly changing reporting staff: Half came from Northwestern University's famed Medill School of Journalism, and the other half came from those with college degrees who applied. I have no idea today if this was so, but it was what I believed at the time. So I went to the City News Bureau's office downtown and filled out an application. No references were sought and I gave none. I was told by a copyboy that I would be called when my name came up. A few months later I changed apartments, without giving a thought to the fact that City News now had an out-of-date phone number for me. A few more months went by, and I continued to sell whiskey, shamefully, and continued, without shame, to enjoy my freedom—a freedom I had not known since my father became ill. I spent my days reading the moderns and the not so moderns—William Styron, Norman Mailer, Philip Roth, Nelson Algren, James Farrell—and keeping a journal with all of the words I did not know, such as "amanuensis" and "sobriquet." My favorite novel for a long time was Saul Bellow's famed *The Adventures of Augie March*, about a Chicago boy, like me, who was not making it.

One Friday night, after work, I was invited to a poker game at the apartment I had recently left, which was now inhabited by a group of graduate students who knew, as I did not, how to play poker. I was busted by two or three in the morning and decided to crash on a couch in the dingy living room I knew well. The next morning, just after nine o'clock—I was dead asleep—the phone rang. I answered it. It was an editor named Ryberg at City News. He was looking for Hersh. I confessed. He asked if I still wanted a job as a cub reporter, pay thirty-five dollars a week, and, if so, could I start immediately. I could. Weeks later, as I was becoming more and more interested in the news business, I watched Walter Ryberg, the day city editor who spent five decades at

City News, seek out a new reporter. He picked up the stack of applications and began dialing. If there was no answer, or the applicant no longer lived there, the application was shoved to the bottom of the pile. My newspaper career began because of a poker game at which I lost all the money I had.

TWO

City News

My first assignment at City News was humbling. I was assigned, as a copyboy, to the evening shift, from five o'clock on, and the demands on me were moronic. My most important task was to speedily churn out scores of copies of dispatches as they were produced. The stories, once edited, were typed onto a waxed-paper stencil that I would wrap around the drum of the office mimeograph machine. I would then begin cranking like hell. The copies I produced were routed into pneumatic tubes and sent flying to the bureau's newspaper, radio, and television clients. It could be madness if there was big news—a double murder or a long-awaited jury verdict in a major criminal trial—and I would invariably be suffused by the end of my shift with the blue ink that I had to feed into the machine.

My other basic chore was even more inane. I could not finish my shift without doing a detailed scrubbing, with special soap, of the desk of Larry Mulay, the early morning editor who had been at City News since the days of John Dillinger and mob shoot-outs in the streets. I could have won three Pulitzer Prizes the night before and still be shown the door if Mulay's desk did not pass his fastidious white-glove inspection the next morning. He would put on the gloves and run his fingers all over the desk, looking for signs that there was a copyboy who was not going to make it. An even more odious task came on Friday nights, when City News was responsible for forwarding the area's high school basketball scores to all of its clients. I spent hours on the telephone recording scores for the bureau's one-man sports desk, whose sullen editor took his miserable job far too seriously, as I would later learn.

Nonetheless, I was smitten. Most of the editors and reporters were cynics and wise to what can only be described as the Chicago way. The cops were on the take, and the mob ran the city. The City News reporters, with rare exception, ignored the corruption and, in return, were given access to crime scenes and allowed to park anywhere they wished as long as they displayed a press card on the dashboard. Chicago's Outer Drive, its main south-to-north highway, was famously depicted by comedian Mort Sahl as the last outpost of collective bargaining. The bars stayed open after hours, and the cops got more free drinks than reporters did. Lenny Bruce was doing his thing a few blocks away at Mister Kelly's nightclub on Rush Street, and Miles Davis, John Coltrane, and Thelonious Monk could be heard, over a beer, at the Sutherland Lounge on the South Side. The ambitious young reporters working the courthouses and police beats understood their mission was to live within the system and somehow help make the city work. The City News street reporters were, so I thought, the ultimate citizen cynics—wise guys full of badinage and constantly mocking all (especially a new copyboy). They lived totally in the moment. I, who spent so much of my life feeling as if I had little control of anything, was dazzled.

My eagerness to get on with it—to escape from desk cleaning and mimeographing and move out onto the streets—was annoying to the editors, especially to Bob Billings, the night editor, my night editor, at City News. Most of the reporters worked outside the main office, with its shabby desks, dirty floors, old typewriters, and marginal lighting. There was a copyboy, an editor, and three or four rewrite men; the important stories were phoned in to the office by the reporters scattered through the city, and put together by rewrite. The life-and-death rule was check it out before calling it in. One of the senior editors, Arnold Dornfeld, who lived outside the city and sometimes wore muddy boots that, to my horror, he enjoyed parking on Larry Mulay's desk, had famously told a reporter, "If your mother says she loves you, check it out." The guys on the street who did not get their facts straight or were consistently being out-reported did not last long. One of my jobs as a copyboy was to read all Chicago dailies for stories or details that our reporters missed, and paste copies of their better stories on the office bulletin board. The notices were known as "scoop sheets," for obvious reasons, and I confess to being delighted to scoop away. There was a constant shuffling of reporters and I wanted in.

There was lots of time for chitchat, which was good, but Billings was almost constantly on my case—partially out of boredom and partially because I was a good foil. I initially saw Bob, a big guy with a square jaw, as a cliché in action. He had played football at the University of Illinois, talked tough, and was dating, as all of us somehow knew, the estranged wife of a Chicago police captain—an awesome feat that, given the reputation of the cops, put him at peril of his life. Bob, then in his late twenties, repeatedly made it clear to me that he was totally incompatible with a punk Jew from the University of Chicago who could not get sandwich orders straight and churned out blurry copies on the mimeograph. But I had begun reading the four Chicago newspapers daily, as well as *The New York Times*, and would occasionally point out information therein that our reporters did not have. I also always had a book, and Bob invariably wanted to know what I was reading. He would then loudly pronounce that the book, especially if it was a novel, was not going to help make me a good reporter. It wasn't difficult to figure out that Billings was well read, far brighter and more open than he wanted others to see.

His interest in me provoked torture, too. One insanely miserable night in Chicago—heavy snow, a vicious wind off Lake Michigan, temperature well below zero—there was a police report of a routine fire in a manhole a few blocks from the office. I jumped when Bob asked if I wanted a reporting assignment—my first—outside the office. Cover the fire, he said. I dressed as warmly as I could and eagerly dashed to the scene of the crime, showed the deputy fire chief in charge my press card, and, taking out a notepad, asked, "What's up?" The chief was mystified. It was just a fire in a manhole. No one was hurt. There was no story. Get the hell out of here, he told me. I returned to the office and reported the nonstory to Billings. What was the name of the fire chief? I didn't know. Get out there and get it, he said. I did so. Write it up, said Bob. And so I did, treating the manhole fire with dignity and extensively quoting the deputy fire chief. Billings edited the story and had me run copies off on the mimeograph—all of which he trashed, as I knew he would.

A few weeks later my days as a copyboy were over. I was initially assigned as the overnight reporter at the central police headquarters just south of downtown, a promotion that clearly emanated from Billings. Over the next few months, I would learn the basics, both good and bad, of my newfound profession while always keeping the faith.

Lesson one came within a few weeks. A squawk on the police radio well before daylight said there were "officers down"—a double shooting on Roosevelt Road, a main thoroughfare just south of downtown. I had a ten-year-old Studebaker that needed a lot of care in the winter— four hours in the cold was more than enough to freeze the battery, and I spent night after night having to run the car every four hours, whether at home or at police headquarters—but luckily it was ready to go. I sped the mile or so to the scene.

What a scene. My police pass got me inside a marked-off perimeter, and someone told me the victims were Feds, two postal inspectors. An unmarked four-door sedan was crumpled up against a light pole. Bullet holes were all over the windows and doors. Two men were inside, heads back, with blood all over. I had only seen one dead man in my life—my father in his coffin before burial—but these two were goners. A very angry Chicago police sergeant was in charge, and I approached him, chirping out, "City News." He said nothing. I asked if the victims were dead. The cop grabbed me by my jacket and shoved me, hard, up against a squad car. "Not unless they're pronounced," adding "you asshole," or "you fuck," or "you shithead." He meant pronounced dead by a police coroner. No coroner was on the scene yet. What to do? I had a scoop, of sorts, because no other reporter had yet arrived. Should I dash to a pay phone and call it in? I was sure my mother loved me; did I need to check it out?

So I waited. The coroner came and made the foregone pronouncement. I then called it in, describing the scene to a rewrite guy and explaining that the names of the two agents—obviously undercover cops, because they were wearing street clothes—were not immediately available. I stayed away from the sergeant, but the coroner was nice.

The lesson? Being first is not nearly as important as being right, and being careful, even if it did not matter in the case at hand. That was in late 1959. The mistakes I made over the next five or so decades—and we all make them—would have been avoided if I always kept in mind what the sergeant had said about waiting for an official pronouncement.

The second lesson came a few weeks later, while on temporary night assignment for a week or two at police headquarters in Hyde Park, near the university. The process had quickly become familiar: hang around with other reporters; ingratiate yourself with the desk sergeant; buy him all the coffee he wants; help him, if he asks, with last week's Sunday *New York Times* crossword puzzle; and wait for the radio to sound off. Late at night comes a report of a deadly fire in the black ghetto a few miles to the west, with many victims. Off I go.

A shabby wooden frame house, twenty or so blocks north of my dad's cleaning store, was a pile of embers by the time I arrived. A cluster of bodies, wrapped in white sheeting, was lying in perfect order on a small lawn. They were wrapped by size—daddy bear, mommy bear, and three or four little bears. I was horrified. A distressed fire chief—or was it a cop?—told me that the best guess was that a father had gone berserk and set fire to the home, killing his wife and children, if they were his wife and children. I asked a lot of questions, but essentially got nowhere, though someone—perhaps a neighbor—gave me the names of those thought to be the dead, and some details about the family, if that was the family lying under the sheets.

What a story, I thought, but I knew how much I didn't know. Still, I had to get to a pay phone and dictate what little I knew to rewrite. It was, I thought, a story that could end up on the front page. As I was yapping away, Mr. Dornfeld, he of the sometimes muddy boots, cut in on the call. There are traumatic events we remember all of our life, and I remember every word he said: "Ah, my good, dear, energetic Mr. Hersh. Do the, alas, poor, unfortunate victims happen to be of the Negro persuasion?" I said yes. He said, "Cheap it out." That meant that my City News dispatch would report the following, give or take a phrase: "Five Negroes died in a fire last night on the Southwest Side." It might also have included an address.

I thought, having worked for years in a family store in a black area, that I knew something about racism. Dornfeld taught me that I had a lot to learn.

There was one final lesson to learn just before I would go off for compulsory army training, after only seven or so months on the job at City News. It was my shameful, but unavoidable, involvement in what we now call self-censorship. I was back on overnight duty at the central police headquarters when two cops called in to report that a robbery suspect had been shot trying to avoid arrest. The cops who had done the shooting were driving in to make a report. Always ambitious, and always curious, I raced down to the basement parking lot in the hope of getting some firsthand quotes before calling in the story. The driver—white, very Irish, and beefy, like far too many Chicago cops then—obviously did not see me as he parked the car. As he climbed out, a fellow cop, who clearly had heard the same radio report I had, shouted something like "So the guy tried to run on you?" The driver said, "Naw. I told the nigger to beat it and then plugged him."

I got the hell out of there, without being seen, called the bureau, and asked for the editor on duty. (It was not Billings.) What to do? The editor urged me to do nothing. It would be my word versus that of all the cops involved, and all would accuse me of lying. The message was clear: I did not have a story. But of course I did. So I waited a few days and then asked for and got a copy of the coroner's report. The victim had been shot in the back. I took a copy of the report to an editor. He wasn't interested. No one was interested. I had no proof that a felony murder had been committed other than what the killer himself had said, and he, of course, would deny it.

So I left the story alone. I did not try to find and interview the cop who bragged about doing the shooting, nor did I seek out his partner. Nor did I raise hell at City News. I shuffled off to six months of army training, full of despair at my weakness and the weakness of a profession that dealt so easily with compromise and self-censorship. I've hated both practices ever since while more than once having gone along with looking the other way. I had found my calling and learned, very quickly, that it wasn't perfect. Neither was I.

THREE

Interludes

My six months as a grunt in the U.S. Army was not a transformative experience. I went through basic training in the summer heat of 1960 at Fort Leonard Wood, Missouri, a forlorn base in the foothills of the Ozark Mountains 150 miles southwest of St. Louis. I did get in great physical shape marching back and forth for hours and doing hundreds of push-ups and jumping jacks daily. I also learned how to fire a rifle and take it apart and reassemble it while blindfolded. There was more to learn: how to force showers—we called them GI showers—upon those poorly educated country boys in my unit who refused to wash their uniforms, and themselves, after long days in the brutal heat of a firing range. There were a few good times, too, bolstered by the relaxing power of the country moonshine that was usually available for purchase outside the base gates.

After basic training, my brief stint at City News got me assigned to the headquarters of the First Army Division at Fort Riley, Kansas, as a journalist. Given the alternatives—such as more combat training—it seemed to me an elite posting. My first morning there was a stunner. Reveille was before 6:00 a.m., and while I was brushing my teeth, a couple of GIs, disheveled and reeking of booze, rushed into the large bathroom in the basement of division headquarters. They were the playboys of the company. Asked why they were so late, one explained that they had driven from Topeka after a night on the town with some women who had cost them a large chunk of money. Someone asked where they got the cash. The soldier answered, with no hesitation, that he and his pals initially had gone to a bar in "T-town"—Topeka—known to be frequented by gay men and gave enough blow jobs to finance their later partying. At first I thought they had to be kidding but was assured later that they were not. I still wonder. Brave new world for this kid, who still had a lot of growing up to do.

Fortunately, the GIs I worked with in the division's office of public information were much less quixotic, and my four months there introduced me to a few experts on army bureaucracy—a relentless machine that eliminated variation and randomness, just as basic training was designed to eliminate individuality. Nine years later, while desperately searching for army lieutenant William L. Calley Jr., the officer initially singled out as the mass killer of My Lai, I learned he had been hidden away at an army base in Georgia. I knew that if I kept on looking at the base, I would find him, because someplace, somewhere there, Calley would be listed by name.

At the end of 1960, I was freed from active duty and went back to Chicago, eager to return to City News. I became the first reporter there in years, perhaps forever, as someone told me, to not be offered a job after military service. I deserved the shaming, for I had decided on my last day of work to pay back the sports editor at City News for the many Friday nights on which I had transcribed hundreds of thousands, so it seemed, of high school basketball scores. I purchased a number of British and Irish newspapers and clipped out dozens of stories dealing with obscure sports for Americans, such as rugby, curling, and cricket, and pinned them to a scoop sheet on the office bulletin board—just as I had done as a copyboy with missed stories by beat reporters. I guess at the time I thought accusing the sports editor of gross dereliction of duty was funny, but I knew, even then, that it was vindictive, unnecessarily so. He cared about his work as much as I did. So I got what I deserved.

Because I was without a job, and without any money, my sister Phyllis, now married with children, let me crash in the basement of her home as I began searching for a new job. I tried the Chicago dailies, and several radio networks, without success. After a few months, I got lucky: A small weekly paper in south suburban Chicago was looking for an editor and paying $110 a week. The weekly circulated in Evergreen Park and Oak Lawn, two prosperous and growing suburbs that I knew well. I had worked weekends and two midweek nights while in law school selling whiskey and beer for a buck fifty an hour in a shopping mall in Evergreen Park. I mentioned that history while being interviewed by the publisher, who clearly knew nothing about the writing and editing of a newspaper—neither did I—and was immediately hired. A major factor, I realized later, was familiarity: to my new boss, having sold booze in the area was more than enough experience.

It was a long commute from my sister's basement north of Chicago to the far South Side, but I did it happily. I was a one-man shop—a reporter and editor responsible for content and also responsible for the makeup of each page of the weekly, which was printed by an offset press. Each page was laid out in type and headlines and, once at the printers, transferred to an ink image and eventually to the press that produced the tabloid newspaper. I was on my own from the moment I signed on, and over the next nine or so months I got a doctorate in small-town newspaper production. I eventually realized that I had been a small pawn in the very tough world of suburban newspaper publishing, Chicago-area style. Our main competition was a well-financed and fully staffed weekly newspaper known as the *Southwest Suburbanite*, whose regional editions were distributed throughout southwest Chicago and its suburbs, including Evergreen Park and Oak Lawn. The *Suburbanite* owned the weekly I worked on. My newspaper existed solely to keep out a competitor who would produce a better product and cut into the *Suburbanite*'s circulation and advertising revenue.

Such details mattered not to me. As an inner-city boy, I was eager to learn how suburbia worked and got hooked on the job. It was a trait I learned from my father; the only way to work was hard. I wrote about school boards and city commissions and found a way to work with the weekly's small coterie of social and gossip columnists—mostly married women with children at home—who filled the pages with chitchat. I found a bright teenager who wrote about local high school sports.

I paid visits to the few local bankers and merchants who were advertisers and was told again and again that they wanted a better newspaper—more coverage meant more readership and more response to their ads. I taught myself how to lay out easier-to-read pages for the printer and actually thought about the headlines. The Chicago mob— then headed by Sam Giancana—controlled many of the unions whose members did sewer construction throughout the region, and I wrote a series of articles supporting a young reformer named Smith who ran for township office on an anticorruption platform. I got a taste of big-city reality, Chicago style, when the reformer was assassinated before the election, shot repeatedly in his car. He had a family, and of course the murder, like many mob murders in those days, was never solved. (I would learn more about his death while working for the *Times* in the late 1970s.) There was no editorial interference from my paper, saddled with a hapless publisher and with no political influence.

During these months, I renewed my friendship with Bob Billings, who made merciless fun of my working for a dinky weekly newspaper. We both loved golf and played often on our days off.* After a while, Bob began talking about the two of us starting a weekly newspaper in the same suburbs, one that would report the hell out of the region and make a difference, as my weekly had not. He had enough money to get us started and knew there was something fishy about my little weekly that kept on going with few advertisements and little income. I had the experience of editing and producing a weekly and, most important, the gift of gab. I knew most of the bankers and small-shop owners in Evergreen Park and Oak Lawn and was pretty sure, young and green as I was, that I could convince more than a few of them to invest in what promised to be a serious weekly newspaper. Our yapping was little more than fantasy until Christmas, when my publisher gave me a holiday bonus of a brand-new ten-dollar bill, enclosed in a corny Christmas card. The guy had no idea how insulted I was, and that was

---

* Golf was a most unlikely sport for a ghetto kid from East Forty-Seventh Street to play, but my brother and I had found some discarded clubs, with ancient wooden shafts, while rummaging around in the basement of our low-end apartment complex. We could not have been more than seven or eight at the time, and one of my sisters, I think it was Marcia, took me to play a few times at a nearby public golf course—fifty cents or so for nine holes. I somehow figured out how to play the game and quickly got good enough to enjoy it.

it. It was time to face the fact that the weekly I was editing was hopeless. So I quit and told Billings it was a go.

The paper we started a month or so later, the *Evergreen Park/Oak Lawn Dispatch*, had an ambitious first edition. A friendly local banker and independent grocer committed to full-page advertisements, and we launched in midwinter, just as registration began for the second half of the school year. Ron Goldberg, a friend from high school days, was a relentless amateur photographer, and he spent a long day at my begging recording the first day of kindergarten at a few local grammar schools. Bob and I were eager to produce a newspaper that would be provocative and have substance, but I understood from my years running my father's business and my year as an editor that we had to start with more advertisers. And more readers. Thus, the centerfold of our first edition consisted of a dozen or more candid photos of timid and excited kindergartners being coaxed by anxious mothers to class, including the carefully collected names of all. Bill Hunt, a colleague from the University of Chicago (he would become a professor of English), joined our staff, after further begging from me, and he agreed to accept the chore of copying local want ads from the *Southwest Suburbanite* and the Chicago dailies and reprinting them in our early editions. All of us would spend a few hours on the day of publication calling those who placed the ads and telling them that we had seen their ad in the new newspaper in the area, the *Dispatch*. Within a month or so, we were publishing two full pages of want ads, which were, until the advent of the internet, a major profit source in the newspaper world. It was validation: I knew I could produce a winning newspaper. The weekly I had edited previously quietly went out of business by spring.

Billings convinced some of his former colleagues at City News to help out by writing a feature story or two, with a local angle, we hoped, and by occasionally covering the real news of the areas—school board meetings and the like. Our unpaid and irregular volunteers included Mike Royko, who would win the Pulitzer Prize for commentary in 1972 as a columnist for the *Chicago Daily News*, and Lee Quarnstrom, who, after a successful newspaper career in California, ended up as a core member of Ken Kesey's drug-loving Merry Band of Pranksters. (After my My Lai dispatches, Quarnstrom was quoted as sardonically

saying he had no idea I was "a great journalist." Correct. My idea of a
solid story then was one that found a way to praise an advertiser.)

Cash flow was always a problem. Many advertisers were more interested in placing ads than in paying for them. I therefore also became a
part-time collection agency. We were printing more than ten thousand
copies of our newspaper every Thursday night, and the printer insisted
on a certified check before running off even one copy. We hired a
driver who dropped off the newspapers by late the next morning to the
150 or so teenagers we'd recruited as delivery boys. Inevitably, mothers
would call the office during the day to report that their son or daughter
was ill and unable to do the delivery. That left it up to me, and sometimes Bob, to spend the afternoon as newspaper carriers.

Despite all, the *Dispatch* remained viable—terrifyingly so. After a
professional circulation audit in the spring, we began getting national
advertisements from the big three auto manufacturers. This was great,
but I was spending more and more of my time selling ads. There was a
payroll to meet, and the rent, and telephone service, and inevitable and
unforeseen day-to-day needs. I did not want to own a press; I wanted to
work for one. So I woke up one morning, in the late summer of 1962,
and realized I'd had it with suburban Chicago, and weekly newspapers.

Billings was right to feel betrayed by my abrupt decision to clear
out. But he knew I was the one who made the paper work, so he did
what I might have done if the situation were reversed: He walked away
before I did. He went on to become press secretary for Chicago mayor
Richard J. Daley, a job he must have hated, and a sports reporter for the
Chicago Daily News, a job I'll bet he loved. He died in 1998.

I took off for California with the woman I would later marry,
dropped her off at Berkeley, and graduate school, and spent the next
few months bumming around in the sunshine with my golf clubs. In
Los Angeles and out of money, I applied for a job with the *Los Angeles
Times.* They weren't interested. I drove back to Chicago and somehow
got an interview with a senior news editor for United Press International (UPI) named Gene Gillette. I liked Gillette and still remember his warmth during the interview. He took a chance on me, but
certainly not because of my credentials. I had been kicked out of law
school; fired, essentially, by the City News Bureau; had walked out on

a newspaper I started; and had crapped around for the past few months in California. Perhaps one of the editors at City News had stood up for me. In any event, my assignment was to cover the annual three-month meeting of the South Dakota legislature in Pierre, the state capital, which was to begin after New Year's Day. The pay was eighty-five dollars a week. I was ecstatic. Finally, I was a real newspaperman. It did not matter that my old jalopy, which now had rotten bearings, broke down en route to South Dakota near La Crosse, Wisconsin, and I had to ask Gillette to wire me a $350 advance. He did it, albeit, I would guess, with trepidation.

I arrived in Pierre on a Sunday night in late October, with no need to sell advertisements or worry about budgets. This was going to be fun. So what if I was the number two man in UPI's two-man bureau in a town that felt smaller than its population of ten thousand? My boss, the bureau chief, was pleasant enough, and reasonably competent, but as I quickly learned, he was intent on staying within bounds. He covered the governor's office and various state agencies and wrote accurate accounts of their pronouncements and decisions. No news beyond that existed for him.

The most important part of my job, from the very beginning, was to file a news summary at 7:00 every morning and throughout the day for UPI's radio and television subscribers in the state. There was no budget in our small office for a teletypist, so I was it. The only sources of information were our day-old wire stories and the morning edition of the local daily. It was reckless at first, because I had no idea what was news on the plains and what was not. I also had a hell of a time typing quickly enough to keep up with the constant demands of newscasters, who read far more than one hundred words a minute. I could not type half that speed with any accuracy, and I resolved the dilemma by typing a few phrases and then drumming my fingers on the pause key while figuring out what to steal next from the morning newspaper. It did not take more than a few mornings for me to realize that there was little gratification to be had in the job for which I had been hired—to rewrite stories from local newspapers and funnel them to clients.

I did come, however, to appreciate the many virtues of small-town life. On many mornings the six or seven journalists who covered the statehouse were invited for coffee and donuts with Archie Gubbrud, the sweet-faced Republican governor who would be reelected to a second term in 1962. Gubbrud was a farmer before he went into politics and went back to his farm when his run was over. One of his major accomplishments was to set up a state budget office—more than seventy years after South Dakota had become a state. The governor, without pretension and guileless, was open to any question, including those about the weather and politics. The local hero was not someone who made it to the major leagues or the National Football League but a rodeo rider named Casey Tibbs, who, so I was told, had been featured on the cover of *Life* magazine. South Dakota was divided between rich farmland that extended east from Pierre to the borders of Iowa and Minnesota and west to the rugged badlands and ranch land bordering Wyoming that was cowboy heaven. It seemed at times as if I was living inside a 1950s Hollywood western with constant political and economic tugs-of-war between the farmers and the ranchers. Pierre and a sister city, Fort Pierre, were separated by the Missouri River, which also served as the dividing line between time zones. In practical terms, it meant that the bars across the river stayed open an hour longer. The young man from Chicago had a lot to learn.

Social life also was . . . different. It was a good thing I had a serious girlfriend because the unmarried secretaries and office workers in the small statehouse were clannish and very protective of each other. In practice, that meant if a guy flirted with one or dated one, that was it. You were forever linked. I ended becoming best friends with a group of bachelor lawyers who worked for the attorney general's office and, like me, did not tangle with the insanity of dating. Weekend nights often were spent with my lawyer buddies in Pierre's sole bowling alley, and drinking. There were a few married couples who were welcoming and invited me to dinner every week. I became especially close to the family of Dan Perkes, a delightful man who was the bureau chief in Pierre for the Associated Press (AP), UPI's bitter and far more prosperous and successful rival. It was fun socializing with the enemy.

It was also fun getting to know the legislators and learning that the cowboys and ranchers who came from the badlands and wide open spaces in the west knew a hell of a lot more about socializing than did the farmers from the east. The good ole boys threw a series of come-one, come-all parties as the legislative season grew near, with sour mash and barbecued venison that never seemed to run out. This city boy heard many strange stories about how to hunt deer, with searchlights blazing away—sure to attract the animals—on the back of a pickup truck packed with shotgun-armed legislators out for the kill. One of the lawyers told me over drinks one night how he ended up working in the statehouse. He was a star high school football halfback who was recruited, all expenses paid, by the University of Nebraska, at the time a football powerhouse. In the fall of his sophomore year, he auditioned for the lead role in the university drama society's production of *Romeo and Juliet* and got it. Swollen with pride, he told the head coach about his success and assured him the rehearsals for the play would have minimal impact on his availability for the team. The next morning, he learned that his scholarship had been canceled and he was no longer a duly registered student in the university. He ended up transferring to a state school in South Dakota and, after law school, came to Pierre to work for the attorney general. This was not a story I would have heard at the University of Chicago.

I had rented a very strange one-room detached cottage—actually more like a shack—a few blocks from the statehouse that included a menacing heater fueled by propane gas. There was a real possibility—to me, anyway—of asphyxiation if the pilot light ever went out. I was constantly checking the goddamn thing that always had to be on, given the subzero weather that often hit central South Dakota. The car I had driven to Pierre was buried under snow by early November, and I did not dig it out until late March.

It would have been lonely except for the fact that I had a chance to do all of the reading I should have done in college and law school. I spent many late nights reading novels and the collections of Carl Sandburg on Lincoln, Winston Churchill on World War II, and Arthur Schlesinger on Franklin Roosevelt. I would often chat about books with A. C. Miller, the quiet, elderly, and self-effacing South Dakota attorney general. One night someone knocked on my door—it literally had never happened before, nor did it later—and there was the white-haired attorney general, with an apology for disturbing me and an armful of history and legal tomes that he wanted to share. You bet I read them.

Things would get more energetic once the legislative session began in January. Ever the enthusiast, I found time over the Christmas and New Year's holidays at the end of 1962 to research and write a four-part series on the legislative history of the South Dakota budget. The crucial issue was whether the state needed to impose a sales tax in order to avoid a deficit. "The legislators have three choices in dealing with the money problem: Raise taxes, drastically slash the budget recommendation, or do nothing until 1964," I wrote.

There was not enough time, even with two of us, for me to competently report on the hearings on the sales tax to which I had been assigned and also write and teletype the obligatory news summaries during the day for UPI's radio and TV clients. More often than not, I would stop by the hearings to pick up the prepared remarks of the various witnesses and legislators and file stories based on those to UPI's subscribers. The witnesses who spoke off the cuff did not make it onto the wire. I often spent weekends—days when I was presumably not working—digging into issues of statewide importance that I had not been able to fully report contemporaneously. My goal was to get beyond the "he said, she said" message that invariably emerged during legislative testimony. Time was always the enemy, along with the space needed to tell more complicated stories, and the lack of interest in such by many of the UPI subscribers in South Dakota.

I kept on plugging on weekends, and one of my stories did make a difference—to my career—although I'm not sure it was widely published in South Dakota. I got interested in Indian tribal history in South Dakota, essentially because of an anomaly, so I thought: South Dakota was the home to no fewer than nine American Indian tribes, including the Cheyenne and Oglala Sioux, with leaders who were of heroic stature—among them, Chief Crazy Horse, the Sioux warrior who led the attack against Lt. Col. George Armstrong Custer's Seventh Cavalry at Little Bighorn in June 1876—and yet there were very few Indians at work in the capitol, and very little, if any, interest by the legislature in their plight. And what a plight it was at the end of 1962. The reservations were broken, with unemployment in some cases approaching 90 percent and high poverty, suicide, and illness rates. It seemed to me to be racism, only those being discriminated against—unlike in Chicago—were kept out of sight. So I did some interviewing, got someone to drive me to a reservation, and in general did what a reporter should do—but on my own time and my own dime. I have not kept a file of the stories I wrote—it was impossible to imagine in early 1963 that I would eventually write a memoir—but vividly recall that at least one of my stories on the difficulties of the Oglala Sioux made it onto the pages of the *Chicago Tribune*, the largest paper, by far, in the region. It was my first big-league play.

At the end of the legislative session, in March, I told the Chicago office of UPI that I wanted out: The response was an offer to transfer me to its bureau in Omaha, Nebraska. I'd had fun and learned a lot about myself and the wire service business, but it was time to get off the plains and get to a big city, any big city, and do the kind of reporting I knew I could do. In a letter that I mailed in midwinter to Bill Hunt, a Chicago friend (he miraculously saved it), I had complained about the cold—it had been below zero for two weeks—and about the oil heater in my house that was burning more and more raggedly. But I also wrote, "I've been here three months and it doesn't bother me. I like the people and I have some very good friends and I'm me. It's sort of a pleasure to be what you are and have people leave you alone. First of all, I'm a good newspaper man." I predicted that there would be job offers in bigger cities and assured Bill, "I will be out of here within one or so months."

Dan Perkes of the AP made it easier to leave by promising to do what he could for me in Chicago, and so I resigned, said farewell to my friends, dug out my old car, and headed east.

FOUR

Chicago and the AP

I arrived back in Chicago in early April 1963, days before my twenty-sixth birthday, with no job, no money, no place to live, and a car in constant need of repair. I crashed once again in my sister's basement, slept in for a few days, ate well, and played with my nephews until it was time to go job hunting. I innocently thought my UPI clips, as published in the *Chicago Tribune*, would be meaningful, but got nowhere at the four Chicago newspapers. I made a call to the Chicago bureau of the Associated Press, and an interview was arranged with Al Orton, the bureau chief. There was paperwork to do and references to be checked, but he hired me. Just like that. I was ecstatic and profusely thanked Dan Perkes. I was convinced it was a letter or call from him that put me over the top. Maybe not. A colleague later told me that at some point shortly before my interview a longtime staff member decided, with no warning, to quit.

Orton had little to do with the workings of the newsroom. His job was to keep the AP's newspaper, radio, and television clients happy and to find more markets for the news service. The newsroom belonged to Carroll Arimond, the city editor who let his sharp pencil and his quiet demeanor speak for him. He'd been in the Chicago bureau since 1937 and would stay on the job there until his retirement in 1974. He'd seen it all, including political scandals and horrific crimes. A punk like me would have to prove he belonged.

My first week was horrendous. I was assigned to what was a new-guy, Tuesday-to-Saturday day shift and spent it, as others had before me, sitting to the left of Arimond—allegedly to get a feel for the rhythm of the bureau. The AP offices, ironically, were in the same downtown office building as the City News Bureau, but with far greater space. There was a separate wing in the office for the photo editor and staff photographers, along with a darkroom. The bureau was a central collection point for what seemed to me to be a confounding maze of desks, reporters, and editors with regional wire stories spewing out of constantly humming Teletype printers. I was figuring all of this out as I sat, mutely, watching Arimond make assignments and edit story after story before they were sent off on the wire. After two or so days, I was given a chance to do what I was hired to do—write a story. Arimond tossed me a four- or five-paragraph dispatch about a fatal automobile accident, as relayed by a regional newspaper in southern Illinois, and asked me to rewrite it for transmission on the Illinois wire. "Make it tighter," he said. I did my best, buttressing it with a quote from a local traffic cop, and watched, with growing anxiety, as Arimond scratched away at the piece. His edited version began with the name of the victim and then cut to "died in a car crash today near Springfield." That was it. He chopped all but one or two words in each paragraph and linked them into a ten-word sentence. I did nothing else for Arimond that week.

Yet I still had some excitement. It was baseball season, and the New York Yankees were playing a day game against the Chicago White Sox, my team, in Comiskey Park on the South Side. The sports department needed someone to call in a running score on the game, inning by inning. I, as the low man on the office totem pole, was it. So I went off to the ballpark early on Friday afternoon, my fourth day at work, with Harry Hall, who had been covering sports and news for the AP for thirty-five years. What fun that turned out to be. Hall, as I learned later, had taken one of the iconic photos of the war years—depicting Sewell Avery, the prominent chairman of the board of Montgomery Ward, being carried, by government fiat, out of his Chicago headquarters in 1944 by two army soldiers. The acerbic Avery had defied a Washington demand that he settle a strike that stopped the flow of war-related goods.

As we drove to the ballpark, Hall learned I had spent much of my childhood playing baseball and going to games at Comiskey. So he defied the apparent office dicta about being anything but civil to a rookie and told me about one of his early experiences covering the Yankees in Chicago. It was a year or two after Babe Ruth, in his prime, had broken all records for hitting home runs. As usual, the Babe was playing catch in front of the first base dugout before a game. Somehow a kid had gotten past the ushers and was parked near the dugout, constantly begging the Babe to sign his scorecard. The kid was about twelve years old, as Harry told it, with a leather cap and the smudged look of the street. The kid's mantra, said over and over again, as he waved the scorecard, was "Sign my card, Babe . . . Sign my card." He was indefatigable. Finally, after half an hour or so of the bleating, the Babe, totally irritated, told the kid to scram and added, "I don't sign scorecards, kid. I only sign balls." With that, the kid flung the scorecard away and, using both hands, emphatically cupped his groin and said, "Oh, yeah. Well, sign mine." As Harry told it, the Babe fell to the ground in laughter and, once the game began, glanced before each at bat toward the dugout where the kid had parked himself, and could not stop smiling. The mighty Babe, Harry added, went 0 for 4 that day.

Okay, I told myself, maybe it wasn't so, but there was no way I could hear a tale like this in Pierre. Working for the AP in Chicago was going to be a kick. So, that Friday night I partied, hard, with some of my old university pals. I woke up in someone's apartment on the South Side an hour after I was scheduled to spend Saturday sitting next to Arimond. I was a hungover mess, with a filthy shirt and a serious stink. Fresh clothes were in my sister's basement thirty miles away. I took a taxi to work and slunk into my chair next to Arimond. My reek was impossible to ignore, but he did. For the next few hours he said nothing to me. I said nothing in return and tried to avoid eye contact. I waited until he left for lunch, which he always did before noon, before dashing for coffee. At the least, I hoped he had figured out that the little eager beaver panting next to him all week was not all work and no play, but someone who showed up for work no matter what. He and I would have issues over the next two years. He was a Jesuit-educated Catholic who endorsed the church's strictures on abortion and other controversial issues, but he kept his religious views out of the news-room. I respected his integrity and the fact that he never interfered with my reporting, even when the stories annoyed him. I later learned he vouched for me with enthusiasm when the AP was considering my promotion to Washington.

My first assignment in Chicago was as a night editor on the radio and television news desk. I was more than well trained for the job, which had the luxury of a teletypist. The job involved some creativity. I was to file a running news summary for the AP clients of the local news stories of the day, and also be alert for bulletins and other special events that called for immediate reporting. I was not merely parroting what the local newspapers were reporting, as I had done in Pierre; I was to edit and summarize, in essence, the news for the scores of radio and television newsmen in Chicago who, in many cases, would simply recite word for word on air what the AP was providing. It did not take long before I started playing with language and trying to make stories less programmed and formulaic. I have no idea whether my efforts were successful or even noticed, but I worked hard at making the stories lively, and it was not long before I was pulled off the job and made a general assignment reporter.

My new job started at five in the afternoon and lasted until one in the morning. The AP had the right to make any use it wished of news articles in the four Chicago dailies, and to my surprise much of the work that was done essentially consisted of rewriting pieces, with credit to the paper involved, for the AP wires. I assumed that the senior editors in New York who controlled the AP's national and interna-tional output would be eager to publish fresh interviews and new data on major stories, and I did all I could to give them what they wanted. And why not take a routine story in one of the papers from time to time and puff it up with whimsy or a pun? Thus, when Sinbad, the lowland gorilla who was the main attraction at Chicago's Lincoln Park Zoo, escaped from his cage and romped around the zoo before being felled by a narcotic, I led my rewritten story with "Sinbad the gorilla nursed a hangover today, just like anyone else not used to being on the town." I did the same with a report on crime in Chicago; my lead read, "Crime—of all things—is falling off in rough, tough Chicago."

A new skyscraper under construction was to be covered with a new form of steel that would oxidize and turn pretty in Chicago's dampness and high air pollution. My lead said, "Chicago's finally found a use for smog. It's going to make the city's new $87 million downtown civic center beautiful." A 1920s ballroom in Chicago closed, and I convinced the night editor to let me flee the desk and take a look. My hokey lead said, "Thousands of Chicagoans, who learned to dance at the Aragon Ballroom, paid dreamy homage to yesteryear Sunday night by waltzing to Wayne King's soft melodies for the last time." The stories all got widespread play in the next day's afternoon newspapers. After a few instances of such silliness, a senior editor in New York began reminding Chicago to add my byline to the stories. The editor eventually made it known he wanted me to get out of the office and find offbeat and feature pieces for the overnight report. I was free to report whatever I wished, within limits. I thought I owned the city.

I quickly found that what editors called human interest stories were hiding in plain sight. I had moved into a cheap room near the University of Chicago, and one weekend night I went with my wife-to-be to a film festival at the school and found an overflow crowd of students oohing and aahing to *The Maltese Falcon*, the 1941 classic film starring Humphrey Bogart as Dashiell Hammett's detective Sam Spade. It was clear something newsworthy was going on. I sought out the guy running the festival and learned that Bogart and his movies were the rage in colleges across the nation. I made a few more calls and wrote a piece for the AP describing the phenomenon, and it was published coast-to-coast, including prominently on the front page of the *New York Herald Tribune*.

I also took advantage of the fact that my years running the family business in Chicago's black ghetto put me in touch with the international importance and vibrancy of gospel music. When the famed Mahalia Jackson fell ill in 1964 with a heart ailment, I telephoned her in the hospital after being refused permission to visit and wrote about the outpouring of letters and flowers she had received. Many were from Europe, where she was widely admired. "There were so many flowers," she told me, with a laugh, "that one morning I woke up and thought I was dead." We did a lot of Chicago talking, especially about

my career as a young white boy trying to make a living running a
cleaning store in the heart of the black ghetto. I also told her how a
few of my father's favorite customers made a point of being around as
I closed up after a busy Saturday night, with the day's receipts in my
pocket. I thought they were there just to chat; it would be years before
I understood they were there to protect me. A few months later, after
her recovery, Mahalia invited me for a fried-chicken-and-corn-bread
lunch at her home on Chicago's South Side and told me her doctors
had assured her that she could continue singing. She had gone to a
Roman Catholic Mass and prayed, she said, "for the Lord to continue
to strengthen and heal me. I'm a Baptist but I believe there is only one
God." I wrote a long feature story for the AP about her recovery, and
her music, and put to use one of the lessons I was learning: My story
was much more readable because I let her good humor, humanity, and
humility come through.

Arimond and his fellow editors in Chicago must have seen some
talent, and they, like others had throughout my early years as a
reporter, just let me run free. I wrote dozens of self-generated feature
stories while in Chicago on subjects that had to have caused my editors angst—including police corruption, birth control, and civil rights
abuses. Chicago, like many big cities in the mid-1960s, was feeling the
pressure of black America for equal rights across the board, including
the housing market. Black families were constantly being told there
were no vacancies in apartment buildings that were continually renting to whites. I wrote a long piece about such discrimination, quoting,
for some idiotic reason, "circles close" to the real estate community.
On the afternoon after the publication of one such piece, I came to
work and saw that Arimond had posted on the office bulletin board a
page from an artist's oversized sketch pad that contained only a large
circle. The caption below said, "Staff: above is an informed circle." I
felt the chill.

Despite such back-and-forth, and my obvious sympathies, the AP
assigned me in my second year in Chicago to be the civil rights reporter
for the region. It was a good call for reasons the AP could not know. I
had worked on and off in the family cleaning store for nearly a dozen
years and had a far closer relationship with the black employees than

did my dad or my mom. I spent many Sundays as a teenager going to Negro League baseball games with a young man who pressed clothes in the store and shared my love of baseball. I understood his frustrations and his sense of limitation, as well as his acceptance of the racism that, so he correctly thought, limited his life.

My new assignment got me in contact with Martin Luther King Jr. These were the days and nights of massive rallies in the North and violent resistance. King was a genius at reading reporters and could spot those, like me, who were eager to fall in love. He was very savvy about the media, and the AP, and thus me, were important to him; my dispatches would be on the front pages of many of the important newspapers in cities where there was racial tension. King, after speaking at one tense nighttime rally in Chicago, caught my eye—how hard was that?—and crooked his finger. That meant hang around and we will talk. King knew that the rally would produce stories for the morning newspapers, but there was another news cycle for the afternoon editions. After ten minutes or so, King drew me aside and provided me with pungent quotes, in one case about his disillusionment with the Johnson administration, that would keep the story alive for another day.

I was doing my thing, for sure, but also learning about my profession, and about the sophistication and resilience of words. On a quiet, hot Sunday night in August 1964, a black woman had been caught trying to shoplift a $2.69 bottle of gin from a neighborhood liquor store in Dixmoor, a middle-class suburb just south of Chicago whose population of thirty-one hundred was heavily black. She had been caught by the white store owner, and the initial reports said that he had thrown the woman to the ground. Tensions grew over the next few hours as word spread, accurately or not, that the store owner also had severely beaten the woman. A crowd of blacks, many of them young, congregated. Police carrying shotguns and firing tear gas dispersed them, amid reports that fifty people, most of them white, had been injured by flying bricks and stones. I quoted Dixmoor's white deputy fire chief as saying, "I'll tell you, it was like savages." The disturbance would become one of the earliest of what would be many black-versus-white urban confrontations in subsequent years, but on that Sunday night it seemed to be a one-off.

Things got much worse on the next night, when the liquor store and nearby shops were looted and set on fire by a much larger, angrier, and more confrontational group of blacks. The AP night city editor, Bob Olmstead, sent me dashing again to the scene. I ended up behind a police line, a few hundred feet from the liquor store. A fire truck was nearing the scene when a volley of what sounded like bullet shots rang out. At that point, a white cop, carrying a shotgun, screamed at me and the few other reporters at the scene to "get back" and added, "They're shooting at us." This was hot stuff. I dashed to a nearby telephone, crawling part of the way, as I had done in basic training, and dictated a bulletin to Olmstead that focused on the cop telling me that the protesters were firing on the police. I took a moment or two to gather myself, reviewed my notes, and then, as AP style demanded, telephoned the office to dictate a new lead backed up with more details of what I had seen and been told. There were no subsequent reports of bullet injuries or deaths, and the police eventually formed a skirmish line and drove off the protesters, while making a few arrests.

I drove back to the AP office downtown feeling a bit heroic. I knew my story, with its vivid quotes and description of the riot scene, would be on front pages all over the world the next morning. By this time I had become an avid daily reader of *The New York Times* and especially its coverage of the expanding Vietnam War. David Halberstam and Charley Mohr of the *Times* were my heroes, along with the AP's Malcolm Browne and the UPI's Neil Sheehan. I got back to the office many hours later envisioning myself as a veteran combat correspondent and prepared to write a longer, more detailed account of the rioting for the next day's afternoon papers. Olmstead had gone home by then but left a file of what had moved from Dixmoor with the overnight editor. The bulletin and lead I had dictated to Bob hours earlier had said, quoting the cop, that Negroes had opened fire on the police amid an expanding race riot. Modest, competent Bob had rewritten my first bulletin to say, "Gunfire broke out tonight" at a riot in Dixmoor. He had conveyed the urgency of the situation without getting into the issue of who started what. Of course I had no way of knowing who shot at whom, or even whether a volley of bullets had been launched. I had relied on a panicked cop despite knowing, from my time at City News, that cops often do not tell the truth, or know the truth. I also realized that I had made no effort to get to the rioters across the police barriers and did not begin to know what they thought the riot was about. Bob Olmstead, who went on to become an editor for the *Chicago Sun-Times*, taught me a master's degree's worth of journalism in one night.

At some point, well into my second year in the bureau, I was asked to fill in as night city editor. It was on a quiet Sunday night. The stories I edited were routine and easily moved to New York or to the Illinois wire for the many newspapers in the state that relied on the AP for their foreign and domestic news.

One of the bureau's sportswriters filed a late report on a Chicago Blackhawks hockey game and then returned to the office, as usual, to write an overnight report, replete with interviews and after-game gossip, for the many newspapers in Canada and New England whose readers dwelled on such stories. The guy who covered hockey was a fine journalist, but he annoyed some of us because he had access to free house tickets for all the sporting events in the city but traded them in for free drinks in a downstairs bar instead of sharing with his fellow reporters. A popular Chicago hockey player named Reggie Fleming had been released at the end of the season, and our reporter filed a story about it, stating that when he sought him out at home for an interview, the door was slammed in his face. It was one of the last stories I edited and sent on its way before going down to the bar with a colleague, Paul Driscoll, for a post-work drink. The sports reporter was, as usual, drinking his free martini. As I walked by his booth, I complimented him, as I thought an editor should, about his story and added, "So the son of a bitch actually slammed the door on you?" No, he answered. He'd called Fleming at home and the guy hung up on him. My first night as the editor and I had just edited a story with a total lie. Should I go back to the office and file a correction? Or should I have a beer and never agree to play night editor again? I chose the latter, but wondered what poor Reggie would think when he read the story. The experience forever wiped away any desire I had to become an editor.

Newsrooms were full of cynical talk about life and death, the lucky and the unlucky, but dealing with the fate of others was a necessary and often brutal part of the profession, as I learned one evening in Chicago. It was just another day at work until we were informed that a jammed passenger plane had crashed hours earlier somewhere in the Pacific, with many deaths. One fatality was a young woman from a suburb north of Chicago. My assignment was to telephone her home and learn what I could about her, including why she was on that plane. I also was to ask for a photograph. I, of course, resisted but was told that it was part of the job and that very often friends and family members were willing to share what they could with the media, even in the midst of their pain. I found the right telephone number and made the call. It was well after the dinner hour. It was clear after a question or two that the gentleman who answered the call had no idea that his daughter had been killed in the crash. The airline had fucked up in a way that was impossible to imagine. Someone else, perhaps a sibling, was eventually put on the phone, and through her tears I was able to share the telephone number of a contact for the airline and left it at that. There was no way I was going to ask any questions or for a photo, and my colleagues in the office agreed. I do not recall whether my anger at myself for agreeing to make the call was greater than my anger toward the airline for its irresponsibility. No AP story about the death was written that night, and I have no idea whether one ever was.

I had gotten married in mid-1964, and by the next spring my wife, a native of New York, was as eager as I was to move east. Chicago had been fun and instructive, but America was getting more and more involved in Vietnam; it was an issue that was not going away, and in Washington I would be much closer to covering the war. I supplemented my daily newspaper reading with Bernard Fall's wonderful work on Vietnam, with accounts of the disastrous French loss to the North Vietnamese at Dien Bien Phu in the spring of 1954. I was also introduced to *I. F. Stone's Weekly* by my mother-in-law and was wowed by Stone's ability to take on, and debunk, the official accounts of events annunciated by the Johnson administration. There was no mystery to how Stone did it: He outworked every journalist in Washington.

A requested transfer to the AP's Washington bureau came through in the spring, and by early summer I was heading east. I've kept in touch with my pal Driscoll over the years, and he reminded me as I was writing this memoir of a note I received from Carroll Arimond before leaving Chicago, praising me with the most generous of words for the work I had done while in the bureau. I cannot believe I did not keep it, and did not remember it, but I'm glad that my vanity led me to share it with Paul.

FIVE

Washington, At Last

I hit Washington in midsummer 1965 and found the city to be slow, southern slow, and the AP bureau to be riveting and fast. I had spent my last year in Chicago monitoring the reporting out of Washington and marveling at the speed and accuracy of reporters such as Frank Cormier, Walter Mears, and Harry Kelly, names little known today, who covered the presidency, Congress, and politics. Their important stories, often initially dictated as bulletins, seemed to me to be exquisite wire service matter—just fact after fact, with no analysis, presented in clean, spare prose under rat-a-tat pressure. The wire services invariably gave America its first knowledge about a vital event at home or abroad, and I was envious of the swagger of the old pros as they dashed from a major news event to the nearest pay phone and smoothly dictated a thousand-word account.

I spent the first week or so obligatorily hanging around the bureau, which was on the ground floor of a creaky office building on Connecticut Avenue eight blocks or so from the White House. My real job, on the overnight rewrite desk, would start on week two. Most of the AP's reporting about the government moved from Washington on the national, or A, wire. I had just spent two years in Chicago scrambling and pleading to get my stories on that wire. Of course there was a municipal government and the city had professional sports teams, but

in general local stories about politics or sports were relegated to a secondary AP wire for lesser matters, known as the B wire. That's where
I began my reporting career in Washington. One afternoon that first
week, I was sent to cover a Shriners parade that threaded through downtown Washington and onto the great mall behind the White House. I
understood that the Shriners did a lot of valuable charity work and supported children's hospitals around the nation, but a parade is a parade,
and it was brutally hot and sunny. I was happy to bump into another
young reporter named Leonard Downie Jr., who, on his first day at *The
Washington Post*, also had been shoved into parade purgatory. (Downie
would end his career as executive editor of the *Post* and the author of a
series of insightful books about the media business.) I filed a much too
cheery story about the parade that ended up, untouched by any editing,
under my name on the B wire—my first Washington byline.

That first week I also met Don Sanders, the day city editor who,
like Carroll Arimond, let his work speak for itself. He wrote occasional
reviews of the performing arts, as seen in Washington, but his skill
at shaping stories and anticipating the news made him the go-to guy
of the Washington editing desk. He would prove to be someone who
shared my dire views about the growing American involvement in the
Vietnam War.

The rewrite desk was a mandatory stop for newcomers like me,
and it involved taking the major Washington stories of the day, as
filed by the bureau's reporters for the nation's morning newspapers—
those with deadlines beginning at 7:00 p.m. on the East Coast—and
rewriting them overnight for the afternoon papers, with deadlines the
next morning. It was easy work if there was a new development—even
something as obvious as writing that "President Johnson returned last
night from a triumphant visit to . . ." But if the story was static, the goal
was to find something new—for instance, by trying to reach senators
and public officials late at night by telephone. Sometimes there were
dozens of stories to be turned around for the next newspaper cycle,
and the overnight crew consisted of me, a fellow rewrite colleague,
and a rewrite editor who was content to funnel our stuff onto the A
wire. It was okay for a month or two, but the work quickly became dry,
rote, and lonely. I started my night shift an hour or so before my wife
returned from her work.

On the plus side, I was in Washington in the serenity, safety, and openness of the mid-1960s. On the Saturday night of my first weekend off, my wife and I wandered into an unpretentious Italian restaurant near my office. I immediately recognized the much older guy seated at the small table next to us as Earl Warren, the chief justice of the United States. I figured what the hell and introduced myself to him, and explained that I was a reporter brand-new to Washington, and my brand-new wife had just begun a job as a psychiatric social worker. Warren introduced his wife and we chitchatted on and off throughout the meal. It was like talking to grandparents I never had. He wanted to know about my job and how it came to be. Brash as I was, I still did not dare ask him about his workday. It felt good, though, to learn that even in the upper stratosphere of Washington people were people. I would soon put that knowledge to work.

We had rented a small condo in a new housing development in Washington's integrated southwest, and, ironically, our immediate neighbors included Thurgood Marshall, another Supreme Court justice, who, on behalf of the NAACP, argued and won *Brown v. Board of Education*, the landmark 1954 case that found racial segregation in public schools to be unconstitutional. Other neighbors included a prominent British journalist and the Pentagon correspondent for *Time*, who would often host what I later learned were off-the-record dinner parties for senior members of the Johnson administration.

Meanwhile, I decided to jump-start my boring job by doing what I did in Chicago—find a story that no one else had and write it while also doing the required rewrites. In early August, six weeks or so after getting to Washington, I tracked down Martin Luther King Jr. on the eve of the signing of the 1965 Voting Rights Act, at the time the high point of the presidency of Lyndon Johnson. The ever-shrewd King told me, and untold numbers of terrified politicians in the South and the North, that he planned within a month to register 900,000 Negroes to vote. He had just finished a tour of Chicago, Cleveland, Philadelphia, and Washington, he said. "It was my first real hard look at the North. I have seen hundreds of thousands of faces, all expressing a great sense of hope in spite of terrible living conditions . . . and I do not yet see the kind of vigorous programs alive in northern communities that are needed to grapple with the enormity of the problems." My story flew off the A wire, and King's remarks were all over America. No one said boo in my office. A few weeks later, once again on my own, I interviewed Bayard Rustin, a visionary of the civil rights movement in America who was deeply involved in organizing the 1963 March on Washington, when hundreds of thousands of whites and blacks gathered to see King give his "I Have a Dream" speech. Rustin told me he was going to take the civil rights fight to Congress. The task of integrating schools and getting more jobs for Negroes, he said, "will require votes, planning, and billions of dollars from Congress. . . . Most of the big problems must be solved by moral and financial aid from Congress." That story, too, made headlines.

I slogged away that summer and fall on the rewrite desk but made it a point to try to reach the key players who were quoted in the various stories I had to rewrite, whether they dealt with a legislative issue, a dispute on military spending, or anything else. My goal was to punch up the story by adding to the inherent controversy, if there was any, or by more fully delineating the issues involved. The high point of my efforts came in late December 1965, after the announcement of a thirty-hour cease-fire in the Vietnam War. Congress was out of session for the Christmas holiday, and many senior administration officials had also left town. There was time to kill on the rewrite desk, so I went on a mini telephone rampage. I cheekily called Vice President Hubert Humphrey at his home in Minnesota and got him—he may have had a hot toddy too many—to talk about extending the cease-fire until Tet, the Vietnamese New Year, which was to begin on February 1, six weeks away. I got calls for peace, with varying caveats, in telephone interviews with John McCormack of Massachusetts, the Speaker of the House; Gerald Ford, the House Republican leader; and Leverett Saltonstall, the ranking Republican on the Senate Armed Services Committee. It was fun to do, made some news, and spread a little more Christmas cheer. The war continued.

My hard work won me a promotion, and in early 1966 I was freed from the overnight desk and put on general assignment. I made a few out-of-town trips to cover conferences at which a major Washington politician, almost invariably Bobby or Teddy Kennedy, was to speak; I also reported for a day or two for one of the AP's client newspapers that wanted special coverage of a congressional debate about an issue of vital local interest. In all, I covered, when needed, politics, Congress, civil rights—I cared deeply about the difficulties and dangers facing those involved in the civil rights movement—and the inequities and other shortcomings of the draft. In the summer, barely a year after I had come to Washington, I was told that Fred Hoffman, the bureau's longtime Pentagon correspondent, was going off on a six-month assignment and I was to start working there immediately, under his tutelage, and then take over the beat. At last, I was going to be writing about the rapidly expanding American commitment in Vietnam. I felt strongly even then that the war was the wrong way to confront Soviet-style communism, but I knew I would be able to separate my personal views from my professional responsibility as a reporter.

Most of the correspondents covering the Pentagon had been on the job for a decade or more and saw themselves as military experts. The key, then and now, was access, and the beat reporters had plenty of it. There were cozy and friendly off-the-record meetings with Robert McNamara, the former president of Ford Motor Company who had been secretary of defense since Jack Kennedy took office, and his deputy, Cyrus Vance, a Yale College and Law School graduate who came from a prominent family. There were also what seemed to be almost daily briefings for the press corps by senior generals and officials on all subjects, from Vietnam to social issues; the American military was praised by social scientists for its progressive role in integration and education. Fred Hoffman, as the senior wire service reporter, had earned the right to ask the last question at news conferences and the like; it was he who decided, often on a cue from a press officer, when to end such sessions. As Fred's replacement, I inherited that responsibility.

I was stunned—even astonished—by the Pentagon pressroom, which had the earmarks of a high-end social club. It seemed stunningly sedate. The correspondents were clustered in an overcrowded ghetto down the hall from the office of McNamara's press secretary, Arthur Sylvester. The hall was known as the "Correspondents Corridor" and featured photographs of past and present war reporters. Most of the guys smoked pipes, or wanted to, I thought. Len Downie would later tell it like it was in depicting the atmosphere in the pressroom when

I arrived there in mid-1965. "Most major stories written by Pentagon correspondents on national issues reflected only the official point of view," Downie wrote in *The New Muckrakers*, a study of investigative reporting that was published a year after the Vietnam War ended. "With a few notable exceptions, Pentagon reporters, especially at the time Hersh was assigned there, have seldom tried to balance that view with more critical appraisals from dissenters within the civilian or Pentagon ranks or from expert outside observers."

I was also as tame as I could be until Hoffman took his leave. By then, the Johnson administration's commitment of troops and dollars was constantly expanding, amid evidence that the war was not going as well as expected. The number of Americans drafted in 1966 reached a staggering total of more than 382,000, and more than 385,000 Americans were on duty in Vietnam by the end of the year. Dissent was growing on college campuses across the nation. I would learn, after doing the My Lai stories in late 1969, that the wanton murdering of civilians began very early, literally within days of the first marine landing on the beaches at Da Nang in March 1965, but nothing of that sort had been published.

My first break with tradition came early, when Sylvester's office trotted out a senior marine general who had returned to his staff job in Washington after a short visit to Vietnam. The general was going on and on about the imminent success of the war but made no effort to back up his opinion with a fact. After fifteen or so minutes, it seemed clear to me that the only story that would emerge would be about yet another general claiming victory in the war. Thus, when the officer finished his presentation and asked for questions, I stood up and, invoking my right as the senior AP correspondent, thanked him for his time and walked out. My gesture made it clear that I felt there was nothing to be gained by asking questions, to which he would have familiar answers. There was a moment or so of hesitation, and my colleagues followed me. There was hell to pay, of course, from Sylvester's office, and muttering about getting me off the Pentagon beat, but I insisted to one of Sylvester's aides that the briefing had been a waste of time and most of my colleagues knew it, but were too polite to say so.

There was a far more important story hiding, as many stories always do, in the open. It revolved around navy pilot retention in the Vietnam War. America was spending as much as half a million dollars to train each navy pilot in the art of landing on and taking off from aircraft carriers, and as the loss rate in the war grew steadily, pilots were putting in for retirement as soon as possible. The targets were increasingly being seen as asymmetrical, in the sense that their destruction was not of much value to the war effort. One key primitive bridge in Thanh Hoa province of North Vietnam was targeted hundreds of times by navy jets, beginning in mid-1965, with significant losses, before finally being put out of commission in 1972.

I picked up on the official double-talking about the aircraft loss rate shortly after getting to the Pentagon when McNamara announced a $700 million investment in more fighter planes, most of them for the navy. I quoted him as explaining that the navy still had a lower loss rate than expected, but more missions were flying and thus more planes were being shot down. I checked out the McNamara analysis with a staff member of the House Armed Services Committee whom I had met while on the general assignment beat. His informed assessment, based on classified data, he said, was much more direct: "We're going to lose more Navy planes than we thought." I reported that.

My continuing interest in the navy losses and McNamara's dissembling on the subject eventually led me to Clarence "Mark" Hill, a navy captain who was at work on a long-term project for McNamara dealing with the shortage of pilots. Hill's deputy at the time was a brilliant junior navy officer named John M. Poindexter, who held a doctorate from the California Institute of Technology. (Poindexter's career would crash two decades later when, as an admiral, he was indicted during the Iran-contra scandals in the Reagan administration.) Hill understood, as I did, that many navy pilots, convinced that their targets in Vietnam were not worth the risk involved, were eager to get out of the service as quickly as possible. It was a story that no one at the top wanted to hear, or have told. But Hill's office had provided testimony and backup statistical data to a committee or two in Congress, and he pointed me to the right committee and the right set of hearings.

The subsequent series of articles in 1966 for the AP on the navy's problems with pilot retention marked me to some at the Pentagon, and to some of my newspaper colleagues, as an antiwar activist. In fact, I also learned a lot about military integrity and honor from Mark Hill, who was as conservative as any officer I knew when it came to social issues. Hill fervently objected to the notion that there was something racist in the navy's tradition of recruiting Filipino sailors to serve as mess stewards for navy officers aboard ship, and he wasn't sure African Americans would make good pilots. But he also valued integrity and truth, and as such he taught me a great deal about the war.

In the fall of 1966 there had been yet another vicious battle in South Vietnam involving a North Vietnamese ambush of an army company—some one hundred soldiers strong—on patrol. More U.S. troops were ordered in, with even greater casualties, before attack planes and helicopters could drive off the enemy. The newspaper accounts of the battle were grim. I, as the senior guy for the AP, was invited for a midday chat with McNamara and Vance, along with five or six other correspondents from the major media. The two key American officials in charge of the war provided a more positive account: Far more enemies than Americans had been killed, they claimed, and the general in charge of the operation had been given a battlefield promotion from a one-star to a two-star general. McNamara explained that, of course, neither he nor Vance should be cited by name or title in our dispatches, which would suggest the two of them were trying to whitewash a bad day. Thus ensued a brief discussion between some of my colleagues and the men running the war about how best to attribute the information. The reporters seemed glad to help out. It was my first background session with McNamara and I kept my mouth shut. I also followed the formula for attribution that had been agreed to— something like "senior officials said."

My article was published in time to make the final edition of the afternoon Washington *Star*, then the main competitor to the more prosperous and highly regarded *Washington Post*. Late in the day Captain Hill showed up in the doorway of the Pentagon pressroom, caught my eye, and signaled for me to join him in the hallway. As we began walking around the endless corridors, Hill wanted to know where on earth I had gotten the information that was published. I did not hesitate before naming McNamara and Vance. Hill was stunned. He was at that time assigned to Systems Analysis, a special unit set up by McNamara that called for military requirements and issues to be reduced to their component parts and analyzed piecemeal for better understanding. There were senior officers in the military who saw the office as a convenient vehicle for McNamara to avoid relying on military advice. I would learn later that Hill had already been promoted to admiral (it was known as being "frocked" in the navy) and was awaiting the right job, at admiral's rank, to become available. With that in mind, what he did next took extraordinary courage and involved an extraordinary trust in me. After swearing me to secrecy, Hill put his promotion at risk by revealing that the involved general had been cashiered—summarily fired—for his refusal to understand the ambush as the crisis it was, leading to a feckless decision to order a second company into the ambush in the vain hope of mitigating the slaughter. The second unit had also been mauled, with high casualties. Hill then told me that the cover-up of the debacle included an on-the-spot promotion for the general, who was then immediately reassigned out of Vietnam. It was a farce.

I remember being angry, of course, but also more than a bit frightened: I had no idea of the extent to which the men running the war would lie to protect their losing hand. I was dealing with a dilemma that reporters who care and work hard constantly face: America needed to know the truth about the Vietnam War, but I had made a commitment to an officer of integrity. Of course I kept my mouth shut because my professional, and moral, obligation was to protect Hill. I should note that Hill, who retired as a three-star admiral in 1973, passed away in 2011; otherwise I would have had to ask for his approval before revealing his role in my education as a reporter—an approval that I believe he surely would have given. Hill got the assignment he was waiting for a few months after our hallway chat, as commander of the USS *Independence*, an aircraft carrier. He and I would stay in touch for the next four decades.

Even if Mark had given me permission at the time to write what he told me, without quoting him by name of course, it would have been very difficult to do so. I had made a number of visits to his office, and Sylvester had ordered all senior military officers and civilian officials in the Pentagon to immediately report every visit by a reporter. In practice, this meant that if I went to a general on a Tuesday and got some relevant information and wrote about it the next day, Sylvester's office would know—whether the general was cited in my dispatch by name or not—that the general had most likely been the source. In order to protect that general, or Mark Hill, if he would have authorized me to use the information he had, I would have had to spend days visiting generals and admirals for spurious reasons in an effort to mask the source. The McNamara/Sylvester edict was a huge element in discouraging serious investigative reporting and essentially forced the reporters to rely more and more on officially arranged interviews and the various news conferences that seemed always to be at hand. Sylvester made it easy for the Pentagon press corps to do the minimum. There was an obvious way to beat the system, of course—contacting senior officers and officials at home. In the year I reported from the Pentagon, that seemed to be done rarely.

IN THESE LAST FEW MONTHS of 1966, I made an important new friend, I. F. Stone. Our first encounter was very typical—for him. My wife and I had been out late on a Saturday night, and the telephone rang early the next morning, before six o'clock. My fear was that it was an AP editor in New York asking me to check out a military story published somewhere in the world. That happened far too often. Instead, the caller introduced himself as Izzy Stone and asked if I had seen the fascinating story on page whatever it was in either *The Philadelphia Inquirer* or *The Baltimore Sun*. Izzy, I soon learned, got up early on Sunday morning and drove to a downtown newsstand that sold national and international newspapers. This call was his way of telling me that he had seen something in my reporting that suggested I might be a kindred soul, in terms of being more than a little bit skeptical of the reporting on the Vietnam War. Izzy was fond of long walks, and we soon began taking them together. We talked incessantly about how to do better reporting, and I was in the hands of a master; it was to the shame of the mainstream media—and my pipe smoker colleagues in the Pentagon pressroom—that his biweekly reports and analyses, as publisher of *I. F. Stone's Weekly*, were viewed as little more than a nuisance.

The most telling crisis of my young career took place at the end of the year. On December 12, 1966, Harrison Salisbury of the *Times* arrived in Hanoi; he was the first mainstream American journalist to be granted a visa since the marines had invaded the South. Two days later he wrote about seeing evidence of massive American bombing in Hanoi, with obvious civilian casualties. The Pentagon's response was immediate and fierce: categorical denials of any American bombing inside the city limits of Hanoi, along with a suggestion, widely repeated in the press, that Salisbury and the *Times* were serving as propaganda agents for the enemy. I was going to the briefings with "American officials"—usually one or two of the men at the top—and reporting their anonymous denials, which eventually included the hard-to-fathom notion that any damage to civilian structures in Hanoi had been caused by errant anti-aircraft missiles that had been fired at American bombers by the North Vietnamese.

A week or so later a Pentagon official reluctantly acknowledged, as I dutifully wrote, that some civilian areas in the North might have been damaged by American bombings, but he insisted that only military objectives had been targeted. Meanwhile, Salisbury, who would stay in North Vietnam until early January, was roaming around the country and consistently providing more evidence of civilian bombing. He further reported on Christmas Day that the American bombing had been going on for months. An "on the spot inspection" indicated that American attacks had led to civilian casualties in Hanoi and elsewhere "for some time past." Four days later Salisbury reported that the city of Nam Dinh, fifty miles south of Hanoi, had been repeatedly bombed for more than a year, resulting in eighty-nine civilian deaths, as many as five hundred wounded, and more than twelve thousand homes destroyed.

I assumed, following the Mark Hill dictum, that there was much truth in the Salisbury dispatches and very little in the official denials I had been faithfully recording, like a good stenographer. I had been invited to a conference a few months earlier on the media and the military at the Naval War College in Newport, Rhode Island, and shared a dinner there with a senior admiral serving in a most sensitive post at the Pentagon. I sensed his ambivalence about the war and expressed my concerns about the lack of integrity at the top of the Pentagon. The admiral made it clear, without saying as much, that he shared my view.

After the New Year's holiday, I spent days interviewing various officers and civilians in Pentagon offices for whatever rational story I could conjure up, with the intent of creating a misleading record for Arthur Sylvester's henchmen. I then telephoned the admiral's secretary and asked for an interview. He agreed to see me, as I thought he might; I was sure he knew what I wanted. He'd had it with the lying; it was as simple as that. He told me that there were many post-bombing photographs (known as BDAs in the Pentagon, for bomb damage assessments) that confirmed the extensive damage to civilian targets that Salisbury had revealed. He also told me that McNamara, in the wake of the Salisbury report, had put a five-mile circle around downtown Hanoi and the navy and air force pilots were under orders not to bomb within that circle.

I knew I had a very important story, but I also understood I had to get confirmation. More pretend interviews were necessary before I contacted a young air force general I knew and liked, for his willingness to be totally open and outspoken about his conviction that only air force bombing missions had been effective in the war. I told him that it was my understanding that navy pilots were convinced that their bombing attacks in the Hanoi area had been far more accurate than the bombs dropped by the high-flying air force. The BDAs, the air force officer said, could not have been clearer in showing the extent of navy bombs that had missed their target inside Hanoi, creating extensive damage to civilian sites. He eventually showed me a few of the photos, pointing out direct hits and bomb craters that indicated a miss. Interservice rivalry had led me to some truth, but I had to provoke it to get there.

I discussed what I had learned with Don Sanders, the editor for whom I'd been writing since I got to the Pentagon, and he said, very simply, "Write it." We both knew that there would be pushback, not only from the Pentagon, but from my peers on Correspondents Corridor. I had not helped matters by publishing a strident defense of

Salisbury, while also attacking McNamara's integrity, in the *National Catholic Reporter*, a weekly newspaper that had been gaining status and a growing audience among Catholics and others for its antiwar stance. I wrote the essay under a pseudonym, at the request of Bob Hoyt, the newspaper's editor. Hoyt had reached out to me before Christmas, presumably because of my AP dispatches, and offered to publish anything I wished. He could not have picked a better time to make the pitch, because I was frantic with frustration at having to file story after story of official denials about the Salisbury dispatch—denials that I felt strongly were lies. I hated to write under a pseudonym, since I believed then and still do that anything worth saying is worth saying in a real voice, but I also knew what I had written for Hoyt would create anger among my colleagues, who would immediately figure out who had written the piece, which was published under the byline of Richard Horner.

The dispatch, published January 4, 1967, under a Washington dateline, violated every understanding about the sanctity of background sessions with McNamara and others in the Pentagon. It began this way:

> One of the very highest Defense Department officials was exercising his not inconsiderable charm at a cocktail party in the department's concrete lair along the Potomac River. At his feet lay a cluster of hard-bitten reporters, ready to laugh at the slightest provocation.
>
> "What about the charges we bombed Hanoi?" asked one newsman. At the time of the party, the U.S. was still steadfastly denying the North Vietnamese charges that American war planes had killed or injured more than 100 civilians during raids on Hanoi Dec. 13 and 14.
>
> Well, said the government official affably, he had learned one thing when he served in World War II: bombs never go where they are aimed. Now, 20 years later, the state of the art has improved, he added with a bright party grin: bombs occasionally go where they are aimed.
>
> Some of the reporters laughed. Others quietly gagged on their drinks.

There was a personal reason for my anger toward McNamara. Earlier that winter my wife and I had gone skiing for a long weekend in Colorado. We had little money to spare and did the trip on the cheap, crashing with a college pal who had rented a condominium at Vail, flying on a low-cost ticket, and renting a car from a budget outfit whose check-in desk was a long bus ride away from the Denver terminal. We landed during a heavy snowstorm, good for skiing but bad for driving. Initially we were the only passengers on the bus to the rental office, but at a second stop another family got on—McNamara, his wife, and their two teenage children. I was knocked out; here was a guy from Camelot who was going skiing on the cheap. There was no Pentagon plane, no security, and no one to help him put on the tire chains that were essential for driving in the mountains in heavy snow. I was pretty sure he barely knew me, if at all—at that time I had seen him up close only a few times and never one-on-one—but I introduced myself as the new AP guy, got a nod, and that was that. I was awed by his integrity—no glitz at all—and his obvious desire to be a good husband and father to his immediate family when on vacation. It was hard for me to accept that this decent-seeming man was so willing to look the other way when it came to war. This added to my dismay at his response to Salisbury.

I knew that publishing the anecdote in the *National Catholic Reporter* was a form of professional suicide. The article quickly made the rounds in the Pentagon, and of course those at the cocktail party knew who had asked the question about the bombing in Hanoi, and of course everyone knew that McNamara had analyzed U.S. bombing efficiency and effectiveness as an air force officer during World War II. I was glad then and now that I had the guts to write the piece.

Enter Neil Sheehan, who had left UPI for the *Times* in 1964 and, after another year in Vietnam, had been assigned a few months earlier as the newspaper's Pentagon correspondent. It did not take long for the two of us to connect. As I said, he was one of my journalism heroes, and he saw me as someone who was trying to cope. I cannot imagine the extent of his shock, as a combat reporter unafraid to challenge his government's conduct of the war, at finding the Pentagon pressroom inhabitants to be so spineless. I made a point of introducing Neil to the few officers and civilians I had come to know who shared my dire view of the chances for American success in Vietnam.

The crunch came when I finished writing the first of what would be two articles that I thought would change or end the debate about Salisbury's reportage: one about the BDAs I had seen and a second about McNamara's order restricting the U.S. bombing in Hanoi. I'd shown a draft of the first article to Neil in advance and told him I hoped that the *Times*, which rarely used wire service copy on sensitive issues, would do something—anything—with it. Don Sanders made sure that the wire service's report for Sunday, January 22, included an advance notice to editors of an exclusive dispatch from the Pentagon about American bombing in North Vietnam. My story, which moved hours later on the A wire, quoted intelligence sources as revealing that the United States had aerial photographs showing extensive damage to civilian structures in North Vietnam. There were specifics provided to me: At least fifty-nine civilian structures near a targeted railroad line close to Hanoi had been bombed, with evidence that many bombs had not hit their primary targets. The photos depicted only three bomb craters inside a targeted rail yard, with no fewer than forty craters found outside the yard's perimeter. The obvious conclusion was that less than 10 percent of the bombs hit their primary target. The story also supported Salisbury's report of major damage to civilian areas in Nam Dinh.

I knew there would be a flurry of action in Arthur Sylvester's office as soon as the story began moving on the A wire; his office included a bank of Teletype machines that provided immediate access to the wire services' reports. I heard nothing from Sylvester but was told later that he had gone to my ultimate boss, Wes Gallagher, the general manager of the AP, to register a complaint about me. Sheehan came up to me after my story moved on the wire and said he'd been asked by the *Times*'s foreign desk to check out my story. In the peculiar language of the *Times*, as I would learn when I worked for the newspaper, that meant that Sheehan, if he were able to independently confirm the dispatch, should rewrite it for publication under his byline for the front page of the Sunday paper. Instead of doing so, Sheehan asked me—I'll never forget his words—if the article that appeared on the wire under my byline was precisely the same as the story I had filed. I said yes, and he said he would wait twenty or so minutes and then tell his foreign desk that he had checked out my story and it should be run in the newspaper. Sure enough, the dispatch, marked "By the Associated Press," appeared prominently displayed on the *Times*'s front page the next morning. That did not happen often. I heard nothing from the AP big shots in New York.

Four days later, I dropped what I thought would be a stunner—an article flatly declaring that McNamara, in response to the furor over Salisbury's dispatches, had ordered the Joint Chiefs of Staff, the men who direct the nation's armed forces, to ban all U.S. bombing missions within five miles of the city of Hanoi. I quoted someone I described only as "the source" as telling me that the new restrictions were "the result of everything that's gone into the press. It shows that we're taking into consideration what's being written" by Salisbury. Don Sanders knew the dispatch would be attacked as soon as it moved on the A wire, and he came up with an ingenious idea. Why not wait until five thirty or so in the afternoon—morning newspapers on the East Coast would be planning their front page by then—and file it as "urgent," assigning the piece a level of importance that was a notch below a bulletin, but one that gave me, as the Pentagon reporter, priority over all other stories moving or scheduled to move on the A wire. The next scene was out of a Mel Brooks farce. The wires around the world were pounding out my story when a wild-eyed Sylvester, then just a few weeks from retirement, came running into the pressroom and jammed his forefinger at me. "We know what you're doing, you son of a bitch," he said. I do not remember his next words, but the gist was that he would call my bosses in New York and that would be the end of me. I did not get mad at him in return; I understood he was a creature of the men at the top—McNamara and Vance.

Meanwhile, my dispatch of more than twelve hundred words had finished moving on the wire, and Neil Sheehan walked up to my desk, totally deadpan, with the same sequence of questions. It went something like this: Is the story you filed to your editors the same one that appeared on the Teletype? I said yes. Sheehan told me he again would tell his editors that he had checked out the story and it should be run on page 1. The next morning I woke up to find my article displayed even more prominently on the front page under a headline that read, "U.S. Bars Attacks in Area in Hanoi." The piece did not hinder the bombing of North Vietnam for very long. McNamara had been scheduled for weeks to give testimony that morning before Congress on the Pentagon's annual posture report—a summary of crises that could arise—and as usual he met with the press beforehand. He immediately denied my story, saying that American bombers had not been banned from bombing within a five-mile limit. He repeated the denial after his testimony. The pressure on me was intense, and I passed a message to my friendly admiral and managed to get reassured, very quickly, that there was, indeed, such a limit, and fought off any possibility that a faint heart in the AP would seek a published correction or clarification. It was not until the Pentagon Papers were published in 1971 that I learned the basis of McNamara's denial. The navy had been assigned the task of drawing up the five-mile ban, but navy ships chart their course, as they have forever, on the basis of nautical miles. The other armed services use statute miles when computing distances. A nautical mile is greater, by 15 percent, than a statute mile. I had written "mile" instead of "statute mile." McNamara's denial prevailed, and the Washington press corps, for varied reasons, shrugged off the evidence that Salisbury, and the smug *New York Times*, got it right. No wonder we lost the war.

I shouldn't have been so surprised by my colleagues. I knew Neil Sheehan was an exception to the rule. I got a good sense of what the rule was when I was invited over the winter to participate in a seminar on the war at, I think, Tufts University. One of the panelists was a senior military correspondent for a leading mainstream newspaper, and at some point a student asked him what he thought of the Vietnam War. "I don't have an opinion," he said, explaining his job was to cover it objectively. I was stunned. Of course he had an opinion; it was a war he supported. It was a classic double standard: If you supported the war, you were objective; if you were against it, you were a lefty—like I. F. Stone—and not trustworthy.

Within a few weeks, I was informed that Gallagher had set up a special investigative unit that would be run out of Washington and I was to join it. I protested, but Fred Hoffman was returning to his job as the AP's chief Pentagon correspondent, and that was that. (Hoffman retired in 1984, during the Reagan administration, and almost immediately returned to the Pentagon as a senior official in the office of public affairs.)

Arthur Sylvester retired on February 1, 1967, after six years on the job as McNamara's senior press aide. He published an essay in *The Saturday Evening Post* ten months later in which he brutally mocked the Pentagon press corps: "I don't know a newsman who has served the government as an information officer in the Pentagon who hasn't been dismayed at the evidence of shabby performance by what he used to think of with pride as his profession. . . . For six years I watched cover stories [promulgated by his office] go down smooth as cream, when I thought they would cause a frightful gargle."

There was no learning curve among the men in the Pentagon running the war.

SIX

Bugs and a Book

Working on the AP's new investigative team would have been a dream job if I hadn't been abruptly pulled away from the dream job I had at the Pentagon. I'd emerged from my brief army experience as a private with skepticism about the officer corps; those for whom I worked were either at the end of an undistinguished career or just out of officer candidate school and inexperienced. The officers on duty at the Pentagon were more intense, more ambitious, and more in the world. I learned a lesson as a Pentagon correspondent that would stick with me during my career: There are many officers, including generals and admirals, who understood that the oath of office they took was a commitment to uphold and defend the Constitution and not the President, or an immediate superior. They deserved my respect and got it. Want to be a good military reporter? Find those officers.

There was a remarkable group of young reporters who would dominate the coverage in the Washington bureau by the end of 1967. Two of them, Gaylord Shaw and James Polk, would leave the AP and win Pulitzer Prizes for their respective newspapers in the next decade. A third colleague, Carl Leubsdorf, would become the chief political reporter for the AP and move on to have a distinguished career as a bureau chief and columnist for *The Dallas Morning News*. But those three were not on the AP's investigative team in early 1967; my new colleagues were strangers to me. It mattered little because I knew enough about myself to know that I was not much of a team player, and the concept behind the new unit was teamwork. I also thought that the initial editor of the group, for whom I'd worked on night rewrite when I first got to Washington, was a misfit—an unambitious, incurious fellow who would take no chances and would not be a success.

I would survive, I thought, if I could get on the road, working on a long-term project that had some connection to the military and would put the Pentagon contacts I had made in play. I had already figured out the core lesson of being a journalist—read before you write—and was a follower of the reporting being done in the news section of *Science* magazine, a weekly publication of the American Association for the Advancement of Science. In mid-January 1967, a gifted reporter named Elinor Langer published a two-part series on the perils of the Pentagon's chemical and biological warfare (CBW) research program, whose budget had tripled between 1961 and 1964. The program, centered on the U.S. Army, was responsible for the Kennedy administration's growing use of defoliants and herbicides in South Vietnam, whose long-term side effects, as I had learned while covering the Pentagon, were not known. Some of the air force units that sprayed the stuff over contested jungle areas and combat zones had a slogan that reeked of sarcasm: "Only we can prevent forests."

I knew that dealing with the pros and cons of CBW would be a safe pitch to make to my new editor. I assured him that the AP would not be the first to raise the issue; someone else had already done the story in a highly respected magazine, and there was a ton of declassified congressional testimony raising questions about the intent of the program. I got the go-ahead and headed back to the Pentagon, but not to Correspondents Corridor. I went to the Pentagon library with a list of the known army CBW bases, as published by Langer, and tried to dig up copies of the weekly newspapers at those bases. I had written for such a paper at Fort Riley and knew that every retirement party for a colonel or general routinely made it into print, invariably with details of where the old-timer planned to retire. I got a list of names and addresses, made some calls, and took off, full of my customary enthusiasm.

I spent much of the next two months on the road, visiting retirees as well as the small towns that were the locales for the secret CBW laboratories and production facilities. Small towns have newspapers, too, and given that the bases themselves were totally off-limits, those offices were my first stop. I learned about unreported deaths of laboratory workers and delivery boys who had gone into the wrong lab at the wrong time. I also learned about animals infected with the most deadly of diseases that had escaped—in one case to the mountains of Maryland near Camp David, the much-used retreat for American presidents. I was led to a newly retired colonel who had spent his career—much of it filled with doubts about the morality of his work—in the U.S. Army Chemical Corps. It did not take long to understand that America was not merely doing defensive research in case of a Russian attack, as constantly claimed—vaccines and all that; additionally, there was an intense drive to develop chemical and biological weapons that had the potential of causing mass destruction.

The scientists secretly involved, I would eventually learn, included some of America's best and brightest—among them, Harvard's Dr. James D. Watson, a Nobel Prize winner who was then serving on a secret Pentagon CBW advisory panel. Watson had earlier won fame for his role in discovering the double-helix structure of DNA.

I ended up writing a five-part series for the investigative unit, totaling more than fifteen thousand words that built on the research Elinor Langer had done, and added to it by finding those inside the CBW program who knew that the program had gone way beyond its constantly stated goal of ensuring a defense against a Soviet attack. I turned in the series to the editor of the investigative team with a note summarizing what I found and why the new information was important. And then I waited. A week went by with no word. A second week. I spent the time pretending to be engrossed in researching a new project, but inwardly I was seething. What was up with the son of a bitch? Finally, the editor called me over, reached into a drawer in his desk, pulled out the CBW series, and told me it was much too long. There was no evidence that he had read the material or made any attempt to edit it. I did not know whether he was acting on orders from on high or whether he was going to show the bosses in the bureau that he knew how to handle Hersh.

The bureau chief and others surely knew, as did a few of my pals in the bureau, that I had transgressed two months earlier, shortly after the Vietnamese had ended their weeklong celebration of the lunar New Year. The annual event, known as Tet, was more important, for a week, than the civil war, and a cease-fire was in effect. My walks with Izzy Stone were continuing and had been augmented by occasional dinners with our wives. Stone had talked often of my finding a way to help him get into the AP's files on the Vietnam War, which included verbatim transcripts of the daily press briefings that took place in Saigon. I had gently asked and was told they were only for AP personnel. I mentioned to Izzy that I was scheduled to work an eight-hour shift on a Sunday night in mid-February, a chore that was rotated among all on the staff. It would be just me and a teletypist in the bureau, with little to do, barring a crisis, except to produce a national weather roundup. Izzy insisted that this was the perfect time for access. We made a date and I opened the office door to him minutes after I arrived. He spent at least six solid hours poring over the daily briefings, taking notes amid yelps of joy. Izzy was an odd-looking duck, short, with thick glasses, unruly hair, and a constantly upbeat manner; he would thank me every few hours and reassure me that he needed nothing—no food or water—and was having a terrific time. At some point I felt I had to explain to the mystified teletypist who he was and what he was doing. Izzy published a piece a week or so later in his weekly newsletter showing that the United States, which heatedly accused North Vietnam of violating the truce, had in fact taken advantage of Tet by vastly expanding the amount of supplies and weaponry it delivered day after day into Saigon's Tan Son Nhat International Airport, with no mortar fire endangering incoming cargo flights. It was typical Izzy, doing what he had been doing for decades: reading and reading and reading before writing. I was thrilled, like a teenager, at being able to help him write it. By opening a door.

In mid-April, my CBW series, shredded down to a single story of slightly more than one thousand words, without consultation with me, ran on the A wire just after midnight on a Sunday morning— the darkest of dark holes for wire service journalism. The lead of the series I had written noted that America was spending $230 million for an aggressive program on CBW research. The lead, as rewritten by someone in the AP, made the same point about U.S. spending but then added that the program was aimed at matching an equally aggressive Russian CBW program. I had no information to support that claim, nor had I made it.

At that point I asked to be reassigned to general assignment. The end was near, I knew, and I made it nearer. I met with Gilbert Harrison and Alex Campbell, the two senior editors of *The New Republic* magazine, whose stance against the Vietnam War had won a wide audience, and wrote a lengthy lead piece about CBW for the magazine, dramatically titled "Just a Drop Can Kill." The article, published May 6, listed fifty-two universities and university research centers that were doing work on CBW under military contract. Much of the research was directly linked to the Vietnam War, I wrote, adding that such work also posed a domestic risk: There was a potential for calamity in case of accident to communities near CBW production centers. The article triggered campus protests and some renewed questions from Congress. I understood that I was violating a basic AP rule by publishing outside the news service without permission, and by so doing I put myself at risk of being fired. But it was then for me, and still is, all about the story, and to the credit of the AP's leadership I heard not one word of complaint about my transgression.

The *New Republic* articles led to at least two serious offers for me to write a book on the CBW dilemma, and I chose a lesser offer from Bobbs-Merrill, primarily a textbook publisher, because the editor who approached me, Robert Ockene, was likable and knowledgeable. I also felt he had clout as executive editor at Bobbs-Merrill. My wife and I were expecting our first child, and the advance, a mere four thousand dollars, allowed me to cheerfully resign from the AP in June and begin crashing on the book. There was no attempt to keep me on the job from anyone in the Washington bureau. And no good-luck farewell party.

I wrote a second piece on CBW in July for *The New Republic*, reporting that I had been contacted since the first essay by dozens of campus newspaper editors who, when confronted by denials about dangerous research from college and university officials, wanted reassurance that my list was accurate. It was, and that led to more campus unrest. I also noted in that second essay that none of the major scientific societies had taken a stand for or against CBW. The debate over the morality of such work was spreading beyond the campus, but the debate was a nonissue for the nation's mainstream media. I was not surprised at the inability of the press to comprehend that America was intent on developing a new strategic weapons system, for I had watched up close as the Pentagon press corps refused to face up to the implications of Harrison Salisbury's reporting from Hanoi. It was much easier, I understood, to accept an official denial than to delve into a difficult and controversial issue.

I had a multitude of reasons to get the CBW book done quickly, and did so by early winter. Ockene did what good editors do: He emphasized outline and organization, and told me I had to have some idea about how the book would end before I began. The book was scheduled for publication in the spring; it was the first of many books I would write and the only one that was not published on a crash schedule. The last chapter quoted Matthew Meselson, a prizewinning biologist at Harvard, as warning in early 1967 that "we have here weapons that could be very cheap, that could be particularly suitable for attacking large populations, and which place a premium on the sudden, surprise attack. . . . You could almost not ask for a better description of what the United States should not want to see happen to the art of war. And yet of all the countries in the world it is the United States which conspicuously pioneers in this area." Our first child, a boy, was born that fall, and my wife told me that she wanted to name him Matthew. I thought it was perfect.

SEVEN

A Presidential Campaign

With the book done, I returned once again to the overwhelming foreign policy issue of the time—Vietnam. The war had become a virtual bloodbath for both sides by late 1967, and the growing antiwar movement was desperate to find a way to block the reelection in 1968 of Lyndon Johnson. One fantasy had it that Senator Robert Kennedy of New York would break with his party and run on an antiwar platform against the President in Democratic primaries across America. There was no sign, however, that Kennedy was prepared to take the political risk of doing so. Thus the "Dump Johnson" movement, led by Allard Lowenstein, who also had been in the forefront of the civil rights movement, was in desperate search of a candidate in late 1967, and he was not having much luck.

My wife and I, in need of more space, had rented a small house in northwest Washington that had two immediate attractions: It was a few dozen yards from the entrance to the official residence of the Indian ambassador, and Mary McGrory lived across the street. India was a close ally of Russia's in the ongoing Cold War and also maintained embassies in Hanoi and Beijing, and its senior diplomats were, by necessity, well informed on America's progress, or lack thereof, in the Vietnam War.* Mary, then a must-read columnist for the Washington *Evening Star*, had emerged as a fearless and moral voice against the Vietnam War. She liked the reporting I had done from the Pentagon while at the Associated Press, and, equally as important, she was a good neighbor. She brought dinner many times to us after the birth of our son, and got a martini or two from me in return. One evening she told me that Senator Eugene J. McCarthy, a Democrat from Minnesota who had been raising questions about the war, was going to jump into the race against Johnson. Mary had been close to President Kennedy and was disappointed because Bobby wouldn't run. Gene was brilliant, but prickly, she said, and would need help with the press and with speeches. Did I want the job?

I didn't know the senator and knew less than nothing about running a press operation for a presidential candidate. Mary urged me to meet McCarthy and said she would vouch for me and set things up. I had a brief chat with McCarthy the next day at his office in the Senate. It was clear he knew little, if anything, about me, but after some laconic back-and-forth he said I would do and ended the interview. The only word for him was "diffident," and the only word for me at that point was "nonplussed." McCarthy's cavalier attitude toward me made it clear that he wasn't very interested in a competent, or even halfway-competent, press operation. I had worked closely on CBW issues with the staffs of two liberal Democratic senators from Wisconsin, Gaylord Nelson and William Proxmire, and knew that the senators took their relationship with the media very seriously. I reported back to Mary McGrory, who told me not to fret and urged me to arrange a meeting with Blair Clark, the former head of CBS News who was going to be—this was all hush-hush—the campaign manager. I had no idea how to reach Clark, a New Yorker listed in the social register, but I

---

* I made it a point to seek out foreign diplomats who had served in Russia, China, or North Vietnam before being assigned to Washington. I became especially friendly a decade later with the Indian ambassador, K. R. Narayanan, who had studied political science after World War II with Harold Laski at the London School of Economics. He joined the Indian foreign service and served in China, Russia, Turkey, and England before coming to Washington. Narayanan, with whom I took many long walks, was elected President of India in 1997, and I had the fun of visiting with him in late 2001 at his official residence, the Viceroy's House, a 200,000-square-foot edifice built by Lord Mountbatten. The modest Narayanan told me he utilized only a few rooms there.

did know his son Timothy, who was a reporter in Washington. We had played golf together, and I told him I was interested in being the press secretary. He called his father, who called me. We arranged a meeting at a Washington hotel, to which I brought a satchelful of clips. Blair, like McCarthy, wasn't very interested in my writing, but he, too, pronounced me hired—"if we can get an okay." The okay had to come from Abigail McCarthy, the senator's wife, who, so I would learn, was doing everything possible to micromanage the campaign through Blair and, of course, through her husband. Mrs. McCarthy was very Catholic, very bright—a Phi Beta Kappa who did graduate work at the University of Minnesota and the University of Chicago—a stay-at-home mom, and totally invested in her husband's career. It was a lethal combination.

McGrory understood that McCarthy's campaign would be crazed and threw me to the wolves in the hope that I could do some good. I could care less what the senator's wife thought, and I felt there were two valid reasons to take the job: No other Democrat seemed interested in challenging the seemingly assured nomination of Lyndon Johnson, and anything in public life was better than being yet another freelance journalist. So I signed up as the campaign's press secretary at the princely sum of one thousand dollars a month. I then learned that most of McCarthy's Senate aides, including Jerome Eller, his longtime chief of staff, the secretaries, and other minions in his office, wanted nothing to do with the campaign staff. I met with Blair in late November 1967, the day McCarthy announced his candidacy in New Hampshire. There was a stunning lack of interest in the announcement because McGrory, after a chat with McCarthy, had revealed in her column the day before that he was going to run. I probably should have made a run for the hills then, but was told, since I had accepted the job, that my first task was to fly to New York with the now-presidential candidate, who was scheduled to make a speech before an antiwar group.

McCarthy delivered his talk off the top, with no text, and it was riveting. He was challenging the post–World War II assumptions about the inherent power of the President to interfere militarily where he thought fit, and raised an issue that remains relevant today by insisting that the office belonged not to the man who holds it but "to the people of the nation." We had a senior senator who was a ranking member of the Foreign Relations Committee attacking a president from the same party over his unilateral decision to prosecute a murderous war. McCarthy went on to depict the war as immoral, something I never thought I'd hear a politician say. The guy knew his history and had guts, brains, and integrity. He also spoke quietly, with total self-assurance and implicit respect for the intelligence of his audience. He did not hector. My ambivalence evaporated. I had made the right choice.

It was going to be one hell of a job. My appointment had been reported in a brief two-paragraph story in the *Times*. Soon afterward a reporter named Jack Cole, who worked for the leading newspaper in Minneapolis, called me on the day of McCarthy's speech and asked me to arrange an interview with him. I was now a real press secretary. I found Jerry Eller, who also had made the trip to New York, and told him of the request. I'll never forget his answer: "Well, I'll tell you what you do. Wait until you get two hundred requests and then throw them over the wall to me. We'll handle them." I felt it was a make-or-break moment for me in the job, so I shoved my way to McCarthy, who was surrounded by a cluster of adoring fans, grabbed him by the shoulder, told him about the request, and asked when the best time was to schedule the interview. We worked it out. I was at war with Eller, the senator's staff, and his wife after that, but it was a war of necessity. McCarthy might have been Eller's man in the Senate office, but he was mine, in a very limited sense, when we were on the road campaigning.

A few days later the senator and I flew to California, a focal point for antiwar fervor. On the flight out I gave him copies of a few recent books critical of the war, with various chapters and pages highlighted. I also gave him some data about local issues that I thought he could use in a speech he was scheduled to give at UCLA. The idea of writing a speech in advance for distribution to the wire services and local press had not penetrated the campaign, but it was a goal. I saw that McCarthy, like many senators, was a quick study. He raced through the packet of materials I gave him, which included critical essays about the war and a long memo on the constitutional issues raised by the pending trial of Dr. Benjamin Spock, everyone's favorite pediatrician, and four others who were accused of conspiring to counsel young men to avoid the draft. We talked about the memo, which had been prepared by Michael Tigar, a brilliant Washington lawyer. I worried that perhaps McCarthy had gone through the materials too quickly. After his talk, though, before an enthusiastic crowd that filled more than half of the UCLA basketball stadium, he answered a question dealing with the Spock trial with a brilliant attack on the indictment, based on the Tigar analysis, and a defense of antiwar protests. His support for Spock made the national news that evening.

The contrast between the brilliance of the man and the chaos created by his Senate office was numbing. McCarthy rarely came to the downtown campaign office, and often I would go nuts because his Senate staff would not put me through to him when I called. I would then have to grab a taxi and race to the Senate to get an audience. But he was mine, so I thought, when we were on campaign trips. In those early days, I often was the only aide who accompanied him, and I was a busy bee, constantly giving him materials to read and keeping him up to date on the war and other issues. My diligence and hustle surely bemused him at first, but he soon came to expect a packet of materials from me before every important campaign stop. My travels were made possible by serendipity, in the name of a bright, fast-talking twenty-three-year-old blond ex-UPI reporter named Marylouise Oates, who had been hired by Allard Lowenstein to be Abigail's press secretary. Oates spent a few days on the job before announcing to me that she was quitting after hearing Mrs. McCarthy express concern about all the "Hebrews" working for her husband. I thought that anyone who could figure out the downside of the candidate's wife that quickly was worth keeping around, and I hired her as my deputy. I also sensed that the senator could not care less about my religious background.

Oates ran the Washington office, did all the hiring, and watched my back for the next three months. But that was the least of it. She had been associated for years as a campus activist with the National Student Association, a confederation of college and university governments whose members totaled in the millions, and she understood the potential and the necessity for organizing students across America to canvass for McCarthy to end the war. She introduced me to Sam Brown and David Mixner, who would mobilize a massive "Get clean for Gene" campaign—a slogan Oates thought up—that put many thousands of college students, with beards shaved off and ponytails gone, at work knocking on doors across America. Mixner and Brown would go on in subsequent years to organize massive antiwar campaigns that attracted hundreds of thousands to Washington.

The campaign had an excellent speechwriter, Peter Barnes, who later went to work for *Newsweek*, and I and a few of the volunteers whom Oates had recruited would add our thoughts to Peter's drafts and get them to McCarthy in the hope that he would be interested enough to make them better. It was an imperfect system because the senator was brilliant at speaking on the fly, with no text, and he was also brilliant when he took time to review a draft, which he always improved. On those few occasions when he did so, we would have an advance text of speeches for distribution to the press, and better media coverage.

I knew my place and understood that McCarthy was a terrific second-guesser. I was constantly drafting short statements for the media about issues in the news, many of them about the Vietnam War, and they were invariably critical of the President. I was careful to get his approval in advance. Most were ignored, but there were occasions when McCarthy would be accused of going too far in his criticism of a president in wartime. The underlying inference was that he was aiding and abetting the enemy. On such occasions, especially in the presence of others, he would tear into me and ask how I could write such thoughtless tripe. I would just take it. I was sure McCarthy liked me—that is, my willingness to work hard and keep him up to date on important new books and magazine articles, along with what was in the newspapers. I also realized how taxing it was to make six, seven, or more speeches a day and constantly be on guard against a gaffe that could damage the campaign and even knock him out of the race. I understood why he was so disdainful of the media, which initially treated his campaign as one of whimsy, but I couldn't fathom why, when there was an important speech to be made, he did not always insist on finding time to sit down with a speechwriter and outside experts to actually discuss what he wanted to say, or in other ways be proactive in terms of making public statements or giving interviews to those reporters he trusted. Did he really want to be President?

Early in the campaign, after a long, exhausting week of McCarthy shaking hands and making the same talk over and over again, I was called on a quiet Saturday afternoon in Manchester, New Hampshire, by a producer for *Meet the Press*, the most popular Sunday morning television interview show, and told there had been a last-minute cancellation. Would McCarthy fly to Washington and be the guest? He resisted, insisting he was just too tired. Of course he had to go. So I assured him I would cancel everything we had scheduled for the day afterward if he did the show. He had to know I was lying, but off we went. I did not cancel, and there was hell to pay. The ultimate truth, which he knew, was that Marylouise Oates and I and the thousands of college students ringing doorbells were not essentially working for him but rather to end the war. He had won us over with his brilliant speeches and the courage to do what Bobby Kennedy was too fearful to do. The senator, however, viewed our respect and admiration for him as an unwanted obligation. I had to beg him to spend time with the volunteers, and he often failed to do so.

On the other hand, there was a night in San Francisco early in the campaign when Jerry Brown, the son of former California governor Pat Brown, came for a visit. Young Brown was a devout Catholic who had studied in a Jesuit cloister, as did McCarthy, a Benedictine (who insisted that his religious views be separate from the campaign), and the two of them began talking about marijuana. Neither had ever smoked a joint, and there was no secret that some of the college-age volunteers who worked for me in the press operation were tokers. What was it all about? they asked. It took me only a few moments to produce a few joints, and the two of them got high, or tried to, for the first time. The stuff did little for McCarthy, so he said, but it did much more for Brown. On another night in San Francisco, after a long round of speeches and meetings, I watched as an exhausted McCarthy revived over drinks with one of his pals from his religious study days in Minnesota, an up-and-coming priest who would eventually become a bishop. I was sent out at some point to the City Lights bookstore in North Beach for a book of poetry, and another bottle of scotch, and as the night wore on, the talk turned from poetry to the Old Testament. The two of them began reading portions of the ancient text aloud to each other, amid much laughter and comments like "Would you believe this one, Gene?" It was fun to watch, and learn, as the two Bible experts went at it.

The nation's first presidential primary, in New Hampshire, was approaching. After some hesitation, President Johnson, worried about his fading popularity, decided to run in the primary as a write-in candidate, and McCarthy's fate, and perhaps the fate of the antiwar movement, would be decided on March 12, election day. The senator worked a hell of a lot harder than even his good friends thought he would. A typical campaign day would begin in Washington before five o'clock in the morning. McCarthy, who lived near our home, would drive over to fetch me, sometimes dashing in for scrambled eggs and a chat with my wife (he was always more interested in women), and we'd fly off to campaign, hoping to shake the hands of factory workers in Manchester as they began their morning shift.

It was very slow going at first. McCarthy had little visibility, as the polls throughout January and early February made clear. But we picked up support from Paul Newman and Robert Ryan, two movie stars who shared our worries about the war and who were willing to do anything they could, no matter how taxing, to help our fledgling campaign. Newman's commitment was immense: He spent day after day making speeches at odd places throughout New Hampshire and afterward would meet with me or Marylouise Oates, who had moved there with our media staff, to discuss questions to which he thought he did not have a good enough answer. He wanted to learn. Ryan was full of surprising information. Over lunch one day, he watched me slather ketchup on a rushed hamburger and fries and asked me where in Chicago I had grown up. How did he know? He told me his father had been a union organizer in that union-dominated city and my use of ketchup made the guess a good bet. Robert Lowell, America's most brilliant poet, also joined the campaign. His affinity with the candidate was obvious: Not only was McCarthy attacking the Vietnam War, which Lowell hated, but he was a poet at heart. McCarthy would bemuse and frustrate me by reading poems by intellectuals such as George Seferis, among others, instead of the briefing books on local issues I and my staff were constantly shoving at him.

The senator was doing six or more campaign speeches and appearances a day, at high schools, at colleges, and in front of church groups, and he enjoyed Lowell's company in between. So did I. The three of us, with a driver, would flow from event to event sipping chilled vodka or some other alcohol from a thermos, and the candidate and the poet would happily trade joyous barbs and insights as I vainly tried to get McCarthy to focus on the next event. At one point, a highway billboard popped up with a photo of Nixon—then a candidate for the Republican nomination—and a slogan saying, "Nixon's the one." McCarthy insisted that the two of them could do better, and within three or four seconds, so it seemed, Cal, as Lowell asked to be called, said, "Nixon's at ease with efficiency."

Writing about it now, I'm not sure why the phrase seemed so impressive, but at the time it hit like a first-round knockout, and McCarthy spent a good hour sulking. Lowell had beaten him to the punch. Cal and I and the volunteer driver (what a story he could share later) dared not glance at each other for fear of laughing. I liked Cal and I'm sure he liked the fact that I knew nothing about poetry and never asked about his chaotic personal life. He spent hours yakking with me about my life— never his—during the seemingly unending McCarthy campaign events, where we sat out of sight. He wanted to know what I learned covering the Pentagon, and at one point he happily informed me, after a call from his then wife, Elizabeth Hardwick, an editor at *The New York Review of Books*, that the magazine had bought the serialization rights to my CBW book and would imminently publish two long excerpts from it.

McCarthy was a man of constant mood swings, best understood by his daughter Mary, the one member of the family who openly supported the campaign and endorsed its antiwar purpose. She was a student at Radcliffe and traveled with us on weekends. I would try hard to find her before presenting her father with a speech draft or a list of journalists who sought interviews. One morning, when my requests were especially fractious, I asked Mary how her father was feeling. Her answer still makes me laugh: "Alienated, as usual."

McCarthy, when irritated, often took off on me, telling me again and again that my job was not "to get the press to like you, but to like me. Everybody thinks you're great. You've got reporters sleeping in my bed, and riding in the back of my car." He seemed to save his harshest indictments until he had an audience that included stars like Lowell or some of his big campaign contributors. I remember one night in which he learned at the end of a long day that I had issued a statement in his name—he had approved the gist of it—in which I quoted him as saying, "I believe." He repeated the phrase again and again, adding, "Everyone knows I don't say those words." Of course he did, but at such moments I was glad for the tough love my father had put me through. I was certainly intimidated by McCarthy and eager to please, but not as much as others were.

There was an occasion, late in the campaign, when I was sure I had crossed a threshold and would be thrown out of work. We were flying on a commercial flight from Washington to Manchester when the pilot approached me to say that George Romney, the moderate Republican governor of Michigan, had just announced he was withdrawing as a presidential candidate. The pilot added that a pressroom had been set aside because there was a huge crowd of journalists waiting at the airport for us. Romney had been mocked incessantly by the media after a visit to South Vietnam when he claimed that he had been "brainwashed" by the briefings he'd received. His withdrawal was a huge break for us; primary rules in New Hampshire permitted independents and unregistered voters to vote for any candidate they chose, regardless of party affiliation, and our polling showed that we were certain to pick up many Romney votes. I told the senator about the withdrawal and wrote him a memo, with statistics from our polling, about the Republican votes that suddenly were there for the taking. I urged him to praise Romney for his great effort and talk about his love of public service. It was complete boilerplate and for sure was unnecessary—McCarthy did not need me to tell him how to win votes. But so what? This was a big deal. The senator read the few pages I wrote and then—as I watched in horror—slowly began tearing them up, with one long strip following another. Trouble was coming; I had told him what to think.

We landed and found a horde of reporters who, ignoring the pressroom, rushed instead to meet our plane on the tarmac. Aircraft in those days landed in front of the terminal, and passengers walked inside. McCarthy was the first off, with me following. Television network correspondents were there, along with more members of the national press corps than we had ever seen. What came next was utter perversion. When all quieted down, he opened his comments by saying—this was in front of a flood of cameras and microphones—that when it came to a question of the brainwashing of Romney, "just a light rinse would do." It took a moment or two for some in the crowd to get it and as laughter was breaking out, I jumped in front of McCarthy waving my arms and said something like "C'mon, guys, we're not having a press conference here." I may have added a line about passengers waiting to get off the plane, but whatever I said worked. The network crews broke down their equipment, and we were all moved to a room inside the terminal. I could not believe the tough national press corps would let a punk like me push them around, but they did.

That night, as I watched in panic, none of the networks used the line about Romney. The one major newspaper that used the quote, and had fun with it, as far as I could tell, was London's *Sunday Times*, whose first-rate Insight investigative team was in America to cover the primary. I was amazed and felt as if I'd protected McCarthy from his own peevishness. He said nothing to me about the event, but he knew I had protected him—from himself. I had a lousy job, so I thought, because I had loved the brilliance of the line—the man was very funny—but his job at that moment was to do everything possible to win the votes of those in New Hampshire who were supporting Romney. The senator had to know that there was no halfway when it came to running for the presidency, and ending a war.

A few days later, during yet another plane ride in which he began gossiping about the Senate, I got the courage to ask about some of his pals who were hanging around the campaign. I knew by sheer coincidence that one of them, Tom McCoy, had been the CIA chief of station in Laos; a neighbor of ours, a local artist, had served under him there. It was hard to dislike McCoy; he was rarely serious and loved playing word games about who he was and where he had worked. He was a devout Catholic, as was McCarthy, and I thought their ties came through the church.

I told McCarthy I knew McCoy had been in the CIA, and the senator said, more or less, so what? Lots of good people had joined the Agency after World War II in hopes of turning back communism and making the world a safer place. I had read enough to know that McCarthy's political party, the Democratic-Farmer-Labor Party, was socially liberal—in favor of unions and state support of railroads and utilities—as well as being hostile to international communism. The senator then volunteered—I did not ask—that he had done favors involving the CIA for President Kennedy. McCarthy had said little to me about Jack Kennedy, but he could be vicious in private about Bobby, telling me and others that he was brighter and a better Catholic than Bobby and then adding that his dog was a lot brighter than Bruno, the high-profile Kennedy family dog. McCarthy went on: He had done some secret missions for President Kennedy, including making visits to Catholic leaders in Latin America—he specifically mentioned Chile— that included the delivery to a prominent anticommunist political leader there of a briefcase filled with fifty thousand dollars in CIA funds. The money, and its delivery, were handled by Jerry Eller. After- ward, McCarthy said, with what I took to be pride, that he would never visit the President in the White House to debrief him, but would meet anywhere else.

I was more than a little troubled by all of this: He had abetted Jack Kennedy in an abuse of presidential power whose continuing abuse in Vietnam, half a decade later, was a major element of his campaign against Lyndon Johnson. I guess, flattered as I was by his trust in me, I applauded him for his change of heart and did not think then and do not believe today that the CIA was in any way running his campaign, nor did it have anything to do with his decision to challenge Lyndon Johnson. But I knew that the CIA was deeply immersed in the killing and maiming that was going on in Vietnam, and thought that there was a hell of a lot about the Agency that needed to be made public— just not during the campaign. (I had already met, through McCarthy, a few other insiders who would be of enormous help to my reporting on the CIA in future years.) I never told McCarthy what I thought of the CIA; in fact, we did not discuss the CIA again.

Our goal was to get rid of Johnson and end the Vietnam War, and we were still floundering by the end of January. We got a huge boost one night in remote Berlin, New Hampshire, after a long day, when

I answered the door of my motel room and found Richard Goodwin standing in the cold. There had been rumors in the press that Goodwin, a veteran of the Kennedy and Johnson administrations who was famed for speeches on civil rights he had written for both presidents, had been disappointed by Bobby Kennedy's refusal to run for the presidency and was thinking of joining our campaign. And here he was, in a run-down motel at a pretty much useless campaign stop. Dick later would tell a different version of our first chat, but I remember his words as well as any I heard from Arnold Dornfeld at the City News Bureau. He walked into my room carrying an electric typewriter, dramatically dropped it on a bed, and said, "You and me and this typewriter, kid, are going to overthrow a president." Goodwin, a Jack Kennedy whiz kid, a guy who finished at the top of his Harvard Law School class and edited the law review there, was volunteering his services to our ragtag campaign. Dick and I bickered a lot; I was jealous of him because McCarthy delighted in talking to someone who was a grown-up and knew the score. How tiresome it had to be for McCarthy to put up with political novices like me whose sole purpose for being in the campaign and working as hard as we were was not, at the core, as I said earlier, about him, or his political success, but to stop a war. That was also Dick's motive. I liked and admired Dick—we eventually shared a suite in the Manchester hotel that was the New Hampshire campaign headquarters—but I quickly tired of picking up the private telephone we both used and hearing Teddy Kennedy ask to speak to Dick. Kennedy called so often he eventually began calling me Sy. It was obvious that if McCarthy did well against the President in New Hampshire, Bobby would enter the race, and it would be bye-bye McCarthy. Goodwin knew everything there was to know about our poll numbers and the campaign funds we did or did not have, and I was convinced he was sharing that information. So one anxious morning I woke up McCarthy earlier than he wanted—not a good idea—and told him what I thought Goodwin was up to. McCarthy, ever droll, even in pajamas, gave me a sly look and said, "Well, I don't know, Sy. It's kind of good to have a traitor around. Keeps you on your toes." That was that. I was again nonplussed. Did the guy want to be president? If not, what was I doing?

A major turning point came on the last day of January when the North Vietnamese army and its allies in the South, known as the Vietcong, began a well-planned and very violent series of armed attacks during the Tet holidays, at a time when a cease-fire supposedly was in place. Over the next two weeks, Americans watched in dismay and horror as South Vietnamese bases and cities fell and the U.S. embassy in Saigon was nearly overrun. It was suddenly clear to many that the war in Vietnam could not be won. Untold numbers of college students began rallying in ever greater numbers for Gene, throughout New Hampshire as well as across the nation. Our poll numbers began rising—faster and more intensely than the campaign chose to make public. My press office was suddenly besieged with requests for interviews and TV appearances. We all began thinking ahead, to the next major primary, in Wisconsin, where McCarthy, a Minnesotan, was far better known.

The campaign continued to be starved for cash, but there was money to be had in Wisconsin. One night a jet was chartered—I had no idea who paid for it—and McCarthy and I flew to a private fund-raiser that had been set up in Milwaukee. We were told that a number of wealthy antiwar businessmen, many of them Jewish, were eager to meet the senator. Also on the flight was Harry Kelly, an AP pal of mine, who was doing a major story on the New Hampshire race. Kelly was bright and a charmer, and he and McCarthy had a terrific time gossiping about books, movies, and the vagaries of various senators—anything but the campaign. I wasn't happy but what the hell. If McCarthy had fun with Harry, it might make it easier for me to get him to spend time with other reporters.

We landed in Milwaukee just in time to get to the fund-raiser, which was scheduled for 8:00 p.m. As we drove into the city, we passed an art house movie theater that was showing a newly released British film version of *Ulysses*, the famed James Joyce novel. McCarthy insisted that our taxi turn around and then ordered me to go to the box office and find out when the next showing would begin. Gripped with dread, I reported back that it would start in the next few minutes. "Let's go, Harry," McCarthy said. "I understand they use the word 'fuck' in the movie." What the fuck, I thought, and asked McCarthy as he climbed out of the taxi what on earth I should tell the men with checks at the fund-raiser. He laughed and said, "Tell them I'll part the waters." He and Harry then walked into the theater.

The fund-raiser was a disaster. I mumbled something about the senator taking ill, and gave a short speech to a lot of insulted rich men. We didn't raise enough cash to pay for the charter—if we had to pay. I was embarrassed by my lame performance but found it difficult to beg for contributions when I was not sure that the money would be well spent. I decided then that I would never write about the campaign— and have not until this memoir. I was convinced McCarthy was showing off for Harry, and I was crushed by his cavalier attitude toward the fund-raising that was vital to his chances of winning the Democratic nomination, and the presidency. We would not do well in New Hampshire if we could not match the Johnson campaign in terms of money raised. The President's campaign, taking no chances, was beginning to spend more and more on television and radio advertisements.

There were other difficulties. We were getting much more media coverage, and I was constantly finding myself having to explain away the senator's penchant for dropping a tough paragraph from a speech that had been distributed in advance. One particularly painful instance involved a gutsy commitment by him to explicitly call for a guaranteed annual income for all Americans, an idea the bright kids on my staff had extensively researched. Stephen Cohen, who dropped out of Amherst College to work in the press operation, produced some terrific data, and when I asked where he got it, he said it came from a telephone chat he had with Wilbur Cohen, who was secretary of health, education, and welfare in the Johnson administration. This was very interesting. Stephen somehow got Cohen's unlisted home telephone number and called him one night, identifying himself as a McCarthy volunteer, and got the cabinet secretary to fill in the blank spots in our proposal. Such antics were not unusual among Oates's volunteers. Nancy Lipton, who was a reliable typist of the early morning speech drafts I wrote for the senator, once pulled me out of the shower to complain about sloppy language and comma faults in the text. Nancy was Mary McCarthy's roommate at Radcliffe and, like Steve Cohen, became a successful academic. The ever-competent Steve became more and more essential to me and Marylouise Oates, and often traveled with us. There was a late night when the three of us, exhausted as usual, found ourselves with one room reserved, instead of three, in a seedy motel somewhere in New Hampshire. We shared the bed, fully clothed.

I should have told the senator about Wilbur Cohen's involvement; it might have made him hesitate before deleting mention of a guaranteed annual income in the speech he delivered. His edit came an hour or so after I had assured a busload of skeptical political reporters that he would indeed say what was in the advance text. The reporters duly filed stories for their newspapers' early editions. They were enraged, as they had every right to be. I took the heat for that, lamely explaining that I had misunderstood the senator's wishes. When McCarthy had finished his speech, he walked past me off the stage and, knowing that he had undercut me, asked me how I liked it. I said, "D minus." When I got to the hotel bar that night, a number of newspaper guys warned me that McCarthy was on the warpath toward me and, once again, my job was in danger. I wanted to say so was his insurgency, but did not.

I also kept my mouth shut about the senator's disdainful attitude toward fund-raising, as well as his amusement at Dick Goodwin's continued private chats with the Kennedys. I would complain like hell to my staff and others, including Paul Newman and Cal Lowell, about the senator, but such was merely the other side of respect, or love, as those who worked with me understood. I confess to also being vocal about my distress at McCarthy's complaints about the volunteers who were rallying more and more to his campaign, and kept on nagging the senator to spend more time at volunteer functions. He continued to resist doing so, on the ground that the students who dropped out of college to knock on doors were not doing so for him but using the campaign to express their anger over the Vietnam War. It was demoralizing to hear such talk.

A far less important nuisance was the venom and paranoia that was constantly being injected into the campaign by Abigail McCarthy. She had called me early in the campaign to object to a photograph of her daughter that appeared in a campaign handout. Was she kidding? I told her that I was not her press secretary but her husband's. Bad mistake. Once on her enemies list, one stayed on it forever. Her power came from the fact that her husband was as frightened of her as was his Senate staff of him. She and the senator would separate the next year. The path to power in the campaign, as two of McCarthy's largest contributors quickly learned, was through Abigail. She also intimidated Curtis Gans, who ran the campaign's political operation and was always having staff meetings that I refused to attend. I saw Gans and his gaggle of aides as typical politicians who would trade principles for votes. I also felt they worried far more about a future role in the campaign and in a McCarthy White House than about the issue that grabbed me and my aides—stopping the war. I had lobbied early in the campaign for the irascible, iconoclastic, and brilliant Harold Ickes to be put in charge of the New Hampshire campaign. It did not happen, so I understood, because Ickes wanted full control and Gans and Blair Clark would not give it up. I always had time for Ickes, who would flit in and out of New Hampshire, because he delighted in mocking me, cheerfully, and would invariably greet me by saying, in a singsong voice, "Chicken Little is here and the sky is falling, falling, falling." He had it right: I took everything to heart, and he did not feel the need to go behind my back to say so.

McCarthy's impatience with his wife came through most vividly one night in Boston. My office had produced a twelve-page campaign brochure full of position papers and the obligatory handsome photographs of a happy McCarthy family that was to be distributed in Sunday newspapers throughout New Hampshire on the last weekend of the campaign. A final proof was rushed from our union print shop in New York to our hotel late at night, and McCarthy and I looked it over before giving the go-ahead to start the presses. The press run was in the hundreds of thousands. I was dragged out of bed hours later by the senator and told to rush to his suite. Abigail, it turned out, had gotten a proof flown to their home in Washington, and she was upset about some of the photographs and language. It had something to do with angering potential Catholic voters or some such. The senator, in his bathrobe, got her on the phone and told her that he had me—the archenemy—sitting in front of him. He then repeated her complaints—she was listening—and told me in a very stern voice that I had to make the changes she wanted. Yes, sir, I said. The alternative was to say, are you nuts? The brochure was being printed as we talked. McCarthy asked Abigail if she was satisfied. She was, I gathered, and he hung up. He rose from his chair, shrugged, gave me a warm smile, and told me he would see me in the morning. It was as close to intimacy as we'd come. He knew he had thrown me to the wolves—that is, his wife— with his cowardly performance and I would suffer the consequences. Abigail, as predicted, told her moneymen that I had deliberately defied her husband. The senator had given me, his press secretary, an order, and I, in Abigail's world, had just lied to his face.

McCarthy stunned America by winning 42 percent of the vote in the March 12 New Hampshire election. Johnson, despite picking up 48 percent of the Democratic vote as a write-in candidate, had to know then that it was over, but he waited almost three weeks, until March 31, to announce that he would not stand for reelection. Bobby Kennedy jumped into the race, and Dick Goodwin left our campaign to join his. Bobby was going to be just as strident about the war as was McCarthy, and I was thinking more and more about going back to what I was good at—being a reporter. My tiny travel staff back in Washington, led by a tireless Joshua Leinsdorf, was now chartering two American Airlines planes, with crews, to fly the senator, our burgeoning staff, and scores of domestic and international reporters from campaign stop to campaign stop. The reporters had to be billed daily for the flights. Lowell had taken time off from the campaign, as had Newman and Ryan. And I was now running a travel agency. Was I really a politician?

There was a chilling moment in Milwaukee that convinced me that McCarthy, with Bobby in the race, felt trapped in a campaign that was no longer viable. The Democratic nomination was still in sight, but there was a lot of political hardball to play. If Irish Catholic McCarthy wanted to win the nomination, he had to deal with Irish Catholic mayor Richard Daley of Chicago. Daley controlled the Illinois delegation to the Democratic convention and was known to be partial to the Kennedys. I had written extensively about police corruption and racism while working for the AP in Chicago and had contempt for the mayor. But I was told by one of our people—I do not remember who— that Daley would be delighted to take a call from McCarthy. I was given a private phone number to call and a time window. My ambiva-

The grungy desks at the City News Bureau of Chicago, circa 1960. I began my journalism career there as a copyboy, and the most hated of tasks was to make the top of one of the desks spotless for the day city editor. *Courtesy of Paul Zimbrakos*

My twin brother, Alan, left, and me at about the age of five. Our two sisters, Marcia and Phyllis, five years older, also were twins. *Courtesy of Cindy Zimmerman*

Celebrating the first edition of the *Evergreen Park/Oak Lawn Dispatch* in the early winter of 1962. Bob Billings, my partner, who also was my former hard-nosed editor at the City News Bureau, is on the left; Paul Zimbrakos, who worked with Bob and me at City News and volunteered to help put out the first edition, is in the middle; and I am on the right. The fledgling newspaper promised to cover both suburbs as never before, from high school sports to city hall debates. *Courtesy of Paul Zimbrakos*

David Halberstam of *The New York Times*, Malcolm Browne of the AP, and Neil Sheehan of UPI in South Vietnam in 1963—three magnificent, courageous, and oh-so-young reporters. Neil and David would become fast friends.
Associated Press

THE NEW REPUBLIC

May 6, 1967, 35 cents

Just a Drop Can Kill
Secret Work on Gas & Germ Warfare
Seymour M. Hersh

My first major freelance article, written in May 1967 for *The New Republic*, as I was ending my AP career.

Senator Eugene McCarthy, right, and his supporter Robert Lowell, the poet, during the 1968 Democratic Party primary race. The two men delighted in each other's company, and I delighted in being a witness to their friendship. The resonance of McCarthy's anti–Vietnam War campaign was a body blow to the presidency of Lyndon Johnson.
Courtesy of Jefferson Siegel

Marylouise Oates, seen here at an antiwar planning session in late 1967, was my trusted deputy when I ran the press office of the McCarthy campaign. She went on to help organize the major anti–Vietnam War rallies of the next few years. *Courtesy of Marylouise Oates*

Ron Ridenhour, in Vietnam in 1970 as a journalist, viewing the aftermath of an American assault in the My Lai area. In late March of 1968, while in the army, Ridenhour had flown over My Lai and seen the destruction and was determined to learn what had happened there. Unlike his colleagues, he chose to do something about the massacre. It was his wave of official complaints that led me to the My Lai story. Ron selflessly stepped back and helped me pursue it. He was a caring man who died after a heart attack in 1998 at the age of fifty-two.
© *1970 Charles Ryan for* The New York Times

FORT BENNING, Ga. -- Lt. William L. Calley Jr., 26, is a mild-mannered, boyish-looking Vietnam combat veteran with the nickname of "Rusty." The Army xsays he deliberately murdered at least 109 Vietnamese civilians during a search-and-destroy mission in March 1968 in a Viet Cong stronghold known as "Pinkville."

Calley has formally been charged with six specifications of mass murder. Each specification cites a number of dead, adding up to the 109 total, and adds that Calley did "with premeditation murder ... oriental human-beings whose names and sex are unknown by shooting them with a rifle."

The first page of the original draft of my first article on Lieutenant William Calley, who ordered the killing of more than a hundred innocent Vietnamese civilians at My Lai in March 1968. In November of that year, David Obst, who ran the Dispatch News Service, wired the completed piece to newspaper editors, seeking publication. He somehow succeeded in convincing more than thirty-five editors to pay one hundred dollars for the right to publish the story.

The always cheeky David Obst in 1992 with a man soon to be president.
Courtesy of David Obst

THE TIMES

US soldiers say 'we saw massacre'

At a time of growing concern in the United States over stories of corruption and atrocities in South Vietnam, three American soldiers have claimed that they saw their combat unit massacre old men, women, and children, in a Vietnamese village.

In Saigon, the United States Embassy and American Command yesterday issued a statement that the American Government did not condone atrocities "in any way, at any time, under any conditions". President Thieu has called for a report from the chief of the province concerned.

'Women and children shot down'

From SEYMOUR M. HERSH

Three American soldiers who took part in the March, 1968, attack on Pinkville—known to the Vietnamese as Son My Village—said in interviews released today that their Army combat

run into resistance at Pinkville and also expecting them (the Vietcong) to use the people as hostages."

A few days before the mission, he said, the men's general

The major play given my second story on My Lai by the London *Times* influenced many American newspapers to reconsider my stories, which they had initially rejected or downplayed.

Charley Company

Charley Company, First Battalion, Twentieth Infantry, ca me to Vietnam in December, 1967, strong, seemingly well-trained and ready to fight. It s men, like GIs in all combat units, considered themselves to be part of the best and toughest outfit in the newly formed Eleventh Brigade. Since December, 1966, the Brigade had been getting ready for Vietnam, at the Schofield Barracks, Hawaii; when the orders came to move out, Charley Company was named to lead the advance party.

Captain Ernest L. Medina, the 33-year-old former enlisted man who was the company's commanding officer, was proud of his men. "We became the best company in the battalion," he would say

The first page of an important chapter from my typed manuscript for my book *My Lai 4*, edited by Robert D. Loomis and published by Random House in June of 1970.

The wildly successful *Harper's* magazine "extra" issue of May 1970 with its almost-book-length insert of *My Lai 4*.

In the barren Dispatch offices in Washington, D.C., I had just learned, in May 1970, that I had won the Pulitzer Prize for international journalism.
AP Photo/Bob Daugherty

Two months before officially joining *The New York Times*, I was sent by the paper to North Vietnam after a stopover in Paris. I was the second mainstream newspaper reporter permitted to report from Hanoi and elsewhere in the North in six years. I took this photo of schoolboys having fun with me in March 1972, outside the Reunification Hotel in Hanoi. They were excited to learn I was an American and made it a point to say "Good morning, sir" whenever we met.

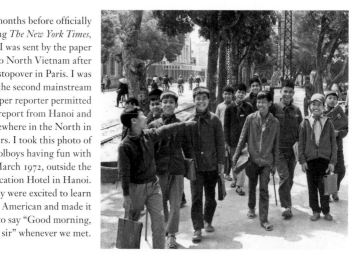

At a news conference in 1971, the top men at *The New York Times*, left to right, executive editor A. M. "Abe" Rosenthal, publisher Arthur Ochs "Punch" Sulzberger Sr., and general counsel James Goodale—all did their best to look somber after learning that the Supreme Court ruled that the *Times* could continue to publish the previously top secret Pentagon Papers. It was a decision, I heard more than once, that cleared the way for me and others at the *Times* to push hard on Watergate and issues of national security. © *1971 Jack Manning/ The New York Times*

8 May 1973

Dear Mr. Hersh,

I am Lt Col Edison W. Miller USMC. I met you in Hanoi while I was a prisoner of the North Vietnamese. I was neither forced or rewarded for meeting with you and expressed my honest feelings to you. I would like to thank you for contacting my family after our visit and reporting to them my good health and spirits. I tried to remain objective while in prison and not succumb to

This is a letter to me from marine lieutenant colonel Edison Miller written in May 1973, after his release from captivity as a POW in North Vietnam. He thanked me for my "frank reporting" on the war. Miller spent more than five years in captivity after being shot down, most of it in the infamous Hanoi Hilton jail.

The strong, silent Major Bo, detailed, clearly against his will, from the army of North Vietnam as my fellow traveler and watcher during my visit to Hanoi for the *Times*. We ended up as friends, though communication was difficult because he spoke Vietnamese and French and I spoke neither. But his dark eyes did a lot of talking.

lence about Daley did not matter; it had to be done. I found McCarthy at lunch with the usual gaggle, including the now-returned Lowell, Mary McGrory, and two of the big money boys. I crouched next to him, waiting for a moment to whisper my message, but McCarthy ignored me. I finally interrupted him and, very quietly, gave him the message. McCarthy, as mean as I'd ever seen him, loudly announced to all that Sy Hersh was here and "wants me to kiss Mayor Daley's ass." He did not make the call.

A few days later, I learned that McCarthy had agreed with Curtis Gans that he would attract a much higher percentage of the white vote in Wisconsin if he canceled a series of already scheduled campaign rallies in the black neighborhoods of Milwaukee. Race was always a complicated issue for McCarthy. He was in no way a racist or a bigot and had been adamant, magnificently so, in his public criticism of the Pentagon's decision in 1966 to lower the standards for enlistment in the armed forces—a move, pushed by Robert McNamara, that resulted in a higher percentage of blacks and Hispanics in the front lines of the Vietnam War. The Johnson administration was "changing the color of the corpses" in the war, McCarthy said again and again in his speeches, as it tried to limit the number of middle-class whites in combat and tamp down the growing antiwar movement. But the senator, in a basic way, did not understand the extent of institutionalized white racism in America. He just could not relate to the anger of black America. Early in the campaign, a young black labor leader from Detroit named John Conyers, who went on to have a long career in Congress, arranged an off-the-record meeting for McCarthy with a number of black civic and union officials. It was a disaster. McCarthy talked about how he had once had a Negro roommate while in a parochial school. I subsequently wrote him a long memo about racism, making the point that he did not have to believe that institutionalized white racism existed; he just had to recognize that an overwhelming number of blacks believed it did. Mary McCarthy, who understood her father in ways many did not, made sure he read it.

This history, along with a lack of respect and distrust for Gans, made Marylouise Oates, and me, and most of my staff, frantic upon hearing that the senator had agreed to cancel appearances in the black community. I couldn't believe McCarthy had signed off on such a dumb move, and I raced to his hotel suite. I almost came to blows with a young man who was then serving as a bodyguard when McCarthy came out. I told him what I had learned and asked if it were so. He told me, very coldly, that it was none of my business. That was it. He was running for the presidency now, and for him moral issues, so I believed, were secondary to getting votes. The Democrats of America had made a statement about the Vietnam War and I had done my part. I left the campaign the next afternoon, along with Oates. We had gone through three months together, protecting each other's back and convinced there was nothing more important than what we were doing, despite the madness.

One of Oates's confidants chose to tell a *New York Times* reporter what had gone on, and our resignations became a two- or three-day television news wonder. Oates would remind me years later that our rumored resignations became official when we literally jumped off a campaign bus before a rally at Stevens Point, Wisconsin. As we fled down the street, with a few reporters following us, we spotted Robert Lowell sitting in the grass, waiting for the McCarthy caravan. As I loped by, Oates said, I yelled, joyously, "Good-bye, Cal Lowell. Good-bye, Poet Laureate."

I flew home, said hello to my family, and went to sleep. I answered no telephone calls and gave no interviews and kept my experience in national politics to myself. I had helped get rid of a president, but not a war. I had a book being published in a few weeks and lots of ideas for magazine assignments and wanted to put national politics behind me.

McCarthy called me a few weeks after the blowup. There was no apology sought, or needed. Instead, he wanted to know if I would return to the campaign to help with speeches and position papers. I told him I was not sure. He said I would get a call to continue the dialogue, but I did not. I had no more formal contact with the campaign, which stayed alive through the assassination of Robert Kennedy and the violent and chaotic Democratic convention that nominated Vice President Hubert Humphrey in Chicago. McCarthy would have been a far better choice.

There was one last hurrah late in the summer when I was asked by Adam Walinsky, who had been one of Bobby Kennedy's aides, if I would call McCarthy and find out if he would agree to a meeting to discuss a fourth party—Governor George Wallace of Alabama also was a presidential candidate in 1968—whose goal would be to deny the election to either Humphrey or Richard Nixon, the Republican candidate. The senator said yes, and Walinsky and I and a few others, Kennedy people, went to his home. McCarthy told us he thought he could win as many as four states if on the ballot—Minnesota, Wisconsin, New York, and California—enough to throw the election to Wallace. I was pretty sure he was putting us on.

There would be no fourth party. Nixon won the election that November and continued the war, as Humphrey would have. McCarthy began a slow drift away from the political mainstream. He formally separated from Abigail in 1969, but their marriage, as many in the campaign knew, had ended long before. There would be no divorce. McCarthy announced in 1970 that he would not be a candidate for reelection to the Senate but, whimsically, so it seemed, staged two halfhearted presidential primary campaigns in 1972 and 1976 in which he performed very poorly. There was a final, doomed campaign in 1982 when he ran in the primary for the Senate seat in Minnesota he had abandoned eleven years earlier. He got 24 percent of the vote.

My wife and I stayed in touch with the senator and made it a point to visit with him, usually over dinner, until he passed away in 2005. We talked very little about the past. His wonderful daughter Mary went on to law school and taught at Yale Law School. She died tragically young, from cancer, in 1990.

EIGHT

Going After the Biologicals

It was liberating to be away from the intensity and irrationality of a political campaign, but there was the glum reality: I was once again out of work. The *New York Review of Books* excerpts from my forthcoming book, spread over a dozen pages, ran in late April and early May, and soon I was back doing what I could do best—being a journalist.

The book was published in early June, and a story about its findings made its way to the front page in the first edition of *The Washington Post* on June 6, 1968, which hit the streets the night before. Bobby Kennedy was assassinated that night, and the friendly dispatch about my book disappeared in later editions of the *Post*, as it should have. Bobby's death, along with the ongoing killings in Vietnam and the earlier murder of Martin Luther King Jr., reignited fears regarding the well-being of our society. McCarthy would keep on campaigning, I knew, but he would make no effort to reassure America. It was not his style.

I spent many weeks that summer promoting my book with talks at bookstores and colleges; campus CBW research remained an emotional issue as the military's growing reliance on defoliation in South Vietnam became more widely reported. Hundreds of American scientists, acting individually or through scientific societies, added their voices to the anti-CBW debate. I struck up an important friendship with Matthew Meselson, the Harvard biochemist who was not interested in another study or any other halfway measure; he wanted an immediate U.S. ban on the development and production of chemical and biological weapons. It took courage for him to be so actively against the weapons, for at the time he was an adviser, with a security clearance, to the U.S. Arms Control and Disarmament Agency. The immediate disarmament goal was to update the 1925 Geneva Protocol barring the use of poison gas and biological weapons in warfare. The U.S. position was that the protocol did not apply to the herbicides and souped-up tear gas agents in use in the Vietnam War.

Enter *The New York Times Magazine.* An editor there—I do not remember who—asked me to do a piece on the CBW issue with the goal of bringing the newspaper's readers up to speed. I was amazed, since there had been no real interest in the issue, or my book, by the daily *Times.* There was good reason for the mainstream news media to be interested: In mid-March, a mysterious event had led to the death of more than six thousand sheep in two valleys adjacent to the army's Dugway Proving Ground, a million-acre top secret CBW test site in rural Utah. As word of the tragedy spread, there were published reports in the Salt Lake City newspapers linking the deaths to "some kind of poison." The military command at Dugway initially insisted to reporters that no tests had been conducted that week and there was no military responsibility for the loss of sheep. It was a preposterous position, but few in the media, outside the two daily newspapers in Salt Lake City, seemed to care. I began my essay for the magazine with an account of the sheep deaths and noted that it took the army more than a month to acknowledge responsibility for the macabre event, and it did so only after a fact sheet sent to a Utah senator for his personal use was inadvertently made public by an aide.

I ended the article with a plea for transparency and disarmament, and the magazine, to my surprise, let me have my say:

The Pentagon should immediately re-evaluate its security restrictions about C.B.W. If Russia is indeed engaged in a major C.B.W. build-up, this information should be made known. The types of agents, their possible effects and the national policy surrounding actual deployment of chemicals and biologicals should be released for public evaluation.

Americans—and Russians—know a great deal about the horrible consequences of atomic attack; this knowledge is as significant a deterrent as the I.C.B.M. rockets shielded deep in their silos. If the world knew more about the potential horror of nerve gases and deadly biologicals, the drive for de-escalation and disarmament would be increased. And the United States, as one of the leaders of C.B.W. research and development, would have an obligation to lead that drive.

The story snuffed out any worries I had about being blackballed or stigmatized by the mainstream newspaper world for having worked, as a Democrat, in a national antiwar presidential campaign. The combination of my book, the *New York Times Magazine* article, and my continued speaking out about CBW at colleges and universities generated what every reporter needs—inside sources. I found a retired senior officer of the U.S. Army Chemical Corps who began telling me about research and production facilities that had not been made public but were known to some congressional committees. That contact led me to a young man who, while in the army, had served as a guinea pig for biological experiments at Fort Detrick, the army's off-limits CBW research facility in Frederick, Maryland, forty-five miles north of Washington. I would learn from a series of letters he wrote to me that he was one of many.

My comfort in getting to know and exchanging views with a wide variety of people generated, I came to understand, from being raised and working in a racially diverse part of Chicago. I had grown up needing to figure out on my own whom to trust and depend on in the community, very likely in an effort to fill in some of the gaps in the parenting I experienced at home. Whatever the reason, I found it easy to be open and connect with scientists, army generals, Republican legislators, and intelligence officials as I moved through my career.

That skill, no matter how useful, did not change the reality: The academic opposition led by Matthew Meselson, my book and other writings, the Elinor Langer essays, and a flicker of campus protest had not created a flood of public indignation. Far from it. But the military, anxious to keep their real secrets hidden, overreacted. The Pentagon's Public Affairs Office arranged for Mike Wallace, a correspondent for CBS's *60 Minutes*, the nation's most watched television news show, to get unprecedented access, with cameras, to three secret CBW facilities. The network aired two segments on germs and gases in late October 1968. The purpose, Wallace explained at the outset, was "to bring CBW into the sphere of rational discussion—sort of delousing it, or debugging it, like kids learning there aren't any ghosts." The network then showed footage of facilities for the massive production of diseases such as anthrax, plague, and tularemia, all potential biological warfare agents. Large concentrations of frozen germs were shown rolling off an assembly line.

My newfound friends from inside the CBW world helped me deconstruct the *60 Minutes* piece in an essay for *The Progressive* magazine. The network did not report who took the footage or where the facilities were located, but I wrote that some of the film had been produced by the army at the Pine Bluff Arsenal, a secret facility in Arkansas. CBS did not report that there were at least 251 cold-storage underground vaults, known as igloos, on the Pine Bluff grounds, many of them used to store biological agents. CBS did not report that there were sophisticated weapons assembly lines at the arsenal, capable of filling hundreds of 750-pound bombs within hours with diseases considered worldwide scourges, nor did it report that there had been thirty-three hundred accidents in an eight-year period at Fort Detrick, resulting in the infection of more than five hundred men and three known deaths—two from anthrax. Most important, in my view, CBS did not tell its audience that more than fifty government officials, representing twelve agencies, were given an advance screening of the two *60 Minutes* segments before they were aired. The officials suggested some "factual" changes, which were made, and offered other objections to the editorial content, not all of which were entertained.

The CBS report prompted a far more critical follow-up in early February 1969 on *First Tuesday*, an NBC network news show that owed its existence to the success of *60 Minutes*. Viewers were told at the outset, very pointedly, that *First Tuesday*'s reporting had not been prepared in consultation with the Pentagon. The show produced heart-throbbing scenes of laboratory experiments involving rabbits and mice, along with the bulldozing of dead sheep into huge pits near the Dugway Proving Ground. Most significant, *First Tuesday* revealed that millions of dollars had been awarded over six years by the Defense Department to the Smithsonian Institution in Washington for research into the migratory patterns of birds near the U.S.-owned Baker Island, a one-square-mile uninhabited chunk of land seventeen hundred miles southwest of Honolulu. The implication was clear: America was on the hunt for a safe place in the Pacific Ocean for a biological warfare test.

There were some stirrings after the November 1968 election of Richard Nixon to the presidency. In December, the General Assembly of the United Nations approved yet another resolution calling for a major report on the possible use of CBW, and Senator Gaylord Nelson, a liberal Democrat from Wisconsin, made a gutsy speech in which he asked questions that had rarely been asked in the Senate: "What is the United States now doing to insure that this totally destructive and little understood aspect of the arms race is reduced? . . . We will need to review the entire scope of chemical and biological warfare." That was his public stance. Privately, a few aides in his Senate office began to fill me in on what they knew was going on, and what they suspected might be. In late April 1969, Meselson was invited by William Fulbright, an Arkansas Democrat and chairman of the Senate Foreign Relations Committee, to brief the committee in closed session—no press or public allowed—and Meselson renewed his call for a comprehensive review of America's CBW policy. Fulbright subsequently wrote to President Nixon urging him to submit the 1925 Geneva Protocol to Congress for ratification. Meselson repeatedly took his plea for a total ban to Henry Kissinger, Nixon's national security adviser. Kissinger and Meselson had been faculty colleagues at Harvard and close neighbors in Cambridge.

There was similar movement in the House. I was put in touch in early 1969 with an ambitious second-term Democratic congressman from Buffalo, New York, named Richard D. "Max" McCarthy, a former newspaper reporter. He was eager to run for Senate and knew he needed an issue. He had watched the *First Tuesday* news show with his wife and children, and all were horrified. His wife shooed the children out of the room, and, as McCarthy recalled in *The Ultimate Folly*, a book he wrote about his anti-CBW campaign, she said, "You're a Congressman. What do you know about this?" He answered, "Nothing." Stopping CBW would be a political plus as well as in the public interest. McCarthy was fortunate to have two skilled aides on his office staff, Wendell Pigman and Peter Riddleberger, who knew Washington and foreign policy. Pigman had worked for Bobby Kennedy until his assassination, and Riddleberger, the son of a prominent postwar U.S. ambassador, had worked for the Senate Foreign Relations Committee.

Wendell, Peter, and I quickly became friends and collaborators. I was in a journalistic catbird seat—getting information from inside Congress as well as from my insiders, who were educating me on where to look for information that the CBW community did not want the public to know. I published five long magazine pieces on CBW between March and June 1969 and continued to get new data. McCarthy, using information supplied by me and his staff, became more effective among his House colleagues in making clear the peril of CBW research, as did Gaylord Nelson in the Senate. By June, my magazine work on biological warfare was focused on the same theme that I had raised in my AP reporting on the Harrison Salisbury bombing disclosures: The military was not telling the truth. America's biological warfare program was far more advanced than was known.

I should note here that I am in no way a fanatic, or a prude about lying, and realize that human beings lie all the time. We all know the clichés about the big fish that one caught or the low golf score. My brother and I learned early in life that our mother lied repeatedly, especially about store-bought cookies she claimed to have baked. Not a big deal. I happen to believe, innocently perhaps, that official lying or authorized lying or understood lying about military planning, weapons systems, or intelligence cannot be tolerated. I cannot look the other way.

I had repeatedly challenged the Pentagon's long-standing defense for its CBW program—that the United States was focused only on defensive research. I reported that the Pine Bluff Arsenal was capable by the late 1960s of producing a full line of ready-to-fire bombs, shells, and even hand grenades filled with virulent, field-tested, lethal anthrax, tularemia, or Q fever germs. Large stocks of anti-crop biological agents, some especially tailored for crops grown in Cuba, also had been manufactured and stored there, as are all biological agents, in igloos that were kept extremely cold. I also learned that CBW agents had been field-tested at Dugway, Utah; at Fort Greely, Alaska; on the Eniwetok Atoll, in the Marshall Islands in the Pacific Ocean; and in isolated areas throughout the Pacific. American-sponsored CBW research has been conducted in Malaysia, Japan, England, Ireland, Canada, Sweden, Cyprus, Australia, Germany, and Taiwan. Fort Detrick, the primary base for research into promising biological weapons, had 120 research scientists with doctorates at work there by 1968, and more than 400 more with lesser degrees. There was also no shortage of young research scientists eager to accept grants from the prestigious National Academy of Sciences to work on exotic projects at Fort Detrick. Detrick was one of the world's largest users, and killers, of laboratory animals; 720,000 animals ranging from guinea pigs to monkeys were put to death each year in experiments. I also learned that thousands of army soldiers and volunteers had participated since the end of World War II as human guinea pigs in experiments aimed at calibrating the impact of various biological agents on human beings. The Seventh-Day Adventist Church had supplied fourteen hundred volunteers by the late 1960s to Fort Detrick for tests involving the spreading of airborne tularemia; the program was known as Operation Whitecoat. At least some of the volunteers, so I was privately told, had no idea what they volunteered for, and consented to, and would learn later what they had been exposed to. Some "volunteers" were given the option after basic training of going to Vietnam as combat medics or joining the Whitecoat program. The diseases they were exposed to included tularemia, yellow fever, Rift Valley fever, and the plague.

I was energized, enjoying what I was doing, but I was still not making very much money. Publishing an article a month in *The New Republic*, *The Progressive*, or *The New York Review of Books* did little more than keep me—now a daddy with rent to pay and a car payment to make—above water. Bob Hoyt of the *National Catholic Reporter* came to the rescue by agreeing to publish a political or foreign policy essay by me each month—I could choose the subject—and paying me too much. I had another source of income, courtesy of a twentysomething neighbor named David Obst who was the Washington representative of Dispatch, a small antiwar news agency that focused, very critically, on the Vietnam War. David was immensely likable and, like me, not very interested in rules. The son of a jewelry store owner near Los Angeles, he had dropped out of the University of California at Berkeley after a year or so and fled to Taiwan, where he learned Mandarin Chinese and fell in love with a local beauty, only to flee for his life when her parents learned what was going on. He was a natural athlete—we bonded over pickup basketball and touch football games—who was not that much interested in sports. He also was a born salesman and easily convinced me to let him try to syndicate my articles for the *National Catholic Reporter* to the Sunday opinion sections of major newspapers. My articles, at a cost of fifty or seventy-five dollars each, suddenly began showing up in Sunday opinion sections of *The Washington Post*, *The Baltimore Sun*, *The Providence Journal*, and other papers.

In April 1969, *Ramparts* magazine, then flourishing amid the expanding anti–Vietnam War movement, agreed to fly me to Utah to learn what I could about the sheep kill at the Dugway Proving Grounds. It was the same old story: A local community financially dependent on the military had kept its collective mouth shut. But a few of those who had stayed mum in the days and weeks after the sheep kill were eager to talk now, a year later, and their account was chilling. The Chemical Corps officers running Dugway had been on alert on the day of the disaster because an advanced airborne aerosol delivery system was being tested. The test was being filmed, in color, with two cameras rolling. The purpose of the mission was not to test the lethal nerve agent involved but to determine how the gas spread when released by a jet into a swirling wind blowing from five to twenty-five miles an hour to the northeast—toward Salt Lake City, eighty miles away. The highly classified film tells what happened: The jet roared over the target at the speed of sound, or above it, and opened its dispersal tanks, which were to close immediately as the jet pulled out of its dive. There was a potentially catastrophic malfunction, and the nerve gas kept on spewing out as the jet climbed to above fifteen hundred feet, where the wind was more active and unpredictable. I was told of one computation indicating that the nerve gas cloud would remain lethal at a range of 394 miles. The army and the citizens of Utah got lucky; the winds shifted an hour later and sheep were the only victims. The cover headline for my reporting, published in the June issue of *Ramparts*, read, "Nerve Gas Was Tested on 6400 Sheep by the Army, Accidentally. It Works."

That June, I also wrote a long piece for *The New Republic* focused on Representative McCarthy and his activism. It told how he broke through on the CBW issue, in terms of public awareness of the peril, a month earlier. McCarthy, in a hearing, had made public a secret Pentagon plan to dump twenty-seven thousand tons of unwanted chemical warfare agents and munitions—twelve thousand of which were nerve gas bombs—into the Atlantic Ocean. More than eight hundred railway cars were to haul the toxic materials from a chemical warfare depot near Denver to Elizabeth, New Jersey. The cars, each one of which was carrying enough poison gas to wipe out a major city, were scheduled to roll through Indianapolis, Dayton, Knoxville, Cincinnati, and Philadelphia before getting to Elizabeth, on the ocean. There was no additional security for the convoy and no advance cautioning notice to officials of the cities along the route. The hearing provoked fear and anger and finally put the CBW issue on the front pages. The army, confronted by a public outcry, quickly announced that the trip was canceled and the toxic goods would be destroyed locally. A major change in American CBW policy was in sight.

I had one more push in late September, revealing all I knew about biological weaponry in a second article for *The New York Times Magazine*. The article's headline said it all: "Dare We Develop Biological Weapons?" I quoted Max McCarthy and paid homage to Gaylord Nelson and came down hard on the Pentagon's now riddled claim that its CBW programs dealt solely with defensive measures. The key question I posed at the end of the piece went to the core in a more focused way than I did in closing the similar article in *The New York Times Magazine* more than a year earlier: "Does the United States really need to invest funds in a weapons system that may not work and will not deter? Unless the military can satisfactorily demonstrate that the C.B.W. threat from an enemy is as real as it thinks it is, the answer seems to be no."

President Nixon, more and more enmeshed in the Vietnam War, tipped his hand on the issue in October by requesting a multiagency review of America's CBW policy. On November 25, he announced that the United States would cease production of offensive biological warfare agents and destroy existing stockpiles. He also renounced the first use of lethal and incapacitating chemical warfare agents and pledged to resubmit the Geneva Protocol to the Senate for ratification. The President had been under pressure from Melvin Laird, the secretary of defense, to get out in front on the issue and ensure that any ban would not impact the continuing use of defoliants and herbicides in South Vietnam. His presidency revolved around the war. He had defeated Hubert Humphrey by telling America that he had a plan to end the war; his plan, as it turned out, was to win it. In his memoirs, Nixon made no mention of his renunciation of CBW but dwelled at length on the burgeoning antiwar movement that fall. Antiwar rallies in October and November had brought out millions across the nation, including an estimated 500,000 marchers in Washington.

I was out of the CBW business by then. Early in the fall, Robert Loomis, a senior editor at Random House, asked if the two of us could have lunch when he was next in Washington. I looked him up and learned that he was William Styron's editor and good friend. Styron's first novel, *Lie Down in Darkness*, about a southern world of which I knew nothing, had overwhelmed me when I read it in college. I was awed by Styron's lush descriptions and vast vocabulary. Bob Loomis was not what I expected—not lush, but precise, careful, and very direct. He ordered a Jack Daniel's on the rocks and ate only half of his lunch, as he would every time we lunched over the next decades. He said he had read and liked my work and had an idea for a book I should consider writing—a study of the Pentagon and its ability to influence society. I could not help but think, *McNamara, McNamara*. I visited Bob Ockene at his apartment in Brooklyn and got his okay—more than that, his approval—to work with Loomis. I also learned that Ockene, then thirty-four, was fighting leukemia. He died a few months later.

I was proud of my CBW journalism, and my role in changing American policy. I had not lobbied anyone in Congress or in the White House about CBW, but had helped force a change by my persistent reporting on an issue that needed public exposure. Many others, of course, were important—and undoubtedly more important. Matthew Meselson, with his determination and lobbying of Henry Kissinger, had brought the issue into the Oval Office, as Max McCarthy and Gaylord Nelson had done in Congress. But I had been in the game and had been a factor. In his book McCarthy acknowledged what he called his "debt to those who have done so much before me in often more comprehensive studies, especially Seymour M. Hersh." The praise that mattered the most, however, came from two brilliant physicists, Dr. Joel Primack of the University of California at Santa Cruz and Dr. Frank von Hippel of Princeton University, who published *Advice and Dissent* in 1974, a study of the role of scientists in the political arena. In a praiseful chapter about the role of Meselson, the book noted that by 1967 a series of questioning newspaper and magazine articles began appearing about CBW. "These were followed by several books," Primack and von Hippel wrote. "Seymour Hersh's *Chemical and Biological Warfare* . . . published in spring 1968, was particularly forceful and well documented and succeeded in raising a considerable furor."

I was thirty-two years old when Nixon capitulated on the CBW issue, and had been in the newspaper business for a decade. I had learned that the U.S. military would choose to lie and cover up rather than face an unpleasant truth. I had learned that some of my colleagues in the mainstream journalism world were equally adept in looking the other way, if need be, rather than writing about an unpleasant and unwanted truth. I had learned that Congress was overflowing with members and staff with integrity and courage who were willing to take a risk and help a journalist whom they respected.

I had only begun researching my new book when, late in September, I got my career-changing tip on an incident in a village known as My Lai in South Vietnam.

NINE

Finding Calley

By the fall of 1969, I was working out of a small, cheap office I had rented—less than one hundred dollars a month—on the eighth floor of the National Press Building in downtown Washington. My neighbor a few doors down was a young Ralph Nader, also a loner, whose exposé of the safety failures in the American automobile industry had changed the industry. There was nothing in those days quite like a quick lunch at the downstairs coffee shop with Ralph. He would grab a spoonful of my tuna fish salad, flatten it out on a plate, and point out small pieces of paper and even tinier pieces of mouse shit in it. He was marvelous, if a bit hard to digest.

The tip came on Wednesday, October 22, as I was doing research into cost overruns on Pentagon projects. I had yet to find an innovative way into the Pentagon book. The caller was Geoffrey Cowan, a young lawyer new to town who had worked on the McCarthy campaign and was an old pal of Marylouise Oates's. He'd been writing critically about the war for *The Village Voice*, and there was a story he wanted me to know about. The army was in the process of court-martialing a GI at Fort Benning, Georgia, for the killing of seventy-five civilians in South Vietnam. Cowan did not have to spell out why such a story, if true, was important, but he refused to discuss the source of his information. His words resonated nonetheless: He spoke with the authority of one who knew more than he was willing to say, or knew someone who knew more.

As I've made clear, I had learned while on the job in the Pentagon of the gap between what the men running the war said and what was going on. The lying seemed at times to be out of control, and there were reasons to believe the war was, too. Even those like Mark Hill, who supported the war, were troubled by the reliance on body counts in assessing progress in the war; it was clear that many of those claimed to be enemy soldiers killed in combat were civilians who may have been in the wrong place at the wrong time, or just were there, living where their ancestors had lived for generations. My many speeches about the perils of chemical and biological warfare had put me in contact with leaders of the antiwar movement around the country, and I was familiar with the war crimes research that had been published by the Quakers and other church groups.

One of the most unheralded critics of the war was Seymour Melman, a Columbia University economist who became an expert on war crimes in Vietnam and directed the research for *In the Name of America*, an extensive summary of reported war crimes that was published in January 1968 by a group known as the Clergy and Laymen Concerned About Vietnam. The dense volume, which Melman pressed on me, reprinted many hundreds of excerpts from American newspaper and magazine reports in 1966 and 1967 that depicted war crimes, including the routine murder of prisoners of war and the killing by hand grenades of women and children who were cowering in their homes during American search-and-destroy missions. The volume included a 1967 *New York Post* dispatch that offered a helpful bit of Vietnamese slang for newly arriving American soldiers—*Co di mo tom*, feeding the lobsters. The newspaper said it meant killing prisoners.

After a speech in Berkeley in early 1969, I was approached by Joe Neilands, a professor of biochemistry at the University of California, who had traveled to North Vietnam in 1967 and participated in the questioning of three American GIs at the Bertrand Russell War Crimes Tribunal that took place that year in Stockholm and near Copenhagen. Neilands, who passed away in 2008, gave me a published copy of the tribunal's proceedings, which included devastating testimony from the three American GIs. One of them, David Kenneth

Tuck from Cleveland, Ohio, who served as a specialist fourth class with the Twenty-Fifth Infantry Division, told of freewheeling raids on villages in suspected Vietcong (Vietnamese communist, or VC) territory in which there routinely were what he called "mad minutes" during which all Americans involved—including machine gunners on tanks—opened fire and poured "everything that they had into this village, because . . . we had assumed that until proven otherwise every Vietnamese was a VC." Tuck's public testimony was summarized by the AP and relayed around the world, but only a few American newspapers published the dispatch, and I found no evidence of any effort by the American media to follow up on Tuck's assertions. More typical of the response was a venomous attack on the tribunal by C. L. Sulzberger, the *Times* foreign affairs columnist, that personally vilified Russell, a Nobel Prize–winning philosopher and mathematician, who was then ninety-four years old. Russell, wrote Sulzberger, had "outlived his own conscious idea and become clay in unscrupulous hands." The tragedy of the tribunal, Sulzberger added, "cannot fairly be laid at the door of the wasted peer whose bodily endurance outpaced his brain."

A question I've been asked again and again by others, and one I've asked myself, is why I pursued Cowan's tip. There was not much to go on. I did not know Cowan. I had not been to South Vietnam. There had been no public mention, not a hint, of a massacre on the scale cited by Cowan. The answer came from my days in the Pentagon pressroom, where such a rumor, or tip, would be dismissed by all, so I believed, without a second thought. My colleagues had scoffed at Harrison Salisbury's firsthand account of systematic American bombing in North Vietnam, and a few had gone further: They had worked with Robert McNamara and Cyrus Vance to undercut the Salisbury dispatches. I chased Cowan's vague tip because I was convinced they would not.

I knew what I was up against: There was a huge difference between testimony at an avowedly antiwar proceeding in Europe and the tip I had been given. If Geoffrey Cowan was right, it was the U.S. Army itself that filed the murder charges. If so, there would have to be some official report somewhere in the military system. Finding it was worth a few days or so of my time.

I had renewed my Pentagon press credentials because my contract with Random House necessitated access to the building. My first step was to review all of the recent army courts-martial that had been initiated worldwide by the Judge Advocate General's Corps, the army's lawyers. I did so, and found no case hinting of mass murder. I hurriedly went through the same process with criminal investigations that had been made public by the military. Once again, no luck. If Cowan was right, the prosecution he knew about was taking place in secrecy. I felt stymied and went back to collecting data for my book.

What happened next was, in a sense, a one-in-a-million bank shot, but it grew out of my respect for those officers who did their job the way it was meant to be done. I was in the Pentagon a few days later, en route to an interview, when I bumped into an army colonel I knew to be a truth teller from my reporting on army training issues while at the AP. He had gone to Vietnam and had been wounded. He was limping as we walked together and he told me, with pride, that he had just learned he had been promoted to general. I teased him about taking a bullet in the leg just to get a promotion, and he laughed, as I knew he would—black humor is a military staple—and we kept on chatting. What was he doing now? I asked. He was assigned to the office of the army's new chief of staff, General William Westmoreland, who had just returned from running the Vietnam War. Wow. If anyone knew about a murder case from Vietnam, it would be someone in that office. I asked the officer what he knew about the mass murder of civilians in Vietnam. I remember the gist of his angry, emphatic answer: "Are you telling me someone who kills little babies and goes around saying he's killing Vietcong knows what he's doing? He's just crazy." I want to believe I betrayed none of the excitement that flushed through me. "This Calley is a madman, Sy. He killed people that were no higher than this," he said, slamming his hand against his right knee, the one that had been injured. "Little babies." He whacked his knee again. "There's no story in that."

I now had a name. There was never more of a disconnect between an honorable military officer and a reporter on the hunt. The newly created general saw Calley as an aberration; I thought he was part of a hell of a story that needed to be told. Needless to say, I did not share my differing view with the officer. I did not want anyone in Westmoreland's office to know I was onto the story.

It took hours of poring over newspapers on microfilm until I found a three-paragraph clip from page 38 of *The New York Times* for Monday, September 8, six weeks earlier, that quoted an information officer at Fort Benning, Georgia—the base Cowan had cited—as revealing that a twenty-six-year-old infantry officer named William L. Calley Jr., of Miami, had been charged with murder "in the deaths of an unspecified number of civilians in Vietnam." The incident took place in March 1968, and the case, as the army was depicting it, involved the deaths of what was said to be more than one civilian. No one in my profession asked any questions at the time, because no reporter then, and now, so I thought, knew what I did about the enormity of the case.*
News of the charges against Calley even made the Huntley-Brinkley evening news, a popular and highly regarded show on NBC, with the network's Pentagon correspondent simply parroting the official press release. He told millions of viewers that Calley had been accused of the premeditated murder "of a number of South Vietnamese citizens. The murders are alleged to have been committed a year ago and the investigation is continuing. A growing number of such cases is coming to light and the Army doesn't know what to do with them."

There was an element of doubt, even with Calley's name and its correct spelling. Geoffrey Cowan had said the mass murder had involved an enlisted man, not an officer. I called the library of *The Miami Herald*, Miami's best newspaper, to see if the newspaper had anything on Calley. There was one clip: A William Calley Jr., then working as a switchman for the Florida East Coast Railway, had been arrested by Fort Lauderdale police in 1964 for allowing a forty-seven-car freight train to block traffic during rush hour for thirty minutes. He was later cleared of wrongdoing.

I owed my next step to what I had learned during my days as an AP reporter in the Pentagon. I'd written about cost overruns and pilot retention—issues that attracted the attention of the defense specialists working for the House and Senate Armed Services Committees. I was especially friendly with a senior aide on the House committee,

---

* I learned later that Charles Black, an experienced military affairs reporter who'd gone to Vietnam five times for the *Columbus Enquirer*, the local daily that covered Fort Benning, had learned significant details of the case against Calley but chose not to publish what he knew until the army went public with the case. He was quoted as explaining after the My Lai story broke that he did not want to embarrass the military.

then headed by Representative L. Mendel Rivers, a Democrat with a locked-in congressional seat from South Carolina. Rivers was an outspoken supporter of all things military, including the war in Vietnam, and I guessed that there was no way the Pentagon would not have given him a private briefing about the mass murders, if there were mass murders, in South Vietnam. Melvin Laird, the shrewd secretary of defense, had served in the House with Rivers for eight terms and had to understand the political importance of keeping a key player like Rivers up to date on the good, and the bad.

I managed to have a cup of coffee with my friend on Rivers's staff. I had also learned from my AP days in the Pentagon that officials with top secret clearances were bored to death by reporters seeking to pry such information from them. (Gene McCarthy hated interviews for a different reason—because he was asked the same question again and again.) So I began my chat with my congressional friend not with a question but by telling him everything I knew about Calley and the charges against him. His response was not to deny the story but to warn me off it. "It's just a mess," he said, referring to Calley by name. "The kid was just crazy. I hear he took a machine gun and shot them all himself. Don't write about this one. It would just be doing nobody any good." I understood my friend's concern, as a senior aide to the very conservative Rivers, but I was not about to stop my reporting.

The story, as I was piecing it together, still did not make sense. One young officer did all the killing? What happened next added to my confusion. I telephoned the public information office at Fort Benning and, as casually as I could, asked the officer on duty for guidance on the Calley court-martial. The duty officer said he would check and, after a few moments, returned to the phone with an out-and-out lie: The Calley incident, he said, involved a shoot-up in a bar in Saigon after a lot of drinking. I understood that the young officer was simply doing his job and relaying what he was told to tell all who asked. Calley was the story, and my man, but something else was going on.

So I had to find Calley's lawyer. The court-martial records for his case were sealed, and I got nowhere asking questions in the Pentagon. I was pretty timid, too, about doing so; I did not want any other journalist to get a sniff of what I was doing. I liked being the best, the leader of the pack, and I sensed there was a game-changing story that revolved around William Calley, wherever he was. I was going to be the first reporter to find him. In desperation I turned again to Geoffrey Cowan, who, so I learned, was a recent Yale Law School graduate who had played a major role in setting up the Center for Law and Social Policy, one of America's early public interest law firms. I told him I was stuck and needed the name of Calley's lawyer. It was a cry for help, a shot in the dark. Two days later, Cowan called with a name: Latimer. Nothing more. I did not waste time wondering what else Cowan could tell me, or where he was getting his information.

I found a lawyer named Latimer in the Washington, D.C., telephone book. He knew nothing about a murder case involving the Vietnam War but thought I might want to get in touch with George Latimer, a retired judge on the Military Court of Appeals who was once again practicing law. Latimer had joined a Salt Lake City law firm, and I got him on the phone. I told him I knew he was representing Calley and added, with some honesty, that I had a hunch his client was being railroaded. (I did not add that I thought he was a criminal.) Latimer, speaking very deliberately, as he always did, acknowledged that yes, Calley was his client and it was a miscarriage of justice. Touchdown. I told the judge I was flying to the West Coast soon and asked if he would mind if I arranged a stopover in Salt Lake City. We settled on a day in early November. I had no need to go to the West Coast but thought it best to hide my eagerness. I also spent half a day in the Pentagon library reading a number of the judge's decisions, and even briefing a few of them; it was a reminder of what I did not do enough of during my underachieving year at the University of Chicago Law School.

I had an American Express card but did not have enough money to start flying around at the last minute doing interviews. I had heard that Philip Stern, an antiwar philanthropist in Washington, was thinking of endowing a fund for investigative journalism, and I called him, told him what I was chasing, and got a commitment within a few minutes for one thousand dollars. It was a relief to have that money in my bank account, but I would have found another way to fly to Salt Lake City, philanthropy or not. Stern eventually endowed the Fund for Investigative Journalism, an important foundation that continues today to finance innovative newspaper and magazine stories.

I took an early flight and arrived at Latimer's modest office by ten o'clock on a weekday morning. I guessed the judge, who was an elder in the Mormon Church, to be in his late fifties. It was clear at first glance that he was not a man full of irony and whimsy. I masked my acute anxiety by telling Latimer that I had reviewed a number of his appellate decisions and asked him to explain why he did what he did in certain instances. He did so. It was an extreme example of the Hersh rule: Never begin an interview by asking core questions. I wanted him to know I was smart and capable of some abstract thought. And I wanted him to like me and, perhaps, trust me.

We got to the case in hand, and Latimer told me that the proceeding against his client was a gross miscarriage of justice but he was bound by the army's version of grand jury rules and could not discuss specifics. He did say that the army offered Calley a plea bargain—one that involved jail time—and he had told the army, "Never." The message was clear: He believed his client was a fall guy for the mistakes, if any, of more senior officers during an intense firefight. It also was clear that the judge was in regular telephone contact with Calley, wherever he might be, in or out of jail. At this point, for reasons I still do not understand, but perhaps having to do with Latimer's sense that the army was piling on his client, I told Latimer that I understood Calley was being accused of killing 150 civilians during the army assault on My Lai. The only number I knew was the vague 75 deaths Cowan had cited, but the army officer and the congressional aide with whom I had discussed the case spoke of wild shootings and insanity. I also knew from my readings of the Russell Tribunal and other antiwar reportage that the senseless killing of hundreds was commonplace in American attacks on rural villages in South Vietnam.

That fictional number got to Latimer, who, visibly angered, went to a file cabinet in his office, snatched a folder, pulled a few pages from it, walked back to his desk—I was seated across from him—and flung the pages in front of me. It was an army charge sheet accusing First Lieutenant William L. Calley Jr. of the premeditated murder of 109 "Oriental" human beings. Even in my moment of exultation—*I knew* it was going to end the war and win prizes—it was stunning to see the number Calley was accused of murdering and the description of the dead as "Orientals." Did the army mean to suggest that one Oriental life was somehow worth less than that of a white American? It was an ugly adjective.

Latimer quickly turned the charge sheet around and pushed it closer to him. I have very little memory of what happened next in our chat, because I spent that time—twenty minutes or so—pretending to take notes as we talked. What I really was doing was reading the document upside down, albeit very slowly, and copying the charge sheet word for word. At some point Latimer broke off the interview and refused to say where Calley was or in any way help me get to him. I was pretty sure the judge sensed he'd gone too far with me, and I did not dare ask him for a copy of the charge sheet, for fear that he would instruct me that I could not use what I had seen. At the door, I thanked him for spending the morning with me and said I assumed that Calley was still at Fort Benning, awaiting a court-martial, and I was going to hunt him down. If I was wrong, I added, he should please tell me. Latimer stared at me for a moment and said nothing, and I flew home. I had to find Calley, and Benning was the place to start.

I was riddled with regret by the time I got back to Washington. How could I not have asked Latimer for a copy of the army charge sheet? A story this big written by someone like me—a fringe player known to be antiwar—could only work if I had a copy of that document. I remember fantasizing about what would happen had I been a reporter for *The Washington Post* or the *Chicago Sun-Times* and called my editor after the Latimer interview to report that I had seen the charge sheet. He would ask if I had a copy of the document. I would say no and then be consigned to the obituary desk for my inability to get the goods.

I was afraid to go to *The New York Times* or any major newspaper with the story. I was a lone operator and feared being overtaken by the large staffs of skilled journalists available to the editors there. I did not see myself as a tipster. It was my story. David Obst, my fun-loving pal from the Dispatch News Service, was desperate for the story, but understood why I had to start at the top. I'd been contacted a month or so earlier by a senior editor at *Life* magazine, America's most famed weekly, and asked whether I was interested in doing some reporting for them. I tracked down the editor and told him, cryptically, that I was working on a story that could change the course of the Vietnam War. Was he interested? Of course he was. We left it at that, and I took off very early one morning in the first week of November for Columbus, Georgia, the largest city adjacent to Fort Benning. The search for Calley was on.

Fort Benning, like most army bases in the United States, was an open facility, and I had no trouble driving onto the main post. I was stunned by its size. The base is roughly as big as all of New York City, some 285 square miles, with an airfield, a series of widely separate training areas, where live ammunition was being fired, and scores of living areas, known today as family villages. There were a hell of a lot of places to hide Calley, as the army apparently had chosen to do. I was undaunted; tracking down people who did not want to be found was vital to what I did for a living, and I was good at it. He was being held on a murder charge, and I assumed that meant he was in a prison, known in the army as a stockade or guardhouse, under the jurisdiction of the provost marshal, who was the equivalent of a chief of police for Fort Benning. My guess was that only a few of the most senior officers there knew about the Calley case, and so I began at the headquarters of the provost marshal's main office. The soldiers working there were helpful and checked their records, but did not find a William Calley listed as a prisoner. Perhaps Calley was being kept under wraps at one of the many stockades that were scattered around the fort.

I got a good map of the base and began driving. The routine was the same at each of the prisons I visited: I parked my rental car in the spot reserved for the senior officer in charge, which was invariably empty, walked into the prison in my suit and tie, carrying a briefcase, and said to the corporal or sergeant in charge, in a brassy voice, "I'm looking for Bill Calley. Bring him out right away." There was no Bill Calley anywhere. It took hours and more than one hundred miles to navigate just a few of the stockades scattered around the fort, and I was beginning to feel the pressure of time. It was just past noon by the time I returned to the main post.

I found a pay phone and a base telephone directory in a post exchange (PX) cafeteria and began calling every club I could find— swimming, tennis, hunting, fishing, hiking. No member by the name of Calley. None of the gas stations I reached on the base serviced a car owned by Lieutenant Bill Calley. I even checked the directory of officers at Infantry Hall, the office that handled all the training needs on the base, whose primary mission at the time was to produce infantry- men for the Vietnam War. There was no Calley booked at any of the army hotels or quarters for junior officers on temporary assignment at Benning. After a frustrating few hours, I still had no clue to Calley's whereabouts, nor did I know if he was still at Benning. I was hungry, running out of daylight, and more than a little anxious. I decided to take a short walk and a huge risk by stopping by the main office of the Judge Advocate General's Corps, whose lawyers would be prosecuting the case against Calley, if he was on the base. It was long after lunch hour, but the office was still empty, except for a lone sergeant. He could not have been more friendly as I introduced myself as a journalist from Washington and said I needed some help. His smile disappeared when I said I was looking for William Calley. He asked me to wait a moment. I asked why. He said he was under orders that if anyone asked about Calley, he was to call the colonel right away. That was enough for me, and I told the sergeant not to worry about it and began walking away. The sergeant got frantic and told me I could not leave. With that I began running out of the office and down the street, going harder with each stride. I did not want a colonel kicking me off the base. The sergeant chased after me for a few dozen yards and stopped. It was a scene out of a Marx Brothers movie.

Judge Latimer had given me the name of Calley's military lawyer, a major named Kenneth Raby. I figured what the hell; I had nothing to lose by trying to find him. Not only was he in the base telephone book, he was in his office at a nearby combat-training unit. He paled when I told him I was a reporter and wanted to find Calley. I remember the major as tall, thin, and most unnerved by my presence. He refused to talk to me, but I was reassured, nonetheless, by the meeting; Calley was somewhere at Benning, and I was not going home until I found him.

I had a hamburger and a Coke at a PX and wondered, as I chewed, what the hell to do next. Then I remembered that Judge Latimer had told me that Calley, still on active duty in Vietnam, had been ordered to fly back to Benning in late August 1969. I recalled from my AP days in Correspondents Corridor that the military produced updated telephone books for the Pentagon every four months, beginning in January. If Benning did the same, and why wouldn't it—there was a war on, and troops were coming and going—the telephone book that I had used hours earlier should be dated September 1969. It was. I dialed the operator and asked for the supervisor on duty, and when she got on the phone, I asked her to check the last batch of new listings for the May telephone book for a Lieutenant William L. Calley Jr. The lieutenant, when he returned from overseas, had yet to be prosecuted, and he would have had to have been parked somewhere on the base—and duly listed as a late entry in the telephone book. After a moment or so, the operator returned, told me she'd found my man, and then quickly rattled off a phone number and an address before hanging up. I did not understand a thing she said, between my jumpiness and her deep southern accent, and wasted precious time reconnecting with her. When I did, she spelled out, letter by letter, Calley's assignment at the fort and his phone number. I had no interest in reaching him or leaving word for him by phone, but I needed the information to be able to physically confront the man.

Calley was attached to an engineering unit located in one of Fort Benning's satellite training camps. The building was only a few miles from the main post, but it took me nearly an hour, through a maze of streets, to find the goddamn place. It was the living quarters for trainees and consisted of two three-story barracks linked by a one-story headquarters office. It was midafternoon, a few hours before the workday would end, and I had a premonition that I would find Calley stashed somewhere inside. Why not start with the office? Its heavy wooden door was divided, military style, into separate upper and lower halves, with only the upper half open. Captain Charles Lewellen was listed as the officer in charge, and I leaned into the office and told a clerk that I was a reporter from Washington and wondered if the captain was around. He was, round-bellied and full of smiles that immediately evaporated when I told him I was looking for Bill Calley. He told me he was not authorized to speak about Calley, and, as had happened before, he picked up a telephone and asked for the colonel as I stood in front of him. Once again, I beat it onto the street. Lewellen followed me outside and asked for a word. He essentially begged me to stay away. He explained that he had been passed over for promotion to major a number of times and would be forced to retire if it happened again, as it would if I found Calley. "Give me a break," he said. "If you've got any questions about Calley, take them someplace else."

Lewellen's bizarre behavior stemmed from the fact that on March 16, 1968, he had been in an operations center that monitored the My Lai operation as it took place and had made a personal tape recording of the carnage—one that he did not turn over to investigators for eighteen months. I knew nothing of that, and I interpreted Lewellen's effort to slow me down as evidence that Calley was very nearby, probably tucked away in one of the barracks I had yet to search. I mumbled some words of acquiescence to the bedraggled captain and began to walk away. After a few moments of scuffling about, I found a back door into the nearest barracks and walked through row after row of double bunk beds on the first floor, all empty and all neatly made up. I raced through the upper two floors, peering into each bed in the hope of finding my man. Nothing. I crossed to the second barracks, avoiding Captain Lewellen by scrambling on hands and knees past the still-closed bottom half of his office door. The eureka moment came on the second floor in the form of a young man, in uniform, with tousled blond hair, dead asleep in a top bunk. It *had* to be Calley. I was all dominance as I raised a leg and banged my foot on the side of the bunk, and said, "Wake up, Calley." The young soldier, not yet twenty years old, yawned and said, "What the hell, man." I do not remember what the name tag on his blouse said—something ending in "ski"—but it made clear I did not have Calley. I sat down in disappointment on a bunk bed facing the GI. What happened next was a vestige of my hating basic training in the army and trying out in the middle of it for the Fort Leonard Wood baseball team, which I made. Doing so enabled me to leave my fellow trainees after lunch to go to practice. It also meant I was in my bunk, dead asleep from the exhaustion of picking up a few ground balls, by the time my colleagues marched back to our barracks. And thus, amid my disappointment, out popped a question to the GI: "What the fuck are you doing sleeping in the middle of the day?"

It was a sad story. He had been scheduled to be released months earlier from active duty, but the army had lost his papers and he was still awaiting them. He was from a farming family in Ottumwa, Iowa, and it was harvest season, and his dad and others were doing his share of the work. Getting released by the army was a day-to-day question mark; meanwhile, he was getting in a lot of sleep. I was curious—how could I not be?—and asked the sad sack if he had been assigned anything to do during the day. Yeah, he said, "I sort the mail." For everyone? Yes. Did he ever get mail for someone named Calley? "You mean that guy that killed all those people?" Yes, that guy.

The farmer-to-be told me that he had never met Calley but had been ordered to collect the lieutenant's mail and deliver it every so often to his pal Smitty, the mail clerk at battalion headquarters. I was flushed with excitement but played it cool. Where's that? Couple of miles away. Take me there. No way, the kid said. Smitty had just lost his sergeant stripes—something to do with too much boozing—and was in no mood to talk to a stranger. I knew this was going to be easy; the kid had seen no action in weeks, and I was going to give him some. We synchronized our watches. It was nearly four o'clock, and I said that I had a rented Ford sedan that was a few hundred feet away and would pull up to the back door of the barracks in precisely seven minutes. Meet me then and take me to Smitty, I said. I raced off. He was where I wanted him to be, as I knew he would be, as I drove up. It took an excruciating fifteen or so minutes to drive to battalion headquarters, and the kid insisted on being driven back. I agreed to do so and hustled back to a parking lot in front of the headquarters.

It was an old one-story building that I knew from my days in the army—essentially a wooden shack with a small porch and a screen door. The door was open and a black sergeant was leaning against it in a chair, taking in the late afternoon Georgia sun, a toothpick in his mouth. I tucked in my shirt, drew my tie tight, grabbed my jacket and briefcase, and climbed out of the car, looking every bit like a lawyer,

I hoped, and said, "Sergeant, get Smitty out here right now." There was a big smile from the sergeant: He was probably thinking, what has that dumb fuckup Smitty done now? Out comes Smitty, not much older than my friend from Ottumwa, with threads hanging from the sleeves of his blouse, where his sergeant stripes had been. I say, "Get in the car," and in he comes. He's scared, but I quickly calm him down by telling him who I am and what I want. Smitty is apologetic and explains he knows little about Calley. Sure, he's heard that the lieutenant had shot up a lot of people, but his contact with him is limited to collecting his mail and giving it to a courier who picks it up. He has no idea where Calley is living or where his mail ends up. I ask, resignedly, so there's nothing on Calley in the battalion files? Well, says Smitty, we do have everyone's 201 files. I knew that a 201 file is the military's essential personnel folder that is kept for both enlisted men and officers. I say nothing. He adds, "I'd have to steal it to get it." There's a long pause. I say, "Well?" "I'll try, mister." Smitty goes inside—the sergeant looks at him but makes no move and asks no questions—and Smitty returns, suddenly much more animated, and slides into the seat next to mine. He opens his blouse and pulls out Lieutenant William L. Calley Jr.'s personnel file. I open it and the first page is the same charge sheet that I had seen days earlier in George Latimer's office. There is more—an address, in nearby Columbus, where Calley is living. I take time to carefully copy the charge sheet, making sure I get every phrase right, and return the file to Smitty. He's glad to have been a help—fuck the army. He leaves and I head for Calley's new home.

It's rush hour and, even with a street map of Columbus, it's after five o'clock by the time I get to Calley's condo in what seems to be a new housing development. The car in front of me pulls in to the driveway to which I am headed. Three young army second lieutenants, dressed in camouflage fatigues, climb out. I park behind them, get out of the car, and explain that I'm a journalist who is trying to find Bill Calley, that I understand he lives here. Not anymore, I am told. I tell them that I've just seen Calley's lawyer and he believes the lieutenant to be guilty of nothing, but was in the wrong place at the wrong time. They invite me in for a drink, share a bourbon with me, and explain that they are June graduates of West Point who are finishing up combat training before heading off to Vietnam as infantry platoon leaders. They are polite, articulate, and very likable. Yes, Calley was their roommate for some weeks but no longer lives with them. Yes, they understand the seriousness of the charges against their buddy, but there is another side. Calley and his platoon were engaged in a horrific firefight with an experienced and tough Vietcong battalion, they say. Bullets were flying and of course civilians get caught in cross fire. It's the inevitable consequence of war. It was the same line I'd heard from George Latimer. The young lieutenants are earnest, and we have another drink or two. Calley stops by occasionally to get his mail, one of them tells me. Of course they know where he's living now, but they volunteer nothing and I ask nothing. It's time to get some takeout, and they offer me another drink and dinner. I tell them I've got to keep on looking for Calley. It's dark outside, and as I prepare to leave, one of them finally breaks ranks and tells me where Calley has been tucked away. (Of course I would have asked.) He's in the senior BOQ—bachelor officers' quarters—for field-grade officers, including colonels and generals who are on temporary assignment to Benning. I was stunned: a suspected mass murderer hidden away in quarters for the army's most elite? I was going to hang around the fort until I got my man, but I never would have looked there. It would have been like finding Calley in a neonatal intensive care unit. I got the address and drove off.

The senior BOQ was a complex of two-story buildings, I think three in all, each housing about forty swank, by army standards, one-bedroom units, with a large parking lot. I got there by eight o'clock and began knocking on doors, calling out as I did, "Bill, Bill Calley?" I kept track of those rooms whose tenants answered—usually with a shouted "Get out of here" or "No one named Bill here"—as well as those doors that needed another try. I got through two buildings over the next few hours, with no luck and much exhaustion. I'd gotten up at five o'clock that morning in Washington and had little to eat and more than I needed to drink. But I was not at all discouraged. Calley was living in the complex, and I was going to find him if it took days. I needed to check into a motel, get an hour or two of sleep, and start knocking on doors again.

It was dark as I walked across the nearly empty parking lot. I noticed two guys working underneath a car a few hundred feet away, with the aid of a floodlight powered by a black power cord that ran the length of the lot. I vividly remember thinking to myself, you do not have to take the last run at the end of a long day's skiing. But I did. As I got close to the car, I apologized for bothering the two guys but said I was looking for Bill Calley. One of the men, perhaps in his late forties, crawled out and asked what I wanted with him. I explained that I was a journalist from Washington and Calley was in a lot of trouble and I was going to write about it. He asked me to wait a second, wiped off his hands, and said something like, "He's not here, but you can wait for him at my place, if that's okay." He muttered something to his pal, who was still under the car, and we walked off. His place turned out to be on the first floor of one of the units, and Calley lived above him. I was warned that it might be hours before Calley would show up; he had gone motorboating at a lake miles away. Motorboating? Yes, said my new friend, who said he was a senior warrant officer who flew helicopters in heavy combat in the war, he knew Calley was in a lot of trouble.

Drinks were offered as we waited; the U.S. Army clearly was running on bourbon. He understood where I was coming from, he said, and acknowledged, sadly, that Vietnam was a murderous, unwinnable war that was taxing his love for the army, which had educated him and taught him how to be an excellent pilot. Calley was frightened, as he should be, the pilot said. His story of a firefight would not hold up. I liked the pilot, and admired his honesty (he mailed me Christmas cards for years), but after an hour or so of pretending to sip a drink, I was done. I had to get some sleep. I said good-bye—I can still see the mosquitoes buzzing around a naked lightbulb outside his door—and began walking to my car. "Hersh," the pilot yelled, "come back. Rusty is here." I was not ready to meet a new friend and said so. "No. No. It's Calley." It turned out Bill Calley was known to all as Rusty.

We shook hands. I told him who I was and that I was there to get his side of the story. He said, as if my tracking him down had been a piece of cake, that yes, his lawyer told him to expect a visit from me. We went upstairs, I had another drink—this time a beer—and we began to talk. I had wanted to hate him, to see him as a child-killing monster, but instead I found a rattled, frightened young man, short, slight, and so pale that the bluish veins on his neck and shoulders were visible. His initial account was impossible to believe—full of heroic one-on-one warfare with bullets, grenades, and artillery shells being exchanged with the evil commies. At one point Calley went to the bathroom to take a leak, or so he said. He left the door—with a full-length mirror in it—partially ajar, and I watched as he vomited bright red arterial blood, the result of a serious ulcer, I would learn.

Sometime after three in the morning, Calley took me to a PX where he bought a bottle of bourbon and some wine. The next stop was an all-night food store on the base, where he purchased a steak. Then we picked up his girlfriend, who was a nurse on night duty at the main hospital at the fort. She was enraged at Calley upon learning that he was introducing her to a journalist, but she drove back to his apartment with us and made dinner. There was more drinking, and as daylight broke, Calley was talking about going bowling. The nurse had fled by then and I'd had it. I had compiled a notebook full of quotes, much of them full of danger for him; his account of the assault at My Lai had become more and more riddled with contradictions as he went on. As I was leaving—by now it was early morning—Calley insisted that I stay and talk to his captain, Ernest Medina, who was in charge of the assault at My Lai. Medina, who would be found not guilty of premeditated murder, involuntary manslaughter, and assault after a court-martial two years later, picked up the telephone after a ring or two. He also was at Fort Benning, presumably going through the same process as Calley. I shared a phone with Calley, and he explained to Medina that he'd been talking with a reporter about My Lai and he wanted Medina to tell me that anything that took place was done under direct order of the captain. Medina said, very simply, "I don't know what you're talking about," and hung up. Calley was stricken; at that moment he knew what I am sure he already suspected: He was going to be the fall guy for the murders at My Lai.

It was too late, or too early, to sleep, and I drove to the Columbus airport and took the first plane to Washington. I began outlining my story as I flew. I had a verbatim copy of a vital document and an interview with the main player. I understood that I had to keep my feelings about the war out of the story.

I was worried by how my story would be received, and remembered as I began to write that my family lived in the last years of World War II in an apartment across the street from the V—for victory—movie theater on Forty-Seventh Street in Chicago and on Saturdays my brother and I would be taken by our sisters to watch heroic war movies. In the best of those films, our guys, flying P-51s in Asia, were in a dogfight with the Japanese, who were flying the hated Zeros. Our guys flew with their cockpits open, no headgear, long white scarves, and their thumb constantly giving the A-OK signal. The bucktoothed Japanese—we called them Nips, of course—flew in closed cockpits, with grim faces and wearing soft dark helmets that tied under their chins (the hated kind we kids were forced to wear in winter by our moms). At a critical moment, one of our heroes dramatically saves the life of another who is under imminent attack by unloading a barrage of bullets into a Japanese plane. We watched as the Zero, suddenly out of control, began its death descent, screeching as it went down. Just before it struck the water, a trickle of blood streamed out of the right corner of the Nip's mouth. We were beside ourselves with cheers as the Zero slammed into the water and blew up.

I was going to try to sell a story that said Americans do not fight war more honorably or more sanely than the Japanese and Germans did in World War II. I wasn't sure what would happen, but I knew it wasn't going to be easy.

TEN

A National Disgrace

I'd been a reporter for a decade by the fall of 1969 and somehow had figured out that the best way to tell a story, no matter how significant or complicated, was to get the hell out of the way and just tell it.

My first My Lai dispatch thus began, "Lt. William Calley, Jr., 26, is a mild-mannered boyish-looking Vietnam combat veteran with the nickname of Rusty. The Army says he deliberately murdered 109 Vietnam civilians during a search-and-destroy mission in March, 1968." I deleted the word "Oriental" in describing the victims after getting assured by an official in Melvin Laird's office that the army would do the same in its case against Calley. Laird, who would become a good friend after leaving office, did so out of fear—a fear I shared—that the overt racism of the initial charge would lead to random violence against GIs in South Vietnam who had nothing to do with the massacre.

I wrote the story to the best of my ability and then telephoned my editor friend at *Life* and said it was all theirs, if the weekly moved quickly. The editor called back within a few hours and said no. He had pushed for it, he said, but there was little interest for such a story by the senior management. I had been in touch earlier with *Look* magazine, another popular weekly that had discussed an assignment for me, and, at the request of an editor there, had written a two-page summary of where I assumed the My Lai story would end up. I called the editor and told him that I had taken it much further than I thought I would and filled him in on the Calley interview. He, too, passed. I was devastated, and frightened by the extent of self-censorship I was encountering in my profession. I feared I would have no choice but to take the My Lai story to a newspaper and run the risk of having editors there turn over my information to their reporting staff: in other words, to be treated like a tipster. In any case, I knew I needed a lawyer to review what I had written for libel. That led me to Michael Nussbaum, a classmate during my year at the University of Chicago Law School. Michael was as brilliant at law as I was opaque, but we nonetheless had become the closest of friends, and he was now a partner in a major law firm in Washington. He was an expert litigator and outspoken critic of the Vietnam War who had just written a handbook on how to avoid the draft legally.

I arrived late one night at his small house in Georgetown just as Michael, then a carefree bachelor, was shooing a woman out the door. He read the story I had written, asked me a series of appropriate questions, recommended some changes that I made, and said, yes, his firm would represent me and stand behind me in case of trouble. There was no talk of fees or obligation. Michael was not new to the world of the First Amendment: His clients included Ralph Nader and a number of *Washington Post* journalists. He would die of cancer in 2011, after representing me, always successfully, in seven libel proceedings during my career. In an essay I wrote after his death for *The New Yorker*'s blog, I told of a suggestion that made that first My Lai story work:

> I'm not sure how it came up, but it was obvious to Michael that Calley's interview with me could be legally disastrous for him, in that it would likely contradict what he had told the Army. Michael's advice was to go back to George Latimer, Calley's lawyer, and tell him everything Calley had told me.
>
> So I did. Latimer was distraught, and said—how right Michael was—that Calley's comments to me conflicted with his prior sworn testimony in the military proceedings. . . . If I published the interview this way, Latimer told me, I possibly would be denying Cal-

ley his constitutional right to a fair trial. He offered a deal: if I would in some manner avoid saying outright that Calley's comments were made directly to me . . . he would go over the story, line for line, and correct any factual mistakes he could. . . . And so George Latimer and I spent a great deal of time on the telephone. He corrected dates, phrasing, the spelling of the names of others involved, etc. He was exceedingly precise, to the point, as I learned years later from an academic's Freedom of Information request, that military analysts had concluded after publication of the first of what would become five freelance articles on My Lai, that I clearly had access to the most secret of Army files.

Latimer had one more inducement. He told me I could tell editors and reporters to telephone him, and he would confirm that he had reviewed the article and that, to the extent of his knowledge, what it said about his client, Calley, was accurate. He lived up to his commitment, although he and Calley never talked to me again.

David Obst was continuing to urge me to let his tiny news service handle the story, but that, even after the travesties with *Life* and *Look*, made no sense to me. I had stayed in touch with I. F. Stone through my recent travails, and he responded to my desperation by telling me that he knew Bob Silvers, the editor of *The New York Review of Books*, would publish it immediately. (I had written another piece or two for the magazine since the serialization of my CBW book there.) I called Silvers—it was on the eve of the closing of an edition of the biweekly magazine—and so he had me dictate the story to someone there. Under Silvers's leadership, the magazine had emerged as a voice of the anti–Vietnam War movement, and Bob, when he and I talked, told me how excited he was about the story and was planning to do what he had done only a few times in the magazine's history—start the piece on the cover. Bob had only one significant editing request: Would I add a short paragraph up high in the piece to explain the meaning of the massacre, in terms of the day-by-day brutality of the war? I was familiar with editors wanting to put their scent on a good story, and laughed him off, saying that surely there was no need to tell readers the political importance of the case against Calley. Bob insisted. I said never. He said he would not run the story without adding the words he wanted me to write. I said good-bye, and that was that.

I was adamant because I knew from my years of being immersed in the war, and the racism and fear that drove it, that the mass murder of civilians was far more common than was known and, most important, prosecuted. We now had a case where the army itself was drawing a line and finally saying, in essence, that there are some actions that cannot be overlooked. There was no way I would let even one paragraph that smacked of antiwar dicta pollute the straightforward report of a mass murder I had written, even if it was to be published in a magazine that was against the war.

The flap with Silvers, someone who was totally on my side, proved to me that there was no way I was going to get the My Lai story published the way I wanted, unless I somehow found a way to take responsibility for publishing it. What the hell, I'd started a newspaper when I was twenty-five years old, and the fact that Nussbaum and his prominent Washington law firm were behind me on libel questions was a good start. I called up David Obst and told him that he had the goddamn story and he'd better not screw it up. I also told him that Dispatch News Service was going to copyright the My Lai story and take full responsibility for publishing it. The newspapers that chose to publish what we wrote would pay a fixed fee for doing so; we settled on one hundred bucks per paper, no matter the size of its circulation—and that would be the extent of each newspaper's responsibility. I somehow had faith that this twenty-three-year-old who could talk himself in and out of trouble with great charm and pizzazz could pull it off.

There were a lot of reasons I could have been wrong. David had been in the streets during the 1968 Democratic convention and was a veteran of hard-core antiwar activity in Berkeley, California, and while he could rattle off the good, and bad, effects of most street drugs, he was now going to be dealing with the senior editors of America's largest newspapers—the same editors who had been ignoring the growing antiwar peace movement. In later years he would go on to help Daniel Ellsberg get the Pentagon Papers published, to become a literary agent for John Dean, Bob Woodward, and Carl Bernstein of Watergate fame, to have his own publishing imprint at Random House, and even to have a role in the filming of *Revenge of the Nerds*, a cult film of the 1980s. But to convince the executive editors of newspapers to publish a mass-murder story?

In its own way, what David did was as much of a miracle as I had managed in finding Calley at Fort Benning. In his memoir, *Too Good to Be Forgotten*, published in 1998, David told how he went about selling the My Lai story, beginning early in the morning on Wednesday, November 12, 1969:

> I got a copy of a book called *The Literary Marketplace*, which listed the names and phone numbers of all of the newspapers in America. I opened to A and began calling. It wasn't until I got to the Cs that I got a hit. The *Hartford Current* [*sic*] in Connecticut said they were interested and requested a copy of the story. . . . I hadn't really thought out how I was going to get it out. I couldn't just mimeograph it and mail it like I did for our Dispatch stories: it would take three days to reach the *Current*. . . . Forget it, I'd figure out how to send it later. I had to sell it first.

As David went along, more and more editors were interested, aided by the fact that he could tell editors that the article had been read for libel by Nussbaum and that George Latimer, Calley's lawyer, had read the story and would attest to its accuracy. One editor he befriended explained to him that my fifteen-hundred-word Calley story could be sent by telex and reach every editor within an hour. Of course, we did not have the money to do so, so the articles, once the editors agreed to read them, went out telex collect.

My only effort to sell the story that day ended in fiasco. I was a good friend of Larry Stern, a star reporter on the national staff of *The Washington Post*, and he invited Nussbaum and me to meet with Ben Bradlee, the *Post*'s magnetic executive editor. We arrived just after lunch and met in the tiny office of Phil Foisie, the foreign editor. Four or five editors and reporters gathered around as I distributed copies of the Calley story. There was quiet as all began to read. It was broken by the effervescent Bradlee, who literally flung the five or six pages he was reading at Foisie and said, "Goddamn it. . . . I've got hundreds of reporters working for me and this has to come from the outside. Publish it. It smells right." This was three years before Bradlee's heroics during Watergate. I could tell at that moment that you either loved the guy or had to leave the paper. (I ended up playing doubles on Sundays with him throughout the 1980s and coming to understand why so many of his reporters admired him.)

Despite Bradlee's drama queen performance, the *Post* totally rewrote my story, adding denials from the Pentagon and other caveats, but did put its article on page 1. The early edition hit the street well before midnight. It was an ignoble beginning, made worse when Peter Braestrup, who had been assigned to rewrite my Calley story, woke me up a few hours before dawn to tell me that I was a lying son of a bitch: No one soldier could be responsible for the murder of 109 civilians. It was just impossible. I thought he was drunk, but he might not have been. I had a lot of trouble going back to sleep; I had seen no video or photographic evidence of a mass murder. I would soon learn that the My Lai story made a lot of people irrational. My telephone at home remained listed, as it still is, and for months after the story broke, I got calls from angry officers and enlisted men, usually drunk, telling me what they were going to do to my private parts. Braestrup's was far and away the most stressful case, especially when I learned of his expertise. He was a former marine officer who had been seriously wounded in the Korean War, and was soon to be the Saigon bureau chief for the *Post*. I obviously anticipated pushback and anger from many in the government and the military, but Braestrup alerted me to the possibility that my fellow reporters would be equally resentful.

I knew I would survive the criticism from Braestrup and the others. Even today, I have flashbacks on stormy days about the wet and snowy mornings on which I, still in my teens, opened my long-gone father's store on Indiana Avenue in the dark of a Chicago winter at 7:00, turning on lights and getting ready to deal with laundry and cleaning while sneaking in a few hours of homework for a later class at the University of Chicago. I survived that beginning, and I would survive any criticism of a story I knew to be true. The streets of Chicago somehow gave me a sense of well-being that stayed with me throughout my career and kept me from falling into a funk when my work was being savaged, as it occasionally was.

Obst and I would have no idea whether the fifty or so newspaper editors around the country who bought the story actually would choose to publish it—this was an era long before the internet—until the middle of the next afternoon, when out-of-town newspapers arrived at the newsstand in the National Press Building, where Dispatch now had an office. David created a miracle, and dozens of major newspapers, including the *Chicago Sun-Times*, the Philadelphia *Bulletin*, and the *St. Louis Post-Dispatch*, prominently displayed the Calley story on the front page the next day, a few even making it the banner headline. The *New York Times* did not buy the story offered by Obst, but the *New York Post* did and gave it dominant play.

The major television networks did nothing with the story, in part because the Pentagon shrewdly refused to make any comment. I was not flooded with the calls that I had imagined would roll in—from energetic reporters eager for leads and from Vietnam vets who had their own horror stories to relay. After a few days, I was reminded of the self-censorship that seemed to dominate the media's coverage of the war. A few editors, instead of assigning their reporters to dig up more dirt, were calling Obst and asking about follow-ups, and he was making promises of further reporting, to my dismay. There was a lively debate in the British Parliament about the Calley crimes, which was extensively reported by the *Times*. The only newspaper, in fact, to actively chase the story seemed to be the *Times*, which sent Henry Kamm, an experienced foreign correspondent, to the immediate area of My Lai, in what once, before the war, had been a beautiful farming community along the South China Sea. He eventually was flown to an evacuation area for the survivors of the massacre and filed a dispatch that was published on Thursday, November 13, quoting survivors as saying that as many as 567 men, women, and children had been massacred by the Americans. There was widespread skepticism elsewhere in the media about my Calley story, with many newspapers—including *The Washington Post*—noting the hardships U.S. soldiers were having in fighting a guerrilla war against an enemy who posed as farmers during the day. The subliminal message was clear: American soldiers were often in a position where they had to shoot first or become victims. Who was I to make such a harsh judgment about the war?

The breakthrough came Sunday night. Obst, in his zany memoir, vividly recalled the moment:

Sy came over to my house. We were both wondering what to do
next—how to follow up. The story . . . didn't have as much of
an impact as we had hoped. *Newsweek* and *Time* both ignored it.
We were looking over the ways the various papers had played
the story . . . when Sy spotted another story in the *Washington
Post*. It was an item about a guy named Ronald Ridenhour who
had announced that he was responsible for initiating the army's
inquiry. Sy jumped out of his seat and began yelling, "The kid!
The kid! The kid!" Suddenly it all made sense to Sy. He hadn't
been able to figure out why the army would air its dirty laundry
about the killings. Why had the army charged Lieutenant Calley?
Ridenhour was the answer.

Sy got on the phone and tracked the kid down. He planned to
take the first flight to Los Angeles to meet Ron, now a student at
Claremont College.

What David did not say was that the item about Ridenhour was a
one-paragraph AP story, datelined Phoenix, Arizona, attached at the
end of a long *Post* story about the dangers facing American boys in
the war. On Monday, I got to Ron's dormitory at Claremont, thirty-
five miles east of downtown Los Angeles, in time for the two of us to
have lunch. Surprisingly, or perhaps not surprisingly, I was the first
reporter to actually meet with him. The *Times* and wire services had
chatted with him by telephone, but no one from the *Los Angeles Times*,
the premier newspaper on the West Coast, had deigned to phone him,
let alone drive the thirty-five miles to Claremont. Ridenhour and I
talked for five hours. Ron had not been at My Lai; he served much of
his year in Vietnam in an advance combat unit known as LRRPs, for
long-range reconnaissance patrols. He told me he had flown over the
My Lai area in late March 1968 and noticed the desolation—"not even
a bird was singing," he would later write—but did not learn what had
taken place until late April, when a member of Calley's platoon told
him that few, if any, of the villagers at My Lai survived the onslaught.
He was determined to find out more, but realized how dangerous his
questioning would be. He told me that he did not take notes as he
gathered information, out of fear for his own safety if they were found.

By November 1968, when his tour of duty in Vietnam was over, he had firsthand information from five members of Calley's company who confirmed the extent of the atrocity. In March 1969, back at his family home in Phoenix, Ridenhour wrote a detailed two-thousand-word letter, replete with names and ranks, about the atrocity and mailed copies to more than thirty officials in Washington. His list began with President Nixon and included fifteen members of the Senate, five members of the Arizona congressional delegation, the State Department, the Pentagon, the Joint Chiefs of Staff, the Department of the Army, and three members of the House of Representatives, including the office of L. Mendel Rivers. Twenty-two of the offices later said they had no record of ever receiving Ridenhour's letter, but the letter worked: The Department of the Army told Ridenhour in April that it had begun an inquiry. The former GI was urged to be patient; his information needed to be corroborated, and it could take many months to do so.

Ridenhour was fearful of a cover-up because he understood that many of those being interviewed—even perhaps some of those who had talked to him—had been participants in the slaughter and would have no incentive to be forthcoming to an army investigator. In late May, he decided he would tell the story of the massacre himself and contacted a literary agent who provided a number of publications with the essentials of Ridenhour's letter, including *Life*, *Look*, *Harper's*, and *The Washington Post*, owners of *Newsweek* magazine, but none responded. When we talked, Ridenhour recalled the name of the editor at *Life* who had been contacted by his agent; it was the same editor I telephoned four months later with a separate account of the massacre, as obtained by my reporting. If there is a journalism hell, that editor belongs there.

Ron was open about his failed journalistic ambitions and made it clear to me that he was ecstatic that I, someone he saw as a real reporter, had managed to find Calley and evidence that the army was ready to prosecute him. We both understood that the issue went far beyond Calley and that most of the men in Charlie Company had joined in the killing, and the cover-up. Ron gave me the names and addresses of those witnesses who might flesh out the story and, most important, dug out a 1967 Thanksgiving Day menu of Charlie Company, then training in Hawaii, that included the correct spelling of the unit's officers and enlisted men. The two veterans I had to see, he told me, were

Michael Terry and Michael Bernhardt. Terry was out of the army and living in Orem, Utah; Bernhardt was still a soldier, stationed at Fort Dix, New Jersey. I left to catch a late flight to Salt Lake City, having made a lifelong friend in the courageous and generous Ridenhour, who did make it as a journalist after all and won a George Polk Award in 1987 after a yearlong inquiry into a tax scandal in New Orleans, his hometown. He died at age fifty-two, far too young, after a heart attack in 1998.

I had an address for Mike Terry but could not reach him by phone, and getting to Orem, forty-five miles south of Salt Lake City, turned out to be hellacious. There was a huge snowstorm, and I was driving in the darkness on twisting, snowy mountain roads of which I knew nothing. Lights were out all over the city, whose population then was twenty-five thousand, and I drove around aimlessly until I finally found an open gas station and got directions. The Terry home was extremely modest, made of wood and warmed, as I would learn, by an indoor oil heater. It was close to midnight when I began knocking. A young boy answered. I asked for his big brother, the one who fought in the war, and was ushered inside, no questions asked. A moment later out came Terry, in pajamas. It was as if late-night visitors were the rule in Orem. I told him who I was and about my visit with Calley and the talk with Ridenhour and asked him to tell me what he remembered. "Do you want me to tell you what I told the colonel?" he asked. Yes. Ridenhour had told me that he had been contacted after writing his letters by an army criminal investigator, a Colonel Wilson, who repeatedly urged him not to do what he had done with me—talk. Terry's next line produced headlines all over the world. "It was a Nazi-type thing," he said, in describing a ditch in which scores of women and children had been slaughtered. I took copious notes as we talked, while also keeping a wary eye on the parlous oil burner, a reminder of my days in Pierre.

I left after a few hours, grabbed some sleep at an airport motel in Salt Lake City, and called Obst and gave him the go-ahead to alert editors all over the world—we'd had inquiries from abroad—that I had another story in the works. I flew to Philadelphia, drove an hour to Fort Dix, and met with Michael Bernhardt. He talked about seeing more than he ever wanted to see and shredded Rusty Calley's self-serving story of a major firefight (as did Terry's account). Ridenhour, Terry, and Bernhardt each recalled—more than that; they needed to share—stunning details of crazed soldiers taking special pleasure in killing little boys and girls by bayonet and other means. It was Bernhardt's first search-and-destroy mission and he said, "It was as if I'd missed a couple days in basic training and this was the way war was, but they never told me. It was like an old joke: You miss something in second grade and you never learn to spell. I got to see everybody killing everybody."

Obst sold my second story. It was especially big in London, following the debate over My Lai in Parliament. The *Daily Mail* headline said, "The Story That Stunned America." Louis Heren, the American editor for the august London *Times*, had praised my earlier work on CBW, and my story ran there, on the front page: The *Times* splashed the Terry/Bernhardt interviews under a triple-deck headline, "US Soldiers Say 'We Saw Massacre'; 'Women and Children Shot Down.' " The *New York Times* chose once again not to pay Dispatch one hundred dollars, and so we sold the eyewitness story, as before, to the *New York Post*. Editors all over America kept calling Obst and asking when the next Hersh story was coming. Given my problems in getting the story in print, I was not surprised that no one else in the American press corps, save for some reporters on the *Times*, seemed to be chasing the story.

I kept on going. I knew there was yet another story that, so I thought, would end any resistance to the obvious truth of My Lai. Terry, Bernhardt, and other platoon members I had talked with told me about a soldier named Paul Meadlo, a farm kid from somewhere in Indiana, who had mechanically fired clip after clip of rifle bullets, at Calley's orders, into groups of women and children who had been rounded up amid the massacre. Calley's company moved on in the late afternoon toward the South China Sea a few miles to the east. Early the next morning Meadlo stepped on a land mine and blew off his right foot. As he was waiting to be evacuated, he chanted, again and again, "God had punished me and God will punish you, Lieutenant Calley, for what you made me do." Calley was shaken and began screaming for the helicopter. I knew how to spell Paul's name, courtesy of Ridenhour's Thanksgiving menu, and I spent hours dialing

Indiana information operators, beginning with cities in the north, looking for a listing for Meadlo. I found one in New Goshen, a small village near Terre Haute, and called. It was the right Meadlo residence, and Paul's mother, speaking in a scratchy southern accent, said it was okay with her if I came to visit, but she had no idea what her son would do.

I don't remember how I got there—I think I flew to Indianapolis via Chicago and drove east for two hours—but I got to the Meadlo farm midday. It was a run-down mess, with clapboard siding and chickens crawling in and out of torn coops, and lots of obvious repair work had not been done. As I pulled up in front of the house, Paul's mother, Myrtle, in her fifties but looking much older, came out to greet me. I introduced myself and asked if I could visit with Paul. She pointed to a second, smaller wooden frame house on the property, and said he was inside. And then this long-suffering mother, who did not follow the news and knew little of the war in Vietnam, said it all: "I sent them a good boy, and they made him a murderer."

I began my talk with Paul by asking to see his stump. He took off his boot and prosthetic device and talked openly and with animation about the treatment he had received in the field, in Vietnam, and the long recuperation he went through at an army hospital in Japan. We turned to the day of the massacre. Paul told his story to me without overt emotion; it was as if he'd clicked from on to off. He'd been asked to stand watch over a large group of women and children, all terrified survivors of the carnage, who had been gathered in a ditch. Calley, upon arriving at the ditch, ordered Meadlo and others to kill all. Meadlo did the bulk of the killing, firing seventeen-bullet clips—four or five in all, he told me—into the ditch, until it grew silent. I would be told later by other soldiers that a moment or two after the firing stopped, and the ditch grew quiet, the GIs heard the sound of a child crying, and Calley's men watched as a three- or four-year-old boy, who had been protected by his mother, crawled to the top of the ditch, full of others' blood, and began running toward a nearby rice paddy. Calley asked Meadlo to "plug him." Meadlo, flooded with tears and confronted with a single victim, refused and so Calley ran up behind the child, with his carbine extended, and blew off the back of his head.

I called Obst late in the afternoon and told him to let editors know we had done it again and now had a front-page story for the world—a firsthand account of the massacre, on the record, from a shooter. I spent the night at Paul's house, with his wife and young son, outlining the story and grabbing a few hours' sleep on a couch. His wife told me how hard it had been when Paul returned from the war without his right foot, and to a little boy he had never met. He did not talk about his experiences in Vietnam, but he was often uncomfortable around the child. One night, shortly after his return, she said, she woke up to hysterical screaming in the baby's room. She rushed in and found Paul violently shaking the terrified infant. It had happened before. I could not help but wonder whether Myrtle was referring to Paul's violence toward his son when she told me that Vietnam had turned her son into a murderer.

Obst, meanwhile, had somehow convinced CBS's flagship nightly television news show, anchored by Walter Cronkite, to pay ten thousand dollars to Dispatch for an exclusive interview with Meadlo the next night, hours before my My Lai story was to be published. There was a huge argument for television exposure, if Meadlo would agree to do an interview, but it would be completely unethical, in the newspaper world, to pay him to do so. You cannot pay for information that the public has a right to know. I'm not sure Obst understood that, but I did. And so I asked Paul if he would do it, and also made it clear he could not be paid for the interview, and that I and Dispatch would be. There was an inducement: I told Paul that CBS would fly him and his wife to New York City and put them up in a good hotel. I was not surprised when Paul readily agreed; he somehow knew, or sensed, that it was time to open up. I flew with Paul and his wife early the next morning to New York, first class, courtesy of CBS.

In his memoir, Obst somehow managed to gloss over the fact that he had made a commitment to produce Meadlo for CBS before we had a commitment. It was all magical:

As a typical baby boomer, I instinctively knew that nothing was real in America until it was on TV. I picked up the phone and called *CBS Evening News*. I told them what we had and they wanted it—badly. When I told them that we needed our expenses covered, they hesitated. "We're not into checkbook journalism," said the *CBS Evening News* managing editor. I politely asked him for NBC's phone number. He asked me where I wanted the check sent.

Sy brought Paul Meadlo to New York. On the way he wrote another installment of the story and we sent it out for morning release to all of our papers. . . .

Sy came over. . . . The phone rang moments after he arrived. It was Abe Rosenthal, head man of the *New York Times*. I'd sent him a copy of our story figuring they'd have no choice but to run it. It was too big a story to ignore and they were America's paper of record. Mr. Rosenthal couldn't have been nicer. He complimented me on the great job Dispatch and Seymour Hersh had done on uncovering the story. . . . Rosenthal continued his banter and then casually mentioned that since the *Times* was the paper of record, he'd kind of like to have one of his reporters come over and interview our star witness. Sy grabbed the phone out of my hand.

"Mr. Rosenthal, it's Sy Hersh. Listen, you want an interview with Paul Meadlo? Well, he's somewhere in New York—find him." Sy slammed the phone down. I stared at him in awe. He'd just hung up on "all the news that's fit to print."

Seconds later the phone rang again. Sy grabbed it.

"Mr. Hersh," Abe Rosenthal yelled, "do you know who I am!"

"Yes," replied Hersh and hung up on him again.

That night Paul Meadlo led the *CBS Evening News*. Mike Wallace interviewed him and Paul calmly told America how he had shot women and children in the ditches of My Lai. It sent a shudder through the nation.

The *Times* ran an account of Mike Wallace's interview with Meadlo on its front page the next day, crediting CBS all the way, with no mention of me or Dispatch. I did not care: I was not going to let Rosenthal and the *Times* turn my Meadlo story into their Meadlo story. I thought I was doing just fine by myself. I would have a testy relationship with Abe Rosenthal and the *Times* for the next two decades. Paul Meadlo's confessional did change America, as I and David Obst hoped it would.

His CBS appearance was broadcast on November 24; on the same day the Pentagon announced that Calley had been formally charged with the murder of 109 Vietnamese civilians. (Richard Nixon chose to announce on the same day that America would unilaterally give up the use, even in retaliation, of biological weapons.)

The harrowing Meadlo account ended the debate, if there was a serious one, about what had happened at My Lai, and it also spawned a wave of Sunday feature stories by journalists about American massacres and atrocities they had witnessed in Vietnam. The one that troubled me the most was filed by an experienced and competent AP foreign correspondent who wrote in great detail of an incident he had witnessed in July 1965, just a few days after a contingent of combat marines hit the beaches in Da Nang, South Vietnam, pursuant to orders from President Johnson. The AP dispatch told how a few marines had gone on a rampage within days of wading ashore and killed a cluster of civilians who had taken refuge in a cave during a firefight. Hand grenades were thrown, and the post–My Lai AP story quoted a marine as calling out, "Whoosh, I'm a killer today. I got me two." A second marine said, "Kill them, I don't want anyone moving." My first angry thought was why hadn't these stories been published at the time; perhaps doing so would have set a precedent and saved untold thousands of Vietnamese lives. After all, I had gotten tough stories published about the war in real time while at the AP, telling of American bombing of North Vietnam and high-level lying about it. It didn't take many days for me to be more charitable; my controversial stories had been written in an office far from Vietnam. Publishing a story from the scene about the needless killing of civilians in mid-1965 would have been seen by many as disloyalty, and the reporter's story immediately debunked by all, including many of the most prominent newspapers.

I continued to race around America well into December, tracking down My Lai participants and witnesses, and produced two more articles on the massacre and its aftermath for Dispatch. There was more than a touch of madness involved. I had arranged to have dinner a few days after Christmas with one of the massacre participants who lived in central New Jersey, seventy miles down the New Jersey Turnpike from New York. My family and I were celebrating the holidays with my in-laws in a suburb of the city. A severe snowstorm hit midmorning, and by afternoon nearly two feet of snow had piled up, with more coming. I took off anyway in my father-in-law's new stick-shift station wagon and somehow made it to the deserted turnpike and to my dinner, constantly gunning the car through snowdrifts. I had a terrific interview with a former GI who desperately needed to tell the truth; he, like many returning members of Charlie Company, was working a job that required little contact with others. I made it back to the snowy suburbs a few hours before dawn but burned out my father-in-law's clutch doing so.

I of course had been in touch with Bob Loomis from the moment I found Calley, and there was no question that a book-length study of My Lai had to be written. Thankfully, there would be no book by me on the Pentagon; I had yet to find a penetrating way into the subject. David Obst was desperate to make my participation in Dispatch a permanent one, and he began talking at the end of the year to other journalists, and newspapers—many of them first-rate—about expanding Dispatch into an independent news organization. It was not for me. I spent the next few months writing, tracking down My Lai participants, and continuing to make scores of antiwar speeches at colleges and political events across the nation.

It wasn't always as easy as the words above suggest. At one point, while writing the book, which was based on scores of interviews with those involved, I wrote Bob Loomis a sad note:

Some will claim that I have attempted to exploit some dumb, out of service, overly talkative G.I.s. But few men are exposed to charges of murder . . . it is not a "naming names and telling all affair." In fact, one of the strengths is that discriminating readers will know how much more I know—and did not tell. I'm convinced that to give the name and hometown of a G.I. who committed rape and murder that day, or one who beheaded an infant, would not further the aim of the book. It is an exposé, but not of the men of Charlie Company. Something much more significant is being put to light. . . . Both the killer and the killed are victims in Vietnam; the peasant who is shot down for no reason and the G.I. who is taught, or comes to believe, that a Vietnamese life somehow has less meaning than his wife's, or his sister's, or his mother's.

I believed those words then, and still do, but it was a hard-earned belief. One GI who shot himself in the foot to get the hell out of My Lai 4 told me of the special savagery some of his colleagues—or was it himself?—had shown toward two- and three-year-olds. One GI used his bayonet repeatedly on a little boy, at one point tossing the child, perhaps still alive, in the air and spearing it as if it were a papier-mâché piñata. I had a two-year-old son at home, and there were times, after talking to my wife and then my child on the telephone—I was often gone for many days at a time—I would suddenly burst into tears, sobbing uncontrollably. For them? For their victims? For me, because of what I was learning?

I tried to avoid sharing the worst in my speeches, but did not always do so. A long-scheduled talk at Tulane University in New Orleans that winter was preceded by a front-page editorial in *The Times-Picayune*, the city's morning newspaper. The editorial was bordered in red—for communist sympathizer, I assumed—and advocated against my appearance. The intervention provoked more interest in my talk, as usually happens, and I ended up speaking to a sea of people in the university's basketball stadium. I saw a large number of Vietnam veterans in the crowd, easily spotted because they wore faded army fatigue jackets laden with VVAW (Vietnam Veterans Against the War) stickers. I was learning more and more about the air war in South Vietnam, and its lack of discipline, and I was more than a little pissed off at the cheap shot in *The Times-Picayune*, and so I improvised with a purpose in mind.

I began my talk by asking if any of the vets in the audience had served in a helicopter unit that saw combat in 1968 or 1969 near the hotly contested city of Quang Ngai, a provincial capital a dozen or so miles from My Lai. A few hands were raised. I asked one of those vets, at random, if he would come onstage and answer a few questions. He came up. After I assured him I was not interested in his name, he told me that he had been a door gunner on a chopper in the right unit at the right time and at the right place. There were lots of tough operations, I said. He agreed. I suggested he often ended his days ferrying dead and wounded Americans from combat zones. He agreed. And after a particularly horrific day, I asked, what did his crew sometimes do—just to cope with the rage—on the way home? I didn't do it, he said, but I know what you're talking about. Is it not a fact, I asked, that choppers in those years and after one of those missions would spot a farmer at work in his field and make a dive toward him? The farmer would begin running, of course, I said, and the pilot, flying lower and lower, would tilt the chopper and try to decapitate him with the propeller blades. There was a long silence. I didn't do it, he said. I assured him that my questions were not about him but about what the war does to otherwise decent men. Did he have any idea what the choppers, once bloodied, would do before returning to home base? The veteran gave his first extensive answer: He understood that the pilot would land outside the unit's landing zone and wash the blood off the rotors. Who would do the washing? I asked. I do not remember if he answered my question or if I just went on to say that the chopper pilot and crew would pay local Vietnamese to wipe off the blood. I did not like what I did to the vet, who was stunningly honest, but I wanted to get back, in some way, at *The Times-Picayune*.

My Lai 4: A Report on the Massacre and Its Aftermath, my second book, was published on June 1. Its publication, to the dismay of many at Random House, was overshadowed by *Harper's* magazine, which published a thirty-thousand-word excerpt of my book, on a different grade of paper from the rest of the magazine, in its May edition, which appeared weeks before my book was available in bookstores. I knew that Willie Morris, the canny editor of *Harper's*, had bought the rights to publish an excerpt of the book from my agent, Robert Lescher, but I had no idea of Morris's definition of excerpt. Neither, apparently, did my literary agent, though he should have. To further hype his coup, Morris titled the May edition a "Harper's extra." My shock was tempered by the fact that there were literally lines of magazine buyers outside drugstores and bookstores on the morning the magazine was released. Morris's coup left Random House with a sure bestseller that did not become one, but his instinct about the importance of the story was a boon for the antiwar movement.

There was another plus of sorts: I was telephoned a few days after the excerpt was published by Robert McNamara's twenty-year-old son, Craig, who opposed the war and told me that he had left a copy of

Harper's, with the My Lai story splashed on the cover, in his father's sitting room. He later found it in the fireplace. (Thirty years later, a senior Pentagon official told me that McNamara had been troubled in 1967 by newspaper reports of American atrocities in Vietnam and ordered the Pentagon's inspector general's office to study the issue. The subsequent 208-page study found that a majority of American troops in combat did not understand their responsibilities under the Geneva Conventions, which set standards for humane treatment of prisoners of war. The report, turned in on August 15, 1967, seven months before My Lai, was ordered rewritten and never published.)

My five pieces on the massacre earned me the 1970 Pulitzer Prize for International Reporting, a rarity for a freelance journalist; as well as a George Polk Award, given by a panel of my peers; the Distinguished Service Award of Sigma Delta Chi (the journalism fraternity); and the Worth Bingham Prize. They also brought me fame and enough money to make a down payment on a small house in Washington. My family were no longer renters. I still wanted a newspaper job, and I had more to say, much more, about the My Lai massacre, how it was covered up, and the many flaws of an internal Pentagon inquiry into the tragedy that finished its work in mid-March 1970. I had been tracking that investigation, known as the Peers Panel, for its director, army lieutenant general William R. Peers, since it began its work in December 1969.

I still had the same dilemma, Pulitzer Prize or not: where to publish and where to work?

ELEVEN

To *The New Yorker*

I had been snotty to Abe Rosenthal because the reporter he wanted to send to "check quotes" from Paul Meadlo was John Corry, one of the aces on the *Times* staff. Did Rosenthal really think I was that much of a rube? Corry wanted to get to Paul to write a front-page interview with him, under his byline, for the next morning's *Times*; the last thing he was interested in was checking the quotes of someone else's story.

But Abe was the executive editor of the *Times*, and I was looking for a job, and so, in late December 1969, after my run of My Lai stories for Dispatch had finished, I sent him a short note proposing that "we could get together, if you want" for coffee or lunch on December 26, if he was going to be in his office that day. I got my comeuppance. Rosenthal wrote back immediately, saying that he might take the "whole damn day off," and added, "Could you possibly call me on the 26th and if I am in, we could have that cup of coffee." I got the drift; paraphrasing what I had said to him when he asked about Paul Meadlo, Abe was going to be in New York and I should try to find him. I did not call, and Abe expressed no regret.

Once *My Lai 4* was published in the spring of 1970, I went job hunting again at the *Times* and *The Washington Post*. I now had a Pulitzer, a bunch of other prizes, and two published books; surely, I thought, it was a hell of a good starting point. I was interviewed at the *Post* by a science editor who chose to focus only on an AP story I had written four years earlier dealing with a highly classified Pentagon study concluding that the United States had the capability to reliably monitor a nuclear test ban treaty with the Soviet Union. The Pentagon's long-standing resistance to such a treaty was based on an insistence that the Soviets could cheat by testing nuclear weapons in an underground cavern in Siberia, or some other place. I remembered my surprise, and irritation, when the *Post* did not publish the story, which was a front-page banner story in the Washington *Star*, the *Post*'s main competitor in Washington.

The editor told me why it did not: He had checked my story with a senior Pentagon spokesman who explained that I had been misled by my sources about the recommendations of the secret study. If I had made one more call, the editor told me, I would have realized the need to do more reporting. I didn't know whether to laugh or cry, because the editor ignored, or chose to ignore, the many direct quotes I published from the report itself. Of course, I did not explicitly state in the article that I had been provided with a copy of the top secret report by a Pentagon scientist, an expert geologist who had been involved in the research and was angered and a bit frightened by the response to the report of the Joint Chiefs of Staff. The nation's top officers had for years been dead set against a nuclear test ban with the Soviets on the grounds that it was technically impossible to monitor compliance. The new study explicitly said that a test ban could be monitored by the addition of high-tech monitoring sites along Russia's borders. After a briefing, army general Earle Wheeler, the chairman of the Joint Chiefs of Staff, stunned the involved scientists by declaring that he and his fellow chiefs would drop their long-standing objection to a test ban treaty on technical grounds, but would now object to such an agreement on political grounds. It was that high-level sleight of hand that led the Pentagon insider to me.

I did not tell my interviewer how narrow-minded he was being. My heart, actually, was set on the *Times*, despite my temper tantrum over the Meadlo story. I went to New York for an interview that, to my disappointment, was not with Rosenthal or one of his senior deputies but with a soon-to-retire editor who wore a green eyeshade in the office, just as some of the old-timers at the Associated Press in Chicago had done. He looked at my clips, acknowledged that I had done some very good work, and then suggested that I try to get a job on a good regional newspaper—he specifically cited *The Washington Post* and *The Boston Globe*—and try again with the *Times* in a few years. The experience was much more bewildering than depressing, and I decided I would have to stick to writing books. I had a good one in mind.

I had been contacted early in 1970 by a senior army officer who was privy to the extensive investigation that was being done as part of the army's inquiry into My Lai. He was convinced there would be a cover-up as the enlisted members of Calley's company provided more specifics about the extent of the horrors and the colonels and generals at the top of Lieutenant Calley's food chain—in the Americal Division—continued to insist they had no knowledge of the massacre. There was little doubt, the officer told me, that the initial investigation in the aftermath of the slaughter was replete with lies that were accepted without question at every command level inside the Americal Division. I had to tell the story, he said.

The Peers Panel would generate forty volumes of testimony and findings by its completion in March 1970, none of which was meant then for public release. My officer friend decided to provide the volumes to me as they rolled off the press inside the Pentagon. His wife commuted by car to her downtown Washington office, and on most weekday mornings for the next few months she would deliver one or two volumes at a time to me, in numerical sequence, at a prearranged point on a city street. I had to exchange volumes with each delivery—the old for the new—and made an arrangement with a print shop in the National Press Building, where I still maintained an office, to rent a Xerox machine at night and run off copies of the Peers interviews, one page at a time. This was going on as I was continuing to report, write, and edit the *My Lai 4* manuscript.

I was overwhelmed with the massacre as I worked my way through the interviews, and I was increasingly troubled by evidence that the investigators themselves had failed to do the right thing upon learning of a second slaughter on March 16, 1968. Medina's Charlie Company was one of three companies attached to Task Force Barker that were in action that day. Task Force Barker's Bravo Company was ordered to attack a village known as My Khe 4 a few miles away from the village of My Lai 4. It was the same story, on a lesser level, as in My Lai: The task force burned, raped, and murdered at will after finding no enemy troops there. As many as one hundred innocent civilians were killed at the second site. The implication was obvious, in terms of how the ground war actually was being fought in that area, but it was an implication that the final army report on My Lai did all it could to muffle. "My Lai 4 was extraordinary, but it was not isolated," I would later write. "My Khe 4, however, was just another atrocity; and that atrocity was covered up—after its uncovering in the midst of the My Lai 4 investigation." I added, referring to General Peers and the civilian leadership of the army, "Even the best general in the Army and its highest civilian officials have a point at which they, like the Vietnamese at My Lai 4 and My Khe 4, become victims."

There was a hell of a book in the full story of the My Lai cover-up. To hell with the *Times* and the *Post*. I knew that Bob Loomis and Random House would readily agree to a contract with me when I got further along in my reporting.

I stayed busy well into 1971 working on the cover-up book-to-be, doing antiwar speeches, and also researching and writing two long dispatches for David Obst's attenuated Dispatch News Service. My army sources inside the CBW community were appalled by the fact that Richard Nixon's renunciation of biological warfare had been more in word than deed; America, as of September 1970, was still maintaining large stockpiles of biological agents and had increased the Pentagon's budget for such work, and I wrote a long piece late that fall for Dispatch about it. A second article, published in January 1971, after more than a month of research, showed that a highly publicized but failed American raid on a suspected prison camp in North Vietnam was based on outdated intelligence data that had been repeatedly manipulated and misrepresented inside the U.S. community. The *Times* and the *Post* may have had their doubts about me, but more and more officials on the inside were talking to me and knew I would deal honestly with the information they shared and protect their identity. The two stories were published in full by many of the newspapers that had carried my My Lai articles, including the London *Times*.

I was not where I wanted to be—at the *Times*, where my reporting would have immediate impact—but I was still being productive. Neil Sheehan had called me months earlier to wonder why I had not been asked to work at the *Times*. I told him my sad story, and he arranged a lunch for me with Max Frankel, the bureau chief and senior correspondent for the paper in Washington. I was a bit worried about the meeting because Frankel had been quoted as expressing a concern about the "peddling" of the My Lai story at a time when Obst and I were essentially doing just that. James Reston, the longtime *Times* correspondent and columnist, also had questioned at one point whether a story such as the My Lai massacre should have been pursued as avidly as it had, given what he said was its adverse consequences for America. But Frankel could not have been more pleasant at our lunch, expressing support for what I had done and pleasure when I told him I wanted nothing more than to be a reporter for the *Times*. There was a freeze on hiring in Washington, Frankel said, but he would get back to me.

I was still jobless, and after an outdoor speech at a publishers and editors' antiwar rally in the spring in Central Park—by God, I thought, full of self-pity, I could lecture them but apparently not be put to work by them—I visited my agent. Bob Lescher was avuncular and gentle, and I had forgiven him for being manhandled by Willie Morris, although there were many at Random House who had not. Bob represented many *New Yorker* writers, and I asked about my going to work there. Would he call William Shawn, the fabled editor of the magazine, and ask him to meet with me? I was told, emphatically, to forget it; I was far too inexperienced for *The New Yorker*. In fact, as Bob reminded me, I had never worked for a newspaper. It was an impossible reach.

I left his office, went to the first pay phone I could find, and called the *New Yorker* offices. I asked for Mr. Shawn and got his secretary. I told her my name and said I lived in Washington but was in New York at the moment and wanted to speak with her boss. Do you have an appointment? she asked. I said no but asked if he was in his office. She said yes. I then asked if she would please just tell him that Seymour

Hersh is on the phone and wants to come see him. She hesitated but did so, and very quickly returned to the phone to ask if I could come right away. I could, and I did.

Shawn was slight and fussy, but he radiated what the military call command presence. He was an intent listener and a watcher; his eyes did not waver as I yapped. I told him what I knew about the cover-up of the My Lai massacre. He listened without interruptions as I rattled off God knows what about the internal army report on My Lai that was in my possession. Yadda yadda yadda. I don't recall a specific word or thought. After about five minutes Shawn raised a hand to quiet me and said—words I'll remember the rest of my life—"That sounds fine, Mr. Hersh. Is five hundred a week enough?" I said five hundred a week of what? He explained he was referring to money, a cash draw to provide expenses for travel, research, and living while I pursued the cover-up. He shook my hand and I did some paperwork with someone at the magazine that day, and off I went. My last paycheck at the AP had been for something like $150 a week. Now I was working for *The New Yorker* at more than three times that pay. My first call was a regretful one to Bob Lescher. I told him what had happened and that I did not think he could be my agent any longer. He had been dead wrong about me and, more significantly, also about William Shawn. He understood.

Bob Loomis was delighted to know that *The New Yorker*, if all went well, would excerpt my book on the cover-up. It wasn't clear what I would find, or how interested the American public would continue to be in a losing war, but Random House's modest advance and my *New Yorker* "draw"—I reveled in that word—would suffice. I had a new agent, Sterling Lord, who had been recommended to me by David Wise, a neighbor and family friend whose extraordinary work on the CIA in the 1960s had set the standard for investigative reporting on the American intelligence community.

I spent the next few months continuing to absorb the forty volumes of the Peers report on My Lai—none of which had yet been released to the public—and drawing harrowing conclusions from the more than four hundred interviews the panel conducted. The panel had recommended criminal charges against fourteen officers, including Major General Samuel Koster, who was commanding general of the Americal Division, and thus was ultimately responsible for the conduct of the units under his command, including Captain Ernest Medina's Charlie Company. Koster had been promoted and was serving as commandant of the West Point Military Academy by the time I published the Dispatch articles, and his involvement in the scandal added to the nightmare for the army, the Pentagon, and President Nixon, who was continuing to escalate the war. The only American Division officer who would be convicted at a court-martial of his peers, and serve time in custody, was William Calley.* The military justice system had failed, but only a few generals were caught up in the scandal, and the Vietnam War, with its violence still targeted on civilians and body counts, would continue apace.

There were extensive rules of engagement for waging war that were provided to all combat units in Vietnam. In his testimony before the Peers Panel, General Koster noted that his headquarters had published seven pages of "criteria for the use of firepower before firing in any civilian areas." But the promulgation of rules was little more than a charade that allowed the system to treat murder, rape, arson, and other war crimes merely as violations of rules. The commanders at My Lai and elsewhere in Vietnam were faced with a choice, one that was repeated again and again in the war: deal with the killings of civilians as murder, and begin a war crimes investigation, and invariably suffer professionally for so doing, or treat the massacre as a violation of the rules of engagement, and punish those who had committed major crimes as rule breakers.

This insanity was dramatically spelled out for me in the spring of 1971 when I was approached by a Vietnam veteran after I gave a speech at the University of South Dakota, in Vermillion, in the far southeastern corner of the state. He had been a clerk in headquarters of the American Division in July 1969 when four American helicopters shot

---

* Calley was sentenced to life in prison at hard labor for the premeditated murder of twenty-two Vietnamese civilians on March 31, 1971. The next day, President Nixon ordered him transferred from the army prison at Leavenworth, Kansas, to house arrest at Fort Benning. In February 1974, he was released from house arrest pending appeal. An appellate court confirmed his conviction, and Calley was returned to Leavenworth on June 13. He was freed on September 25, 1974, when his sentence and parole obligation were commuted to time served, leaving him a free man. He spent three months and thirteen days behind bars for the murder of twenty-two civilians in cold blood.

up two hamlets in a restricted fire zone ten miles north of the division headquarters, killing ten innocent civilians and wounding fifteen. The crews claimed that they had detected gunfire from one of the hamlets, but it was widely known that the war, for some reason, had not come to the area, which was dotted with small fishing villages just west of the South China Sea. There were complaints from the Vietnamese, and an investigation was ordered by Major General Lloyd B. Ramsey, the commanding general of the division. The official record of the inquiry was replete with what, at best, could be called contradictory testimony about the threat to the gunships. At its end, General Ramsey issued official letters of reprimand to three of the four command pilots involved. The men were guilty of a violation of rules, Ramsey concluded, and the letters of reprimand were to remain in their personnel file until the pilots completed their tour of duty in the division. If no further violations of the rules took place, Ramsey wrote, the letters would be removed from their files and destroyed.

The army clerk's contempt for Ramsey's decision to treat the clearly unwarranted attacks as a rules violation, especially given the division's sordid My Lai history, drove him to copy the files involved and take them to South Dakota with him. In March 1971, a month before my visit to Vermillion, Ramsey had been promoted to provost marshal general of the army, a promotion that added significance and drama to the story I would write; he was now the officer in charge of all military police functions. The former clerk gave me the files and wished me luck. I called Shawn from South Dakota, told him what I had, and got his okay to chase it. It took a few months, but I got to General Ramsey and some of the pilots and crew members involved, and wrote a twelve-thousand-word article for *The New Yorker*. I ended the account by quoting a senior army lawyer who said officers such as Ramsey find themselves caught in "a system of rules and regulations that have no relationship to what goes on in Vietnam. It's a little like the Ten Commandments—they're there but no one pays attention to them. . . . We're trapped by a system we created."

I called Shawn to tell him I had finished the piece and apologized for its length. He responded, "Oh, Mr. Hersh, stories are never too long or too short. They're too interesting or too boring." I had spent ten years in the business being told stories are always too long. My editor at the magazine was Pat Crow, a shrewd Arkansas boy who wore jeans and boots to the office and had little patience for chitchat—of which I was a master. These were the days at *The New Yorker* when the writer was dominant, and an editor with a different point of view about a paragraph or structure, or a cut that was needed, would not impose his will, but discuss a change that was wanted, and explain why. I quickly learned that it was suicidal to avoid the logic and common sense of Pat's recommendations. He, like Bob Loomis, was full of grace. The story was easily fact-checked—having a chunk of documents helped—and soon ready for publication. Crow called me in Washington to say that Shawn wanted to read the proof; he assured me such was standard operating procedure for a first story by a new writer.

The proof came by mail a few weeks later, very long weeks. A *New Yorker* galley back then contained something like four hundred words, and the first thing I did was count galleys. There were more than thirty of them, about right for a twelve-thousand-word story. That was good. I started reading the galleys. There was nothing from Shawn on galley one. Good. He liked the lead. There was nothing on galley two. On galley three, however, Shawn circled a cliché—a routine figure of speech I had used. He drew a line from the offensive phrase to the left margin and wrote in his tiny and very legible hand, "Mr. Hersh—pls use words."

My Reporter at Large piece, titled "The Reprimand," was published in October 1971 in a two-hundred-page edition of the magazine that had my reportage sandwiched among work by Donald Barthelme, Whitney Balliett, Calvin Trillin, and Pauline Kael. The police reporter from the South Side of Chicago had made it to Broadway, but the war was still on and I was going to stay on it.

Three months later, *The New Yorker* excerpted the gist of what would be my book on the My Lai cover-up in two issues. Each excerpt ran more than twenty-five pages in the magazine, and Shawn took no chances of a dumb mistake that could turn an innocent soldier into a murderer. The two articles were fact-checked, line by line, by two experienced young women who essentially moved to Washington for weeks. The process taught me humility, or what passes for humility for me; I had made many errors, the bulk of which arose when I was summarizing material that had been published or printed elsewhere. I learned from the checkers that every detail—essential or otherwise—matters. The *New Yorker* articles and the book, which was published by Random House a few months later, produced no lawsuits or threats of such, and no need for a published correction. I've been an avid supporter of fact-checking since then.

The two excerpts attracted the attention of someone at the *Times*, and Doug Robinson, a reporter in the Washington bureau, who got an early proof, spent time on the telephone with me, and wrote two cogent articles on the cover-up. In the midst of this, I learned that a visa application I had sought years earlier from the North Vietnamese government had been approved, and I was going to be the first mainstream Western reporter going to Hanoi since Harrison Salisbury's momentous visit in late 1966. I was excited and Shawn was all for it. I told Robinson about the visa, and he, so I gathered, passed the word inside the newspaper. In any case, I was telephoned sometime in February by James Greenfield, the foreign editor of the *Times*. He complimented me on the *New Yorker* series and wondered whether I would consider doing reporting for the *Times* when in North Vietnam. Greenfield also asked if I would be willing to have a visit with Abe Rosenthal. That was more than a little odd: Did Rosenthal really think I would say no if he extended an invitation? On the other hand, perhaps I had been a little peremptory by hanging up on him twice.

I told Shawn about the call, and he urged me to talk to the *Times*. So I did. Greenfield greeted me and introduced me to Abe, who promptly walked me into a small annex to his office. It was modeled, so I thought, after a Japanese tearoom, or some such. I learned later that Abe had reported for the *Times* from Japan and had been enchanted by the experience. His first sentence to me was a stunner: Why hadn't I ever approached *The New York Times* for a job? What? I could understand that he had forgotten our exchange of letters two years earlier, and perhaps he did not know I had been told to get a job somewhere else in an interview a year earlier. But surely Max Frankel had told him about our meeting, and the fact that there had been a job freeze imposed on the Washington bureau by none other than, I had to believe, the man sitting across from me. (I learned years later that Frankel had written to Abe more than a year earlier, on December 9, 1970, that I was eager to join the newspaper and he, Max, was persuaded that "the talent, energy and sources this man possesses ought to be in the service of the Times. . . . [H]is ability could bring us great rewards." Max also dealt with my obvious personal political biases, writing that "regardless of his opinions on this or that issue, he is a reporter first of all. I think he not only recognizes the *Times'* standards of fairness and nonpartisanship but has shown, above all in his Mylai work, that he has mastered the techniques of marshaling factual evidence and muting the crusader's instinct." It was a very generous assessment for a man whose instincts, in terms of being a crusader, would always be the opposite of mine.)

Anyway, in what I think was one of my finest hours, I told Rosenthal I did not know why I had not applied for a job. The truth seemed pointless. The gist of his message to me now was that *The New Yorker* was swell but there was nothing like the *Times*; I should go to North Vietnam, write for him, come back, and then we could talk about my joining the Washington bureau. Greenfield subsequently told me that if I agreed to file from the North, the *Times* would supply me with ten thousand dollars and a money belt that could be hidden. The cash was needed, he explained, because the North Vietnamese insisted that I pay one dollar per word for articles filed through their telegraph system that would be relayed by the Reuters news agency to New York, and read, so I assumed, by all along the way. It sounded mysterious and wonderful. But what would Shawn say?

Shawn was amazing. He urged me to go to work for the *Times* for the best of reasons: I had far too much energy for his magazine, he said, and he knew he would not be able to publish as much as I would write. I was worried about my brush with presidential politics and my obvious antiwar beliefs and asked him whether I would be okay at the *Times*. He said, "Yes. You will be fine there." I knew what Shawn meant by the word "fine": I was a reporter who believed in hard work and facts and understood the difference between a story and a nonstory. He also was convinced, as I was, that I could cope with the mechanics of writing on deadline for the *Times*.

So off I went to Hanoi in late February, money belt tucked away, via Bangkok and Vientiane, Laos, where I was to be met by a North Vietnamese official and put on one of the irregular flights from Laos to Hanoi. The flight on Air Lao from Bangkok was beyond chaotic: on an ancient DC-3 loaded with terrified goats and other animals, passengers scattered on the floor, and a balky engine—one of only two—that stopped running while climbing over a mountain range. My short layover in Vientiane turned into days of waiting because, as I later learned, there was turmoil among the leadership in Hanoi over the timing of my March visit. The buildup for an offensive was in the works, and there was worry that I might pick up on it. They had no need to worry. This ace *New York Times* foreign correspondent spent more than two weeks in the North without figuring out that the constant rolling of trucks going south had a particular meaning.

I had no expectation of a game-changing interview with Vo Nguyen Giap, the defense minister and commander in chief of the North Vietnamese army, or with Le Duc Tho, the senior Communist Party leader who was Henry Kissinger's counterpart in the onetime secret Paris peace talks. Harrison Salisbury had been given no such access on his visit to the North, but he had been able to produce a series of vital stories about the war. My admittedly ambitious goal was to write about asymmetrical war—to try to explain how a small nation with no air force could stand toe-to-toe with mighty America and come out ahead.

My host was Ha Van Lau, a former army colonel whose importance, I would learn, was in the political sphere; he had been a delegate to the inconclusive Paris peace talks on ending the war. He dropped me off at my hotel, the Reunification. It was state run and had seen far better days, but its location—near a city park and the historic Hoan Kiem Lake—almost made up for the fact that it took hours to draw three inches of greenish water for a bath. I met my interpreter, whose English was superb, and my minder, a silent, hulking army officer I knew only as Major Bo; I constantly fantasized about his success in killing Americans in combat in the South. It was odd being with the enemy, and being in their control, and also depositing thousands of dollars in an account in a Hanoi post office and wondering whether my dollars—that is, *The New York Times*'s dollars—would buy bullets that perhaps could, in some future battle, kill my countrymen.

I was told to rest, that interviews and meetings would begin the next morning. No way. I grabbed the interpreter and we took off to explore the city. It was early March and Hanoi was shockingly serene, with few checkpoints or other signs of a war-dominated society. There were posters exhorting vigilance and promising victory, but the center city streets were full of bicycles, motorcycles, children, and beautiful Vietnamese women. I had been forewarned about the extent of Communist Party control, but with the help of my interpreter I was led to pockets of entrepreneurship in the fast-food industry that dominated Hanoi's side streets. I saw no restaurants, but there were superb noodle soups available for sale all over. I wandered into a bookshop and encountered a young man on crutches with one leg missing. He told me he was a veteran of the famed North Vietnamese siege of Khe Sanh, in South Vietnam, where a group of American marines held out for six months in 1968 before retreating. We chatted and I was unnerved, truly rattled, to learn this young Vietnamese soldier knew the name of the marine lieutenant colonel who was in charge of a battalion that had trapped his unit in an ambush that cost him his leg. It was difficult to imagine Lieutenant Calley or one of his peers having any information at all about the other side. I filed a story early the next morning to the *Times*, via Reuters, about the one-legged soldier, and the editors there wisely decided it was not the kind of story with which I should begin my visit to Hanoi.

So I dutifully did my thing, following the schedule of interviews, museum visits, and historic sights that had been prearranged. Westerners were rare in Hanoi, and I was quickly spotted while waiting for my morning pickup by a group of neatly dressed teenagers walking to a nearby school. A ritual evolved: They would walk by and say, with smiles and giggles, "Good morning, sir," and I would wish them a very good day. I made it a point, when possible, to be outside at the right time every morning. I was determined to strike out on my own, despite my shadows. I felt no one would interfere with me; I was, after all, the American reporter who wrote about My Lai. So I got a list of the diplomatic missions in Hanoi and began making visits. The Indian ambassador had served in Beijing and Moscow and was delighted to give me his take on the North, the prospects for the war, and the Paris talks. He had a superb cook and a supply of something even more important—

novels by V. S. Naipaul. Jean-Christophe Öberg, the Swedish ambassador, was a scholar on Southeast Asia and provided the background and context every foreign correspondent must have—especially those who parachuted into a crisis, as I had—to judge the claims of his hosts. Öberg, who died in 1992, also had a feel for day-to-day life in Hanoi and told me at a lunch of his soccer-loving son's despair over the fact that he had joined a local schoolboy Vietnamese team, only to discover a curious form of diplomatic immunity: Every one of his shots on goal, no matter how weak, would be untouched by the opposing goalkeeper. Both Öberg and the French ambassador urged me not to be taken in if, as I expected, I was allowed to interview American prisoners of war. They had good reason to believe that some of the prisoners at the infamous Hanoi Hilton prison had had very bad times.

I had a raucous dinner with a detachment of Canadian soldiers who were assigned to Hanoi as part of a moribund peacekeeping mission. Early the next morning I somehow managed to stagger back to my hotel, having gotten drunk, watched bad pornography, and learned nothing about Hanoi or the war. I had a meeting that morning, and Ha Van Lau laughed when he saw me and asked, in English, "How was your night?" I mumbled an answer and he said, "You know the Canadians are more Yankee than the Yanks." I'd like to think that the Vietnamese's careful watch on me had been aimed solely at protecting me from the unruly Canadians, but of course it was more than that.

My first published piece in the *Times* described a newly opened war museum in Hanoi that depicted the failed South Vietnamese invasion of Laos in early 1971 as a turning point in the Vietnam War, a victory that was seen as a "test case" against the Nixon administration's policy of Vietnamization—the turning over of the war to the South Vietnamese army. I was able to check the heavily propagandized presentation with an unnamed "Western diplomat" who was quoted as agreeing that the victory came at "a critical time" for the Hanoi government. The byline on my dispatch described me as a freelance journalist who was currently in North Vietnam.

The stories flowed over the next few days as I began to move around, always under the watchful eye of the silent Major Bo. I traveled ninety-five miles east, to the heavily bombed city of Hon Gay,

a major coal-mining site, and was told how local villagers had inge-
niously found uses for the precious aluminum and other metals from
the airframes and engines of the downed American aircraft. The
materials were used to repair bicycles, make kitchen utensils, and even
fashion decorative jewelry. After much persistence, I was taken to the
infamous Thanh Hoa Bridge that had survived being targeted by U.S.
planes for the past five years, with horrific losses on both sides. I was
urged to get to the bridge by officials in Washington who told me that
as many as one hundred American planes were shot down while trying
to score a direct hit. The bridge, a key relay point from north to south,
was riddled with shrapnel holes and blackened from bomb blasts on the
afternoon I was given a tour, but it was still in daily use. I had learned
about the bridge, and its almost mythic invincibility, while reporting
for the AP.

On one of my trips to the east from Hanoi—a horrid ride along a
much-bombed road laden with huge water-filled craters—I witnessed
asymmetrical war at work. U.S. Navy pilots had bombed a railway line
near Haiphong an hour or so before we drove there, and work crews
had filled in the craters and were beginning to lay new track, which
had been stockpiled every few miles or so. My fellow Americans would
fly through heavy anti-aircraft fire to demolish rail lines that, even
if successfully struck, would need to be attacked again in subsequent
days.

It was on this dark day that I finally resolved my impasse with Major
Bo. While waiting for the road to be cleared, I began taking photographs of the far-off Annamese Mountains, a low-lying range that
extends from Laos to the South China Sea. I heard Bo say something
to the interpreter, and both men cracked up with laughter. What's so
funny? I asked. My interpreter said it was nothing. I asked again and he
shrugged and remained silent. I went into a tirade about being on my
own with no knowledge of Vietnamese and very little French and I had
to have confidence in him. He shrugged and said, "Major Bo says you
are a very, very shitty photographer." I had to laugh; he was of course
right, and it was good for me to learn that the strong, silent major had
a sense of humor—and for him to know that my temper tantrums were
little more than my way of coping.

I came to grow fond of the Reunification, whose rickety furniture, ancient toilet, and bed covered by mosquito netting had me fantasizing about Vietnam in the ethereal days of Graham Greene and French intrigue. The only other guests when I arrived were a Chinese delegation and a few Russians. A few days after my arrival, I came down to breakfast to find Pete Seeger, the famed antiwar folksinger, and his wife, Toshi, sitting nearby. I did not know him, but we had something in common: My wife had been a counselor at an upstate New York camp that offered needy New York City children a chance to spend a few weeks in the woods in the summer. Seeger lived near the camp, for which he had a great affection, and often led the campers in song. The next morning I came down to find Seeger telling all the waiters and the kitchen staff, via his interpreter, about an amazing handmade musical instrument he had seen, and played, the prior afternoon. It was shaped something like a flute, he said, but with a much different sound. None of the workers had any idea what he was talking about, so Seeger replicated the sound with his voice. It was a moment of pure musical genius, viewed by half a dozen awed—no, actually stunned— Vietnamese. And me.

A few days later, March 16, was the fourth anniversary of the My Lai massacre, an event about which I had repeatedly refused to do a talk for the North Vietnamese radio network. Seeger told me at breakfast that he had been asked to discuss his feelings about the war in a radio interview that day. He asked for my advice. I told him his critical views on the Vietnam War, and all wars, in fact, were well known, and if he wanted to do a sing-along on the radio, he should go right ahead. But he was not going to affect the course of the war by telling the North Vietnamese public he was against it. Moreover, thousands of young Americans, many of whom shared his views on the war, were killing and being killed a few hundred miles to the south, and inevitably he would be accused of backing the wrong side. I felt bad, I added, about telling someone who always stood up for what he thought was right not to do a crummy radio interview. He told me a few days later, with a touch of resentment—aimed at me, or so I thought—that he had not done the interview. I never saw him again.

I did not make page 1 of the *Times* until I had left Hanoi and was en route home via Bangkok, but there my byline was, along with the same "Special to *The New York Times*" tagline that the dispatches of all of the newspaper's foreign correspondents were given, over a long story about the status of American prisoners of war that included interviews with two Americans, one of whom told of steadily improving treatment and an end of isolation. I was careful to note that even the sophisticated Ha Van Lau "did not seem to realize that interviews with a few selected pilots in a less than open atmosphere fell short of demonstrating the adequacy of treatment."

I understood what the routine byline meant: Abe Rosenthal had decided to hire me, albeit without formally doing so and without discussing any of the usual stuff, like where I would work and how much money I would be paid. I knew without his saying that he wanted me to go to Washington to write stories that would make a difference.

I returned to the *Times* office in New York, dropped off a few rolls of film, agreed that I was to start my career in the *Times* Washington bureau on May 1, and wrote a long story, datelined from Hanoi, that was published in late March. I had spent more than fifteen hours discussing Hanoi's view of the Paris peace talks with Ha Van Lau and Hoang Tung, editor of the North's official newspaper who had been a revolutionary since the age of seventeen. There was no pretense that I was being given a new peace proposal; I was being provided instead with a firsthand account—Ha Van Lau had been a delegate to the talks—of the back-and-forth in the talks with the American delegation, headed by Henry Kissinger. The basic thrust was that the South Vietnamese government, headed by the former South Vietnamese army general Nguyen Van Thieu, had to go before any serious talks could take place. The interviews gave me a superb understanding of the other side's basic demands.

My second book on the My Lai massacre, titled *Cover-Up*, was published in early April 1972 by Random House. The two-part serialization in *The New Yorker* had focused on the cover-up as it took place in the hours and days of the massacre, as thoroughly explicated by the Peers inquiry, but I had done scores of interviews for my book in an effort to describe what the officers in charge of the inquiry were unable to see—the day-by-day disconnect between Samuel Koster, the general in charge of the division, and the men in the field doing the killing:

> High-ranking Army officers traditionally pride themselves on the quality of the meals served at headquarters. . . . Nothing was spared to make General Koster's mess an excellent one. . . . [D]inner was an elaborate affair, served by uniformed GIs wearing white waiter's coats. There was wine, engraved china with the Americal Division emblem, a well-stocked bar, and excellent French food on occasion. Steak and lobster were often served. Up to fifteen officers would attend, including Koster, his deputy commanding generals, the key headquarters staff, and occasional guests—very often Red Cross nurses. After dinner the dining hall was darkened and those officers who chose to stay were treated to private screenings of movies. . . . The normal work schedule of General Koster and his key aides, like that of their social life, seemed to have little relationship to the realities of the guerrilla war going on a few miles away. Koster lived in an air-conditioned four-room house on a hill at division headquarters. . . . [H]e was served by a full-time enlisted aide and a young officer. A few yards away was a fortified bunker with full communications in case of attack. Most of his workday was spent in a helicopter visiting the brigades and battalions under his command. . . . Even with these visits, the general was far removed from the problems and fears of the "grunts," the ground soldiers . . . under his command. When problems and complaints did arise, they often would be deliberately withheld from the general by his aides.

I also tracked down those witnesses, now out of the army, whose testimony before the Peers Panel had unsettled the investigators. Among them was Father Carl E. Cresswell, an Episcopal minister in the Americal Division at the time of the My Lai massacre who subsequently resigned his commission. He told the panel, "I became absolutely convinced that as far as the United States Army was concerned there was no such thing as murder of a Vietnamese civilian. I'm sorry, maybe it's a little bit cynical. I'm sure it is, but that's the way the system works."

Cresswell was still angry when he and I talked more than a year later at his parish in Emporia, Kansas, and he told of being assigned in late 1967 to an infantry brigade that was en route to the war by ship. The ship was slowed by heavy rains, and the colonel in charge of the voyage called out to Cresswell at one point, in front of other officers, and said, "Hey, Father. Why don't you ask your boss to do something about this?" The officers laughed, Cresswell recalled, and he responded, "I'm not sure God is in that much of a hurry for us to get to Vietnam to kill people." There was silence and that evening Cresswell's place at the colonel's dining table was removed.

There were many prominent reviews of my book, but the one that pleased me the most was written for *The Washington Post* by Ron Ridenhour, who had done more than anyone to help me expose the horror of My Lai. "'Cover-Up,'" he wrote, raised "serious questions that cut to the core of the military as an institution" and laid "open to question the integrity of our top military and civilian leaders as well as the American brand of justice." Ridenhour ended his essay by speculating that in future years questions would be asked about why the vital questions posed in my book "were allowed to go unanswered—as they surely will in a nation that has had the war up to here."

Ron got it dead right, in terms of America turning away from the war. It certainly turned away from *Cover-Up*. The book was slow to sell, despite the advance *New Yorker* serialization and the reviews. It surely did not help that North Vietnam had initiated a major and immediately successful offensive on April 1 and pushed farther south with each day. The continuing failure of the South Vietnamese army to stand and fight, even with the support of American soldiers and American airpower, was beyond dispiriting.

I was sorry about the poor sales, primarily because I wanted more people to know that the insanities of the Vietnam War originated at the top of the chain of command and that the GIs doing the killing were being poorly served, in many instances, by their superiors. All of which made my May 1 date with the Washington bureau of *The New York Times* so enticing. I'd be reporting and writing for millions of daily readers. Bliss.

As it happened, my *Times* career began with a roar—at the Paris peace talks.

TWELVE

Finally There

My first day as a *New York Times* man was Monday, May 1, 1972, and I spent it at the newspaper's headquarters on West Forty-Third Street. I was to stay most of the week in the third-floor newsroom to meet the editors and my fellow reporters and get a feel, from the inside, of the energy that went into every day's edition. I had not been in a newsroom since I fled the AP in 1967, and I hung around the foreign desk early that morning, listening to the editors check in with their foreign correspondents to discuss story ideas and begin shaping the next day's news. I played it cool and spoke only when spoken to, but it was a long way from my days covering midwinter manhole fires for Bob Billings at the City News Bureau.

The news from Vietnam that morning was grim. The North Vietnamese and the Vietcong, whose political wing was known as the National Liberation Front (NLF), were continuing to make headway in their monthlong offensive and were sweeping down Highway 1, the main north-south drag, toward Saigon. Abe Rosenthal rushed up to me late in the morning and asked if I had my passport with me. I said of course not and his answer was out of a Ben Hecht play, something like "Go home, get it, pack a bag, fly to Paris, talk to the North Vietnamese delegation at the peace talks, and find out what the hell is going on." I was taken to an office and handed an American Express credit card, an international air travel card, and a list of telephone numbers that would help in case of trouble.

Abe apparently assumed that my reporting on My Lai would guarantee me access to the Vietnamese. I wasn't sure of that, but I did exactly what Abe wanted. Paris meant a late-night business-class flight from Washington to Paris, a plush room at the five-star Hôtel de Crillon on the Place de la Concorde, a visit to the *Times* bureau, and my first meeting with two brilliant journalists, Anthony Lewis and Gloria Emerson. They took me to lunch at an offbeat joint near an outdoor French market, and we talked and talked about the war, about the paper, and, of course, about Paris. (Gloria later took me to lunch with Mary McCarthy, the famed novelist who hated the Vietnam War, as did Gloria, and was then writing incessantly about it.) Gloria and Tony would become dear friends and comrades in arms fighting the war inside the *Times*, but it never occurred to me that I would outlive both.

I had alerted someone I knew in Hanoi's delegation to the United Nations of my trip to Paris, and shortly after my arrival I was invited to an off-the-record lunch—a commitment that is sacrosanct, or should be, in my profession—with Nguyen Co Thach, a senior deputy to Le Duc Tho, Kissinger's counterpart at the talks. There were many reasons to agree to what could be seen as a courtesy meeting with the American journalist who had just returned from Hanoi. I was sure I would be told details of the current stalemate that were not publicly known, and at a minimum I would be able to privately fill in Rosenthal and the foreign desk about the impasse, as seen from the other side. The *Times* always had access to Kissinger, as Thach and his colleagues surely knew. I also guessed that at some point there would be at least one on-the-record meeting between me and a senior member of the opposition while I was in Paris, and what I learned from Thach would enable me to ask far more pointed questions.

The public dispute at the time between Washington and Hanoi still revolved around Hanoi's insistence that President Thieu had to be replaced before serious talks could begin. The reality was that the war was being won on the ground by the North Vietnamese and Vietcong and no amount of American bombing and support for the outmatched and beleaguered South Vietnamese army was going to lead to a change in policy. The leaders of the North and Vietcong believed their people could withstand the American bombing and they were going to win the war. My extensive discussions two months earlier with Ha Van Lau and Hoang Tung in Hanoi had also left me with a solid understanding of their willingness to suffer to win the war.

I worked around the clock during my week in Paris. There was a large Vietnamese expatriate community there—perhaps as many as twenty thousand, some of whom supported each side—and their leaders had lots of contact with the North and South delegates to the peace talks. I shared terrific Vietnamese meals with as many expat leaders who would see me and wrote a story about the community, and the split therein, before leaving Paris. I was granted a background talk with a significant North Vietnamese official at his delegation's villa at Choisy-le-Roi, a Paris suburb. It was a kick listening to him as chickens cackled in a courtyard somewhere behind us. A background conversation, however, didn't do for the *Times* foreign desk. My story about our conversation, with its new details about the impasse, would have made headlines if I could have named the official, but it was shunted to an inside page, where it belonged. I needed Le Duc Tho or someone of equal stature to give me the lowdown on the record. I'd had a coffee a few days earlier with someone known to the *Times* to be a well-informed member of the CIA station in Paris who was undercover as a consular officer. (Such info was one of the perks of being a *Times* man.) I told him what I thought was going on, and he, understanding I would not attribute any information and insights to him, gave me an honest, and negative, view of the prospects for a breakthrough in the talks. I of course had requested a meeting with Kissinger or one of his deputies at the peace talks, but it was not agreed to; Kissinger, I would learn, chose to do much of his talking, on background, with James Reston and Max Frankel.

On May 8, President Nixon responded to the on-the-ground military success of the North Vietnamese and Vietcong with expanded bombing of the North and a warning that the American escalation would include the mining of harbors in North Vietnam and an all-out effort to prevent the shipping of war goods from China and Russia to the North. He also called for an immediate cease-fire through-out Southeast Asia and the release of American prisoners of war in exchange for a commitment to withdraw all American troops within four months. I sensed I was going to get what I wanted even before I was granted an on-the-record interview two days later with Mrs. Nguyen Thi Binh, the charismatic head of the Vietcong delegation to the Paris talks. Madame Binh, as she was known, tore into Nixon and what she called his "speech of war" and mocked his conditions for a settlement—in the face of a successful enemy offensive—as even more bankrupt than previous offers.

Madame Binh's criticism was unrelenting, and the story I filed later that day was equally so; I included none of the usual verbiage from Kissinger or someone in the White House suggesting that the President's proposal offered a route to peace. The interview led the paper the next morning with a four-column headline, "Vietcong Turn Down Peace Plan," and there was no effort by the editors to mitigate the Vietcong's ferocious response to Nixon. I wrote a few more sto-ries from Paris about the ongoing talks, including an analysis of the prospects for peace. Such opinion stories, not based on a specific news event, were known as Q headers inside the paper; they had rarely, if ever, been done by a reporter less than two weeks at the *Times*. I had made my presence known on the paper with a perhaps unprecedented splash, and I understood that Abe Rosenthal had made it happen. The paper's coverage of the war itself, and the lack of progress, led by David Halberstam, Neil Sheehan, Charley Mohr, and others, had always been edgy, skeptical, and brilliant, and Rosenthal wanted more of the same from the Washington bureau. I sensed he was beginning to turn on the war and wanted his Washington bureau to do so, too, and I was to be his vehicle for change.

I finally got to my nirvana in mid-May: the Washington bureau of the *Times*. The city was humming with presidential politics. Many reporters were out of town, and I was given a temporary desk next to a longtime reporter for the paper, one of the few people actually at work in the bureau. There were a few pieces of mail for me and a large carton, full of books. It was from Erik Erikson, the famed psychologist and psychoanalyst whose first major book, *Childhood and Society*, with its concept of an identity crisis, had seemingly been on half the reading lists of the courses I took during my years at the University of Chicago. Erikson was preparing a series of lectures at Harvard and wanted permission to quote from my description, in the opening chapters of *My Lai 4*, of the slow descent into hell. It was not a surprise that Erikson was able to perceive what I had tried to do, aided by some sage advice from my psychoanalyst-to-be wife—describe without using any psychiatric or medical terms how a group of American kids could end up doing what they did at My Lai. I quoted Gregory Olsen, of Portland, Oregon, describing his shock soon after arriving in Vietnam when he and his colleagues "saw an American troop carrier drive by with 'about twenty human ears tied to the antenna. It was kind of hard to believe. They actually had ears on the antenna.'" I wrote that a few weeks later "the company began to systematically beat its prisoners, and it began to be less discriminating about who was—or was not—a VC [Vietcong]." I quoted Michael Bernhardt, who grew up in a suburb of New York City, who said that the company's officers thought that "everything that walked and didn't wear any uniform was a VC." It would take three months for Calley's GIs to morph from occasional violence, always unpunished, to the massacre. In anticipation of my agreeing, Erikson wrote, he was sending me autographed copies of his published works. I was floored: Erik Erikson wanted to quote from my work.

Washington, amid an unpopular war and with a disliked president, was teeming with stories, and within a few weeks I was in the middle of a good one. Many in the military and Congress were mystified in early June by the sudden dismissal and demotion of General John Lavelle, who ran the air force's bombing operations in the war. Four-star generals rarely got fired in wartime, and the Pentagon, which announced his firing and demotion, was refusing to answer questions from Representative Otis Pike, a Democrat from New York and former marine pilot who was a member of the House Armed Services Committee. I got an early taste of the power of the *Times* when Pike, who was convinced there was much more to the story, telephoned me—I did not know him—and urged me to find the mysterious Lavelle, who had gone into hiding, and get the truth.

No one in the media had interviewed Lavelle, and officials in the

Nixon administration were not talking. The action against him was unprecedented in modern military history: Lavelle had been summarily fired and demoted one rank, but he had not been prosecuted. I'm not sure how diligently anyone in the Washington press corps worked the issue—summer was coming—because it turned out to be easy to track down the guy. All generals have a personal aide or two—bright young captains with ambition—and Lavelle, in his climb to four stars, had served in many commands in Washington and abroad that published telephone books; I knew how important military telephone books could be from my reporting on My Lai. Sure enough, I found the names of a few captains who had served as his aide over the years, and one of them, now a major, was on duty in the Pentagon. I telephoned the major at home, explained that I was a reporter for the *Times* and wanted to find Lavelle and get his side of the story. Being direct with someone in the military, I'd learned, invariably produced a direct answer. The officer, who was as curious as Otis Pike about what had happened to his former boss, gave me the general's home address and telephone number in suburban Maryland.

I reached the general by phone the next morning and, as he lamented to an air force historian six years later, "conned" him into meeting with me. My memory of our talk is much different, of course. Four-star generals do not get "conned" or bullied into an interview. In fact, Lavelle readily agreed to meet me at a local golf course later in the day. I found him there with his two sons practicing on the driving range and I joined them. After a while, he asked his two sons to wait in the car, and we went into the clubhouse for a beer. I remember Lavelle took a big swig out of a bottle of Miller High Life, and I figured what the hell and asked right off why he was fired but not court-martialed. I'll never forget his answer, given with a smile: "When was the last time a four-star general was court-martialed?" At that moment, I began to like him. He said he would tell me what happened if I did not directly quote him, since he had been cautioned not to speak publicly for fear of undermining the war effort. Because of that issue, he said, he could not tell me the truth on the record. I agreed and was glad I had done so, for the truth was startling: The war was going badly, and he had been fired for ordering the pilots in his command to bomb strategic targets in North Vietnam that were not on the approved target list. He added that everything he did was known to all in the chain of command, who looked the other way when the unauthorized bombings became known inside the government. He had taken it on the chin for the war effort. I told him I had to raise the issue of higher authority and somehow suggest in print that he had attacked unlawful targets at the request of someone high up in the Nixon administration. Jack Lavelle knew that I was referring to Henry Kissinger.

My dispatch was splashed all over the front page of the Sunday *New York Times* a few days later under an imprecise headline stating, "General Bombed in North Before President's Order." Some of the targets struck by Lavelle—anti-aircraft missiles, fuel depots—were no longer restricted by the time I got into the story. There were rules authorizing air force pilots to take aggressive action if attacked by North Vietnamese anti-aircraft rocket fire or if there were signs of radar activity at the North's more sophisticated and more lethal surface-to-air missile sites. The procedure was known as protective reaction. Lavelle's pilots had been cheating for three months—bombing with or without a prior enemy response—before getting caught. This was at a time when all air operations over the North were under constant monitoring. There was something wrong with the Lavelle story, as I wrote: "Was it possible for a battlefield commander to grossly violate operation orders and not be detected for three months?"

All reporters operate on instinct, and I was convinced that this guy was straight; there was no way he would cheat so egregiously without knowing that he was doing what a higher authority wanted. My job, so I thought, was to find out who at the top had pushed Lavelle to violate the rules. I had flown to New York on Saturday morning to go over a proof of the story with Lavelle and to reassure him that he would not be directly quoted in the next day's story. He took no issue with what I had written and even added an illegal target to the list I read to him. He had forgotten to mention it earlier, he explained. He was not ashamed of what he did.

I felt I was Abe Rosenthal's hired gun and therefore free to make a crusade out of the Lavelle story. I wrote seven more articles about the issue in the next eleven days, aided by similar accounts from three present and former air force veterans who served under Lavelle in the Seventh Air Force. I had been given their names and contact information by an airman who was still on active duty in Southeast Asia. A former sergeant named Michael Lewis, then a student at the University of Michigan, who had been a photointerpreter in Lavelle's command, described the activity as little more than a cover-up of obvious wrongdoing throughout the air war. That story led me to other photointerpreters who said that they were involved in the cover-up of as many as twenty illegal raids a month on off-limit targets in North Vietnam. I was contacted by a few Democratic members of the Senate Armed Services Committee who wondered, as I did, whether Nixon and Kissinger were somehow involved. A disheartened air force lieutenant on active duty then formally filed court-martial charges against Lavelle and held a news conference in Washington to voice his anger at the official cheating and breaking of rules. By now the story was getting widespread newspaper and television coverage, and the *Times* editorialized the next day that the officer's charges should impel Congress "to take a harder and deeper look" at the Lavelle case.

My work brought me into contact with usually reclusive John C. Stennis, the conservative Democratic senator from Mississippi who was chairman of the Armed Services Committee. I didn't know Stennis but sensed that he would be appalled by the cheating that was going on, and keep his concerns to himself, just as I had correctly guessed years earlier that L. Mendel Rivers, the conservative chairman of the House Armed Services Committee, would be troubled by the massacre at My Lai. I was told Stennis was an early bird who got to his office by 7:00 a.m., so I called at that time one weekday and he answered the phone. He had been following my stories, and he and I began a series of early morning telephone conversations that went on for years. He would talk to me, he said at the beginning, about the Lavelle matter and my splurge of stories about it if we kept what was said between ourselves. It was reassuring to know that Stennis was deeply troubled by the command-and-control issues involved, especially because, as he said to me one morning, we were in a war that he thought had to be won. He said he was going to authorize hearings on the case and wanted me to know that if I kept going on the issue, as he knew I would, my *Times* stories could—I cannot forget these words—"destroy the Pentagon." I suspected then that he knew that Lavelle had been given authority to conduct the bombings. It was a bit hard to fathom, given his reputation as defender of everything military, but Stennis repeatedly encouraged me to write the truth as I knew it.

The Lavelle story lingered through the end of the year. The Senate held a series of public hearings in the fall, and Lavelle finally acknowledged, during his testimony, that he had received higher authority. All above him in the immediate chain of command—the air force chief of staff, the army general in charge of the war effort, and Mel Laird, the secretary of defense—denied in subsequent testimony that they had any knowledge of Lavelle's actions.

Decades later, the real story emerged in the White House tape recordings and it was ugly. In February 1972, Nixon had ordered his generals, through Kissinger, to expand the air war by bombing North Vietnamese anti-aircraft missile sites at will. By then, as Nixon and Kissinger knew, Lavelle had been attacking those sites, without a formal order, for months. On June 14, 1972, two days after publication of my first article on the issue, Nixon was upset about the leak of the illegal bombing and about Lavelle's firing. "I just don't want him to be made a goat," he told Kissinger. Twelve days later, with the first stories about the Senate hearings, Nixon again expressed guilt about Lavelle and told Kissinger, "I just do not feel right about pushing him into this thing and then he takes a bad rap." Kissinger urged him to stay out of it, and Nixon agreed to do so, saying, "I want to keep it away if I can, but I do not want to hurt an innocent man"—it was as if he had no power to intervene. Lavelle was drummed into an early, and unfair, retirement.

I was never in touch with Jack Lavelle again—he passed away in 1979—but his wife and two of his children did occasionally write to me, including a son who told me that he was one of the two boys who had waited an hour in the family car as his dad and I talked at the golf course. In late October 1972, when it was clear that there would be no absolution for his father, the oldest boy, Jack Lavelle Jr., wrote me a note that I will keep forever. "It is amazing how things can be distorted in the free press," he said. "I guess that implies freedom from accuracy and license to accuse from the hip if you're aiming below the belt. Gen. Lavelle didn't ask for mercy, just honesty. You were fair and honest . . . didn't moralize or make implications. On behalf of my family and myself, I thank you . . . for your impartial hard work." One letter like that in a decade is all a reporter can ask for.

My initial splash of Lavelle stories ended in late June, just as the first Watergate story broke in *The Washington Post*. By then, I had been moved into the bureau's foreign policy cluster and was sitting across from Bernard Gwertzman, the very competent point man for stories involving Henry Kissinger and his National Security Council (NSC). There was a near-daily ritual involving Bernie that stunned me. On far too many afternoons around 5:00, Max Frankel's secretary would approach Bernie and tell him that Max was at that moment on the phone with "Henry" and the call would soon be switched to him. Sure enough, in a few moments Bernie would avidly begin scratching notes as he listened to Kissinger—he listened far more than he talked—and the result was a foreign policy story that invariably led the paper the next morning, with quotes from an unnamed senior government official. After a week or two of observing the process, I asked the always affable and straightforward Bernie if he ever checked what Henry was telling him with Bill Rogers, the secretary of state, or Mel Laird at the Pentagon. "Oh no," he said. "If I did that, Henry wouldn't speak to us."

Frankel was paying little attention to me, but I worked closely with Bob Phelps, the deputy bureau chief and a wonderful editor whom I came to trust totally. I continued to focus on everything that was wrong with the war, and Frankel seemed to have no issues with that. I wrote a few front-page stories that summer about the CIA's alleged role in running drugs as part of its covert operations in Southeast Asia, as reported in a new book by Alfred McCoy, then a graduate student at Yale University. An academic publishing a book is one thing, but for the *Times* to give wide exposure to his findings was unexpected and traumatic for the CIA. As a result, I received a visit from a senior officer in the Directorate of Operations—the Agency's so-called dirty tricks bureau—who could not quite understand why I published such stories given that the Agency had denied it all. It did not help, I guess, that I had quoted a former CIA officer with years of experience in

Vietnam as saying that McCoy's work was "10 per cent tendentious and 90 per cent of the most valuable contribution I can think of." It was clear that from the CIA's point of view I was running amok.*

In early July, I wrote an article that led the paper about the Pentagon's previously unknown cloud-seeding program in Southeast Asia whose goal was to create storms that would hinder, so the military hoped, enemy troop movement and suppress anti-aircraft fire. It turned out, as I wrote later, that Secretary of Defense McNamara had in 1967 ordered an end to such efforts, whose long-term impact on the environment was not at all understood. The Pentagon, however, continued to seed clouds until late 1971. There was another summertime series of articles dealing with allegations that the United States was targeting dikes in North Vietnam. In fact it was the anti-aircraft sites built on top of the dikes that were the targets. In late July there were more front-page stories based on testimony from war veterans who told of knowingly targeting North Vietnamese and Vietcong hospitals. I wrote a long piece for *The New York Times Magazine* about the exploits of a former air force captain who had spent eighteen months working out of a secret office in Laos on the clandestine bombing campaign there. The magazine, like the daily paper, was totally supportive of me. The headline of the story was "How We Ran the Secret Air War in Laos." By the end of the summer I had become the point man for those in the military and, more important, for those inside the CIA who were troubled by what they knew.

I was making Rosenthal happy—and more than a little anxious about my personal politics. At one point in the fall, while visiting the Washington bureau, he snuck up behind me, ruffled my hair, and said, "How's my little commie?" He then added, "And what do you have for me today?" It was his way of telling me he knew I was keeping my per-

---

* In a critical study of American global power published in September 2017, McCoy, a history professor at the University of Wisconsin, recalled an important role—not remembered by me—I had played in initially getting his book published. Cord Meyer, the deputy director for covert operations, had gone, very early, to McCoy's publisher, Harper & Row, in New York, and asked that they not publish it. Harper & Row refused, but did agree, to McCoy's horror, to allow the CIA to review the manuscript prior to publication. At that point, McCoy, as he wrote, went to me: "Instead of waiting quietly for the CIA's critique, I contacted Seymour Hersh, then an investigative reporter for the *New York Times*. The same day that the CIA courier arrived . . . to collect my manuscript, Hersh swept through Harper & Row's offices like a tropical storm and his exposé of the CIA's attempt at censorship soon appeared on the paper's front page. Other national media organizations followed his lead. . . . The book was published unaltered."

sonal politics out of my reporting. There was always residual anxiety about those of us on the paper who were open about their dislike of the war. At one point in the mid-1970s, with Saigon on the verge of falling to the North, I was going to lunch in New York with Gloria Emerson, Tony Lewis, and Richard Eder, a brilliant colleague who shared our feelings, and we bumped into Abe and Arthur Gelb, the city editor, who was Abe's close friend. "Ah, the cell is meeting," Gelb said. My hatred of the Vietnam War stemmed not from an ideology but from what I had learned in reading and reporting on it—on-the-job training, in a sense.

I stayed busy and kept the hell away from the Watergate story. I knew nothing about the Nixon White House or the presidential aides who worked there. Bob Woodward and Carl Bernstein, the two *Washington Post* whiz kids—neither one was thirty years old in 1972, and I was all of thirty-five—were onto an issue that I felt could doom the Nixon presidency. The *Times* Washington bureau, though, was doing little on the story. Frankel and his senior editors seemed unperturbed as the *Post* kept on banging away. Gwertzman told me more than once that summer that Frankel and other higher-ups in the bureau had been assured by Kissinger that the *Post* was making a huge mistake in pushing the stories by the two young reporters. There was nothing to it, and the *Post* would be embarrassed.

The tension between the Washington bureau and the home office in New York had been the stuff of gossipy magazine and newspaper reports for nearly a decade, but I did not understand the depth of those feelings until 1980, when Harrison Salisbury, who spent more than twenty-five years at the *Times*, wrote *Without Fear or Favor*, a book on the paper's history that he described as uncompromising. By the end of the day on Saturday, June 17, 1972—the break-in at Democratic National Committee headquarters in the Watergate office complex in Washington took place early that morning—the *Post*, Salisbury wrote, had eight reporters assigned to the story. At the Washington bureau of the *Times*,

no alarm bells rang. . . . Not many members of the forty-man Washington bureau worked on Saturdays. It was an assignment everyone tried to avoid. They wanted to be away for the weekend, to their houses in the West Virginia hills, the Blue Ridge of Virginia, the eastern Maryland shore, or by mid-June in Martha's Vineyard or Nantucket where half the staff spent the summer. . . . Nothing was more un-chic than to stay in grubby Nixonian Washington over a weekend at any time from June 15 to September 15. *Nobody* worth knowing possibly could be in town.

Salisbury was exaggerating, of course. Frankel had brought a bunch of first-rate young reporters onto his staff—among them, Walter Rugaber, John Crewdson, and Christopher Lydon—who were chasing the Watergate story, but the *Post* had the inside track and was holding it dear. Salisbury's mean-spirited words were imprecise, but the gist of what he wrote was not. Abe Rosenthal was enraged and embarrassed by the success of his main competitor, and changes were coming. I knew nothing of this.

THAT FALL, after a family vacation that included a visit with Erik Erikson and his son Kai, then teaching at Yale, my merry way with the *Times* got more complicated. I was continuing to report on the Senate hearings on the unauthorized bombing issue, watching sadly as one senior general after another dissembled in a successful effort to put the full onus for the unauthorized bombing on the disgraced Jack Lavelle. By then I had become friendly with Daniel Ellsberg, of the Pentagon Papers fame, and he, as one of Kissinger's early advisers, told me that the Pentagon, at Nixon and Kissinger's insistence, had systematically bombed Cambodia in secret for more than a year in an effort to deny the Vietcong a sanctuary. I talked to former Kissinger aides who knew the story—the illegal bombing would later become an item of impeachment for Nixon—but none of them would go on the record. I was aware that someone had to be quoted by name to enable the *Times* to publish a story of such import within two months of an election that Nixon was heavily favored to win.

I was invited to a dinner hosted by one of Eugene McCarthy's Irish Catholic cronies from the 1968 campaign, a retired senior operative for the CIA. I had made contact earlier with a number of former and present CIA officers with a story or two to tell; the fact that I was able to publish the critical stories I had in the *Times* obviously was a factor in their coming to me. I asked my host at one point during the dinner—there were a few other old hands from the Agency there—about the CIA's highly secret plans to use a salvage ship owned by Howard Hughes to recover a Soviet submarine, with three nuclear warheads aboard, from the bottom of the Pacific Ocean. I used the then current code word for the operation and the table froze. My host responded that he hoped I would not write the story until the mission was completed.

Washington certainly worked in strange ways, but the dinner table confirmation enabled me to go back to those former agents, who shared a lot of disturbing information with me, with renewed confidence in their status as insiders; an inevitable fear for any reporter who is critical of his government's policies is being fed a false story that would be professionally catastrophic. I resolved early that I would never publish information from someone on the inside without verifying it elsewhere, even if a second source insisted I had to pretend that he did not exist. Abe Rosenthal made a point, after I was hired and began writing inside stories for the *Times*, to speak privately to me and ask for the names of all of the sources involved, including those not cited in any way by me. I had no hesitancy in telling all to him. In some cases, the unnamed source was a senior official in the White House or even in the CIA. One source led to another, and I learned of three major issues that were creating controversy inside the Agency, led by Richard Helms, the urbane old-timer who meshed brilliantly with the Washington establishment. One involved the recovery of the downed Soviet submarine, an operation whose budget was estimated at $750 million at a time the federal government was cutting back milk subsidies for public school lunches; the second dealt with the CIA's frantic efforts to undermine the government of Salvador Allende of Chile, a socialist who was unafraid to speak out against American foreign policy; and the third was total dynamite—the existence of Operation Chaos, a secret project authorized in 1967 to collect intelligence inside the United States on anti–Vietnam War protesters and other suspected dissidents. Such activity was in direct violation of the CIA's charter, which explicitly forbade the Agency to operate inside the United States.

The stories would take time, lots of it. I understood that going that deep into the Agency was a hell of a lot more complicated than writing about the unfair cashiering of a general. I had relied on Bob Phelps to keep Frankel aware of what I was doing, but the CIA was a formidable target, and I wrote a long memorandum to Frankel about the three stories, explaining what I knew, what I needed to know, and something about my sources. I did not remember that Frankel had published a series of articles in early 1972 about the Nixon-Kissinger foreign policy, obviously with a great deal of help from Kissinger, one of which told how Nixon had successfully resisted pressure from the CIA to be more aggressive in opposition to Allende. Even if I had recalled the stories, I would have sent the memo; Frankel was far too bright and competent not to realize that stories evolve.

A month went by with no answer. I kept busy in the interim. I had gotten to know and respect Mrs. Cora Weiss, a leading New York City activist against the war who, through her contacts with the North Vietnamese, had become a funnel for mail to and from the American prisoners of war in Hanoi. She filled a natural void, since the U.S. government refused to acknowledge the North and thus was unable to handle mail for the prisoners. In September, Cora flew to Hanoi to accept in her care three American prisoners who had been released by the North. She was accompanied by Mrs. Minnie Lee Gartley, whose son, navy lieutenant Mark L. Gartley, was one of those released. The flight from Hanoi stopped in Moscow, and from there the five of them flew on a commercial flight to New York, via Copenhagen. I was invited by Cora to join the group in Copenhagen. The *Times* allowed me to do so, and I was able to spend useful time with the former prisoners and also witness a very tense standoff at John F. Kennedy Airport after the regular passengers had departed. The three men were to go directly to a nearby military hospital for evaluation, and a team of Pentagon officials, on edge because the prisoners had been freed by Cora Weiss, and not by the U.S. government, boarded the plane to begin the process. Mrs. Gartley stunned all by insisting on taking her son home for a few days before he was to report to the hospital. A senior Pentagon official angrily told her that the lieutenant, prisoner or not, was still a navy officer and was obligated to go where he was ordered. At that, Mrs. Gartley burst into tears, and said, "I haven't cried since the day you called me and said my son was shot down." As I watched and took notes, another senior Pentagon official whispered to me, speaking of the Pentagon's insistence that Gartley could not go home with his mother, "I told them not to do it." I of course began my story for the next morning's *Times* with Mrs. Gartley's tears.

A few days later, I wrote a far more significant dispatch, based on information I learned in talking to the pilots en route from Copenhagen, about the high standard of discipline that was being maintained among the prisoners in Hanoi, including an internally adopted code of conduct. I coordinated closely with the Pentagon in preparing the article, as any journalist would—hundreds of Americans were still in captivity—and many of the ingenious ways the prisoners found for communicating with one another remained a secret.

My first six months at the *Times* had been exciting and I was proud of the work I did, but I understood I was still on the fringes of even more significant stories. An air force general bombing unauthorized targets and a mother crying for her prisoner son made great reading, but there was, so I was learning, another level of Nixon and Kissinger wrongdoing in foreign policy. Woodward and Bernstein were continuing to make headlines in their relentless hunt for the Watergate truth, but I still wanted no part of a story those two owned. I knew nothing of the war between Washington and New York over Watergate coverage, but I was convinced that the three stories I had proffered to Frankel would be as important, if not more, than the continuing Watergate saga. There was a secret world in Washington, and I wanted to write about it.

I finally got my answer from Frankel late in the fall. In a one-paragraph memo to "sh" from "mf," I was told that my story ideas were interesting and should be written in a single dispatch that described the lengths the national security establishment had gone to to protect American interests and monitor Soviet gains in technology. Be sure to run it by "Henry [Kissinger] and Dick [Helms]," Frankel wrote. I was crushed, and then horrified, and then realized that if I could not find a way to get what I knew into the newspaper, I would have to resign. Run it by Henry and Dick? They were the architects of the idiocy and criminality I was desperate to write about. I could not imagine how a senior editor, one as bright and supportive as Frankel had been, could not grasp the implications of what I was proposing. (I would be even more confounded by Max's indifference when I learned later of the pressure he was under because of the bureau's failings on the Watergate story. My stories offered the guy a chance to show New York, at a difficult time, what his bureau could do.)

I do not remember whom in New York I bitched to, but I was bitching aplenty. It may well have been something I said to Bob Phelps that made its way north. In any case, in the midst of my doldrums, I got a call from Clifton Daniel, a senior *Times* editor who was primarily known to me as the husband of Harry Truman's talented daughter, Margaret. I recall the gist of the one-way conversation well: "Sy, this is Clifton Daniel. I know you're unhappy but don't go anywhere. I'm coming down—this is private—to run the bureau in a few weeks, and I promise that you will be able to write any story you have." A few days later it was announced that Max was moving to New York to become Sunday editor of the newspaper, a job that got him out of Washington and put him in the running to eventually become the executive editor, the top job that every editor on the newspaper, for reasons I could never fathom, dreamed about. How could anyone want to edit when there was so much fun to be had reporting? I stayed put.

Clifton was a North Carolinian who was always gracious and polite. It would be hard to locate anyone on the newspaper, or perhaps on the planet, who could be more of a contrast than I was. He always dressed well and oozed charm and very pointed humor. At an end-of-year reception for the staff and families, I introduced Clifton to my wife and he said, with a big smile, "Oh my, Mrs. Hersh. You have my heartfelt condolences." A few days later he walked into the newsroom and dumped half a dozen boxes full of Brooks Brothers shirts and sweaters on my desk and said only, "Dress better." As different as we were, we had two things in common—a love of stories that pained Nixon and Kissinger, architects of a mutually despised war, and two young children of the same age, all of whom adored McDonald's. The two of us eventually set up a standing date to take our children there on Saturday mornings, and occasionally to a very bad kiddie movie. I would be dressed as I usually was, in a T-shirt and chinos, and Clifton was always in a suit. The odd couple.

Just before the end of 1972, with Nixon reelected by a landslide—his opponent, the liberal Democrat George McGovern, won only 37.5 percent of the vote—and the Democrats in total disarray, Clifton gave me the bad news: Abe Rosenthal wanted me to drop my obsession with Vietnam—an obsession I thought Abe shared—and focus on Watergate. Nixon may have won, I was told, but Abe was convinced the story was far from over. There would be investigations not yet envisioned, and he did not want Ben Bradlee to continue humiliating the Washington bureau as many in New York were suggesting. I protested but Abe insisted he was doing me a favor by giving me a chance to show the newspaper world that my skills went beyond trashing the Vietnam War. Unfortunately, I knew nothing about the White House or the Watergate story, other than what had been published.

Over the Christmas holiday Abe had made another radical move, hiring Leslie Gelb to begin work in January 1973 as a reporter in the Washington bureau. I knew Gelb as someone who had worked as director of policy planning and arms control for the Pentagon and also served as director of the top secret Pentagon Papers project that was authorized by Robert McNamara. Earlier, while working on a doctorate at Harvard, Gelb was a teaching assistant for Henry Kissinger. I had interviewed him while he was at the Brookings Institution, a Washington think tank, about the Paris peace talks, about which he was knowledgeable and helpful. It all sounded pretty bad to me, especially because he had never worked for a newspaper and had worked on the war.

Gelb was assigned a desk a few feet from me, and he turned out to be the most fun-loving guy I had met on the newspaper. He was brilliant, no fan of the war, and innately suspicious of Kissinger—although respectful of Henry's intelligence and cunning—and understood the soul of bureaucracy in a way no one who spent his life as a reporter could. If I learned of a new highly secret document, Les would get it within a few weeks. He was a marvel. We became fast friends and active pranksters. I not only had a bureau chief who would have my back, but I had a new best friend.

All I had to do was figure out Watergate, six months after Bob and Carl had done so. That story, by the end of 1972, seemed to be at a dead end. In fact, it had just begun.

THIRTEEN

Watergate, and Much More

I had one thing going for me as I slunk into the Watergate scandal. It came off a tip I had received a month or two earlier but had ignored. A friend from the New York publishing world told me that a freelance writer named Andrew St. George, who had ties to the anti-Castro Cuban community in Miami, was circulating a book outline about the experience of Frank A. Sturgis, one of the five men who had been caught burglarizing the Democratic National Committee offices in Washington.

My initial response had been, more or less, "What does this have to do with the war in Vietnam?" Now, given my new assignment, I began calling around to get a copy of the outline. One of St. George's most explosive claims, based on what he said were a series of interviews with Sturgis, was that Sturgis had done political surveillance of Democrats in Washington as well as being part of a team that was investigating drug trafficking in Central America. I wondered whether investigating meant smuggling. All of this allegedly was done at the direction of Howard Hunt, a former CIA officer who was linked to the Watergate break-in team. St. George's reputation in the New York publishing world was spotty, but he had won prizes in the late 1950s for his photographs of the Cuban revolution and apparently had gotten a contract, for minimal money, for a book based on interviews with Sturgis. I called him and we had a meeting at which it became clear that the likable St. George was extremely eager for me to write a story about his book project. I told him that would never happen unless he could produce Sturgis for me and prove that the two had the relationship he claimed. A few days later St. George, who died in 2001, told me that a meeting with Sturgis was on; the three of us, if I was still serious, were to have dinner in a few nights with Sturgis at Joe's Stone Crab, a famous high-end seafood joint in Miami Beach.

We met, had a drink, and St. George told a sullen Sturgis that I was a hotshot who was interested in writing a story about the book they were doing. Sturgis, craggy-faced and deeply tanned, did not seem very interested in anything St. George said. I had done some home-work and knew Sturgis had fought with Fidel Castro in the late 1950s to overthrow the dictatorship of the U.S.-supported Batista regime but had turned against Castro when, as Cuba's leader, Castro embraced communism. By 1972, Sturgis had been involved in anti-Castro activi-ties for more than a decade, with or without the help of the CIA. After a drink or two, St. George got up to go to the bathroom. Sturgis gave me a look and asked if I had a rental car. I said yes. He said, "Let's go," and began to slide out of our booth. It was a very brief moment of truth for me. Can I screw St. George to get what could be the story I need? Sturgis gave me the answer, of course. I dropped a few twenties on the table and we split. I drove him to my hotel. We had another drink, and dinner, during which he began telling me what actually had taken place, but only for a few moments. He abruptly announced that he had someone he needed to meet and asked if he could borrow my car. Since it wasn't my car, and I knew there was only one way to respond if I wanted to get this guy's story, I said yes. He promised to be back for breakfast the next morning, or something like that. It was a charming introduction to the anti-Castro world of Miami Beach.

Sturgis returned the next day with the car intact, and we renewed our talk. He confirmed that he and others on the Watergate break-in team had been paid hush money since their arrest. He had wanted more money and did not get it, which was the sole reason, so I surmised, he had talked to St. George and was now talking to me. I returned to Washington knowing that Andrew St. George would be mad as hell at me, and he had a right to be, but I had the beginning of what could be a hell of a story. I also had information to barter with the lawyer who was representing Sturgis and his break-in colleagues as well as the Feds in the U.S. Attorney's Office in Washington who were prosecuting the case.

Sturgis had told me he thought John N. Mitchell, Nixon's attorney general, had knowledge of earlier political dirty tricks targeted at the Democrats, which included spying, or attempts to spy, in 1971 on Senators George McGovern and Edmund Muskie, then the leading candidates for the Democratic nomination. I learned later, not from Sturgis, that $900,000, far more money than was previously known, could not be accounted for by Nixon's 1972 reelection committee. There was no proof, but there also was no question in my mind that some of the unaccounted-for money had ended up, through cutouts, in the hands of the break-in team.

The story I wrote about all of this was the *Times*'s first big exclusive on the Watergate scandal, but it was a bitch to get into the paper. For all of Abe Rosenthal's angst about Ben Bradlee and *The Washington Post*'s preeminence on the story, the editors drove me nuts in a way that had not been the case with any of my prior stories about the Vietnam War. There was a strange *Times* pathology when it came to stories that touched the presidency.

Bill Kovach, a colleague in 1973 who later became the Washington bureau chief, explained to *The Washington Post* years later that one of the biggest problems he had as an editor "was managing Sy at a newspaper that hated to be beaten but didn't really want to be first. It was scared to death of being first on a controversial story that challenged the credibility of the government." It was this attitude, Kovach added, that was "part of the culture of the institution that Sy was breaking down. Journalistically, Abe Rosenthal and the others wanted to be there. They *wanted* to be there. But historically, culturally, viscerally, they *hated* it. . . . [T]he arguments and the debates and the rassling back and forth on every Sy Hersh story were almost endless. It wasn't because Sy was sloppy. It was material they didn't want to be out there with."*

Salisbury, in his book on the *Times*, recalled, as I do not, that I had originally proposed that my Watergate debut be a three-part series,

* Kovach, after his retirement from the *Times* in 1989, spent twelve years as curator at the Nieman Foundation for Journalism at Harvard University.

but my new information was consolidated into one long piece that ran on Sunday, January 14, 1973, with a modest headline on the left side of the front page. I had used the word "source" repeatedly throughout the story, without identifying who the sources were. Of course Abe knew their names, but I insisted on being as opaque in print as possible; this was just the first step up a big hill, and I wanted everyone involved in that first story to keep on talking. Salisbury said that another issue was a threat of a lawsuit from John Mitchell. He wrote, "But in the end the story was published, including the Mitchell part. There had been trouble in both New York and Washington over the sourcing, it was not as clear and complete as *The Times* liked, but Hersh remembered telling the editors that 'at some point you will just have to believe me and trust me. A number of guys had told me about the story.' *The Times* did trust Hersh. . . . At long last the great investigative story and the great investigative reporter had been linked. They would stay together for the duration of Watergate."

One of the first calls I got on Monday morning was from Bob Woodward. We had never met or talked, but he congratulated me and thanked me for doing the story. The *Post* could not do it alone, Bob said, and he knew he needed the *Times* with them. Nixon's landslide reelection, despite the brilliant work he and Carl Bernstein had done, obviously rankled. I've liked and respected Bob ever since, although we differ on many issues. He did not have to make that call.

There was no lawsuit from John Mitchell or anyone, and I sensed—as I was pretty sure Abe did, too—that there would be none as I kept on going. I focused over the next few months on learning what I could about the White House and the men who ran it, and I had a few long talks with senior Republican Party insiders who supported Nixon politically but were fearful of what he might have done. The Senate Watergate Committee was voted into being in early February by an ominous, for the White House, vote of 77 to 0, after which I was able to make useful contact with a few senior senators and staff, Democrat and Republican. I was trying to find truth in a White House sodden with lies, deception, and fear. Being the *New York Times* guy on the beat surely helped—no other newspaper in America had its authority—but it was still Bob and Carl's story.

I wrote a few suggestive articles about the inevitable sacrifice of lower-level aides who worked directly for Bob Haldeman, Nixon's hard-driving chief of staff. The aides had been stupidly funneling money and messages for much of the past year to college chums they recruited to carry out a series of jejune dirty tricks on behalf of the President. I was convinced that Haldeman and his partner in the White House terror, John Ehrlichman, the domestic adviser, had to know they were going to be eventual targets. I also made contact with investigators and staff members of the U.S. Attorney's Office who led the federal government inquiry; they did far more to bring down Nixon than history has given them credit for. There were also a few good guys in the Nixon cabinet and White House who were appalled by what had been authorized, in one way or another, by Nixon. The most important of those for me was Elliot Richardson, a State Department official who was named secretary of defense in January 1973 and served less than four months before being appointed attorney general in May by an increasingly desperate Nixon.

I got to where I needed to be by mid-April, in terms of contacts inside the Nixon White House, Congress, and the agencies doing the investigation into Watergate. From April 19 to July 1, I published forty-two articles in the *Times*, all of them dealing with exclusive information moving the needle closer to the President, and all but two of them on the front page. The high point was in early May; in six days I wrote four stories that led the paper with banner headlines and a fifth that was the off lead—the front-page story at the top of the far-left column. Reviewing them for this memoir reminded me how half-nuts I must have been with exhaustion and anxiety and lack of sleep. On May 2 it was a three-deck banner headline saying, "Watergate Investigators Link Cover-Up to High White House Aides and Mitchell." A sub-head said, "6 May Be Indicted." On May 3 it was a three-deck headline reading, "Investigators Term G.O.P. Spying a Widespread Attempt to Insure Weak Democratic Nominee in 1972." On May 5 my off-lead dispatch linked a senior Nixon attorney to the destruction of campaign data. On May 6, I brought CIA wrongdoing onto the front page; there was a three-column headline that day saying, "C.I.A. Officials Summoned to Explain Agency's Role in Ellsberg Break-In Plot." On

May 7 there was another three-column headline: "Marine Corps Head Linked to C.I.A.'s Authorization for Ellsberg Burglary."*

It was an unimaginable explosion of news as Nixon was being fed to the wolves by his friends and enemies. Amazingly, it all took place before the existence of the White House taping system was known. It was nirvana for me, marked by halcyon days without second-guessing by editors in Washington or New York. I also felt I was responding, in a totally appropriate and professional way, to Nixon's cavalier attitude toward the My Lai massacre, his support of Lieutenant William Calley, and his unwillingness to protect General Jack Lavelle, whose sin was doing what he had been ordered by the President to do. The national desk in New York, and its editor, David Jones, became my best friends. I would be called midday by someone on the desk in New York and asked if I thought I would have a story for that day. If the answer was yes, I would be asked if it was front-page material. I always said yes, of course. On occasion, as the evening wore down, I would be asked by a late-shift editor whether I thought a story was worth a two- or three-column headline.

Many years later I told Bob Thomson of *The Washington Post*, who wrote wonderful stuff for the paper's Sunday magazine, "There will never be a period like that in our business again. Nobody can understand what it was like. Boy wake up. Boy hear story. Boy get story. Boy put story in paper. No trauma." Salisbury, always generous to me in his

---

* I was completely immersed in my work that spring and was persuaded—forced might be more apt—to join my wife one evening at a party at the nearby home of the Reverend Paul Moore, the Episcopal bishop of Washington. Moore, along with the Reverend William Sloane Coffin, had led the church to its unconditional support for civil rights and unyielding opposition to the Vietnam War. I noticed a huge crowd of teenagers outside the Moore home but thought little of it. Once inside I was eventually approached by a pleasant Brit and his Japanese girlfriend who knew I worked for the *Times* and they told me of the guy's problem in obtaining a green card and permanent residence in the United States because of his opposition to the war and a previous conviction in England for smoking hashish. I had a teenage niece named Laura whose best friend was one of the Moore daughters, and I could not help noticing as the three of us talked that Laura's pal was hopping up and down and making gestures to me and signs about . . . what? Of course, it turned out the Brit was John Lennon and his friend was Yoko Ono. How was I to know? Neither had anything to do with Watergate. Lennon called or came to see me the next day at the *Times* offices, and the paper eventually wrote stories about what was clearly a Nixon administration vendetta against him because of his Vietnam War stance. A few years after Lennon's untimely death in 1980, Yoko Ono gave me and my wife a breakfast and tour of the apartment she had shared with Lennon in New York. It was filled with dozens of framed drawings by the Beatle, all suggesting the world had yet to see the best of him.

book on the *Times*, said simply of my Watergate reportage, "It was as though Sy Hersh had been born for this moment."

It was, in those months, a self-perpetuating process. I was getting stories because I was finding and writing stories, and people inside the government or Congress with something they thought important or pertinent to say wanted to talk to me. It was inevitable that I would end up in close contact with the honorable men in that disgraced administration; for example, I could reach Elliot Richardson or one of his senior deputies whenever I needed in the month or so after Richardson's appointment as attorney general.

There is a story behind my contact with Richardson that I have not told, until now. After his reelection in 1972, Nixon nominated a White House aide named Egil Krogh to be undersecretary of transportation. It was a big leap for a thirty-three-year-old aide who lacked any experience in transportation issues; he was known only as someone who had worked on drug abuse and internal security issues for John Ehrlichman. I had paid no attention to Krogh or his appointment until I got a call from Michael Pertschuk, a quick-witted Democrat who was chief counsel of the Senate Committee on Commerce, Science, and Transportation. Pertschuk told me he and a colleague were monitoring Krogh's confirmation before the committee and found something off about it. There was something wrong with the guy, Pertschuk said. I do not recall the exact words, but the message was that this seemingly upstanding White House nominee was very troubled. One did not ignore such a hint from Pertschuk, who would go on to serve with distinction as head of the Federal Trade Commission in the Carter administration, so I made an appointment to visit Krogh before the full Senate had scheduled a vote on his confirmation. He was still at work in the White House, and my pretext was the international drug issue; Krogh and a colleague, a former aide to Kissinger named David Young, had traveled to Southeast Asia in late 1972 to ask questions, and we talked about that. I asked a bunch of leading questions but came away thinking that there was no hidden agenda in Bud, as he was known; he seemed to be earnest but unhappy.

Then, one day in the spring of 1973, Krogh telephoned me at the *Times*. He had a problem and wondered if I would meet him at the office of a lawyer named William Treadwell in downtown Washing-

The New York Times masthead with headlines:

VIETCONG TURN DOWN PEACE PLAN; LAIRD CAUTIONS FOE'S SUPPLIERS; RAIL LINES TO CHINA BOMBED AGAIN

This May 11, 1972, interview, datelined Paris, was my first major piece as a full-time *Times* employee. It was published ten days after I formally joined the paper. © *1972 The New York Times*

My three closest and most adored friends from my *Times* days: Anthony Lewis as he appeared in the mid-1960s; Gloria Emerson in 1970; and Leslie Gelb when we first met at the *Times* bureau in Washington in early January 1973.
© *1972 George Tames*/ The New York Times; © *1970 John Hartnett*/ The New York Times; *Courtesy of Judy Gelb*

The New York Times

LATE CITY EDITION

VOL. CXXII...No. 42,102

NEW YORK, WEDNESDAY, MAY 2, 1973

15 CENTS

WATERGATE INVESTIGATORS LINK COVER-UP TO HIGH WHITE HOUSE AIDES AND MITCHELL; EHRLICHMAN ORDERED '71 ELLSBERG INQUIRY

6 MAY BE INDICTED

U.S. WARNS HANOI MILITARY ACTION COULD BE RESUMED

Sullivan, Leaving Paris After Talks, Calls for an End of Cease-Fire Violations

NIXON ROLE CITED

F.B.I. Quotes Aide as Saying Hunt, Liddy Were Given Job

F.B.I. Guard Put on Files Of 3 Departing Nixon Men

Biaggi Now Asks Of Jury Record, bi

The New York Times

LATE CITY EDITION

VOL. CXXII...No. 42,103

NEW YORK, THURSDAY, MAY 3, 1973

15 CENTS

INVESTIGATORS TERM G.O.P. SPYING A WIDESPREAD ATTEMPT TO INSURE WEAK DEMOCRATIC NOMINEE IN 1972

Army and Palestinians Clash in Beirut

Heavy Fighting Kills 12 Soldiers—Rich Toll of Guerrillas Indicated

PRESIDENT ORDERS TIGHTER CONTROLS OVER PRICE RISES

But Nixon Says Increases Will Probably Continue "For Some Months"

CHARGES ON FUNDS

Justice Department's Action in Vesco Gift Cites Financial Panel

TEARS OF AGENTS

Drive Viewed as Way to Help McGovern Get Nomination

The New York Times

LATE CITY EDITION

VOL. CXXII...No. 42,104

NEW YORK, FRIDAY, MAY 4, 1973

15 CENTS

KALMBACH LINKED TO DESTRUCTION OF CAMPAIGN DATA

Nixon Attorney at Time Reportedly Acted Before New Financing Law

DONORS WERE SHIELDED

KISSINGER VIEWS CAMBODIA PARLEY AS POSSIBLE SOON

LEBANESE JETS AND TANKS ATTACK PALESTINIAN UNITS AFTER A CEASE-FIRE FAILS

4 in Mackell's Office Got Free Car Use, Avis Says

2D TRUCE REPORT

Haldeman and Ehrlichman Testify Before Grand Jury

ELLSBERG JUDGE ORDERS HUNT DATA

EXCHANGE TO SEEK BROKERS FEE RISE

Revised Narcotics Measure Is Voted 80-65 in Assembly

INDUSTRIAL PRICES SPURTED IN APRIL

My *Times* splash on Watergate in the spring of
1973—five page-one news-making stories in six
days, from May 2 through May 7. I still am not sure
how I survived the week. © *1973 The New York Times*

My favorite portrait of
Henry Kissinger.
Courtesy of the Estate of Gene Spatz

September 24, 1974

C̶O̶N̶F̶I̶D̶E̶N̶T̶I̶A̶L̶

To: The Secretary

From: Lawrence S. Eagleburger and
          Robert J. McCloskey

The CIA in Chile

We believe Seymour Hersh intends to publish
further allegations on the CIA in Chile. He will
not put an end to this campaign. You are his
ultimate target.

Bill Colby told Brent Scowcroft this morning that
Hersh's articles of today, last Friday, and Saturday
are false and that he is prepared to say so. We believe
that a direct and public denial from Colby is the most
effective method of countering Hersh.

Nat Davis and Harry Shlaudeman have drafted the
attached statement which represents the truth as they
know it. With your authorization we would ask
Scowcroft to give it to Colby for him to check, verify
absolutely, and issue if justified. Time is of the
essence since the longer Hersh's allegations go
uncountered, the more credibility they assume. Can
we proceed?

A memo to Kissinger from two of
his aides meant to spur efforts to
officially challenge my reporting
on events in Chile. I had written,
accurately, that Kissinger, obviously
at the behest of President Richard
Nixon, was pressuring the CIA to
be more aggressive in its activities
against the socialist Salvador
Allende, who had won the Chilean
presidency in 1970.

My December 22, 1974, CIA domestic spying story. © *1974* The New York Times

The cover of the program from Bob Kiley's memorial service in New York City, 2016. He had been a special assistant to Richard Helms, the CIA director, and he had become increasingly troubled by American lying about the Vietnam War and the CIA's most secret domestic spying program on dissident students. Thinking of his two grown sons who knew little of their father's CIA years, I decided to talk at the memorial service about how important Kiley's guidance was to me.

Alternatives —
1.) FBI investigation of NYT, Hersh
4/c possible govt. sources.
2.) Grand Jury - seek immediate indictments of NYT + Hersh
3.) Search Warrant - to go after Hersh papers in his apt.
4.) Discuss informally w/ NYT -
5.) Do nothing

Richard Cheney's handwritten memo of May 28, 1975, suggesting that the FBI get a search warrant "to go after Hersh papers in his apt." I had written that U.S. submarines had been in Soviet waters, and obviously it hadn't gone over well in some circles. Cheney was then an assistant to Donald Rumsfeld, President Ford's chief of staff.

DAVID HALBERSTAM   229 EAST 48 STREET, NEW YORK CITY, N. Y. 10017

February 23, 1974

Dear Sy,

    My own instinct tells me that it is probably a difficult time for you and that the pallid clerks who control your destiny (in the immortal words of Homer Bigart) are probably an immense pain in the ass, but I do hope you keep in mind the importance of what you are doing. You are, my friend, a national resource. Bless you

One of many supportive letters David Halberstam wrote to me, with his warning about *New York Times* editors!

This photo of me, my wife, Elizabeth, and our two oldest children, Matthew and Melissa, was taken by a young Annie Leibovitz, on assignment for *Rolling Stone*, after being told by me that my family was off-limits. She shot it early in the morning through a window of our home in 1976, and I had no choice but to reward her cheekiness by letting the magazine publish it. *Courtesy of Annie Leibovitz*

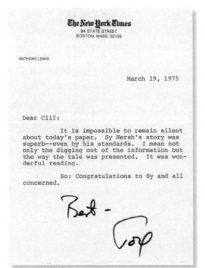

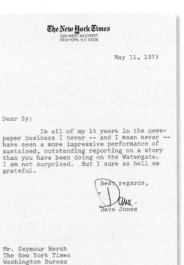

Two of many letters of praise for my reporting on Watergate from *Times* colleagues: one from Anthony Lewis sent to Clifton Daniel, then the *Times* Washington bureau chief, and one to me from Dave Jones, national editor.

Washington, D.C., police photos of four of the key players in the White House, clockwise from top left: Bob Haldeman, John Mitchell, John Ehrlichman, and Charles W. Colson, in 1974 at the time of their arrest for involvement in the Watergate affair.

The front-page *Times* story on the *Glomar Explorer.* The vessel was the key element of a $750 million covert CIA program to recover the remains of a sunken Russian submarine that, it was hoped, would contain Soviet codebooks as well as nuclear torpedoes. It was a classic CIA boondoggle. © *1974* The New York Times

Sharing a sometimes argumentative panel with William Colby, then the CIA director, at the Associated Press's managing editors' annual convention in 1975. I had respect for Colby as someone who understood that the CIA would not survive, given its misdeeds, unless he and other senior agency officials talked honestly and openly, up to a point, about its wrongdoing.
Associated Press

This is one of hundreds of pages I obtained from Admiral Elmo Zumwalt, who was chief of naval operations in 1972, that described, from the inside, the insane level of bureaucratic turmoil in the National Security Council at a critical moment in the Paris peace talks with North Vietnam. Kissinger and his deputy in the White House, army general Alexander Haig, were constantly betraying each other's confidences to President Nixon. After retiring, the admiral had the purloined data transcribed. The markings are mine.

dictation on 7 March 1975

At a meeting in December the President decided that Haig should go with Kissinger to the negotiations—Haig came Saturday to go to Saigon—Kissinger thought that he had a deal—ready for signature on the 8th or the 12th—Kissinger therefore called for a Verification Panel meeting on Monday—to ratify—then Hanoi stalled—Kissinger stayed until Wednesday—the President, whose mind is being poisoned by Haig on the subject feels that Kissinger is screwing the negotiations up—Haig told the President that Kissinger would get yo-yoed by the North Vietnamese—Haig called Kissinger to relay this as the President's judgment—Kissinger was furious—Al reported to the President that Kissinger wouldn't come home—the President held firm—

My wonderful *Times* colleague and friend Jeff Gerth, whose ability to absorb and recall the most demanding of corporate documents was unparalleled. I had been led to him by aides of Robert F. Kennedy, who told me in 1976 that Gerth was the go-to guy if I was interested in reporting on organized crime, which I was.
Courtesy of Jeffrey Gerth

ton. Treadwell turned out to be a prominent member of the Christian Science Church in the Washington area, and Krogh, as a committed member of the faith, had turned to Treadwell for guidance. Krogh explained that he had a crisis of conscience because he had not told me the truth when we met earlier and, after consultation with Treadwell, it had been determined that he could absolve himself by doing so now. So, on a bright sunny day in late April, or early May, I was stunned by what he told me—that he and David Young had been members of a secret internal security group in the White House, known formally, as I learned later, as the Special Investigations Unit, and informally as the Plumbers, that in 1971 recruited G. Gordon Liddy, a former FBI agent, and E. Howard Hunt, a former CIA operative, to assemble a trusted team to do whatever was needed—provided there would be no link to the White House—to find out what else Daniel Ellsberg knew that could be damaging to Nixon's reelection. What the Hunt-Liddy team did, of course, was break into the office of Ellsberg's psychoanalyst in Los Angeles. The two men later orchestrated the famed Watergate break-in in June 1972. Krogh told me that he was also going to confess all to federal prosecutors and asked that I not write about our conversation until he had done so. With that understanding, I agreed to treat his absolution as a private matter between him and me, as the person he wronged, in front of a representative of his church. His goal was to free himself from his burden that, as Pertschuk saw, was tormenting him. After my hour or two with him and Treadwell, I knew that the emerging Watergate scandal was going to get much darker, as did Bud Krogh. He subsequently did agree to cooperate with federal prosecutors and spent four and a half months in jail after being given a two- to four-year sentence for his role in the Los Angeles break-in.[*]

I honored my agreement with Krogh, but I did privately relay much

[*] I left a series of messages for Krogh with one of his good friends when I decided to write about our extraordinary meeting and relayed the essence of what I would say. He did not respond. I sent a similar summary to Bill Treadwell, who is retired and resides in North Fort Myers, Florida, and he responded with his recollection of our meeting. He told me that it was Krogh's idea to meet with me and correct the record. "I did not want him to talk to you, or anybody from the press," Treadwell wrote me in August 2017. "Bud insisted you were a 'straight shooter,' knew you from your work, and felt he could trust you. I finally agreed so long as it was in my law office and only the three of us. . . . Bud decided the time had come to completely 'come clean,' cooperate with the prosecutors . . . and tell honestly all that he knew and had done himself." I later called Pertschuk to check his recollections, and he said then what he had not before—that Krogh had spoken of the existence of the plumbers in his initial talks with the committee.

of what I learned to an aide to Richardson soon after Nixon appointed him attorney general in May 1973. Richardson had been given the job by Nixon, so I assumed, with the understanding that he would protect the President and Kissinger from the hell that was coming their way. I have no idea whether the information I relayed was useful, but Richardson and I talked many times, always on background, during the next year or two.

He understood early, as I did, that Watergate was going to get much uglier.

FOURTEEN

Me and Henry

One of my most memorable stories that spring came on Thursday, May 17, 1973, and it created turmoil inside Kissinger's National Security Council office as well as inside the *Times* Washington bureau. I reported, without naming sources, that Kissinger had personally provided the FBI with the names of a number of his closest NSC aides and of newsmen to be wiretapped. Among them was Helmut Sonnenfeldt, perhaps Kissinger's closest friend on his staff, who had just been nominated to be undersecretary of the Treasury Department. All hell broke loose.

A few days earlier William Ruckelshaus, an honorable guy who was the acting FBI director, had revealed that thirteen government officials and four newsmen had been wiretapped at various times from 1969 until 1971. The story set off the usual mad scramble to learn who had ordered the FBI to do what, and it quickly became known that a number of Kissinger's closest aides on the National Security Council had been overheard on the tape. Kissinger acknowledged that he had seen summaries of some of the conversations but insisted that he had not asked that the taps be installed and had not approved any of them in advance. Until this point, Kissinger, beloved by the media because he was always accessible, had managed to escape much of the obloquy being directed at the President and his senior aides, although Nixon's machinations, including the yet to be determined authorization of the break-in on the Democratic headquarters, were linked to his preelection anxiety over his and Kissinger's continuing endorsement of the Vietnam War.

I was far from a Kissinger advocate at the time. My suspicions about his role in setting up John Lavelle as a fall guy had grown as I reported on that unresolved saga the year before. I had met with Henry only once, shortly after I returned from my trip to Hanoi in late March 1972. We talked for half an hour or so at his invitation in his White House office; John Negroponte, an aide who worked on Vietnam issues as well as the Paris peace talks, sat in. Kissinger was more than pleasant—I was, after all, going to be at the *Times* to do investigative reporting, and he was having his way with the Washington bureau—and there was nothing special about our chat. He asked about morale in Hanoi, and I told him what he already had to know: that I had seen no evidence that the American B-52 bombings and other attacks had diminished the intensity of popular support. It was a boilerplate comment, but at that point Kissinger turned to Negroponte and exclaimed that this young reporter had told him more about what was going on inside the North than all of the secret CIA reports he'd seen. It was malarkey and I remember wondering how Kissinger had managed to get away with such fulsome flattery with the White House press corps. I thought the reporters assigned to that beat were at the top of the game and could not be as easy to please as was the Pentagon press corps in my days there. I was wrong and Kissinger was right.

It was only after the Ruckelshaus admission on Monday, May 14, that I got involved in the wiretapping saga, and how I did it was hardly a brilliant feat of investigative reporting. I was called shortly after the Ruckelshaus disclosure by William C. Sullivan, a longtime FBI official who had been pushed out of the bureau by the despotic J. Edgar Hoover in the fall of 1971. At the time, Sullivan, whom I had met years earlier, was in charge of all of the bureau's investigative activities, including wiretaps. Bill, who died in a hunting accident in 1977, invited me to a late lunch at a restaurant very near the FBI headquarters downtown. I innocently took it to be purely a social occasion, because I knew the restaurant would be full at lunch, as it always was, with senior FBI officials. We did the usual chitchat, with me more than a little anxious to get back to my Watergate madness, and at the end of lunch

Bill asked me to let him leave first. There will be a little something for you on my chair, he said. Sure enough, he'd been sitting on a manila envelope that I grabbed, trying hard to be very cool. I opened it as soon as I got back to the office and found seventeen formal White House wiretap requests for the FBI, sixteen of them signed by Henry Kissinger. They included newsmen with whom he chatted frequently, and many of his close NSC aides, as well as the senior aides to Mel Laird, the secretary of defense, and Bill Rogers, the hapless secretary of state. Kissinger was wiretapping friend and foe—especially his foes—in the bureaucracy.

Sullivan's portfolio also included documents indicating that the wiretaps had been put in place on the home telephones of those targeted. The papers listed the names of the FBI technicians who had done the work. I found a few of them at home that Monday night, and they confirmed, with some asperity, that yes, they had done the deed. I told the national desk Tuesday morning what I had, called the White House press office, told someone there what I was planning to write, and left word for Kissinger to call me. A few hours later the trouble began. Scotty Reston, who had an office in the far reaches of the bureau, padded up to my desk in slippers and asked if it were indeed so that I was going to target Kissinger in my next story. His message was very direct: Do you understand that if you do this story, Henry will resign? I had not had much to do with the estimable Scotty, though I knew he had been more than a little irritated earlier when one of my stories was based on traditionally secret grand jury testimony. Scotty's position was very direct: *The New York Times* does not violate the sanctity of grand juries. He was right, up to a point. The paper had hesitated a few weeks earlier to run a good Watergate story I proffered because it came from someone linked to a grand jury. A few days later Carl and Bob published the same story, clearly with the same source, all over *The Washington Post*'s front page. My discarded story was flung into the *Times*'s second edition, and it was clear to me that any important Watergate story, if it checked out, was going to be published on page 1. The old rules were gone.[*]

---

[*] Reston was always a little mystified by me but eventually ended up, so Harrison Salisbury put it, admiring my chutzpah. I wasn't so sure. On Christmas Eve in 1973. I had volunteered, as one of the office Jews, to work late that night. It would be me, a clerk, and a tele-

I did not worry about Kissinger's rights; his immorality and deceit, and power, made him fair game, so I thought. In the midst of the Watergate onslaught, however, *The Times* of London accused the *Times* and the *Post* of interfering with the judicial system by publishing "vast quantities of prejudicial matter" that would lead to "lynch law" in the trials of those accused. I had discussed the issue in an exchange of memos with the retired Lester Markel, a famed *Times* editor who had invented the Sunday magazine, which had boosted my confidence as a freelancer by publishing every story I suggested. Markel also was the man behind the Sunday "News of the Week in Review" section, for which I constantly wrote; it gave me a venue for analyzing the stories I was reporting, asking questions that I could not in the news sections. Markel retired from the newspaper in 1968 but maintained a strong interest in the day-to-day reporting, and he was worried about trial by newspapers and wanted to meet with me and ask whether, in my drive to match Woodward and Bernstein, eagerness had not eclipsed scruples. I thought he was right when it came to grand jury issues, but also understood that going after a president, as the grand jury was doing, was an extraordinary event that also happened to be highly competitive. I begged off a meeting by saying I was too exhausted to be "other than discursive on any subject, let alone the propriety of blasting away at (perhaps) innocent people every day without due process. In particular," I added in a memo, "I do not wish to participate in my beheading." I was aware that Rosenthal and his deputies were letting me run now, when they needed me, but I did not like being seen as a hit man.

---

typist until well after midnight. At some point very late, Scotty, in black tie, walked into the bureau with his wife and two other bedecked couples, one of them being the Paul Nitzes, he of arms control fame. Scotty had had a few and I assumed he was there to collect a fresh bottle from his office, since liquor stores had long closed. Reston spotted me and exclaimed, "Hersh, aren't you going to get that exclusive interview with Jesus for the second edition?" I was, to put it mildly, nonplussed. Was Scotty making fun of my constant hustle? Or was he pissed at me for breaking the rules by going after his high friends in government? I got my answer a few weeks later. Ernst Klein, my wife's garrulous and sometimes cranky grandfather, who had immigrated to New York, allegedly from Hungary, as a youth and prospered enough to be able to escape to Miami Beach for the winter, suddenly strolled into the bureau. He wanted to see me at work, he said, but admitted that he actually was there to meet Scotty Reston, whose columns he admired. I was on deadline but happily walked him to Scotty's office and introduced Ernie, who was in his mideighties, as a fan. Scotty waved him to a chair and I left. I forgot about the two of them until after I had filed, hours later. I dashed to Scotty's office and found them deep into a quart bottle of vodka and having a grand time talking about the old days. No question that Scotty was a street reporter at heart, as I liked to think I was. But we never had lunch.

I spoke to Kissinger by telephone about the wiretaps before filing my story. He insisted that all of our conversations had to be off the record, or he would have nothing to do with me, so I of course agreed, only to learn decades later from an academic who filed a Freedom of Information request that Kissinger was provided with verbatim typed transcripts of our very infrequent talks within hours. He insisted then, according to the transcript, that his motives in authorizing the wiretaps "were honorable." The wiretaps "had to be conducted in the interests of the country. It turned out to be a protection for innocent people [in] the way it was handled." Needless to say, those who were wiretapped did not see it that way. One aide, Morton Halperin, had a special reason to take offense at Kissinger's decision to put him on the list. He had been one of Kissinger's most trusted associates in early 1969 and had drafted many of the more important NSC decision papers for Kissinger. Halperin sued over the wiretapping and did not drop his case until he got a public apology two decades later from Kissinger. He also got a copy of the FBI transcripts of the wiretap and learned in late 1969 that Ina, his then-wife, had been overheard complaining that she thought the house telephone was wiretapped. The FBI wiretap log showed that after her complaint about a beeping on the telephone, the agent monitoring her phone wrote, "There isn't any beeping on the line. Ina has a complex her phone is being tapped."

I was not above flattery, of course, in my telephone chat with Kissinger, but he outdid me when it came to posturing. I began our chat, not knowing he was recording it, by saying, "Hi, Dr. Kissinger. I know we're driving you half-crazy. All of your friends are telling us if we don't stop, you're going to leave and you're a national asset and I think we all agree. I know Scotty certainly does." Kissinger responded, "It's a little disconcerting for me to have to spend all my time answering phone calls." Me: "Well, let me tell you the more bad news I have. . . . Everybody is leaking everything, as you know." We talked about those who were wiretapped, and I said, "Well, it's not going to be a nice story." I added at a later point, innocently enough, I guess, because I do think I meant it, "The only spirit is truth, as you know, Dr. Kissinger, and I assume that's the one we all work on." Kissinger's answer was ingenious, if sheer pap: "Look, at this point the only thing that needs to concern us all, whatever our different views may be, is to presume some integrity and dignity for this country. . . . And to get us back to some things that we can be proud of. . . . And that's what, you know, in my own way that's what I'm trying to do here." I was doing a lot of double-talking for sure, but he, with his practiced cant, far outdid me.

Kissinger knew that few, if any, would believe his motives for the wiretapping of his aides and others were altruistic, including me, and so he sicced General Alexander Haig, his sometimes loyal deputy, on me. Haig called me a few times during the afternoon to inquire whether the story directly linking his boss to the wiretaps was going to be published the next morning. Yes, I said. There was an astonishing final call at deadline, around 7:00 p.m. "You're Jewish, aren't you, Seymour?" In all of our previous conversations, I'd been Sy. I again said yes. "Let me ask you one question then," Haig said. "Do you honestly believe that Henry Kissinger, a Jewish refugee from Germany who lost thirteen members of his family to the Nazis, could engage in such police-state tactics as wiretapping his own aides? If there is any doubt, you owe it to yourself, your beliefs, and your nation to give us one day to prove that your story is wrong." I remember staring at my phone in astonishment. The story ran and Kissinger did not resign.

Kissinger was named secretary of state by Nixon that September while continuing to serve as national security adviser. It was an unprecedented bit of double-dipping that moved Kissinger close to absolute control of the foreign policy process. It also signaled Nixon's conviction that Kissinger's popularity with the press was Nixon's greatest asset in his fight to stay in office. The saga of Kissinger and the wiretaps dragged on for another year or so, as the Senate Foreign Relations Committee commenced hearings, and Kissinger, as he had done with the Lavelle matter, escaped any sanction after insisting that he would resign unless the hearings erased what he called a stain on his "public honor." The most dramatic threat came in June 1974 during a trip to the Middle East by President Nixon, one seen by many as a futile last hurrah in an effort to avoid impeachment. My colleague John Crewdson, who had continued, with Walter Rugaber, to expertly cover the Watergate inquiries, had alerted the White House to the fact that the *Times* was going to publish an internal FBI memorandum directly linking Kissinger to the placing of wiretaps whose purpose was uncovering those on his NSC staff who were leaking information. Kissinger summoned newsmen to a news conference in Salzburg, Austria, on the eve of the Nixon trip, to make a preemptive strike. It was the same old, same old: "I do not believe it is possible to conduct the foreign policy of the United States under these circumstances when the character and credibility of the secretary of state is at issue. And if it is not cleared up, I will resign." My view was that staying in office was the best defense Kissinger would have to ward off a prosecution for perjury—the man lied the way most people breathed—and worse.

I spent most of my time between the summer of 1973 and the fall of 1974 on three more issues that had Kissinger's markings on them—the secret bombing of Cambodia, the activities of the White House Plumbers, and the CIA's clandestine war against the Allende government in Chile. I helped make the issues public, found new material that made headlines, and put malfeasant cabinet officials in jeopardy—helping to make Nixon's presidency unsustainable. I never got to Kissinger in any legal or moral sense, but I did get his attention.

In July 1973, I began a series of stories about an illegal and astonishing—absolutely the right words—fake bookkeeping system that was authorized somewhere in the upper reaches of the Nixon administration to hide fourteen months' worth of secret B-52 bombing in Cambodia. The bombings, aimed at disrupting the flow of arms to Vietcong and North Vietnamese troops in South Vietnam, ended in May 1970, when the Nixon administration invaded Cambodia and officially recognized the neutral regime of Prince Norodom Sihanouk. The long-running bombing attacks had been disclosed earlier by the press, but not the fact that their existence was hidden by a double-entry bookkeeping system that permitted only a very few in the military and the White House to know that the bombs were not falling inside the borders of South Vietnam, as falsely reported in all of the Pentagon's classified records, but in Cambodia.

The existence of the cooked books was made known in a letter sent by a just-retired air force major named Hal M. Knight to Senator Harold Hughes of Iowa, an antiwar Democrat who was on the Senate Armed Services Committee, then still dealing with remnants of the

Lavelle affair. Hughes and I had become friends during the Lavelle matter—the man could put away a dozen pork chops over lunch—and he forwarded the letter to me. Knight's disclosure went right onto the front page for Sunday, July 15. In an interview, Knight, who had served in the U.S. Air Force's Strategic Air Command, told me he had begun to falsify B-52 bombing records shortly after arriving in South Vietnam in February 1970. The former major quickly got to the crucial issue: The Strategic Air Command's main function, along with dropping bombs from B-52s in the war, was to carry nuclear weapons and stay on constant airborne patrol on the edges of Russia and China. The B-52 pilots were only a verified presidential command from raining nuclear hell on Russia and beginning World War III. "We were all SAC," Knight told me. "If somebody [in the Nixon White House] could have punched the right number into the right spot, they could have had us bombing China, if they so chose, instead of Cambodia." The integrity of America's nuclear deterrent was being put at risk by someone at the top of the Nixon administration, then immersed in a losing war, who was ordering pilots of the Strategic Air Command to lie.

I called Kissinger two days later, shortly after noon on July 17, and according to a transcript put together by his office, I began by saying my call "is in the nature of here we go again." On background, I told him what I knew about Hal Knight's recollection. I was hoping, naively perhaps, for a serious discussion, given Kissinger's expertise on arms control and related issues, and what I got was a series of lies. "What I read in your story was total news to me. . . . I don't know anything about the goddamned reporting system," he said. "So I wouldn't even know how to give an order to falsify it if I wanted to. . . . If my life depended on it, I couldn't tell you how the reporting is done." Kissinger urged me to talk to Al Haig about the issue and promised he would tell him to get in touch with me. He added, almost plaintively, "You know there are a lot of people who have tried to do the right thing, even the moral thing and the right thing, and it's getting awfully tough when everything—when constantly every action has to be interpreted four years after an event." Among the very few Kissinger telephone transcripts I obtained years later was one depicting a Kissinger-to-Haig call four hours later that dealt with his talk with me. Kissinger asked, "Did we ever tell them [the Strategic Air Command] how they should do their report?" Haig: "Hell no." Kissinger: "That is what I said." Haig: "Why should we even talk about that? Why should we even tell Seymour Hersh anything?" Kissinger: "Well, you can take that attitude but I can't. I knew about the operation." I did not need a transcript at the time to know that Kissinger had been lying to me.

The Senate hearings, which were authorized by chairman John Stennis, began the morning of my talk with Kissinger and produced a quick confirmation of the falsified bombing reporting from James R. Schlesinger, the new secretary of defense, who had just replaced Elliot Richardson. The fun began as Kissinger, Laird, and other officials, including retired army general Earle Wheeler, who was chairman of the Joint Chiefs of Staff at the time, initially deplored the fake book-keeping system and insisted they had no knowledge of it. Amid all this, I revealed that Secretary of State William Rogers had told Congress three years earlier in a secret hearing that Cambodia was one Southeast Asian nation "where our hands are clean and our hearts are pure."

The truth finally dribbled out in early August, when the Senate committee released a highly classified memorandum showing that Laird and Wheeler knew about and authorized the phony bookkeeping. Those top officials then began ratting out those responsible in the White House. Laird told me that orders for the falsification came from Kissinger's National Security Council, and Wheeler, recanting his earlier testimony, told the Senate committee that Nixon had personally ordered that the raids be held "with the greatest secrecy." It took another decade, when I was at work on a book about Kissinger, before I learned that the secret bookkeeping system had been organized, with the help of an air force colonel, by Al Haig, Kissinger's most trusted confidant on the NSC staff, with Kissinger's complete knowledge.

In a summary of the matter for the *Times* that summer, I could not resist the obvious opening sentence, "It always begins with a letter"—a reference to Ron Ridenhour's tip-off about My Lai. It took only a few days of Senate hearings before the denials fell away as the risk of tampering with the Strategic Air Command's sense of mission became clear. Nixon's authorization of the military cheating and lying to shield the B-52 bombing of Cambodia became the fourth item of impeachment promulgated by the House Judiciary Committee against Nixon in July 1974, a month before he left office, but it was not adopted.

There was more evidence late in the year of the extreme chaos and lack of respect for the law inside the Nixon administration, and this time Kissinger was both the cause of the disarray and its main victim. Much of Kissinger's diplomacy was done in secrecy out of sight of the media, a fact that for some mysterious reason seemed to titillate many in the Washington press corps. Only those few aides who had an immediate need to know were being kept up to date as Kissinger conducted the secret peace talks in Paris and also secretly set the stage for Nixon's triumphant visit in 1972 to Beijing. Admiral Tom Moorer, a southern hawk who was chairman of the Joint Chiefs of Staff, had been cut out of the loop, as were other military officers and civilian officials who should have been consulted for their take on such issues as a visit to China, and the end to the impasse between Washington and Beijing.

Kissinger and Haig also eschewed the civilian professionals who usually served as note takers and stenographers on secret trips, and turned to the military, who were seen as less likely to leak. The two national security leaders thought they had found the perfect fit in a navy yeoman named Charles E. Radford, a sometime submariner and top-notch stenographer who was assigned to Kissinger's office in late 1970 and was still at it by the end of 1971. Radford accompanied Kissinger to secret talks in early 1971 in Islamabad with the Pakistani president, Yahya Khan, who was a close ally of China's. The arrangements for Nixon's Beijing visit in early 1972 were made formal via the good services of President Khan. There was a very dark side to the secrecy: Khan was also a murderous despot whose army slaughtered anywhere from 500,000 to 3 million of his own people in suppressing a secessionist revolt in late March 1971 in what was then East Pakistan (now Bangladesh). The world recoiled over Khan's brutality, but Nixon and Kissinger remained mute for reasons not understood by the State Department bureaucracy and the rest of the world at the time, to protect their lifeline to the Chinese leadership. Kissinger would devote nearly eighty pages in his memoirs to an unconvincing rationalization for his inaction in the face of Khan's brutality. Radford, of course, knew the secret; he had the full confidence of Kissinger, who had no idea that the yeoman was making a copy of his notes and papers prepared for the President and relaying them, through a senior admiral on duty in the White House, to Admiral Moorer.

Some of the inside information about what became known as the White House's "tilt" toward Pakistan began showing up in December 1971 in the daily columns of Jack Anderson, the longtime Washington muckraker. The leaking of such embarrassing top secret data led to an internal security inquiry headed by David Young, Egil Krogh's sidekick on the Plumbers team, that quickly found its way to Radford. Anderson was a Mormon and so was Radford, who acknowledged under questioning that he had a church-based friendship with Anderson; there seemed little doubt that Radford, immersed in the spying, was putting in some overtime work for the columnist, who won a Pulitzer Prize in 1972 for his many news-breaking columns.

There were obvious questions for Kissinger in all of this, because the secretive Young, who held degrees from Oxford University and Cornell Law School, worked for more than two years with Kissinger's NSC staff before joining John Ehrlichman's domestic council and, ultimately, the Plumbers. There was yet another inquiry into the scandal by a John Stennis–led Senate committee, and Radford and all of his superiors in the military initially denied what was obvious—that there was a concerted military spying ring, with as many as five senior officers involved, along with Radford, that had been triggered by Kissinger's secrecy. The sordid mess was buried until January 1974, when I learned that the White House had informed the Senate Watergate Committee of what it wrongly believed to be a blackmail threat by W. Donald Stewart, then the inspector general of the Defense Department's Investigative Service. Stewart, a former FBI agent, had applied earlier to be head of the bureau, and there were some in the rattled administration who feared he was seeking to trade his information about the military spying for a high-level job. (Stewart laughed off the allegations, which were dismissed, in a subsequent interview with me; I later learned that he had futilely gone to Secretary of Defense McNamara in 1967, a year before My Lai, with evidence that things were getting out of hand in the Vietnam War.)

I was joined in the chase by the hardworking Bob Woodward,

who was also on top of the story. He and I had begun playing tennis together as Watergate moved from scandal to impeachment, and that led to a few late-night pizzas over which we decided that we would stay in touch and share, as much as possible, what we were learning.* The thought was that it would be much more efficient if we would no longer chase the same story—I once found a "Kilroy was here" note from Bob outside the office of someone I'd hoped to interview—but do separate stories and push our editors to run the gist of each other's work. The agreement freed both of us to work on our own stories and no longer be responsible for trying to "match"—a hated word in our profession— each other's exclusive report. Of course there was no sharing of a truly vital story, but those were dwindling as the Watergate saga entered its third year. Bob eventually told his editors about our arrangement; he also insisted, tongue in cheek, that I never paid for the indoor tennis court time (not so). The time had been booked for the season by Katharine Graham, the *Post*'s publisher, a Georgetown socialite who, in private, could be as foulmouthed as Ben Bradlee—and me. She, like Woodward, could ignore the fierce *Post* versus *Times* competition when a need arose, and at the height of my Watergate run she summoned me to her top-floor office to help draft a speech on investigative reporting, bitching all the while about the fact that Bradlee would never give the paper's biggest advertisers a break when they got in trouble. It was impossible not to admire her directness.

The military spying scandal led to an obvious question, as I wrote: Why didn't the President, with his oft-stated concerns about the need for national security, insist on a real investigation? The paper trail,

---

* By this time David Obst somehow had befriended Woodward and Bernstein—he would later become their literary agent—and he arranged a dinner meeting with the three of us, then, so we thought, at the top of our game, with Jann Wenner, the editor and publisher of *Rolling Stone* magazine. There was the usual drinking et cetera, which Bob eschewed, and at a hazy moment late at night the talk turned to the conspiracy theories about the assassination of John F. Kennedy. Obst, or was it Wenner?, in their wacky genius, came up with what seemed at that hour to be a fantastic idea: *Rolling Stone* would announce a joint investigation by Woodward and Bernstein and Sy Hersh into the JFK assassination—one that would be publicly financed and completely divorced from any outside influence. Stock in the venture, which would produce newspaper stories, a book, and a TV documentary, would be sold through the magazine for twenty-five dollars a share. All in America and around the world could buy in. There was frenzied talk of raising scores of millions of dollars. Needless to say, what seemed to be a terrific idea in the middle of the night proved to be less interesting the next morning. I called Obst and told him not a chance, and I assume Bob and Carl did the same.

as disgorged by Radford in interviews with me, led directly to Admiral Moorer and others, but no prosecutions took place and all stayed in their jobs. I wrote about that aspect, of course, but could not say what I really thought, since I wasn't being paid by the *Times* to convey my unsubstantiated thoughts. They, in fact, were very dark: I was convinced the White House would cover up any scandal in fear that the really important ones, whatever they were, would be uncovered. I was focusing once again on Kissinger, in part because of Kissinger's triggering role in the mess with his secrecy, but also because I was convinced that the very quiet David Young had filled him in all the while, along with details, perhaps, of other Plumbers operations still unknown.

I thought so because Kissinger had been emphatic in his denials about any such knowledge during his Senate confirmation hearing four months earlier on his nomination to be secretary of state. "I have no knowledge of any such activities that David Young may have engaged in," he told the Foreign Relations Committee. "I did not know of the existence of the plumbers group by that or any other name. Nor did I know that David Young was concerned with internal security."

It was a lie he had to tell, for Young and Krogh were responsible for the hiring of E. Howard Hunt and G. Gordon Liddy for the Plumbers team, and both, as said earlier, were involved in the illegal break-in into the office of Ellsberg's psychoanalyst in Los Angeles in mid-1971, as well as the break-in at the Watergate. Young cooperated with the prosecution in the Plumbers trial and spent no time in jail. He left America to return to Oxford, got his doctorate, and kept his mouth shut, as Kissinger, so I thought, had to know he would. Kissinger, questioned further three days later by the Foreign Relations Committee about his knowledge of the Plumbers, repeated his denials and added a new element: "I was not aware even of the location of his [Young's] office or duties, nor did I have any contact with him."

Ten days after my first story about the military spying scandal, Kissinger dropped his pretense about his ties to Young and acknowledged, in a news briefing at the State Department, that in late 1971 he had listened to a tape recording Young had made with a junior admiral who had been involved in the funneling of documents from his office to the Pentagon. The admission directly contradicted his testimony during his confirmation hearings and, as Kissinger surely knew, would do him little good with the many people in the government and media who viewed him as a serial liar. He did his best to muddle the issue, initially stating that it was John Ehrlichman who "let me see, or rather listen to, the interrogation." He later conceded, under questioning by the press, that the interrogation had been conducted by David Young. Kissinger could not stop himself, however, and sought to convince the journalists that "one could not suppose that David Young was conducting an investigation" because *he* was doing the interview, and not the young admiral. He "assumed," he said, that Young had simply been asked by Ehrlichman to do the interview. "I reaffirm here every word that I have said to the Senate Foreign Relations Committee [in his confirmation hearings] and I assert that they were fully consistent with the allegations of the unnamed sources that have been made."

It had come to this with Kissinger—just another day and another briefing and more misrepresentations. I was still in touch with John Stennis, and he made it clear that the Radford mess was an investigation that would go nowhere, in terms of punishing wrongdoers. It was another story, he said, like the phony bookkeeping that hid the Cambodian bombing, that could destroy the Pentagon. Woodward and I continued to write about the scandal, but the public seemed to have had its fill of the White House shenanigans. Nixon's constant wrongdoing and Kissinger's way with words were pretty established by then, and the pro-military Senate Armed Services Committee held a few pro forma hearings and let the matter drop. In a later interview, Radford told me something that he had not told the committee or publicly said earlier—that he moved no fewer than five thousand secret documents from Kissinger's office to the Pentagon during his thirteen months in the White House.

By early 1974, Les Gelb, who constantly saw humor in the White House madness, was telling stories to all who would listen about my interviewing antics on the telephone. The one I liked the most, whether true or not, involved a time during the crisis over the Plumbers when I was desperate to reach Charles Colson, the Nixon aide who was deeply involved in much of the wrongdoing that went on. He'd been indicted on some matter, and everyone in the press corps was looking for the guy. As Les tells it, I had Colson's private home phone number, but no one was picking up. So I spent hours dialing again and again every few moments, allegedly reading a transcript of a congressional hearing while doing so. Finally, Mrs. Colson answered and said that Colson was not available. "He's still in Washington?" I said, and then added, "Well, Mrs. Colson, if I were your husband, I'd have put on a mustache and flown to South America." She laughed and I then went on and on about how much I admired Colson for not running away. She said she would have him call me back, and he did.

Les understood the intricacies of nuclear bargaining strategy, a rarity among newspaper correspondents—it was his beat at the *Times*—and Kissinger worked hard to keep him, a former academic associate, in the loop and on the team, as Kissinger saw it. Les and Kissinger talked often, leaving a trail of transcripts that showed Kissinger's sense of mortality and, perhaps, doom. At one point in a 1974 telephone talk about one of Gelb's arms control stories that suggested deliberate deception—this talk was classified—Gelb said, "It's hard . . . in Washington today not to believe that every government official isn't trying to pull your ear"—that is, trying to mislead. Kissinger, hearing the word "ear," had a revelatory response: "I'm not talking about wiretapping." At the time, questions about his responsibility for such were still pending before the Senate. Gelb: "I'm talking about in general . . . including the wiretapping." Kissinger: "Sy Hersh is out to get me." The ever-loyal Gelb: "All I'm saying . . . if you have a conversation with him, you will explain your notion of reality. Sy Hersh will print it and he will take that into account. He will be bound by it." Kissinger: "I will defend substance. If in order to keep in public office, I have to turn myself into a constant defense of my integrity I won't keep public office."

Les was a lifesaver for me amid the pressures of the Washington bureau, and it was sometimes hard to say no to one of his antic schemes. For instance, one miserable winter day I tagged along, very reluctantly, when Les had a late morning appointment in the State Department to review the text of a Kissinger background briefing on arms control. As Les later told a journalist, he casually asked a Kissinger spokesman if he "could bring a friend in, too?" The answer was yes. We arrive and Gelb, who is having the time of his life, says after shaking hands with the spokesman, "This is Sy Hersh." The spokesman, as Gelb recalled, "begins to tremble, physically tremble. Sy is reading a newspaper. [The spokesman] can't keep his eyes off him. He might as well have been Dracula." The guy was completely unnerved, but Les quickly said something like I was there on another mission and had nothing to do with the appointment at hand. The aide did not get around to shaking my hand. Les and I laughed about the scene for weeks.

It was wonderful to have a laugh or two in the office, but we were dealing in the early 1970s with a corrupt president who was fighting to stay in office and perhaps would do anything to do so. I got a brutal taste of the power of the presidency and the complicated responsibility of the press a few weeks after the military spying scandal evaporated. Nixon's internal taping system had been revealed the summer before, and federal prosecutors handling the various Watergate cases were successfully suing for access to conversations that could be relevant. In early May, a federal employee I knew slightly sent me pages from a Nixon tape that had been subpoenaed and received for use in the criminal trial in New York of two of Nixon's cabinet members, Secretary of Commerce Maurice Stans and former attorney general John Mitchell.* On the nighttime tape, Nixon was perhaps showing off, or perhaps after too many martinis, mouthing off about minorities. He talked repeatedly and disparagingly about "those Jew boys" in the Securities and Exchange Commission (SEC) who "are all over everybody. You can't stop them." There was similar talk about "stopping those Jews in the U.S. Attorney's Office" in Washington that were involved in proceedings against him. He referred to Judge John Sirica, who skeptically handled the original Watergate break-in case, as "that Wop." I

---

* I knew Mitchell slightly, having interviewed him a few times, and was surprised when he showed up with two of his lawyers for a late lunch in downtown Washington amid his 1974 Watergate trial on charges of perjury, obstruction of justice, and conspiracy. I nodded at him but left the group alone until the end of his meal. The lawyers had departed, and Mitchell was signing a credit card bill—clients always seem to pay for lunch with their lawyers—when I sat down. Mitchell had a terrible reputation, based on his fervent support for Nixon, but he was hard to dislike. I asked how it was going. He tore off the credit card receipt, wrote something on its back, folded it, handed it to me, and said, "This will tell all you need to know in life, kiddo." I waited until he left the restaurant before looking at the note. It said, "Next time take the Fifth." He was convicted the next year on all counts and spent nineteen months in jail, the only senior Nixon administration official to do so.

spent many days verifying that such language came easily in the Oval Office and was far from being used, as the White House would later contend, "in a spirit of good humor among friends."

The story ran on the front page of the *Times* and created the expected wave of protest from the White House and the President's supporters. A number of White House officials, obviously being egged on by a furious president, attacked the story publicly and privately in letters to various editors at the *Times*, including Clifton Daniel, still the Washington bureau chief. All of that was expected, but what happened next was not. Tom Wicker, the wonderful reporter, editor, and columnist for the *Times*, pulled up a chair next to my desk in the noisy newsroom and asked if I had a minute. Of course I did. He hunched closer and said my story about Nixon's language, and the White House's over-the-top denials of such, amid attacks on me and the *Times*, told much about Nixon's irrational state of mind and reminded him of a story he did not write. He had become the paper's Washington bureau chief in 1964 while also covering the White House. At some point late in 1965, as the Vietnam War was, even then, stalemated, he filed a tough analysis piece about the war and its dangers a day or so before he and his colleagues in the White House press corps flew down to the Johnson ranch with the President for a long weekend. There was a routine press briefing midmorning on Saturday, and the reporters were told that the "lid" was on, meaning that there would be no official presidential events that day. At some point the President, driving, as he often did, a white Lincoln convertible, drove up to the press pool at breakneck speed, slammed on the brakes, opened the right front door—all eyes were on him—yelled "Wicker," and made a come-hither motion. Tom got into the car and the two of them sped off down a dusty dirt road. No words were spoken. After a moment or two, Johnson once again slammed on the brakes, wheeling to a halt near a stand of trees. Leaving the motor running, he climbed out, walked a few dozen feet toward the trees, stopped, pulled down his pants, and defecated, in full view. The President wiped himself with leaves and grass, pulled up his pants, climbed into the car, turned it around, and sped back to the press gathering. Once there, again the brakes were slammed on, and Tom was motioned out. All of this was done without a word being spoken.

I of course do not remember all of Tom's precise words, but I remember some, and all of his pain. Johnson was passing a very obvious message about what he thought of Wicker's newspaper analysis. But what he did was crazy, just as Nixon's use of language and his insistence, through others, that the words were meant to be affectionate was crazy. "I knew then," Tom told me, "that the son of a bitch was never going to end the war." He added that he thought then, and still thought, he should have found a way to write about what happened, and what it said about Johnson's blind insistence that he was right and those who disagreed were wrong, shit-kicking wrong. The Vietnam War would go on and on.

I would have my own Wicker-like moment, but without the regret, shortly after Nixon left the White House in disgrace on August 9, 1974, to return to his beachfront home in San Clemente, California. A few weeks later I was called by someone connected to a nearby hospital in California and told that Nixon's wife, Pat, had been treated in the emergency room there a few days after she and Nixon had returned from Washington. She told doctors that her husband had hit her. I can say that the person who talked to me had very precise information on the extent of her injuries and the anger of the emergency room physician who treated her. I had no idea what to do with the information, if anything, but I went along with the old adage from the City News Bureau: "If your mother says she loves you, check it out." I had gotten to know John Ehrlichman well enough by mid-1974, so I called him and told him, with more specifics than I am writing here, about what had happened to Pat Nixon in San Clemente. Ehrlichman stunned me by saying that he knew of two previous incidents when Nixon struck his wife. The first time was in the days after he lost the race for governor of California in 1962, when he bitterly told the press that it was his last political race and they would not have "Richard Nixon to kick around anymore." A second assault took place during Nixon's years in the White House. I did not write the story at the time, and I do not recall telling any of the editors in the Washington bureau about it. I did think about turning what I knew into a footnote in a later book on Kissinger, but decided against doing so. I raised the story once again during a talk in 1998 to that year's journalism fellows at the Nieman Foundation at Harvard University. The issue was the merging of private life and public life, and I explained that I would have written about the attacks if they were an example of why his personal life impinges on policy, but there was no evidence of such a link. I added that it was not a case where Nixon had gone looking for his wife with an intent to hit her, could not find her, and bombed Cambodia instead. I was taken aback by the anger my decision generated among some of the female fellows, who noted that battery is a crime in many jurisdictions and wondered why I did not choose to report a crime. "What if it's another crime that he's committing?" I was asked. "What if he went in and robbed a bank?" All I could say was that at the time I did not—in my ignorance—view the incident as a crime. My reply was not satisfactory. I did not comprehend then, as the women who challenged me did, that what Nixon had done was a criminal act. I should have reported what I knew at the time or, if my doing so would have compromised a source, have made sure that someone else did.

In early September 1974, I was slipped a letter, written by Michael Harrington, a member of Congress, telling of top secret testimony that William Colby, the CIA director, had given five months earlier about CIA economic and political activities aimed at imperiling and eventually overthrowing the government of Salvador Allende, the socialist president of Chile who had been elected to office in 1970. Allende had been assassinated the previous September, and a coup leader, General Augusto Pinochet, instituted martial law and moved the nation to the far right while murdering, jailing, and repressing much of the leftist opposition. Colby told Congress that most, if not all, of the CIA's clandestine activities had been approved by the Forty Committee, a high-level State Department covert intelligence panel that was headed by Henry Kissinger. Colby, in his testimony, depicted the operations against Allende as being a test of the use of cash payments to bring down a government viewed as hostile to the United States. The budget for the operation was eight million dollars, Colby testified. Kissinger, in his confirmation testimony before the Senate Foreign Relations Committee, had been asked whether the CIA had been involved in any way in Allende's overthrow. He did what American officials are taught to do at such moments; he responded with a qualified lie, saying, "The CIA had nothing to do with the coup, to the best of my knowledge and belief."

I tore into the story over the next month or so, quoting those involved as saying that the policy was Richard Nixon's, but Kissinger had emerged as the key strategist in the economic fight against Allende. There had been repeated allegations of American influence in the overthrow, bolstered by the Nixon administration's immediate recognition of the Pinochet government, and the refusal of Washington to insist that Pinochet's murderous recriminations against Allende supporters be ended. Representative Harrington's letter essentially said that Nixon and Kissinger had been lying for years with their insistence that the United States was not intervening illegally inside Chile, and that the Allende government's inability to get loans and credit was not a result of Chile's poor credit but the result of American policy. Within a few weeks, I had been given access to secret documents showing that the CIA's activities went beyond economic pressure and involved the funding of violent extremist groups inside Chile that staged strikes aimed at disrupting the economy. There also was talk of assassination, and at least one senior Chilean army general who was pro-Allende was murdered with arms smuggled in by the CIA station in Santiago.

It was obvious that some in the CIA were talking to me and doing more than that. Kissinger must have known why: The pressure on the Agency to do something about Allende was constant and had come from Nixon, as relayed by Kissinger. The CIA, battered by the Vietnam War and by its disturbing role in the Watergate scandal, was not going to go silently into the night when it came to Kissinger. Neither was I. Kissinger was their target, and mine. There was no doubt about my intent inside the State Department. A September 24, 1974, memorandum to Kissinger, later declassified, written by two close aides, Larry Eagleburger, Kissinger's executive assistant, and Robert McCloskey, the State Department's spokesman, warned,

> We believe Seymour Hersh intends to publish further allegations on the CIA in Chile. He will not put an end to this campaign. You are his ultimate target.
>
> Bill Colby told Brent Scowcroft [Nixon's military assistant] that Hersh's articles of today, last Friday, and Saturday are false and that he is prepared to say so. We believe that a direct and public denial from Colby is the most effective method of countering Hersh.

Nat Davis and Harry Shlaudeman [diplomats who served in Chile] have drafted the attached statement which represents *the truth as they know it* [emphasis added]. With your authorization we would ask Scowcroft to give it to Colby for him to check, verify absolutely, and issue if justified. Time is of the essence since the longer Hersh's allegations go uncountered, the more credibility they assume. Can we proceed?

The articles cited dealt, in part, with internal CIA directives that I had seen, dealing with the Agency's efforts to get funding to support anti-Allende extremists, such as the Patria y Libertad, a reactionary group that openly boasted of its involvement in military efforts to overthrow the Allende government. Colby issued no denial.

Three days later I wrote about a stunning Kissinger rebuke to David Popper, the U.S. ambassador to Chile, who had discussed torture and other human rights violations during a meeting on military aid with representatives of the Pinochet government. "Tell Popper to cut out the political science lectures," Kissinger had scribbled over a cable he had received from Popper. I wrote that Popper and other diplomats in Chile and in the State Department's Bureau of Inter-American Affairs, which is responsible for diplomacy in Latin America, were angered and "amazed" by the Kissinger rebuke.

Kissinger immediately convened a meeting of the department's leadership after reading my dispatch and went on a rant, according to a verbatim transcript that somehow ended up in the files of the State Department's Office of the Historian:

I want it to be made very clear that the party is over. I don't want to hear from you what I am doing wrong anymore and anyone who doesn't like what I am doing can leave. . . . I am simply fed up. . . . The Foreign Service is a disgrace to itself. . . . I don't care about the leaks because I will be gone anyway. I want Popper's explanation of what his role was in this Hersh thing. . . . I don't feel obligated to explain myself to Sy Hersh. If a Secretary of State cannot write a note on a cable without it being leaked . . . then you don't have a Foreign Service, but a rabble. . . . These leaks are simply unmanly, cowardly and disloyal. If they had guts, if there was one person who had the guts to resign, it would be something. But there must be something wrong with this system and how we take them in.

Kissinger's tirade, before at least eight senior State Department officials and a note taker, did not leak. His role in Chile would be a focal point of many investigations to come, including the most significant and far-reaching inquiry into the role of the CIA and the American intelligence community since the Agency came into being after World War II.

FIFTEEN

The Big One

M y December 22, 1974, story about the CIA's domestic spying was the most explosive of my years at *The New York Times*. It carried a startling headline that ran across three columns on the front page that Sunday:

HUGE C.I.A. OPERATION REPORTED

IN U.S. AGAINST ANTIWAR FORCES,

OTHER DISSIDENTS IN NIXON YEARS

The story produced widespread public dismay and anger over the CIA's spying at home, as well as two major congressional investigations that uncovered further evidence of wrongdoing, but the congressional pressures for reform were outmuscled by the new Ford administration, managed by Chief of Staff Donald Rumsfeld and Dick Cheney, his deputy, who were intent on protecting the Agency. The CIA is still doing today what it has done in secret around the world since the end of World War II.

None of this, however, diminished the hard work, patience, and inside help I had chasing the illegal spying story, and how deeply I was able to delve inside the Agency in doing so. The best way—that is, the least self-serving way—to tell the story is to let the CIA itself do it.

In 1993 a CIA historian and analyst named Harold Ford, who began his career in covert operations, published a secret history of William Colby's controversial career as CIA director in the Watergate years. Ford's work was declassified in 2011 but, like many such histories, attracted little attention. Ford, whom I did not know, included an eleven-page chapter on me in his history that began with quotes from Ray Cline, a longtime CIA officer who served in the Kissinger era as the State Department's director of intelligence: "I like Sy in a way. He's an arrogant son-of-a-bitch. . . . He's one of those whimsical, skeptical iconoclastic fellows who's interested in a good story and has a shrewd nose for people and events and who's doing his thing."

Ray, who passed away in 1996, shared my views about Kissinger's machinations and the CIA's monumental stupidity in spending seven years, from 1967 to 1974, spying on American citizens inside the United States in direct violation of its charter. I'd like to believe, from Ford's nonjudgmental and surprisingly detailed account of my reporting, that he also saw value in what I had done in tracking down a most secret internal CIA compilation—known internally as the "family jewels"—of illegal activities. Here's how Ford began his account:

> Hersh's charges against the CIA did not suddenly drop from the clouds at the end of December 1974. Behind his indictment of the Agency lay months of journalistic effort. Suspicious at first that CIA had participated in illegal actions related to Watergate, Hersh's search expanded once he began to get scraps of information about the CIA's "family jewels." Hersh's allegations were based largely on the "family jewels" compilation [of wrongdoing] that DCI James Schlesinger [Colby's predecessor as director] had ordered in the wake of May 1973 Watergate revelations.
>
> As far back as November 1972, Hersh had told House intelligence subcommittee chairman Lucien Nedzi that he had information that the CIA was engaged in "extensive domestic operations." [I had cited this issue, among others, at the time in the note about potential stories that Max Frankel ignored.] In February 1973 DCI Schlesinger learned that Hersh was working on an article for the New York Times that was apt to expose sensitive intelligence operations. . . . In March, Hersh asked for an interview with Schlesinger

but was refused. In May, however Schlesinger did order all CIA officers to report whether the Agency was now, or had been in the past, involved in any illegal activities. This was the first of several steps taken by Schlesinger and Colby to draw up what became the "family jewels" list. . . . That listing ran to a startling 693 pages of possible violations of or at least questionable activities in regard to the CIA's legislative charter.

That autumn, soon after becoming DCI, Colby learned that Seymour Hersh was making inquiries about past CIA operations and instructed all CIA deputies not to honor Hersh's requests for an interview. . . . For some months after that all was fairly quiet concerning Hersh's inquiries [I was reporting then on CIA operations in Chile] until that journalist telephoned Colby on 9 December 1974 to tell him that he was now embarked on a wholly different undertaking—a big news story on past illegal operations within the United States. . . . Later that same day, Colby informed House oversight Chairman Nedzi of this conversation and learned that Hersh had seen the Congressman that afternoon with the same story.

At this point, Ford's history noted that two highly respected CIA officers—the current head of the CIA's clandestine service, the famed "dirty tricks" directorate, and one of his processors—told Colby that I had telephoned them to warn that I was prepared to write about the domestic spying and cite James Jesus Angleton, the famed head of counterintelligence, as the officer in charge of violating the CIA's charter and the Fourth Amendment to the U.S. Constitution, which barred unreasonable searches. On December 18, Ford wrote, "Hersh began to turn the screws. 'I figure I have about one-tenth of 1 percent of the story which you and I talked about,' he warned in a phone note he left for Colby, 'which is more than enough, I think, to cause a lot of discombobulation, which is not my purpose. I want to write it this weekend. *I am willing to trade with you. I will trade you Jim Angleton for 14 files of my choice. I will be in my office at the* Times *in 30 minutes.'* " [Emphasis in original.]

Ford could not make sense of my facetious telephone message, which was understandable because Colby and I had talked more than once on his unlisted telephone at home, which apparently had no recording device, about the danger posed by Angleton. Angleton was a fabled character inside the CIA for his belief that the Russians had completely penetrated the Agency and for his willingness to investigate anyone, especially Soviet spies who had defected. The domestic spying operation was his baby, and he and a deputy named Dick Ober met frequently with Richard Helms, a Colby predecessor, for guidance and support. I had gone to Angleton with my information, and he had stunned me—not by denying all, but by offering to make a trade: If I dropped the story, he would tell me in great detail about current spy operations in North Korea and Russia. He was drinking heavily at the time, and his offer to trade secrets for my silence, whether the secrets were true or not, was inappropriate and, if true, treasonous. I gleaned from Colby's horrified response that he saw the danger in such loose talk, especially if one of the operations was still ongoing; Angleton was attempting to buy me off by betraying his fellow agents.

It got worse. I telephoned Angleton again as I was writing the December 22 story—it ran seven thousand words, enough to fill a newspaper page of type—and this time he insisted that he'd had nothing to do with the domestic spying. The program was Ober's responsibility. I found Ober at home and told him what Angleton had said. Ober was far from an innocent—he'd been involved in the illegal spying on Americans since the program began in 1967—but I knew from a superb source that it was Angleton who was considered the chief actor in the operation. In any case, Ober denied any knowledge of CIA domestic operations. A few hours later he called me back and made it clear that Angleton indeed was the boss. (In all of this back-and-forth, Colby, as the CIA director, and Ober, who was still undercover as a clandestine officer, understood without saying that I was not going to quote them by name.) By this time, I was getting sympathetic to Colby because it was becoming clear to me how much Angleton and Helms despised Colby and were working against him because Colby was intent on coming clean about the extent of CIA domestic spying. He did so knowing the risks. Angleton was known for his closeness to Helms, who had been fired by Nixon in late 1972 but kept inside the tent by the President, who appointed him ambassador to Iran. I knew from someone who worked with Helms that the CIA director had destroyed many files before leaving for Tehran. As I learned more about the Agency, I'd become convinced that Nixon's responsibility for the Watergate break-in was, perhaps, merely a footnote to the real criminality of my government.

Harold Ford noted that Colby did not return my call on December 18. Instead he telephoned Nedzi, who had been talking to me about suspected CIA abuses for more than a year, something Colby apparently did not know. The conversation was taped, and it is priceless:

> NEDZI: I talked with him [Hersh] a short time ago, and I guess that is about the message [regarding my sardonic offer to Colby to trade Angleton for fourteen CIA files]. Who is Jim Angleton?
>
> COLBY: He is the head of our counterintelligence. He is kind of a legendary character. He has been around for 150 years or so. He is a very spooky guy. His reputation is one of total secrecy and no one knows what he is doing. We know what he is doing, but he is a little bit out of date in terms of seeing Soviets under every bush.
>
> NEDZI: What is he doing talking to Hersh?
>
> COLBY: I do not think he is. Hersh called him and wanted to talk with him, but he said he would not talk with him.
>
> NEDZI: Sy showed me notes of what he said and claims he [Angleton] was drunk. . . . There is a bit of a problem for you. . . . All of a sudden a guy [Hersh] is telling things about . . . that meeting we had in which you briefed me on all the—he used the same term, incidentally, "jewels."
>
> COLBY: Hersh did?
>
> NEDZI: Yes.
>
> COLBY: I wonder where he got that word. It was used by [only] a few people around here.

Ford adds that on the same day "Hersh got through to Colby on the phone, telling him he was writing a story that would come out on Sunday, 22 December. . . . Colby took the fatal step and agreed to see Hersh."

I liked Colby well enough—reporters always like officials who take our calls—but there was no way I was going to indicate to him how much I knew in our meeting, which took place early on Friday morning, December 20. It was a given that any interview in Colby's office would be taped, but that was not a concern; there was no way I would compromise a source, and I was only interested in CIA operations, or any intelligence activities, that were stupid or criminal. In Ford's account of what he depicted as "a fateful meeting," I gave Colby a partial summary of what I knew and said I was planning to write about the Agency's long-standing "massive" domestic operations against the antiwar movement and other dissidents. Colby, wrote Ford, "realizing that this story was a garble of the 'family jewels' list that the CIA itself had compiled . . . sought to correct and put in perspective Hersh's exaggerated account. . . . 'What few mistakes we made in the past have long before this been corrected.' . . . There the matter rested for the moment. Or so Colby thought. He clearly believed he had pulled the teeth of the forthcoming article."

Ford did not attempt to interview me for his historical paper. If he had, I'm sure I would have told him that I did not understand how Colby could not know that I had far more information than he assumed; I had interviewed many people inside the Agency who had been appalled about the domestic spying and other activities for years, but only chose to do something about it after Dick Helms was fired by Nixon. I knew Colby as a tough-minded CIA operative who had been in charge of the CIA's cold-blooded Phoenix assassination program during the Vietnam War, when more than twenty thousand civilians in South Vietnam were murdered after being accused—often falsely—of ties to the Vietcong or North Vietnamese.

Self-delusion was not in Colby's makeup, so I assumed. He knew from Nedzi that I knew the very secret in-house word for the files dealing with illegal domestic activities. Ford cited a series of taped conversations at the time between Colby and Larry Silberman, the deputy attorney general, that made it clear, or should have, that I was getting inside information—lots of it. I knew Silberman and respected him as an honest officer of the law and had briefed him long before writing the December 22 article about what I had found out. No one at the CIA had bothered to inform the Justice Department, or the White

House, about the smoking bombs contained in the "family jewels," or about the fact that I was hot on the story. Did Colby truly believe that my information was exaggerated?

In a later chapter of his history, Ford recounted a conversation Colby had with Silberman in late December, a few days before my article was published, to see whether a decades-earlier agreement that gave the CIA the right to determine for itself whether to report a crime was still in force. Silberman was dismissive, as Ford wrote. "Come on, Bill," he said. "You're a lawyer. You know better than that." Twenty-five years of CIA connivance and criminal activity without worry was abruptly washed away. Silberman also gave Colby a sharp warning about how deeply inside the Agency I had gone. Colby's meeting with Silberman had been on December 19. Two days later, in another taped telephone conversation, Silberman told Colby what he had not said earlier, Ford wrote, "that Hersh had phoned to tell him in advance of Colby's meeting with Silberman on the 19th."

COLBY: I am absolutely staggered that he knew that I was going to see you.

SILBERMAN: The SOB has sources that are absolutely beyond comparison.

COLBY: He knows more about this place than I do.

Of course Colby knew that was not so, but my December 22 exposé cited seven different categories of sources, without naming one. I mentioned an individual who was involved in the initial CIA inquiry into domestic spying; past and present CIA officials; high-ranking American intelligence officials (not in the CIA); one official with close access to Colby; men with firsthand knowledge of the CIA domestic activities; CIA officials who began waving the "red flag" inside the Agency; and a former high-level aide who worked closely with Dick Helms in the executive offices of the Agency. I can name one of them now—Bob Kiley, who died at the age of eighty in August 2016 of Alzheimer's disease. Kiley, among the brightest of the young men who worked closely with Helms in his heyday as CIA director, was a Notre Dame graduate who joined the Agency in 1963 and worked undercover with student groups for Dick Ober until he joined Helms's personal staff. By 1970, when he resigned in dismay from the Agency, he was the manager of intelligence operations for the CIA and Helms's executive assistant. There were few secrets at the time that Kiley did not know, or could not know. He moved to Boston and began working for the then mayor, Kevin White. In 1975, Kiley, now a deputy mayor, was assigned to reorganize Boston's troubled mass transit system. He did so successfully and was recruited in the early 1980s to do the same for the New York transit system. His continued good work there led to an appointment overseas in 2001 as London's first commissioner of transit. He was widely publicized for his success in getting results in all three cities.

I was introduced to Bob in 1972 by a mutual friend who worked for Mayor White. I decided to talk in public about my longtime relationship with him—initially as a reporter but later as a friend and confidant—after being asked by his wife, Rona, to give a eulogy for him at a memorial service at the University Club in New York a few months after his death. His two grown sons had never been able to get much information about his days in the CIA, and I thought they ought to know something about why he quit the Agency and why he chose to help me. My sense of the man—he never discussed his reasons for leaving—was that he believed deeply in America and in the Agency, but he did not believe in the Vietnam War and the Agency's role in domestic spying. As I said at the service, "I did not need Bob Kiley to tell me secrets. I had plenty of those, but I needed someone to give me context—to tell me who were the good guys on the inside and what programs were worth keeping secret." He and I shared many late-night dinners in Boston.

There were others with long ties to the Agency who also helped me during the two years I worked on the story. It was the quality and integrity of my sources that enabled me to have the confidence to tell Colby on Friday, December 20, that I would be in print on Sunday. I had yet to write a word.

Abe Rosenthal knew I was at work on what I assured him was a great intelligence story, but it was not until I spent time with Colby on the twentieth that I telephoned Abe from a pay phone near the Agency to say it was about CIA spying inside America and I had enough from Colby to start writing. Abe ordered me, as I knew he would, to get to the office and get to work. I promised I would get the story done before leaving the office that night, and he said he would alert the weekend editors to expect a strong story about the CIA for the Sunday edition.

There was an element of luck in this. A few months earlier I had arranged a meeting at the CIA with Colby for Abe, and at his request I accompanied him. It was impossible for the two of us not to notice the hostility directed at me by the Colby assistant who ushered us into the elevator that brought us directly to Colby's office. The guy never stopped glowering at me. Colby was cordial, as he always was, and the three of us sat around a large table over coffee. Abe told Colby he hated communism and everything it stands for, and was proud to be kicked out of Poland in the late 1950s for his reporting on the party. Colby responded with a big smile and said, "Oh, we know, Mr. Rosenthal, we know." Abe went on to say that he also hated all forms of fascism and repression. So what he wanted to know, he now asked, was why his country supported the nail pullers and torturers who ran South Vietnam, South Korea, Indonesia, the Philippines—and a few other places I do not recall. Colby, very calmly, responded by saying in essence that it was not the CIA's place to make judgments about world leaders who were our allies. The CIA does what the President tells it to do, he said. Sometimes the Agency supported wonderful leaders who ruled by example, and other times it worked on the side of the nail pullers. The meeting was soon over, and Abe was quiet as we rode the elevator down, the dark-eyed Colby aide still glowering. When we began rolling down a parkway back to Washington in my car, Abe exploded. He was enraged by Colby's refusal to differentiate between a democratic government and one run by a despot. I don't recall all of Abe's words as he fulminated, but I remember his final instructions to me: "You keep on writing—keep on—about those sons of bitches."

I loved the guy at that moment, but things had gotten very tense between Abe and me after Nixon's resignation in August 1974. I was continuing my freewheeling, above-the-fray ways in Washington, but I was now back in the bureau and the world of all my colleagues, not only Gelb. Any good reporter knows which of his colleagues are the real thing—people who work hard and care about being fair while also getting it right. Denny Walsh, who'd had a marvelous career writing for *Life* magazine, had been hired a few months or so after me. Denny was not a fast-talking, hotheaded operator like me; he was simply a wonderful reporter—careful, meticulous, and an expert on organized crime and political corruption. He was also unselfish. He went out of his way at one point early in the Watergate mess, when I knew little and was struggling, to put me in touch with an old friend of his, someone high up in the Nixon world. I was happy to have Denny as a colleague and friend. In the summer of 1974 a political corruption exposé he had spent many months researching and writing was suddenly killed by Rosenthal, with no explanation. None of us could figure out what had gone wrong, and I volunteered to help Denny sell the story to a major magazine. I made the initial call to an editor I knew there. Rosenthal falsely declared after the fact, upon learning of Denny's intention to sell the story elsewhere, that he had not killed the piece but merely delayed publication. Denny was fired and Abe, who knew of my support for Denny, wrote me a long, soulful letter saying he did not hold me responsible in any way for "the whole unhappy thing" and inviting me to come visit him in New York to talk things over. I wisely did not respond, though I thought Abe had behaved despicably, as he was wont to do, because there was nothing I could say or do that would get Denny reinstated.

A few months later, I gave a talk on investigative reporting at a conference sponsored by the American Press Institute, a nonprofit group that does media research. I talked honestly about the pressure I was under as a reporter designated by Rosenthal, as I saw it, to save *The New York Times* from itself, in terms of its initial failure to comprehend the importance of Watergate. I was asked by the editor of a major newspaper whether I agreed it was essential to get multiple sources for important investigative stories, and I remember my laughing response—something to the effect that at the height of the media frenzy over Watergate if I overheard something important from a guy standing next to me at a urinal, it would go right into the newspaper. I was obviously joking, but there was an element of truth in it; once I got going on a story, I was rarely questioned about the sourcing, although

I always answered every question Rosenthal and other senior editors asked about sources. A few days after Thanksgiving 1974, Abe wrote me a very sorrowful note, saying that a fellow editor had relayed my comments at the conference and was astonished to hear a reporter be "so devastating in public about his own newspaper." His goal in writing was to ask whether "this is indeed what you indeed said or think." I had hurt his feelings and he deserved better, but I did not tell him that. Instead, I childishly wrote and asked him if he really wanted to know what I "think."

The underlying issue between us revolved around Abe's profound love of everything about the *Times* and his need for me to be in love, too. He had repeatedly told me how much I enriched the paper and how he envisioned "years of mutuality" between the two of us. I thought the paper had been great to me and for me, and was ecstatic to be there, but there was much about its America-first coverage of foreign affairs I disagreed with, and Abe sensed it. I never responded to his requests to fly up to New York and talk about my future. At one point I had encouraged Brit Hume, who had done amazing work for Jack Anderson in the early 1970s, to come to the *Times*. Hume was politically conservative—he would have a long career as the evening news anchorman for Fox News—but he knew how to get a story, and that skill superseded politics in my view. Brit was skeptical, but I told Abe he had to see him and, sure enough, Brit did go for a one-on-one interview. There was no job offer. I asked Brit later what happened, and still nonplussed by the encounter, he told me that Abe at one point had said that those who worked for the paper had to learn to love it. "I told him," Brit said, "Mr. Rosenthal, I don't want to fuck your newspaper. I just want to work here." That was it.

This background makes what happened early on December 21, 1974, a Saturday morning, my favorite story about the most complicated editor I've ever worked for. I had returned to the *Times* office by early Friday, having had my talk with Colby, and began writing. I had years of interviews to review and dozens of people to call for comment, or for more information, or to check quotes with the few who were to be cited by name in the story. I also placed a call to Sandy Berger, a key aide to Senator Edmund Muskie, then considered a major candidate for the Democratic presidential nomination in 1976. Sandy, who later became Bill Clinton's national security adviser, was a pro who understood the importance of the story. It was going to create a national debate. I asked if Muskie wanted to be the leader of a reform-the-CIA movement. Muskie said no.

I wrote until early evening, dashed home for a meal, and returned to the near-empty bureau to keep on pounding out copy. Novelists talk about getting into a book and finding that the main characters develop their own voice and do the writing, and in a sense the storytelling, for the author. I felt the same way about the domestic spying story. I had outlined it, of course, but after a few thousand words the story was writing itself. By midnight, the night editor had left, and I was alone in the bureau, just me and a member or two of the building's janitorial crew. The lights and heat were on; I don't think they were ever turned off. It was not the first time I'd stayed into the early morning at the office, and I liked the quiet. I began filing takes; stories in those days were written on flimsy paper with four carbon copies and relayed, take by take, to the bureau news desk or, as in my overnight case, directly to New York for copyediting. Sometime well after midnight, a night editor named Evan Jenkins telephoned me to ask what in the hell I was doing. I had filed nearly five thousand words and was still sending copy. There was no room in the Sunday paper, Jenkins said. My story had been budgeted to run two thousand words. I urged him, to put it mildly, to reconsider. He said at the most he could find space for another five hundred words. It was my choice, he said: The story could run at that length or be held for the Monday paper; there was no other option.

I went nuts. I didn't know Abe socially or in any personal way, but I had once met his wife, very briefly, and remembered her name was Ann. I also knew that in the bureau there was a list of editors' home phone numbers. I found Abe's private number, took a deep breath—it was past two in the morning—and called. The phone rang and rang. I did not hang up. Ann eventually answered. I apologized for calling, told her who I was, and said I needed to speak to Abe right away. Well, she said, with much bitterness, you've called the wrong person. Abe's left me. You'll have to call him at his girlfriend's house. I'd staggered into a soap opera. I mumbled something and hung up. And then—I was not going to give up—I called again and asked Ann if she knew the name of the girlfriend. I got an earful, but she was an editor's wife, and she came up with a name.

I don't remember whom I telephoned next, but I came up with an unlisted telephone number for Abe's girlfriend. I called—it was close to three in the morning by this time—and the phone rang a few times and then cut off. I called again and Abe's girlfriend picked up. I said, very quickly, I don't care what the hell is going on there, but you've got to tell Abe Rosenthal that Sy Hersh is on the phone and needs to talk to him urgently. There was no response, but she did not hang up. Do it please, I said. A minute later Abe got on the telephone. He was very angry but I didn't care. I interrupted his bitching to say that his fucking newspaper had its head up its ass and I had been told there was not enough space for the CIA story. How much do you need? he asked. I said at least seven or eight columns, seven thousand or more words. What's your phone number? he asked. I said, What number? Numskull, he roared. The phone you're using in the office. I gave the number to him and hung up. A few moments later Abe called and said I want you to know that tomorrow's *New York Times* will have an extra page in every one of its 1.6 million copies. On one side will be a house ad and on the other side your cockamamie story. I muttered my thanks and he said, in response, "I am telling you right now that you are not to tell anyone, and I mean anyone, about what happened tonight. You got that?" With that, he hung up. And we never discussed it again.

Of course I told a few of my *Times* colleagues about Abe's remarkable response to my insane three o'clock in the morning call. I left out a few details, though.

To this day I still cannot understand why Ed Muskie did not want to get involved in the domestic spying issue, because his Senate Democratic colleagues sure did. I began hearing from liberal senators within days of the December 22 story. It was clear that a major Senate inquiry was a must, but the issue for them was how to make sure that it would not be led by John Stennis, since he was the conservative head of the intelligence subcommittee of the Senate Armed Services Committee. I could not say publicly that Stennis might be the best bet, because the other senators did not know of my many chats with him, which convinced me that he would always do the right thing. In early January, I was invited after the New Year's congressional recess to brief a group of senators about my story and what else I knew. I had worked on other issues with five or six of them, most notably Harold Hughes of Iowa and William Proxmire of Wisconsin, but was more than a little chary of operating as a political insider. I talked it over with Clifton Daniel and Bob Phelps, whom I relied on in the bureau, and they said go. At the time I knew nothing about the CIA's assassination attempts on Fidel Castro of Cuba and at least four other foreign leaders, which were among the as yet unknown revelations in the "family jewels," but I had learned that there was at least one CIA-authorized request to take "Executive Action," a phrase depicting assassination that the Agency used at the time in internal memorandums, against a domestic informer who had gone rogue. I went to a Sunday morning meeting, held in the Watergate apartment of Senator Alan Cranston of California, and talked off the record, so I thought, with a group of eight or so senators. I was asked at one point where else a no-holds-barred inquiry could lead, and I mentioned the possible murder of an insider in America. I also said my reporting on that element was very much a work in progress. In a floor speech the next morning, Cranston exhorted his fellow senators to vote for a full investigation and blithely claimed—to my shock and anger—that the inquiry could lead to a domestic CIA murder. That was it; being an insider was not in my DNA, and I never met privately with a group of senators after that and chose never to testify at a congressional hearing.

I continued to report on the CIA domestic spying story for months after my initial piece was published, with growing unease: It was more than a little self-serving to write articles bolstering my initial story. But a scoop was a scoop; I was the first to report Jim Angleton's firing, which was accompanied by the inevitable resignations of two of his senior deputies in the CIA's counterintelligence office.* I was also get-

---

* Angleton blamed me for much of his troubles, including his firing. He had telephoned me at home early on Sunday morning, December 22, after he read my domestic spying story, to ask, "Do you know what you have done? You've blown my cover. My wife, in thirty-one years of marriage, was never aware of my activity until your story. And now she's left me." I was stunned, and initially felt guilty. But I also remembered hearing of an awards

ting leaks from inside the Ford White House and learned that Colby had acknowledged in a memo to the President over the New Year's holiday that his Agency had maintained files on thousands of American citizens, but insisted that did not amount to a "massive" program of such spying, as I had written. In return, I raised an obvious question in an early January 1975 essay in a *Times* Week in Review piece: Given that the existence of the domestic spying program was known to a few members of Congress and in the government, and that all understood the potential criminality of the CIA's activities, why did it take a newspaper story to provoke the firing of James Angleton, White House briefings on the wrongdoing, and a congressional hearing or two?

I was, alas, initially mauled by some of my erstwhile newspaper colleagues on the national security beat, who had raised no objections when I was constantly breaking anti-Nixon stories a few years earlier. There seemingly was a love, or an admiration, for the CIA that I did not share. Not surprisingly, *The Washington Post*, the *Times*'s main competitor, was the most vocal, and snarky, noting early on that "most CIA activity can be fitted under the headline of 'spying,' and while CIA activities undertaken on American soil can be called 'domestic spying,' it remains to be determined which of these activities has been conducted in 'violation' of the agency's Congressional charter or are 'illegal.'" Larry Stern, my pal who covered intelligence for the *Post*, wrote that it was not the CIA that was keeping files on dissident or suspect Americans, but the Federal Bureau of Investigation. *Time* magazine began a profile on me, titled "Supersnoop," with a plaudit: My prior writings on My Lai, Kissinger's wiretapping, and the secret

---

ceremony at the CIA at which Cicely, Angleton's wife, was present. I called a longtime CIA operative—someone I knew from my days working for Eugene McCarthy—and relayed the gist of Angleton's call. My pal laughed and said, "I can tell you that Cicely did leave him, but not because of you. She left him about three years ago to go live out in Arizona." Three years later I began working on a long profile of Angleton for *The New York Times Magazine* and called him; it was our first talk since his firing. "He refused to grant me a formal interview," I wrote at the opening of the magazine piece—code language indicating that we did talk, but on background. He did allow me to say, though, "You just go ahead and do what you want to do. The damage is pretty much irreversible." He also insisted, so I wrote, that the damage to American national security that I had done by my domestic spying revelations, and his dismissal, was far more extensive than I could possibly realize. I found Angleton impossible to fathom; he was obviously brilliant but also childish, paranoid, and petty. The magazine's cover said it all, I thought: It featured an enlarged close-up of Angleton's face, buried in a deep shadow, with a black background. The photograph was slightly out of focus.

bombing of Cambodia, among others, "read like a historic road map to a generation." But not the CIA revelations: "There is a strong likelihood that Hersh's CIA story is considerably exaggerated and that the Times overplayed it." I won many prizes for the spying story but not the Pulitzer, and it was explained to me by someone on the jury that Ben Bradlee, a fellow juror, successfully argued against the prize for me, stating that the CIA disclosures were, in some order, "overwritten, overplayed, and under-reported."

I was aware that I was not, to put it mildly, everyone's cup of tea. The always witty Gloria Emerson once told a reporter, in her inimitable style, "There's nothing silky about Sy," adding that I bitched about one of her stories at our first meeting in 1972 in Paris. "No hoping that you'll *like* him—*Oh, forget it.*" The irony of all of this is that I was saved by the honesty of Bill Colby, who would eventually publicly admit that his Agency had done what I had written, even to the extent of maintaining files on a hundred thousand American citizens.

My psychiatric social worker wife, Elizabeth, had decided to become a psychoanalyst and was persuaded by others, among whom was Erik Erikson, the most prominent lay analyst, that going to medical school was the best way to get there. After a year or two of premed studies, she had been accepted at New York University's medical school, and the Hersh family was planning to move to New York in the fall. I spent my last few months in Washington making trouble about other issues for the CIA and the navy, and I made a new enemy in so doing—Richard Cheney, the deputy to Donald Rumsfeld, Ford's chief of staff. Cheney's powerful intellect and ultraconservative views made him, even in early 1975, a powerhouse inside the White House.

SIXTEEN

Off to New York

My domestic spying story, important as it was, had at least one unintended and unfortunate consequence: It brought Richard Cheney into the world of national security. I learned that decades later by reading *Cheney*, a very informative 2007 biography of the then vice president that was written by Stephen Hayes of *The Weekly Standard*. Hayes wrote that the White House aide "had not previously worked on intelligence issues. As Cheney's notes at the time anticipated, the [Hersh] article would have long-term implications for the future of American intelligence and for the relationship between the executive and legislative branches of the U.S. government." Cheney's initial take was to protect the CIA from Congress—and then go after me.

I had no idea at the time who Cheney was or that I was on his to-do list. I had my own problems. Since few, if any, in the Washington press corps seemed to be interested in adding to my domestic spying account, I did not take my family on a New Year's holiday. I instead pounded out story after story over the next month with the goal—never stated, of course—of ensuring that Alan Cranston and his colleagues in the Senate would agree to set up a special investigating committee to look into CIA abuses. I felt I owned the story, as I had with the My Lai disclosures, and accepted the pressure and responsibility of continuing to elaborate on a story that I had written, one that was under attack by my peers.

Amid all this, I felt I was double-crossed by the top editors of the *Times*. On January 16, 1975, Abe Rosenthal, Clifton Daniel, Scotty Reston, and a few others, including Tom Wicker, were invited to join President Ford for a lunch at the White House. I was not invited or included, nor was I told of the lunch. The issue of whether the meeting would be on or off the record had not been discussed beforehand. Ford, hoping to head off a Senate inquiry, had announced the appointment of a commission headed by Vice President Nelson Rockefeller to investigate and report on the alleged CIA abuses. The group was dominated by conservatives. Rosenthal, in a memorandum I found years later, explained that as the editor responsible for my stories he had felt obligated to ask the President why he had selected "such an obviously loaded commission." Ford responded that he needed to appoint those who could be trusted to keep those secrets that had to remain secret. "Like what?" asked Rosenthal. "Like assassinations," the President said. He added, "That's off the record."

It stayed that way, although Wicker came away from the lunch convinced, as he wrote in his 1978 memoir, *On Press*, it was "intolerable that the American government should sponsor such criminal and indefensible acts as political assassinations, and I saw no reason why the *New York Times* should protect Ford against his own disclosures of such acts. If the people had a right to know anything, surely they had a right to know murder was being done in their name." The story was sure to come out eventually, he told Rosenthal and the others. "It couldn't hold. Why not give the information to Hersh—he wouldn't have to be told where the lead came from . . . and let him take it from there?" Ford *had* asked that his comment be off the record, but he had done so after the fact. Wicker's question—"did we have a right to keep that secret to ourselves?"—was left hanging.

I shared Tom's concern about morality, but there was a more practical argument to be made. If Rosenthal and his colleagues had brought me into the discussion, I would have pointed out that Ford had surrounded himself with staff aides and operators such as Dick Helms, Bill Colby, and Henry Kissinger who had spent their careers telling lies and keeping secrets from higher-ups. If I had been turned loose on the assassination story, the odds were high that the intelligence community officials—fellow moralists, one could say—who had helped me get the domestic spying story would keep on talking and tell me about operations that had been hidden from presidents and the Justice Department. In the long run, therefore, my reporting could have done Gerald Ford a lot of good by getting the truth out early in the inquiry and preventing the White House from being sandbagged by the CIA, as it had been with regard to domestic spying.

It's also possible that Ford knew what he was doing by talking about assassinations. Declassified memorandums of secret White House conversations made public decades later showed that the President and his key advisers were obsessed with the political implications of my story and knew that the Kennedy administration had been deeply involved in attempts to murder Castro. There was a risk of collateral damage in going after Kennedy, however. In one meeting, on January 4, 1975, Kissinger told President Ford, "What is happening is worse than in the days of McCarthy. You will end up with a CIA that does only reporting, and not operations. . . . Helms said all these stories are just the tip of the iceberg. If they come out, blood will flow. For example, Robert Kennedy personally managed the operation on the assassination of Castro." At this point, the declassification memorandum noted only that Kissinger "described some of the other stories." Kissinger, always anxious about his public persona, also told Ford, "The Chilean things—that is not in any report. That is sort of blackmail on me. . . . This will get very rough and you need people around who know the Presidency, and the national interest. What Colby has done [in talking to me] is a disgrace."

The private attitude of the White House toward full disclosure made a mockery, as Wicker understood, of the high-minded response of the *Times*'s senior leadership to the President's belated request that his comment about assassination be kept off the record. (Wicker closed his memoir with a plea for an end to self-censorship.)

Rosenthal phoned me a day or so after the lunch and urged me to keep on reporting on the domestic operations story, but also to think more about "foreign intelligence matters." I had no idea what he was talking about and told him so. There was a moment of silence. Then he said, "Never mind," and hung up. It was not like Abe, but I figured everyone was entitled to a senior moment. A few days later Wicker again pulled up a chair next to my desk and filled me in on Ford's mention of assassination, and the later conversation among the newspaper's big shots at which it was agreed that I would not be told about it. I made some calls and learned, for the first time, that Fidel Castro had been high on the CIA's hit list, but I could not write that without overriding the decision that Abe and the others had made in respecting Ford's request for secrecy.

Talk about unrequited love. The guys running my newspaper who for years had showered me with praise and raises had a higher loyalty to a president who had just appointed a weak-kneed investigating commission than to someone who had pulled them out of the Watergate swamp. Sure, I understood there were more charitable ways of looking at the dilemma of Abe and his colleagues, but I was distraught at being—there is no other word for it—censored. There was no way I could pursue and write the important assassination story for the *Times*, but it had to be made public. So I did what Wicker had done: He had leaked to me, and I would leak to a neighbor and family friend, Daniel Schorr, of CBS News. I told Dan about the lunch with Ford and what little I had learned about the efforts against Castro. I understood he had his own contacts, and CBS was a hell of a good place to break the news that the CIA had been involved in political assassination. Dan got the story and it was a winner.

I finally was able to move off the CIA beat when the *Times* hired from *Newsweek* Nicholas Horrock, a serious professional, to handle the ongoing investigations. I felt that the halcyon days in the newsroom were over. With Nixon gone, the pendulum had swung back to a place where a president's argument that national security trumps the people's right to know was once again carrying weight with editors and publishers.

I spent my last few months in Washington taking long overdue vacation time and joining my wife in looking for schools for our two children and a place to live in New York while also giving the intelligence community a few farewell licks. I was trying that winter and spring to finish the trifecta I had told Max Frankel about—Chile, CIA spying, and the attempt to recover a submerged Russian submarine. In the fall of 1973, Colby, then the new CIA director, had called me to ask if we could meet. Of course we could, and he came to the *Times* bureau soon after to ask me if I would forget all about that submarine. I had asked Bob Phelps to join the meeting and did not hesitate to engage in some low-level extortion in front of him. Colby always thought I knew more than I did and I told him I would do what he wished, but I needed something on Watergate and the CIA in return. Colby did not hesitate and told me that Lucien Nedzi's House intelligence subcommittee had stumbled a year earlier into some vital Watergate data that was overlooked. I had a lead on a good story.

Flash forward to February 1975, when the *Los Angeles Times* revealed the existence of the CIA's submarine recovery program and the fact that—as I did not know—the Agency had contracted with a firm owned by the mysterious Howard Hughes to build a multimillion-dollar rescue ship that was thought to be capable of bringing the Russian submarine to the surface. Watergate was over, but I had forgotten about the submarine story. I was enraged at myself for so doing and frantically renewed my reporting. I was no longer covering the domestic spying scandal and it felt great to be working again, and I soon accumulated enough information to fill a page full of type. There was much more than the initial *Los Angeles Times* story had reported—such as the fact that a recovered portion of the submarine included the bodies of Russian sailors. I also learned that Colby had begun going around to Washington news bureau chiefs and urging them, with total success, not to report on the story and let the operation proceed. He was bragging to editors and reporters that I and the *Times* had gone along earlier with such a request, without mentioning—there was no reason for him to do so—the trade we had made. I further learned that Colby, to my horror, had convinced Abe Rosenthal to lay off the story, which he did without consulting me. Abe surely had to know I was at work on it. Why else had Colby gone to see him? I wrote a testy note to Clifton Daniel, asking him to forward it to Rosenthal, bitching about the decision, and telling Abe that I knew about their betrayal on the assassination issue a month earlier. I was pretty mouthy in that March 4,

1975, memo: "Lest I seem cavalier about secrets, the fact is that I know almost every major on-going reconnaissance operation . . . and have for years. I'm not going around shooting off my mouth about it"—except to my editors, obviously—"but when one of the programs seems risky and overpriced and there's a legitimate news peg, it doesn't make sense not to tell the American people about it." I was such a purist.

I had stopped working on the story after learning of Abe's acquiescence in the Colby ban and ignored Clifton's insistence that I update the work I had done on the submarine story and get it ready for publication in case someone decided to ignore the embargo. Clifton renewed his request. I said no way; if the *Times* wanted to play ball with the CIA, it was their business and not mine. Daniel didn't bat an eye. He telephoned my wife at home that night or one soon after and told her that I was being a baby, and would she tell me to grow up. She did and I spent a day or two finishing a long version of the story that was quickly edited and readied for publication.

A few weeks later Jack Anderson broke the embargo on one of his nightly news broadcasts and reported many more details of the submarine retrieval project; he also revealed Colby's success in persuading dozens of newspaper editors and publishers to suppress the story. He had called me before going on the air to ask if it was true, as he had heard, that I had a much more comprehensive story ready to go and had been censored. I said yes, because I liked Jack. I was also agog at his ability to obtain important documents; he and Les Gelb were the best I'd seen in being able to raid the federal bureaucracy. I had a lot of dealings with Jack while researching a book on Henry Kissinger years later and learned, firsthand, that he had an up-to-date lending library of top secret White House documents that was dazzling.

I told Daniel that Anderson was going to break the submarine story that night; his show was broadcast at 9:00 p.m., too late for the first edition. Jack, as anticipated, did break the embargo, and I was asked to update our story to include that fact and have it ready for the second edition, whose deadline was a few hours off. There was more petulance from me. I called Rosenthal and argued that Jack Anderson was not a force and the *Times* was—I had been told my second-edition story would be given a triple-deck headline across five columns at the top of the front page—and wouldn't Bill Colby's argument about national security still be valid? The august *New York Times* was taken far more seriously by Russia than Jack Anderson, was it not? Why run the story? Abe ignored my whining and said, simply, "Shut the fuck up and get the story ready."

I wasn't helped in my self-pity by the late David Halberstam, whose brilliant reporting for the *Times* from Vietnam in the early 1960s had changed the perception of the war for many Americans. David somehow figured out that I was having a problem or two at the *Times* and began writing me fan letters that were so wonderfully rancid about the paper that I dared not share them with anyone outside Gelb. The most zestful, and generous, was one written in 1974: "My own instinct tells me that it is probably a difficult time for you and that the pallid clerks who control your destiny . . . are probably an immense pain in the ass, but I do hope you keep in mind the importance of what you are doing. You are, my friend, a national treasure. Bless you." David had left the *Times* in a huff in 1969, for reasons not clear to me, to begin his successful career as a biographer and historian.

The *Times* redeemed itself in my eyes a few months later by publishing an article of mine full of secrets that were sure to make trouble amid the ongoing Senate hearings into CIA spying. The article told how the U.S. Navy had been spying inside the territorial waters of the Soviet Union for at least fifteen years. The mission's initial goal was to tap into Soviet underground communication lines as well as to monitor the travels of the Soviet submarine fleet, but over the years the intelligence gathered was far more easily obtained by other means—primarily electronic intercepts—and the inherent risks of the illegal mission were considered by many too high to justify their continuance. I was warned by a federal agent before leaving Washington that summer to watch my step; the Ford White House had gone bonkers over the story and wanted to prosecute me. I wasn't worried, because, so I thought, I knew much more about the spying program and how it began and the many things that had gone wrong and been covered up. Going after me would bring a lot of dirt to light.

Enter Cheney. After the publication of the story he fought hard to get me punished, not only for my perceived transgression, but also to prevent reports of other possible intelligence wrongdoing from being revealed during the Senate intelligence hearings chaired by Frank Church, a liberal Democrat from Idaho. A stash of Cheney memorandums and other notes were declassified in 2000, twenty-five years after their origin, and they showed that Cheney, beginning on May 29, four days after publication of my article, had been in the forefront of those wanting to shut me up. One of his memorandums proposed five courses of action, including doing nothing, obtaining a search warrant to go after any classified papers I might have at my home, and the convening of a grand jury to obtain my immediate indictment. In the end, the Ford administration chose the first option, but I had made an enemy for life.* The few times over the next decades when I was introduced to Cheney—including one instance by Donald Rumsfeld—Cheney ignored my proffered handshake and walked past me without a glance.

It took guts for Abe to run the submarine story and a later one in July—perhaps the last one I wrote from Washington—that reported that the navy's special fleet of spy submarines had the wherewithal in case of a collision or a similar troublesome incident to falsify official logs to avoid alerting higher-ups of the error. The story, like many others I wrote in my four years in the Washington bureau, attracted little attention from my colleagues.

By late August, I was ready to leave Washington for New York City, which was then in financial meltdown. I had enjoyed reporting on the military and intelligence world, and now I was eager to see how I measured up when it came to the world of Wall Street and high finance.

The one worry I had about the New York bureau was being in much closer contact with the editors there, including Abe. I was coming as a lone wolf and being provided with a private office, a rarity

---

* Cheney's hard-line suggestions were immediately shot down by Edward Levi, the former University of Chicago Law School dean who was then the attorney general. Levi explained to Cheney that the legal actions he sought would force the government to "have to admit—and indeed prove—that the undersea communications intelligence operations both existed and was classified. This would put the official stamp of truth on the article." Levi ended his memorandum by stating that "the most promising course of action" would be to talk to publishers about the dangers of printing material detrimental to national security. He was as direct with Cheney as he had been with floundering me in 1959 when I stopped doing any work in the final quarter of my first year in law school. He asked me then, very simply, whether I wanted to be in law school. I said no, without hesitation.

that separated me from the other reporters on the paper, but I did not want to be pampered or given special treatment. I wanted to be part of the *Times*'s team that was reporting on a New York that was unable to collect enough taxes to keep the city going and was in dire need of a huge bailout from the federal government. What had gone wrong and why was a great story. Robert Caro's fascinating book about Robert Moses, *The Power Broker*, had been published the year before, and it convinced me that there were stories to be had in the city. I also remembered that Harrison Salisbury had returned to New York in the 1950s after winning a Pulitzer Prize for his coverage of Russia for the paper, and it was decided, so legend has it, to take him down a peg by assigning him to cover the city's sanitation department. He turned the assignment into a prizewinning three-part series delving into the city's inability to keep its streets clean despite spending millions more than any other American city on garbage collection. New York was there for the taking.

My first day on the job told me it was going to be an idiosyncratic ride. There were family issues: I was to report for work after Labor Day 1975, but the city's teachers were on strike and we had yet to find a suitable caretaker for our children. My wife's classes at NYU had been under way for a week, and so I took the little ones with me to the paper. It was a kick for them to ride the subway, and the three of us arrived at the *Times*'s lobby at nine o'clock in the morning, just as Abe did. "What's this?" he asked of his new man from Washington. I explained the situation and told him the children would take care of themselves while I took a day or so to get organized. That's fine, he said, with a perfunctory nod to the kids. A few hours later, I was storing files in my office, which was located beyond the sports department in the huge third-floor newsroom. My five-year-old daughter was drawing in a corner, and my seven-year-old son was playing kickball with a couple of sportswriters who were seven years old at heart. I heard a noise at the door. I look up and it's an unsmiling Abe. "Seymour," he asked, "what do you think would have happened if, on that fateful day two thousand years ago, Mrs. Moses had told her husband that he had to stay home and take care of the kids? Do you think the waters would have parted?" I gave him a look and realized he was not kidding. All I could say was "I dunno, Abe." With that, he left. Well, I thought, the guy certainly wore his heart on his sleeve. We found a caretaker within days, and I was able to report such to Abe in a note at week's end. (I did not add that the waters would be able to be parted, once again.)

In those first few weeks in New York, I tried like hell to get Abe to assign me to the team dealing with the city's budget crisis and the Ford administration's refusal to provide any bailout funds. The very man who insisted that I had to expand my reporting skills to compensate for the paper's failings on the Watergate story was absolutely not interested in turning those acquired skills to reporting on the city's crisis. Abe simply saw me as a go-to guy on national security. As such, I was told I was free to fly back and forth to Washington as much as I needed.

I pouted. I still had weeks of accumulated vacation time, so I began playing a lot of midday tennis with some new *Times* colleagues who loved the game. The group occasionally included James Goodale, the paper's general counsel, who had a significant role in the paper's decision to publish the Pentagon Papers. Goodale was a terrific athlete who did not worry about taking long, long tennis lunches. I traveled on and off to Washington and wrote occasional stories about the clumsiness of the Senate's investigation into CIA abuses or about a new tell-all book by a burned-out former CIA agent. It was blah-blah stuff until I again ran into Adam Walinsky, the bright lawyer who had worked for Bobby Kennedy when he was attorney general and in the Senate and knew me slightly from my days in the 1968 McCarthy campaign. Walinsky was an organized-crime buff, as was Kennedy, and he challenged me to do an exposé of a low-profile Los Angeles lawyer named Sidney Korshak. Walinsky depicted him as one of the major players in organized crime. He had ties to many corrupt leaders of organized labor, and especially to the Teamsters Union, long before it was taken over by Jimmy Hoffa. Korshak, who grew up on Chicago's West Side, had been a common street thug as a youth but had expanded his authority and influence after going to law school. He was a fixer and middleman who had never been indicted, although many grand juries had considered doing so. If I decided to take him on, Walinsky added, I'd be wise to hire a guy named Jeff Gerth, a graduate school dropout from Columbia University who had written some of the best stuff on the mob for various alternative media.

The *Times* was ecstatic that Hersh was finally getting off his ass to do a juicy story, and I was given carte blanche to do what I wanted. If I needed some kid to help out, so be it. I went looking for Gerth and found him playing the piano in the middle of a sunny afternoon in Berkeley, California, and realized within a few minutes that Walinsky had been right—the kid had it. He was a lot younger than I was, unattached, willing to travel, and totally sure of himself when it came to facts about organized crime. I hired him and off we went. We were both loners, and we both wanted to get things right the first time. Within a few weeks, we had tracked down a highly secret FBI file on Korshak that told how he had morphed from a small-time lawyer and fixer in Chicago in the 1930s into a big-time lawyer and union fixer in Los Angeles who was socializing a few decades later with the likes of Lew Wasserman, a leading theatrical agent in Hollywood, and the leadership of the Democratic Party. Korshak could stop a Teamsters strike on a Hollywood set with a telephone call and had enough power to save Frank Sinatra's career by ordering that he be cast for a major role in *From Here to Eternity*. Korshak was considered essentially untouchable by 1976. The late Jimmy Breslin, the New York columnist, was said to have always insisted that the mob was run by nine Italians and a Jewish lawyer named Sidney.

The FBI files showed that Korshak had made one big mistake in his career: He had betrayed a leading Chicago businessman by testifying against him in a divorce suit. The businessman owned a chain of department stores in Chicago, a strong union town, and had turned in the early 1940s to Korshak, still a small-time fixer, for help in bribing the Teamsters Union. The leadership got rich while the cost of shipping dropped and the rank and file earned less.

The businessman became a source for the FBI but knew better than to testify in court or on the record about their joint criminal activities. The guy still wanted payback, though, and we offered him a safe way to get it. Betraying a key mobster is not done lightly, to be sure, and so Jeff and I did all we could to mask our informant's identity as he led us to others who had been screwed by Korshak and were willing to talk about it.

I had no idea how deeply the mob had penetrated society until one evening in the spring of 1976 when I got a call at home from John Van de Kamp, the Los Angeles County district attorney who was doing what he could to support our investigation. My wife was studying at med school, and I was making hamburgers for two grumpy children who wanted a better meal. Van de Kamp's message was succinct: "Get to a pay phone now, and call me. It's serious." He gave me his personal number. I do not remember what I told the children, but they got the message and did not move until I returned. There was a pay phone at the local candy store that also doubled as a bookie joint, and I called John from there. He told me that he had learned that Korshak's people had all of my travel and telephone records from inside the *Times;* this meant, he said, that any confidential sources I and Jeff had were compromised and could be in danger. I had been using *Times* credit cards for travel and a telephone whose monthly bill, with each call listed, was paid by the paper, which meant, if Van de Kamp was right, that everyone who had been talking to me and Jeff was screwed.

We warned those who needed to know to protect themselves and learned, after a very cautious and quiet inquiry by the newspaper, that one of the clerks in the *Times* treasury office, where the reporters' monthly expense account receipts were sorted and paid, was from Chicago and had a family connection to the mob. He was to be fired, but not immediately, so I was told, and I was given another method of getting my expenses reimbursed.

As we worked our way around America, Korshak's Los Angeles lawyers wrote a series of threatening letters to Abe Rosenthal while continuing to refuse our requests for an interview with the big guy. Rosenthal and the editors seemed to be behind our story all the way, although I knew the six months Jeff and I had been working together had been very costly. On our last trip to Los Angeles, a few weeks before our four-part series was to be published, I figured what the hell and once more dialed the telephone number we had for the Korshak house. Someone answered. I said who I was and asked to speak to Mr. Korshak. There was a pause, then Korshak, speaking softly and calling me Mr. Hersh, accused me of having slandered him "from one end of the country to the other." "Mr. Hersh," he said, "let me ask, why are you interested in me? You are a specialist in writing about mass murders, with blood filling ditches." He talked for a few more minutes about blood, death, mayhem, slaughter; it did not take me nearly that long to get the drift. He had threatened me without doing it. I was rattled, and impressed.

Our series was edited and reedited because of appropriate legal concerns—Korshak had never been indicted—as well as by ambitious deputy editors eager to show Abe that they could make a Hersh series sing. It was a problem I had not had while in Washington, and the constant fiddling with the series—invariably only with the first few paragraphs—led me one afternoon, amid great disgust at the editorial mischief, to toss my typewriter through the glass window in my office and go home early. I arrived the next day to find the window replaced, and my office cleaned of glass, and not one word about it was said to me. I never bothered to throw my typewriter again, but I did write Abe a note bitching about the process. I got a note back from him within an hour or so, and it made me laugh.

It began,

Speaking of memos: It should interest you to note that at this moment a good part of *The New York Times* has come to a stand-still because the deputy managing editor, one assistant managing editor, one acting national editor and one assistant national editor are tied up as they have been all day, and for days past, in try-ing to get your series into printable form. It seems to me that if I were a reporter whose work needed that much attention, I would be slightly embarrassed and hugely grateful. Unlike you and me, the editors involved are polite and civilized individuals.

"Unlike you and me." Abe did have his moments.

The series finally was scheduled to be published on a Sunday in early June, and, sure enough, the Teamsters Union staged a wildcat strike the afternoon before, and half a million or so Sunday editions did not make it outside New York for days. It seemed clear that some-one inside the *Times* was still in touch with the boys. Ironically, the edition did not have the first of the Korshak series in it; it had been pulled at the last moment for yet another look by Abe's staff and the lawyers. It ran two weeks later, with no trouble from the Teamsters.

The sense I had was that Abe and his senior staff did not think the series was worth the cost in money and time—mine and that of the editors assigned to bludgeon it. Gerth and I had done our job, and nearly all of the most significant allegations of political and financial corruption ended up in the series, but neither of us had heard a kind word since we began our work. The first compliment I got, on the Monday after the series began, came from a senior editor who had not, to my knowledge, been involved in the processing of the series. He called me into his office and told me, with both excitement and awe, that the high-end corporate players in his Sunday morning doubles game in suburban Connecticut were full of praise for the takedown of Korshak. One of the foursome was the chief executive officer of a major corporation that had a Hollywood division. The division had a film ready to go into production when there was a dispute and the Teamsters Union struck the set. The show did not go on. The CEO was asked if he could help. He made a few phone calls and learned that the guy to go to was Korshak, who was tracked down at a country club in Los Angeles. He told Korshak his problem; Korshak took down the data and said he would look into it. A few hours later the CEO's men in Hollywood called with congratulations: He had worked a miracle; the union dropped its protest, and production was starting. The CEO called Korshak, who immediately waived off the question of a fee; not a problem, he said, adding that sometime in the future he would need a favor and the CEO would owe him. The matter rested there for a year or so, until Korshak telephoned the CEO and said he was in New York and wanted to stop by. He arrived with a well-known blond movie star on his arm. What can I do for you? asked the CEO. I'd like to be on your board of directors, Korshak said. The CEO of course knew who Korshak was and what he represented, and he also knew there was no way he could put him on the board. He was terror struck. Eventually, a cashier's check for fifty or a hundred thousand dollars—the editor could not recall which—was delivered to Korshak's hotel. And that was it, the editor told me. Great story, eh? I asked for the name of the CEO. The editor said it did not matter. I then told him that his tennis partner had violated a series of federal antiracketeering and antiunion laws and needed to be exposed for doing so. The editor's resistance to naming names was why bums like Korshak could continue to prey on businessmen and the innocent. Corruption was corruption. It was a very bad moment and got worse when the editor angrily ordered me out of his office.

I personally was thrilled with the Korshak series. It was about an ugly America that few knew about and even fewer wanted to do something about. I wasn't going after a high-level intelligence operative buried deep inside official Washington who would not stop what he was doing after a critical story but find a better way to mask it. My target went beyond Korshak to the corporate wheeler-dealers who were his enablers and protectors. I also hoped the series would embarrass those newspapers in Los Angeles that chose not to tell it like it was; let them feel anxiety. The reporters who followed organized crime understood what I and Gerth had done. Sidney Zion, a New York journalist with a working knowledge of the seedy, wrote an essay in 1996 for the New York *Daily News* that depicted Korshak as an untouchable "man of mystery." An FBI agent once cautioned him, Zion said, "never to bother to try to get him. 'We had Bobby [Kennedy], the Justice Department, we had the newspapers, we had the Senate and we got zero. Sidney Korshak is immune, don't waste your time.'" He described me, aided by Jeff, as "the first journalist to go after [him]." Zion then told of a party at Lew Wasserman's home in Los Angeles that took place on the day the first of the Korshak series was published. The story, he wrote, had

> bloodied Korshak's nose, exposing him as a major underworld and overworld figure in the universe of show business, labor, politics and finance. . . . I got a call from a guy who was at [the] party. . . . "Nobody wanted to talk about the *Times* story on Sidney," my pal said. . . . "But all they did was whisper about it. Then suddenly Sidney walked in the door. Silence. You could hear the proverbial pin drop. Then Lew Wasserman walked over to Sidney, threw his arms around him. Everybody breathed again, and the party went on."

The editors of the paper might have sniffed at what six months' work and many tens of thousands of dollars had delivered, but the *Times* editorial page got it right, in my view: At the close of the series it noted, "A basic responsibility of the press is to lay out the evidence when it points to a serious threat to the public interest and when that evidence shows chronic problems and major weaknesses and deficiencies in national institutions. The series on Mr. Korshak does just that."

We talk often in the newspaper business about stories having legs—that is, they generate more information, sometimes years later. It happened two times with the Korshak series. Jeff and I—and the FBI—could never pin a murder on Korshak, though it was widely believed, or known, that if Korshak gave a thumbs-down, someone lost his or her life. We had tried to get one of Korshak's nieces to talk to us after learning that she was estranged from the family, and especially from Uncle Sidney. She gave us coffee but explained that she was just too frightened to talk.

Some months after the series was published, I got a telephone call at home from the niece and was told a story that put to rest my question about what had happened in the spring of 1960 to a local politician, a reformer, whom I had written about while I was still editing the useless weekly. He had been murdered in a gangland slaying. The Korshak niece said she would give me a taste of her uncle's hypocrisy and ruthlessness, but only if I promised not to write it, which I did. The incident took place twenty-five years before, when she was about twelve years old, and it was in the spring—Passover seder time at the home of a Korshak relative in a suburb north of the city. She was picked up in a Cadillac driven by Uncle Sidney, the patriarch of the family who, she understood even then, was a man of menace. She was in the backseat with Sidney's two sons, both roughly her age, and they were playing word games. She was singing a song that went, "Eenie, meenie, miney mo; catch a nigger by the toe." With that word, Korshak slammed on the brakes, turned around, and slapped her hard on her cheek, saying, "We don't want them talking about us that way, and we don't talk that way about them." She was terrified and wept hysterically. Later, as Uncle Sidney was leading the seder, there was a call and a family member brought the telephone to him, saying it was urgent. Korshak listened for a moment and then said, "Good. You got the goy." The seder went on. The next day's newspapers were filled with stories of a reformer in southwest Chicago who had been executed in what clearly was a gangland slaying. I wanted to believe—I did believe—that the goy was my man.

Korshak's name came up years later at a Washington lunch with a onetime fund-raiser for Democrats. He knew I wrote the Korshak series and told me the following story. Things were not going well in a crowded primary race for a presidential candidate he was supporting, he said, and money, lots of it, was an immediate necessity. The desperate fund-raiser was told to get in touch with someone named Lew Wasserman in Los Angeles. He could help. The fund-raiser had never heard of Wasserman but made the call. He was told to get in touch with someone named Korshak and given a phone number. He made that call and reached Korshak, who was in Las Vegas, and they arranged to meet the next day. The fund-raiser proposed 11:00 a.m.; a bemused Korshak told him that no one in Vegas meets that early. The fund-raiser arrived at 4:00 p.m. at the designated hotel on the Strip and was taken to a meeting room where Korshak was holding forth, surrounded by a collection of hard-looking men. You're the guy from Washington? Korshak asked. Yes. Korshak pointed at two men and told them to take care of the fellow from Washington, and explained that he was going to stick around with the other guys and have a little party. The two thugs walked the fund-raiser into the casino, swarming with bettors, and shooed a group of gamblers away from a craps table. It was just the fund-raiser, a croupier, and the two thugs. "You ever play craps?" one asked. The fund-raiser said no. Just do what we tell you, he was told. The thug then told the croupier to put ten thousand dollars in chips on the table. She did. Roll the dice, he said to the fund-raiser. He did so. The dice came up with one dot and two dots. "Lucky you," said the thug. "A seven." A much larger chunk of chips was placed on the table. "Roll again." The fund-raiser, knowing nothing about a winner-take-all pass line bet if a seven or eleven is rolled, was confused and hesitated. "Throw the fucking dice, you moron," he was told. He did so. A three and a six came up. "Another seven," said the thug, and the pile was overflowing. The fund-raiser was told to collect the chips, take them to the cashier, and go home. He did so, with enough cash to keep the campaign alive for many weeks. It was a terrific lesson in the working of democracy.

The Korshak series got me hooked on the interplay of organized crime, politics, and big business, as well as the workings of America in the 1970s. I was desperate to look into more of it. One of the fringe players in Korshak's world was Charles Bluhdorn, the chief executive officer of Gulf and Western (G&W), one of America's largest conglomerates, whose holdings included Simon & Schuster, a major publisher; Paramount Pictures; and the Madison Square Garden Corporation, owners of New York's professional hockey and basketball teams. G&W, which was widely known for its on-the-edge business practices, by early 1977 was under no fewer than fourteen separate investigations by Washington's Securities and Exchange Commission, whose enforcement division was headed by Stanley Sporkin, a charismatic federal official who was not afraid of the big boys. Sporkin had a huge edge: One of Bluhdorn's key associates had been convicted of embezzlement and was cooperating with the SEC, in lieu of beginning a prison sentence.

I'd been a New Yorker for two years and had worked my way around, which included occasional tennis games with Robert Morgenthau, the district attorney of New York City, and a few of his associates. They all knew who the dirtiest mogul in town was; Morgenthau's office was then running its own investigation into Gulf and Western's corporate practices—to the profound annoyance of Sporkin. Competition among investigating agencies was very good for journalists, as was the fact that few in the publishing world, with the notable exception of *The Wall Street Journal*, had taken on Bluhdorn. The company was an obvious target; Mel Brooks had gone so far as to call an evil corporation "Engulf & Devour" in *Silent Movie*, his 1976 slapstick film. Nonetheless, I was lobbying inside the *Times* for permission to work on the story with Gerth when I was told that Arthur "Punch" Sulzberger, the publisher of the *Times*, had socialized with Bluhdorn, which included previewing soon-to-be-released Paramount movies in Bluhdorn's home theater. It took months of intense research before Gerth and I were able to present—"confront" might be a more accurate word—the top editors with specific evidence of Bluhdorn's financial wrongdoing. We got the go-ahead, began finding past and present senior G&W officials to interview, and walked into four months of sheer hell.

There was a constant stream of letters to Abe Rosenthal and Punch and others at the paper from Bluhdorn and Martin Davis, a G&W vice president, accusing me of character assassination and gangster tactics. It was a theme that I had been living with for nearly two decades, that my success as a reporter was in part due to my incessant bullying of sources. Profile after profile had depicted me as a kamikaze reporter who terrified generals and cabinet officials into revealing the gravest of secrets. I often wondered why my media colleagues thought that anyone could induce a battle-tested general or senior cabinet official to open up by yelling at them. I was once seriously quoted as saying that I would run over my mother to get a story. It was just silly stuff that I had no choice but to endure. So it was not surprising that Gulf and Western, masters of invective, would jump at the chance to depict me as a journalistic terrorist. Their letters all reinforced that theme, such as one sent to the *Times* leadership by Davis on May 6, 1977:

> We are not a company writing to try and kill what may turn out to be an unfavorable story. . . . We want to stop these vicious, prejudiced attacks [from me] masquerading under the name of a newspaper that is known throughout the world for its aggressive, but responsible ferreting out of information. Your name gives weight, dignity, support to these sick, twisted, malicious, hateful attacks. . . . We believe you have an obligation to investigate Mr. Hersh's tactics in the same way we would expect you to investigate any other story.

The letter then included a list of some of my alleged comments to present and former officers of G&W, as related to the *Times*'s management:

> "You'd better see me . . . [said to a former G&W employee]. Otherwise you are going to jail."
>
> "Why is G&W like the Mafia where no one (former employees) wants to talk to us?"
>
> "Every transaction they enter into, they do so with tax fraud in mind."

"I know all about Bluhdorn perjuring himself in the A&P case."

"I know that Levinson [a lawyer and G&W vice president] shredded documents."

"Levinson holds Bluhdorn's coat, lights his candles."

"Bluhdorn lied to me."

"G&W is a piece of shit—garbage."

I did not see the letter until years later. Why it and others like it were not shared with me and Jeff at the time remains a mystery. We were never given a chance to respond to them, and thus were unable to note that they were supposedly based on remarks I allegedly made to unnamed others, as relayed by them to G&W's management, with no evidence provided by Bluhdorn and his gaggle of proxies that I had indeed threatened a former company official with jail time, depicted the company as a piece of shit, and all the other nonsense. If I had been shown the letters when they arrived, I would have told my bosses that there was no question I often took umbrage when someone lied to me or misstated our conversations—I still do—but I would never have threatened anyone with going to jail for not talking to me, nor would I tell someone who worked for Gulf and Western that his company was "a piece of shit." I learned early in my career that the way to get someone to open up was to know what I was talking about and ask questions that showed it. Humor and persistence often would work, as it did with Charles Colson's wife, but being threatening or aggressive never would.

We heard nothing about the many G&W complaints from the *Times*'s management before Jeff and I met for three hours in early May with Martin Davis and an outside lawyer for the firm and were subjected to repeated insults and threats of legal action for doing what I had been doing all my career: reporting. I told Seymour Topping, the managing editor, what had happened. "It was the most disturbing interview I've had in more than seventeen years in the business," I wrote. Some of the remarks directed at me and Jeff were little more than school-yard trash talk. The series on Sidney Korshak had "diminished my reputation," and the story was "a rathole" that some *Times* editors had privately told G&W officials was below the newspaper's standards "for fairness and accuracy."

Gulf and Western later warned Jeff and me that they were doing research on our families and knew that one of my wife's aunts had flirted with the Communist Party in the 1930s. They also suggested that Jeff's father, who was a broker in the steel business in Cleveland, had some unsavory business ties. One offensive senior officer of the company taped a deservedly tough call from me—he had lied to us and about us and was continuing to do so—and sent it to Sulzberger, who was a most gentle man and surely was upset about the dialogue, which did not include all of the conversation. Rosenthal was pissed about the drama enveloping the corporate offices over our investigation, and the tape sent to the publisher, but he told me, with a smile, that I was lucky that the dummies at Gulf and Western went over his head to the publisher, because he then had no choice but to defend me.

This went on through the spring and summer until Gerth and I finally delivered our fifteen-thousand-word bill of attainder. At that point, there was a new element, one that I and Jeff were not to be told of. Our story was submitted to John Lee, the editor of the *Times* business news section that had been renamed something like Business Day. Jeff and I had our own sardonic name for the tepid section—biz/millennium. We did not like or respect Lee and his ass-kissing coterie of moronic editors, and they surely did not like us. Lee savaged us in a confidential memorandum to Topping, Abe's chief deputy. In the memo, which did not mention either me or Gerth by name, Lee acknowledged that "We"—who in the hell was "We"? I wondered—"have the unique opportunity to detail the practices which are a focus of a major SEC investigation. . . . As for the material on hand, it is excessive, diffuse and poorly organized. Much closer sourcing is needed. The anonymous quotes are unusable." The last was a kiss-up to Abe, with whom I had been arguing for years about anonymous quotes, which he hated and which I insisted had to be published, especially because he knew who the anonymous sources were, if we were to get to the truth.

Lee's timing was perfect: It was the right moment to lay into me, because the top echelon of the paper was having fits about the letters from Bluhdorn and Davis and my memos about the threatening and abusive telephone calls we were getting from the company, and the direct abuse we got when we interviewed those corporate officials who were sanctioned to talk to us. We eventually came to believe, fairly or not, that all of G&W's senior employees had been warned of severe sanctions if they talked to us. (The threats inevitably propelled some to talk to us, of course.)

The series, when published, had been lawyered to death, but it managed to tell the newspaper's readership about a corporation that had misrepresented its financial standing in every legal and illegal way it could, and had been caught, to a large degree, by the Securities and Exchange Commission. I was particularly proud of the fact that we were able to tell, with firsthand (and anonymous) accounts, of how a group of corporate officers had worked through the night in the summer of 1968 moving the firm's tax records from midtown Manhattan to Stamford, Connecticut, where Bluhdorn and others were convinced they would be subjected to less informed and intrusive Internal Revenue Service auditing. The story quoted one unnamed senior corporate official as explaining that G&W was "afraid of the New York tax people who were more sophisticated." Many *Times* readers undoubtedly shared that sentiment, but they did not have the luxury of changing their location, for IRS purposes, overnight.

I was proud of our series, which fulfilled our initial promise to Rosenthal—that a serious story on the methods of Gulf and Western would "help explain how things work in this nation." At one point in our research, Jeff decided on his own to take a look at the *Times*'s corporate filings with the SEC—that type of thing was why I hooked up with the guy—and discovered that Rosenthal had taken a loan from the newspaper's board of directors at one-half of the prime rate to purchase a penthouse apartment on elegant Central Park West. Punch Sulzberger and the newspaper's board were generous with many of its reporters and editors: I was later given a short-term bridge loan by the paper to help my transition back to Washington from New York. But I had no responsibility to the newspaper's board of directors, as Abe did. He was beholden to the newsroom and the men and women in it, and the loan he sought and received from the board compromised that obligation. Jeff and I had discovered a few weeks earlier that Bluhdorn had borrowed millions of dollars from the G&W board at a ridiculously low interest rate and used the money to buy G&W stock a week or so before a two-for-one stock split. His unethical insider trading was matched by the dumbness and obviousness of his greed. In any case, we felt we could no longer cite that chunk of greed because the executive editor of our paper, who was supposed to be independent of its board, had acted in a questionable manner.

I was enraged when Jeff showed me the SEC filing that noted the loan, and headed for Abe's office. He was talking to Robert "Rosey" Rosenthal, a well-liked onetime *Times* copyboy on the foreign desk, who was seeking a reporting job. (Rosey would go on to become the editor of *The Philadelphia Inquirer* and director of a California reporting consortium.) As Rosey described the scene to me for this book, the encounter took place in the newsroom. He was chatting with Abe when I came "pouring" into the newsroom: "You looked your normal disheveled look, hair mussed up, shirt half out, and you were holding copy . . . your story. You came up to Abe, upset about something. He was talking to me and you started yelling, shaking the copy, your story, in his face. I don't recall anything you said about the story you were holding, but you were pissed off. After yelling at Abe, you looked at me and said something like 'He's nuts,' pointing at Abe, and said, 'Don't come to work at this fucked-up place.' After that you stormed away."

I remember the scene as having taken place in Abe's office. I had told Abe about Jeff's research, with Rosey watching, and asked him how in hell he could do such a dumb thing as getting a financial break from the paper's board of directors. Abe's answer was out of the corporate textbook: "I asked my lawyer and he said it was okay." I will never forget my answer: "That's what they all say. The Bluhdorns of the world; that's why they have lawyers." I told Abe that because of him we were forced to pull some great stuff out of the article. I began a morally superior strut out of his office. At the door, Abe stopped me by saying, "Seymour," in a stern voice. My full name again. "What?" "Do you think you have the right to investigate anything, anybody, in this newspaper?" I hesitated and said, "No." He said "Good" and turned back to the interview with poor Rosey. A few weeks later his secretary dropped a large manila envelope from Abe on my desk. It was a copy of his new mortgage from a local bank, at the mandated rate of interest, with a note stating that his monthly payment was now doubled. How could anyone stay mad at the guy?

I'll let another voice discuss the outcome of our Gulf and Western work. Mark Ames, a freelance journalist who did much admirable work in Moscow, analyzed the G&W series and its impact in 2015 for an online journal. His finding was brutal, but pretty much on the mark:

> Hersh's massive Gulf & Western exposé was . . . 13,000 words long, in three parts, revealing a private labyrinth of corporate fraud, abuse, tax avoidance schemes, and mobbed-up malfeasance. And yet—in spite of all the pre-publication hype, the story landed with a whimper. Something Hersh wasn't at all used to. For one thing, the article's language was unusually cautious and dull for a Hersh scoop. As *New York* magazine quipped, *[T]he general reaction has been a big yawn.*
>
> [U]nlike Hersh's stories going after the CIA and the military, the Times was far more afraid, and careful, of the consequences of taking on a powerful private company . . . and getting sued out of existence. . . . [T]he Times saddled Hersh with a team of editors and lawyers to vet his reporting, sucking the life out of the piece until it was almost unreadable. Among other things, the Times cut out all the colorful anonymous quotes that made his muckraking bombshells on the CIA . . . such memorable reads.

The critique had it right about the cowardly editing, but the story had legs in ways that were not immediately seen. I could tell from the mail I received that there were many experts, far more knowledgeable about corporate business practices, perhaps, than Ames or the editors of *New York* magazine, and even the editors of the *Times*, who understood how far Jeff and I had raised the bar. For example, John Kenneth Galbraith, the Harvard economist who had served as ambassador to India for President John F. Kennedy, wrote me to say, "The pieces on Gulf & Western are excellent—better than most readers will know. Extracting usable information from these characters, as I can attest from slight experience, is more difficult by a factor of ten than from the CIA." He signed it, "Thanks again." Charles Nesson, a longtime professor at Harvard Law School, told me in a note that the stories were "extremely important . . . the first I know that have attempted to give a picture to us laymen of the financial machinations of a mogul who is still riding high. I'm struck by how unexplored the territory seems to be in terms of lawyers and business ethics. You've done a great job." Galbraith and Nesson apparently understood that the price of delving into a major corporation would be cautious editing and excessive worry about retribution—the factors that kept our series from being more colorful or lively to read. Bill Kovach, my former colleague in Washington who became the bureau chief, would later tell Bob Thomson of *The Washington Post*, who wrote a long profile of me in 1991, that the issue was that I and Jeff were writing about private power, as opposed to government issues. The reality was, Kovach added, that had my story been about a public institution, it "would have been in the paper the first time he wrote it, the first way he wrote it."

The experience was frustrating and enervating. Writing about corporate America had sapped my energy, disappointed the editors, and unnerved me. There would be no check on corporate America, I feared: Greed had won out. The ugly fight with Gulf and Western had rattled the publisher and the editors to the point that the editors who ran the business pages had been allowed to vitiate and undercut the good work Jeff and I had done. I could not but wonder if the editors there had been told about Bluhdorn's personal connection to Punch. In any case, it was clear to me and Jeff that the courage the *Times* had shown in confronting the wrath of a president and an attorney general in the crisis over the Pentagon Papers in 1971 was nowhere to be seen when confronted by a gaggle of corporate con men who were struggling for their existence in the face of a major SEC investigation about which Gerth and I knew far more than we were allowed to write. There was no way the frightened, arrogant, and mouthy men who ran Gulf and Western would dare bring a lawsuit against the *Times;* they knew Jeff and I had penetrated deeply into their wrongdoing, and the discovery that would be allowed in a lawsuit would be extremely damaging.

After that experience, I was ready to leave New York. My wife had agreed to finish much of her last year in medical school at Georgetown University, and we would be returning to Washington.

I spent my last months in New York as an overpaid beat reporter, traveling back and forth to Washington to write about the Carter administration's seemingly endless foreign policy debacles. I managed to do a good turn for Jeff Gerth, which shouldn't have required my intervention. I had been lobbying the *Times* to hire Jeff as a full-time staffer since the Korshak series, with no response. No one said no, and no one said yes. Jeff told me late in the summer that he had been contacted by a senior editor of *The Washington Post* and asked to come in for an interview. When I heard that, I exaggerated a bit and told Arthur Gelb how wonderful it was that Gerth had received a terrific job offer from the *Post*. The suddenly desirable Gerth was immediately offered a job on the *Times* and went on to spend thirty years making whoopee in Washington.

I kept busy during the two-month newspaper strike that shut down every paper in New York in late 1978 by writing a few Talk of the Town pieces for Mr. Shawn. Nonetheless, I still saw myself as a newspaperman and still relished the power of the *Times*. Washington would still be fertile ground, I thought. But the city had changed: The Vietnam War was over and so was Watergate. No one in the CIA had been prosecuted for the crimes that had been committed against the American people and the Constitution. Richard Helms, who had flatly lied to Congress about CIA activities in Chile, was hailed as a hero and a patriot upon being allowed to plead nolo contendere in 1978 to a misdemeanor charge of not being completely truthful in his testimony about CIA activities to Congress. He received a two-year suspended sentence, paid a two-thousand-dollar fine, and was greeted by a cheering crowd when he left the courthouse. The *New Yorker* journalist Richard Harris, in a report about the Helms case, saw the absurdity of the concept of nolo contendere: "The government accused Helms of committing crimes but declined to specify what they were or to prove them, and Helms refused to admit any guilt but allowed a judgment of guilt to be recorded against him." I was still suffering disillusionment over the Gulf and Western process, and Harris's shrewd analysis of the import of the Helms plea did not help.

It got worse for me when the *Times* editorially praised the plea, as did far too many in the press, noting, "Helms was caught between his duty to obey the law and his duty to protect the secrets. . . . And so the government was caught—between the need to enforce the laws against lying and the continuing need to keep secrets." In other words, every CIA officer who took the oath of secrecy was now exempt from testifying truthfully to Congress. The intelligence community had survived a yearlong media blitz and the Church Committee inquiry and was once again where it thrived—in the gray area between right and wrong, legal and illegal, honor and dishonor. It was a gray area, I thought, that was shared by many American corporations.

The Washington bureau did not work out for me. Clarity came a few months after my return to the bureau when John Finney, a marvelous old-time reporter there who had been promoted to editor, showed me a confidential back-channel message that had been sent to him by one of the editors on the biz/millennium desk warning about my bias against American corporations. Finney was appalled at the utter stupidity of the note and the insult to me therein. I resigned immediately, without saying why, and took a long-standing offer to write a book about Henry Kissinger. I would never work regularly for a newspaper again.

SEVENTEEN

Kissinger, Again, and Beyond

The offer to take a critical look at Kissinger's diplomatic record had been on the table for more than a year. It was a book that needed to be done, I knew, but the idea was especially attractive because it came at the right time and from James Silberman, who had been editor in chief of Random House when I did the My Lai books. Jim now had his own imprint, Summit Books, and an uncanny instinct for bestsellers.

In my letter of resignation, I did not tell Abe the real reason for my resignation—although he had to know I was discouraged by the paper's lukewarm, at best, support for the Gulf and Western series—but cited the need for a critical study of Kissinger. I asked for a formal leave of absence, and Abe said no. I was not surprised; rumors of my leaving the newspaper had made the gossip columns in New York and had to be a sore point. Abe felt I not only never loved the newspaper but had used it, in his view, to get a book contract and move on, as had David Halberstam.

The irony is that over the next decade, until Abe's retirement as executive editor in 1988, I wrote a dozen or so major freelance articles for the *Times*, bylined as if I were still on the staff. It was as if the words each of us spoke to the other had no meaning; we were ensnared by our love for good journalism. My first dispatches came in August 1979, just four months after my resignation. I had returned to Hanoi, now the capital of the Democratic Republic of Vietnam, to conduct interviews for the Kissinger book about the secret peace talks in Paris with Nguyen Co Thach, who would become Vietnam's foreign minister in 1980. After the interviews, I chose to stay in Vietnam to write about life in Saigon under communism. Like many of my newspaper colleagues, I was a Vietnam junkie, endlessly obsessed by the wrongheaded American war. I ended up writing half a dozen dispatches for the paper about postwar Saigon, crudely renamed Ho Chi Minh City, in an effort to give a glimpse of the many difficulties facing those who had been unable to flee the South after its collapse in 1975. One piece provided details about the burgeoning black market; another reported on a flourishing noncommunist newspaper in Saigon. I interviewed Red Cross and United Nations officials in Hanoi and Saigon and wrote a long piece about the plight of the more than two million Cambodians who were facing starvation. It was as if I had never left the staff.

My interview with Thach and others for the Kissinger book went well, but the highlight of my visit came at a lunch at the still-operating rooftop restaurant at the Caravelle Hotel in Saigon, which was the hangout for many foreign correspondents during the war. I had arranged to meet there with one of the wartime leaders of the National Liberation Front. He was a nationalist, not a communist, as were many NLF leaders, but was now a ranking administrator in Ho Chi Minh City.

There were two remarkable moments. Our waiter, upon learning I was an American journalist, told me he had worked throughout the war serving my colleagues and as a special treat would dig out a still-frozen steak from the last days of the South, which fell in 1975. After weeks of Vietnamese food, as wonderful as it was, the four-year-old defrosted steak tasted great. The second moment came when my lunch partner, after getting my assurance that we were speaking privately, told me he had been stunned after Saigon fell to learn how many hundreds of millions of dollars had been spent by America on infrastructure projects—including roadways and water and sewer systems—to support the South Vietnamese army, and society at large, during the war. The Russians, he said, took over the American role as economic partner and consultants to the new government at the war's end. One of the earliest Russian projects involved the construction of a processing plant in Ho Chi Minh City that was capable of converting powdered medicines, such as aspirin, into pills and packaging them for Russia's trading partners in Eastern Europe. Russian ships began arriving in the city's busy harbor filled with drugs in bulk and returned with packaged medicines. The new plant was a success, but the Russian government had not paid for the work, and after a year or two of such my lunch partner was assigned the mission of collecting the funds due. He was told by the authorities in Moscow, without a trace of irony, that the Russian government would be delighted to deduct the cost of the packaging from the Vietnamese debt to Russia for arms and other supplies it provided the North during the war. We shared a shrug—what could one say about the vagaries of both America and Russia?—and moved on.

I got important material on the peace talks while in Hanoi, much of it supported by back-and-forth internal memorandums that provided what the American press had not had during the war—a Vietnamese point of view. The beauty of my Kissinger project was that it did not matter whether Kissinger agreed to talk with me or not; he had given me what amounted to an extended, revelatory interview in the first volume of his memoirs, *White House Years*, published in 1979. His book of more than fifteen hundred pages was intended, far more than most readers could perceive, to answer all of his critics. It was a gold mine of new information about all of the important (and unimportant) issues he faced, along with an astonishing amount of misrepresentation and outright lies. I spent nearly a year reading his version of events alongside the published information at the time; I also had the luxury of comparing Kissinger's account with the published memoirs by other government insiders, including *RN*, Nixon's far more honest—and thus revelatory—presidential history.

It was hard work, and I took time out to produce a two-part series for the *Times* magazine about the old boys' network at the beck and call of two former CIA operatives who were supplying the renegade regime of Libya's Muammar Qaddafi with arms and explosives at huge profit. Edwin P. Wilson and Frank Terpil had convinced a third former CIA employee named Kevin Mulcahy that they were legitimate. Mulcahy eventually figured out the scam, which resulted in millions of dollars in profit to Wilson and Terpil, and eventually made his way to me with the story. The series won an unprecedented fifth Polk Award for me in 1981, a prize that was shared by two *Times* reporters, Philip Taubman and Jeff Gerth, my old pal, who also had written about the Wilson-Terpil scam. (Richard V. Allen, a former Kissinger aide who was then Reagan's national security adviser, sent me a copy of the magazine on which the President had written a note asking Allen to look into the allegations therein.*)

The contradictions in the Kissinger memoir were glaring, and I learned more about them in interviews over the next few years. Writing a nonfiction book involves the same principles I sought to use in my daily journalism: Read before you write, find people who know the truth, or a truth, and let the facts tell the story. There were some on Kissinger's National Security Council staff who did not want to talk to me, but the vast majority did, many of them on the record.

I also benefited from the essential evil of the Nixon/Kissinger foreign policy. My reporting in 1974 for the *Times* on Chile produced a

* The series also led me to a huge embarrassment. After the series was published, I was contacted by yet another alleged CIA operative who told me he had specific information about nuclear materials that had been smuggled by Wilson and Terpil into Libya. By then I was back at work on the Kissinger book, and I decided, with the operative's permission, to pass his information to Dick Allen, who had been very helpful to me on my book before joining the administration. I told him the story and the operative's name. He said he would check him out and get back to me. He did so and a meeting was arranged in the Situation Room of the White House. I was invited by Allen to attend the meeting but had mixed emotions, to put it mildly, about doing so. One part of me said it was none of my business; on the other hand, I had never seen the top secret Situation Room while often writing about it. So I joined the meeting. It was agreed my presence would be off the record—another mistake. At one point, a senior official at the meeting told my operative that he understood there was nothing that he had not done for country. The idiot I brought to the meeting said yes and added that there were many times that he had done the utmost. It was clear to all that the two were talking about sanctioned assassinations. I was appalled and angered by the exchange and by the fact that it took place in front of me. I was now a participant and not a reporter. Things were said that I could not, and did not, write about. I walked a block or two toward my office with the operative and expressed my anger at participating. He, with a sly smile, asked if I wanted a transcript of the session. It turned out that somehow he had managed to smuggle a small tape recorder past the Situation Room security by burying it high up between his legs. I got the hell away from him as fast as I could and called Allen to tell him that he may have been betrayed. Allen said not to worry, and we maintained a friendship that continues today. I never heard from the operative again, nor did the context of the meeting ever become public. I also have no idea whether the operative's information was valid and, if so, was acted on. Off the record was anathema to me after that, and I learned once again not to allow myself to become a participant in a government function.

series of anonymous letters to me from someone inside the CIA's clandestine service who had firsthand information about the administration's desire, from Nixon and Kissinger on down, to get rid of Allende. The letters were astonishing—full of highly classified inside cable traffic and policy concerns, and as such they tested, but did not alter, my determination to never publish information provided by people who did not identify themselves.

One of my quirks as a reporter, however, has been to keep track of the retirement of senior generals and admirals; those who did not get to the top invariably had a story to tell in explaining why. I also watched death notices, which proved surprisingly full of detail on the foreign postings of CIA operatives who passed away. A brief *Washington Post* obituary of a retired CIA officer named John C. Murray in 1979 intrigued me because it mentioned that Murray had served overseas in Latin America before his retirement. His widow's name and address were listed. I found a phone number for her and kept a reminder to call on my to-do list (the one in my head). Six months later I called and struck pay dirt. Yes, his wife said, her husband was the one who had been writing to me in anger and frustration over the Agency's criminal activities in Chile; and yes, her husband did have a box or two of documents that he kept in the basement; and yes, I could come and retrieve them; and yes, why not publish his name? He had been appalled at the Agency's willingness to carry out the criminal orders of Nixon and Kissinger.*

Kissinger's instinct for deceit also helped. Roger Morris, one of Kissinger's most trusted aides in his first years—he was a liaison for the most sensitive intelligence in the government—had much to say on the record about Kissinger and Africa as well as Kissinger's interest in the pluses and minuses of the use of a tactical nuclear weapon in a crisis. The code word for the option was "Duck Hook," and Morris had kept copies of his memos about it. Kissinger was perceived by some on his staff to take credit for the work done by others, and thus

---

* A few years later, with the publication of an excerpt on Chile from my soon-to-be-published Kissinger book, I received a letter from Murray's daughter, Marea, then living in Massachusetts, thanking me for my work and adding, "Finally, I know what my father's role was in this 'CIA business'—at least with regard to Chile—and I am proud."

some aides smuggled home copies of their papers, highly classified or not, as a hedge against misrepresentation of their work. Others, such as Dick Allen, who left Kissinger's staff early for an appointment at the Hoover Institution at Stanford University, rewarded my constant visits and my willingness to chase down details by telling me, after a few years of contact, how he had been in the middle as Kissinger passed confidential political and national security information to both sides in the 1968 presidential race between Nixon and Hubert Humphrey. The result was that either man, if elected, would have chosen him to be his national security adviser. I verified Allen's account, and, as amplified, it became a much-publicized opening chapter of the Kissinger book.

Government memoirs are ghastly affairs, invariably self-serving and full of untruths, but one of the better ones was written by a retired admiral named Elmo Zumwalt, who served as chief of naval operations, the navy's top job, from 1970 to 1974. In his memoir, *On Watch*, published in 1976, the admiral wrote critically of Nixon's cynical willingness, as he explained privately to the Joint Chiefs of Staff, to ignore the explicit wording of the late 1972 breakthrough peace agreement with Hanoi. "We will keep the agreement if it serves us," Zumwalt quoted Nixon as saying. I remember admiring the memoir, but do not recall any conversation about it with the admiral, who passed away in 2000. What I do remember is getting a call in late 1982 from Zumwalt, then living and working in Milwaukee, and being invited to come for a visit over a weekend. I moved with alacrity, and we met in a suburb along Lake Michigan on a late Saturday afternoon. Zumwalt told me that he had some papers he wanted to share with me, and to do so, we needed to find a photo shop. We did, and I paid the manager for after-hours access to a copying machine. When all was quiet, I spent a good part of an hour copying one page after another on the primitive machine, with Zumwalt feeding pages to me and handling the collating. It felt great to have a four-star admiral as my wingman. It turned out that in mid-1972, with the quickening pace of the secret peace talks with Hanoi in Paris, Zumwalt wanted to know what was going on inside Kissinger's NSC and found a novel way to do so: He planted a young navy officer on Al Haig's personal staff, someone who was trusted to monitor and take notes on many of Haig's personal calls, as directed. Haig was known to have his aides, invariably a junior military officer, listen to his calls on a third phone. What Haig did not know is that the young navy officer to whom he gave that assignment in 1972 was recording notes of the calls on a cassette and supplying them directly to Zumwalt, who had them transcribed. I used only a few lines from the tapes in the Kissinger book, in fear of tipping off Haig to the source, who had left the navy by then for a career in business.

The full extent of the vile, vindictive, and paranoid atmosphere as Kissinger sought a peace agreement with a stunningly unstable president was vividly apparent as I read through the transcripts. The main leverage Nixon and Kissinger had, or thought they had, in the floundering peace talks by the summer of 1972, with an election looming, was massive B-52 bombing. "Three more months," Zumwalt was told in June, "and then pull the plug with an all-out bombing campaign or bug out." A few months later, with no progress in Paris, Zumwalt was told that Nixon "is presently on a dovish track. . . . The President said take anything that Hanoi will give. The President is afraid that the war will do him in. Kissinger is worried that his reputation will be dragged down." Some weeks later, Zumwalt was told that Nixon, "whose mind is being poisoned by Haig on the subject, feels that Kissinger is screwing the negotiations up. Haig told the President that Kissinger would get yo-yoed by the North Vietnamese. Haig called Kissinger to relay this as the President's judgment. Kissinger was furious." Kissinger got his revenge later, when Haig was out of Washington, by going to the President and saying, "It was important to get Haig back in the Army because nobody was watching Abrams [army chief of staff General Creighton Abrams] from within the Army. . . . Haig said, 'Henry is trying to promote me out of the White House.'"

The internal madness continued after a peace agreement was reached with the North Vietnamese—and immediately violated by all sides, as was anticipated—and it went on after Kissinger became secretary of state, while continuing as Nixon's national security adviser. As the Watergate scandal unfolded in 1973 and 1974, Zumwalt was told that Haig, then the army's deputy chief of staff,

was in bed with Haldeman and Ehrlichman and was aware of the Plumbers operation. . . . The President wants to say [regarding the wiretapping of aides and others] . . . that all Presidents did it. He wants to justify the motive, not the act. . . . Kissinger keeps insisting that he was not involved in Watergate . . . that he didn't know about the wiretaps. . . . Kissinger asked if [David] Young [who with Egil Krogh ran the Plumbers team for Ehrlichman] was loyal to Kissinger. . . . Kissinger wanted to bring David Young back to the NSC staff. . . . Nobody gets to the President. Some of his old political advisors have tried to get in and he refuses to see them. . . . There are five coups a day as various power centers try to take over.

It was very reassuring data to have as I was finishing my book on Kissinger in Nixon's White House. As the memoirs of both made clear, I noted at the end of my book, "neither man ever came to grips with the basic vulnerability of their policy: They were operating in a democracy, guided by a constitution, and among a citizenry who held their leaders to a reasonable standard of morality and integrity. . . . The dead and maimed in Vietnam and Cambodia—as in Chile, Bangladesh, Biafra, and the Middle East—seemed not to count as the President and his national security adviser battled the Soviet Union, their misconceptions, their political enemies, and each other."

It took four years of constant reading, interviewing, and writing and rewriting, before the book, far too lengthy, was published in June 1983. Its title, *The Price of Power*, was suggested by the ever-loyal Halberstam. The reaction was predictable: Those in the media whose success and insights were derived, in part, from their closeness to Kissinger, hated the book; others admired it. Noam Chomsky, whom I knew only slightly and respected greatly, sent me a warm note saying, "It is really fabulous, apart from the feeling that one is crawling through a sewer. It sets a new standard for far-reaching and insightful analysis of the making of foreign policy, one that is going to be very hard to equal." The ever-droll Russell Baker wrote a column in the *Times* titled "The Hissing of Hersh" that depicted another point of view:

Among the well-tailored group headed for Seymour Hersh's house, I recognized Endicott. "Come join us," he cried. "We're all going to stand outside Seymour Hersh's house and hiss."

Well, he didn't have to tell me what that was all about. I knew

Hersh had just published a book of 698 pages. . . . Personally, I hadn't read it and didn't see how I could for a while. . . .

Still, I'd read in the papers that Hersh's book wasn't very flattering to Kissinger; and knowing that Endicott considers Kissinger the greatest diplomat since Talleyrand, I wasn't surprised that he might dislike opinion to the contrary.

"But is it bad enough to justify hissing Hersh en masse in front of his own house?" I asked. "Worse," said Endicott. "It is a pack of slimy lies." "That's terrible. What are the things Hersh lies slimily about?" "How should I know?" said Endicott. "I haven't had a chance to read the book yet."

Baker's inspiration came from an interview I did the day after publication with Ted Koppel, the distinguished anchor of ABC-TV's *Nightline*, a hugely popular late-night news program. Kissinger had been interviewed by Koppel the night before my appearance on a different issue, but Koppel raised the subject of my book, whose opening chapter about double-dealing was splashed all over newspapers that day. Kissinger's response was ferocious, and undoubtedly sold thousands of copies of my book. "I haven't read the book," he said, adding, "What you read is a slimy lie." But it was he who lied when asked if he knew me or my work, telling Koppel, "I don't know him at all."

Koppel's introduction of me the next night set the tone for an ugly hour that managed to produce something unusual for me—sympathy.

Koppel: "Mr. Hersh's book paints a savage portrait of a wildly ambitious and largely unprincipled man, charges which Kissinger has denounced as 'slimy lies.' . . . Sy Hersh, what's the point? What purpose is served by the book?"

I remembered thinking that this was going to be bad. Easy answer, though: "Oh, truth, for sure . . . simply to tell what happened in that first Nixon administration."

Koppel: "Truth without having spoken to him?"

Hersh: "A reporter is often able to get truth without speaking to some of the people directly involved."

Koppel: "You must forgive me. I guess everyone's in the same boat on this one. . . . No one has quite had the time yet to read the entire book. . . . I get the impression that beyond a grudging first couple of paragraphs about the China opening and the SALT talks there isn't a great deal of admiration left in the book."

It went on like that for a few minutes, with Koppel continuing to suggest that my book was focused on a Kissinger who was "almost Rasputin-like in his ability to fool everybody, until Sy Hersh comes along and rips the mask from him." It was impossible to say much about what I had learned about Kissinger's real foreign policy since Koppel had no idea of what was in the book, nor did he know just how Rasputin-like all in that White House had been.

Enter two more guests on the hour-long show: Larry Eagleburger, who was Kissinger's undersecretary in the State Department and one of those who warned Kissinger that he was my "ultimate target" for his role in overthrowing the Allende government in Chile, and Winston Lord, whom I knew slightly from a few poker games at Les Gelb's home. Lord, one of Kissinger's most trusted aides, had my respect as someone who remained totally loyal to Kissinger on a staff full of malcontents. I had wanted both men to talk to me, but they would not.

Eagleburger went first. At one point in 1974, while working for Kissinger, Larry had invited me to the State Department and said, sardonically, that "Heinrich" wanted me to see some top secret documents about the CIA operations in Chile in an effort to prove that a former CIA official who had been talking to me had supported the mission at a critical time. I of course skimmed through the sensitive papers and realized, as Larry perhaps had not, that they included a summary of an earlier secret meeting at which yet another heinous covert operation against the Allende government had been approved by Kissinger, and wrote a story the next day about it for the *Times*. I had been glad to make a mockery of yet another Kissinger gambit that demonstrated his essential contempt for the working press. Remembering all this, I was hard-pressed not to laugh when Larry said, "What we have here is a total ignorance, or attempt to avoid . . . the fact this was a massive intellectual effort and a great foreign policy. . . . I suffer also from not having read the book."

Lord tore into me personally. He acknowledged that he had not read the book but depicted me nonetheless as a know-nothing who ignored Kissinger's achievements in China, on arms control, and in trying to end a war with honor. "Are we better off" with Kissinger serving as an anchor for the American people and the world during Watergate? he asked rhetorically. "I submit the answer is yes. That will be the verdict of history long after hatchet men have slunk back into their holes." Lord had to know he was playing fast and loose by bringing up the 1972 Kissinger and Nixon breakthrough visit to China. The middleman in the secret negotiations was, as I said earlier, the murderous Yahya Khan, the president of Pakistan, and Nixon and Kissinger looked away as the Pakistani army slaughtered untold numbers of innocents. Lord was famed on the inside in those days for his ability to know which aide had been told which set of lies by Kissinger. I quoted a rare on-the-record interview in my book that Lord gave about the slaughter, in which he managed to claim that Kissinger's refusal to crack down on Khan's attacks in East Pakistan, despite waves of protest inside the United States, was aimed at China: "So it was not so much a 'Thanks, Yahya, for helping us with China' as a demonstration to China that we were a reliable country to deal with."

At that point, I was sure that Koppel would defend me, if only to suggest that I did have enough standing as a journalist to merit spending an hour on his broadcast. He did not and I was left having to say, "I'm a little tired of talking about my book to people who haven't read it. . . . I certainly hope . . . when Mr. Eagleburger and Mr. Lord were in government, they didn't conduct foreign policy on the basis of what they read in newspapers."

I had been exposed to tough love from CIA operatives, Sidney Korshak, Charles Bluhdorn, and a variety of thugs in my career, but nothing would match the face-to-face hostility generated by Koppel and the others, with millions watching on television. I knew Koppel had been a longtime admirer of Kissinger's, and was open in describing him, as he did in a 1989 interview, as "one of the two or three great secretaries of state of our century." In 2005, after his retirement from ABC, Koppel went further and told a public television interviewer that Kissinger, after being appointed by Nixon to be secretary of state, asked him to become the State Department spokesman with the rank of assistant secretary of state. "It was a nice offer," Koppel told a reporter for the

PBS *Frontline* documentary series. "I struggled with it for about three or four weeks" before turning it down.

The book did what it was meant to do: expose some of the truth about Kissinger. There were bad reviews, but more good ones. The one I thought caught both the good and the tedious in the book was written by Christopher Lehmann-Haupt, a *Times* daily book reviewer, whom I did not know. What was most impressive about the book, he wrote, was

> its exhaustive detail, its seeming objectivity and, most striking of all, its ultimate thesis. This is a book that doesn't just gossip and tattle, but reconstructs four years of American foreign policy in far greater detail than Mr. Nixon did in his own official memoirs, and almost rivals the exhaustiveness of Mr. Kissinger's two volumes. . . .
>
> This is a book that through its factual density avoids the typically hectoring tone of the investigative reporter or the ideologue with an ax to grind. Indeed, Mr. Hersh manages to sound like a historian, a morally objective one at that.

Lehmann-Haupt went on to explain the ultimate difficulty with the book. It was a hard read, he said, in essence. "So densely detailed that it must test the tolerance of anyone who has grown even slightly weary of reading about the Nixon Administration." Besides, he added, the book ultimately "is depressing, especially to anyone grown weary with Watergate. Foreign policy and Henry Kissinger were supposed to be two of the redeeming features of the Nixon Administration. If Mr. Hersh is wrong, then there is still cause for comfort, but if his monumental study stands the test of future scrutiny, then we will no longer have even that solace."

I SAW BOTH the good and the tedious one day early in the summer of 1983 when my family was invited to swim at a YMCA pool in suburban Maryland. As we got settled, I saw a young woman reading my book while sunbathing. Thirty minutes later she was fast asleep, with the opened book shielding her face from the sun.

With the book behind me, Les Gelb thought we should combine on a column. There was no question that we would be able to sign up many newspapers for the venture. Les, though, brilliant as he was at getting hard-core information, was a bit lazy at heart and would have been clever and seductive enough to get me to do most of the writing, or at least the first draft. My real concern was that it just wasn't for me: I thrived on long projects and would have gone nuts writing two or three seven-hundred-word columns week after week. Les did fine without me and ended up with a column at the *Times.**

Meanwhile, there was a lot of crazy stuff going on inside the White House. The consequences of President Reagan's inability to control, or desire to control, William J. Casey, the CIA director, were not being reported, and I knew there was some important work I could do for the *Times*, if the paper would have me. I had a talk with Abe about me, the *Times*, and his hurt feelings, and we both knew then it would be a mistake. He wrote me a long letter afterward saying, "It would have been awfully nice if you had stayed and built with us, but since that didn't work, I think it's best to leave it at that." He was right—although, once again, that didn't stop him from publishing some pretty important stories I wrote over the next few years. The pieces

- helped keep Kissinger out of a White House job in 1984 by revealing that a commission on the future of Central America he headed had concluded, farcically, that the Soviet Union was threatening a "strategic coup of major proportions" in the region. No such coup took place, and the commission dissolved amid controversy about its main conclusion. A draft of the commission's

---

* Ben Bradlee called me amid my scheming with Gelb and invited me to lunch at an upscale French restaurant in downtown Washington. He told me that Bob Woodward, then in charge of the ten-man *Post* investigative team, was going on leave to write a book and would I consider taking over for him? I would be free to write, too. I said nothing to anyone about the offer, as Bradlee had urged, and had a pleasant meeting about the job, and about money, with Katharine Graham. Bob learned within days that I was to be his replacement—secrecy does not exist when it comes to newspaper gossip—and offered to stay on and help me get adjusted to the job. I liked and respected Bob—he is one of the very few reporters I've shared a source or two with—but I was a loner at heart and always had been, whether in my father's store or at the *Times*. I had surprised myself by working well with Jeff Gerth, but collaboration, even with those as talented as Bob Woodward or Les Gelb, wasn't for me and I told Ben that. He understood, and our Sunday morning tennis games went on for many more years with no more discussion about my coming to work at the *Post*.

Times managing editor
Abe Rosenthal's testy, albeit
funny, response to my, in turn,
testy complaint about the tedious
editing of one of my stories.

A trio of photos of Abe Rosenthal as he
read the Hersh/Gerth series on Gulf
and Western, the conglomerate run
by the sleazy—in our view—Charles
Bluhdorn. Our reporting provoked
anxiety because of Bluhdorn's friends at
the top of the *Times* management. Abe,
who could be more than a little impish
when he saw fit, sent the photos to me.
He was reading during a power failure
in New York City in 1977.

A *New York Times Magazine* cover story from 1982 about two former CIA operatives, Edwin P. Wilson and Frank E. Terpil, doing improper business with Libyan leader Muammar Qaddafi. The story caused a furor inside the government.

National Security Adviser Richard Allen's note to me about the Wilson-Terpil story, "a remarkable document," in his words. He asked to meet with me. I knew Dick both as a presidential adviser and as a friend; the two did not mix well, and the only meeting we had while he was in the White House was a disaster.

THE WHITE HOUSE
WASHINGTON

Dear Sey:

Over the weekend I managed to find time to read your two-part series in the New York Times Magazine on Wilson and Terpil. This is a remarkable document, and you have my congratulations on bringing it to light.

Your story raises important questions to which I had not been paying attention. I think that, even now, something remains to be done in this case. I doubt that there is anything I could do to accelerate the momentum of justice, but I would be very interested in receiving your specific suggestions.

That Mulcahy could be treated this way is believable but it is at once believable and impossible. The assurance that your article has

The Kissinger Antimemoirs

THE PRICE OF POWER
Kissinger in the Nixon White House
By Seymour M. Hersh.
698 pp. New York:
Summit Books. $19.95.

By STANLEY HOFFMANN

The cover of *The New York Times Book Review*, with a provocative title, featuring Professor Stanley Hoffmann's essay on my book on Kissinger, *The Price of Power*, in 1983.
Courtesy of The New York Times Licensing Bureau

A devastating cartoon of Kissinger by Richard Guindon of the *Detroit Free Press* that appeared upon publication of my book.
Courtesy of Richard Guindon

Another *New York Times Magazine* cover story, this one in 1987, on the attempted assassination of Qaddafi by U.S. bombers.

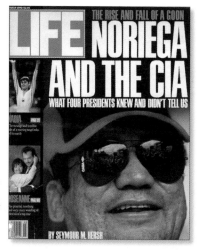

My only article for *Life* magazine, in 1991, on Panama's despotic head of state, Manuel Noriega.

I was photographed for the front page of the London *Times* during my very
public fight in 1991 with Robert Maxwell, the British publisher, over an
allegation I made in *The Samson Option*, my book on the U.S. role in the making
of the Israeli nuclear bomb. I won a large settlement from the Mirror Group for
its complaints against me.

The *Time* cover referring to
The Dark Side of Camelot, my
very controversial 1997 book
on John F. Kennedy

Key Excerpts

April 10, 1961

MEMORANDUM FOR THE PRESIDENT

SUBJECT: Cuba: Political, Diplomatic and Economic Problems

1. Introduction. The operational planning for the Cuban project seems much farther advanced than the political, diplomatic and economic planning which properly should accompany it. As a result, preparations to deal with the political, diplomatic and economic repercussions of the operation are inadequate. Unless we speed these preparations, we run the risk that a successful military result may be to a considerable degree nullified by seriously adverse results in the political, diplomatic and economic areas.

8. The United States line. The impending Stevenson speech in the United Nations represents our first effort at a political-diplomatic counter-offensive. The essential elements of this speech are (a) that Castro is threatened, not by Americans, but by Cubans justly indignant over his betrayal of his own revolution, (b) that we sympathize with these patriotic Cubans, and (c) that there will be no American participation in any military aggression against Castro's Cuba. If our representatives cannot evade in debate the question whether the CIA has actually helped these Cuban rebels, they will presumably be obliged, in the traditional, pre-U-2 manner, to deny any such CIA activity. (If Castro flies a group of captured Cubans to New York to testify that they were organized and trained by CIA, we will have to be prepared to show that the alleged CIA personnel were errant idealists or soldiers-of-fortune working on their own.)

10. Protection of the President. The character and repute of President Kennedy constitute one of our greatest national resources. Nothing should be done to jeopardize this invaluable asset. When lies must be told, they should be told by subordinate officials. At no point should the President be asked to lend himself to the cover operation. For this reason, there seems to me merit in Secretary Rusk's suggestion that someone other than the President make the final decision and do so in his absence — someone whose head can later be placed in the block if things go terribly wrong.

Arthur Schlesinger, Jr.

A stunningly cynical memo to JFK—uncovered by an academic and mailed to me—that was written by Arthur Schlesinger Jr., then a White House aide, a few days before the doomed Bay of Pigs invasion in 1961. He recommended finding "someone whose head can later be placed in the block if things go terribly wrong," to protect the President.

The cover of *The New York Times Book Review* featuring *The Dark Side of Camelot.*

IRAQ:
STATUS OF WMD PROGRAMS

- **We assess Iraq is making significant progress in WMD programs**
- **Our assessments rely heavily on analytic assumptions and judgment rather than hard evidence**
- **The evidentiary base is particularly sparse for Iraqi nuclear programs**
- **Concerted Iraqi CCD&D have effectively negated our view into large parts of their WMD program**

> *We don't know with any precision how much we don't know*

DECLASSIFIED IN FULL
Authority: EO 13526
Chief, Records & Declass Div, WHS
Date: JAN 0 6 2011

71432002
5 Sep 02

~~SECRET//NOFORN//X1~~

In the late summer of 2002, Secretary of Defense Donald Rumsfeld was briefed on the Pentagon's most recent assessment of the Iraqi nuclear weapons program—the famed WMD used by the George W. Bush administration to justify America's invasion of Iraq. A second page read, in part: "Our knowledge of the Iraqi nuclear weapons program is based largely—perhaps 90%—on analysis of imprecise intelligence."

A photo mailed to *The New Yorker*—"protect Seymour Hersh" the sign begins— showing a 2004 anti–Iraqi War demonstrator in Western Europe.

A photograph taken at Abu Ghraib prison in Iraq in 2004, as published in *The New Yorker*. *Courtesy of* The New Yorker

New Yorker editor David Remnick interviewing me at the 2007 New Yorker Festival in Manhattan. It was a serious talk about serious issues, but David, as is his wont, found a way to make it fun. I first wrote for *The New Yorker* in 1971, after being hired following an interview lasting no more than five minutes with the famed William Shawn, who edited the magazine for thirty-five years. After my *Times* years, I began writing again for *The New Yorker* in the early 1990s when Tina Brown became editor. My most significant years there came after Remnick was named editor in 1998. *Courtesy of* The New Yorker

A My Lai survivor, Pham Thanh Cong is now the director of the museum at My Lai, which opened in 1978. For decades I had turned down repeated invitations to visit the museum and chat with Cong, but I finally went, at the insistence of my family, in late 2014. *Courtesy of Katie Orlinsky*

One evening during our visit to Hanoi, when I was at a meeting, my wife and children were given a tour of the best of the city's family-owned "street food" restaurants, featuring great food and no pretension. From the right, my wife, Elizabeth; daughter Melissa; and sons Joshua and Matthew. None of us can remember the name of the smiling tour guide.

report had been leaked to me, and much of it was reprinted in the paper.

- revealed highly classified evidence reporting that Iraq had used a nerve agent in its war with Iran—the United States supported Iraq at the time—and had been buying laboratory equipment for the production of the agent from a West German company. The intelligence, gathered from satellite coverage, had been presented three times within a week to President Reagan without any indication he had read it, forcing CIA officials to redline the most pressing issues in the President's daily intelligence brief that they prepared, which he apparently was not reading. (I was told at the time, but did not verify, that the White House's national security aides eventually found a way to engage the President—by having the daily CIA intelligence brief recorded on a videotape and screened on TV for him.)

- detailed a successful Pakistani operation over nine months to smuggle nuclear triggers out of the United States for its burgeoning nuclear weapons program. The story, which included an interview with the Pakistani agent involved in the operation, was published a few days in advance of the airing of a PBS *Frontline* documentary on the Pakistani smuggling that I had worked on with Mark Obenhaus, a New York filmmaker.

- told of the secret role of the U.S. intelligence community in providing the South African government with intelligence on the banned and exiled African National Congress (ANC), which was then immersed in an ultimately successful fight to end apartheid. The sharing of such intelligence, which led to the jailing of ANC leaders, was shut down by President Jimmy Carter. (I was unable to learn whether it had been reinstated under Reagan.)

The most troublesome article I did, as someone not on the staff of the newspaper, came in June 1986 and dealt with American signals intelligence showing that General Manuel Antonio Noriega, the dictator who ran Panama, had authorized the assassination of a popular political opponent. At the time, Noriega was actively involved in supplying the Reagan administration with what was said to be intelligence

on the spread of communism in Central America. Noriega also permitted American military and intelligence units to operate with impu-
nity, in secret, from bases in Panama, and the Americans, in return,
looked the other way while the general dealt openly in drugs and arms.
The story was published just as Noriega was giving a speech at Harvard University and created embarrassment for him, and for Harvard,
along with a very disturbing telephone threat at home, directed not at
me but at my family.

I also wrote three more detailed magazine articles in those years
for *The New York Times Magazine*. One told of a secret army spy unit
that had been corrupted by money and lack of supervision; another
described the attempted assassination, by American F-111s flying out
of England, of Libya's Muammar Qaddafi, and a third dealt with the
Iran-contra scandal of 1987, which revolved around the White House's
secret agreement to sell arms to Iran in return for American hostages.
That article, which relied on interviews with staff members of the separate House and Senate committees, as well as with some members,
raised significant issues about the reluctance of the legislators, Democrats as well as Republicans, to delve deeply into the specific role of
Reagan and Vice President Bush in the sordid affair that tarnished the
last years of the administration.

The newspaper and magazine articles for the *Times* involved intensive interviewing and reporting and reminded me of the power and
importance of long-form journalism. But my main projects in the
decade after the Kissinger book revolved around writing two more
books and doing a second *Frontline* documentary, in 1988, with Mark
Obenhaus that depicted the many failures of intelligence and tactics
during the problematic American invasion of Grenada in 1983. I also
got dragged into another profession during that time by David Obst,
who had drifted into the film world and helped produce *Revenge of
the Nerds* in 1984. David nagged me relentlessly and finally persuaded
me to take a few hours off on my next reporting trip to Los Angeles
and join him in visiting with Martin Bregman, a successful producer
whose most recent hit had been *Dog Day Afternoon*, starring a very
young Al Pacino. I thought the movie was terrific and so off we went.

We were to discuss a possible movie based on a Kissinger-like character that David and I had spent perhaps half an hour discussing as we drove to what is known in Hollywood as a pitch meeting. After ten or so minutes of meandering chatter with Bregman, he stunned both of us by saying "Fine" and asking us to have our agents call. As I would learn, we were meeting amid a short-lived period of milk and honey when studios put up serious money on the basis of loose talk, without a script in hand.

It did not work out with Bregman, but David and I soon had a contract at Warner Bros., and I had something new to learn. We ended up writing five scripts over the next few years for a number of serious filmmakers, including Oliver Stone, Sarah Black, and Ned Tanen. My weeks of flying back and forth between Washington and Los Angeles had nothing to do with journalism, of course, and were best described by my wife as accomplishing three things: a chance to get to the West Coast and play tennis with my brother; take my mother to dinner; and never get embarrassed by having anything made. I did learn how to write a reasonably competent script, mostly through our association with the brilliant and very patient Tanen, a longtime studio executive who was involved in a series of hit movies that included *The Deer Hunter*, *American Graffiti*, and *Top Gun*. As Ned told us again and again, it's all about character.

I wrote two more books after the Kissinger opus. *"The Target Is Destroyed,"* published in 1986, was an exegesis of the 1983 Russian shoot down of Korean passenger Flight 007, and *The Samson Option* was a 1991 history of America's secret acquiescence in the Israeli decision to go nuclear. Both were edited by Bob Loomis of Random House.

They both had much to say that went beyond the facts. The 007 book dealt with the Reagan administration's willingness to immediately conclude, without evidence, that Russia had shot down the airliner in full awareness that it was a passenger plane, when it inadvertently flew into Russian territory. It turned out to be pilot error, but America went into a White House–generated spasm of Cold War hysteria over the shoot down. With the help of Major General James Pfautz, the head of air force intelligence, I got deep into the air force's first-rate reporting on the mistakes that were made. The remarkable Pfautz, who flew scores of missions in the Vietnam War, was a strong-minded officer who essentially forced the system to realize that the Russians had simply mistaken the Korean airliner that had gone off course for an American spy plane that was constantly flying off the Russian coast tracking radar and other signals. Pfautz grew to trust me because, in my reporting on the shoot down, I had uncovered some facts that he requested that I not publish, and I did what he asked. In turn, he helped me find a number of people inside the American intelligence community who knew the truth and shared it with me. My book ended with this sentence: "A tragic and brutal Soviet mistake—never acknowledged by Moscow—was escalated into a tinder-box issue on the basis of misunderstood and distorted intelligence, while the NSA, which knew better, chose not to tell others in the government what they didn't want to hear." The book's greatest sales were in Japan, whose citizens learned from my book that the National Security Agency (NSA) had a signals monitoring site, known to only a few in the Japanese hierarchy, on one of the country's northernmost islands.

The journalist Thomas Powers, in closing his review of the book for the *Times*, got the message:

> Mr. Hersh has no quarrel with the collection of intelligence, has clearly been impressed with the seriousness and ability of the people who gather and analyze it, and has made no effort to compromise their work. But he has gone a long way toward exposing the most closely held of all intelligence secrets—the fact that the ultimate consumers of intelligence, the officials at the top of the pyramid of government, are political in their instincts before they are anything else, and sometimes use it for entirely personal political ends. They are accustomed to getting away with it. Mr. Hersh has caught them at it, and they don't like it.

It was not surprising that an experienced national security reporter got the point of the book, but I was even more pleased when I was asked by an intelligence analyst at one of the most important, and secret, NSA collection stations in Japan if I would donate a few autographed copies of *"The Target Is Destroyed"* for the annual fund-raising book fair for the base's charitable programs. I also was told it was a must-read there, and at other NSA installations in the Far East.

My book on the Israeli bomb, and what America knew about it, benefited from the surprising victory of Menachem Begin's Likud Party in the 1977 national elections in Israel. The defeat of Labor, which had merged in 1968 with the center-left Mapai Party, meant that moderate liberals would not dominate Israeli politics for the first time in twenty-nine years. The result was something that could only happen in Israel: Some of those out of office began to talk about the unknowable—how Israel got its bomb, and how America chose to do nothing about it. I could not name those former members of the Labor Party who talked to me here in America and elsewhere about the early days of the bomb, just as I could not identify those CIA officers who were appalled by what they knew of America's secret support for the Israeli research.

I also walked into an inside account of how Robert Maxwell, the prominent British publisher of the bestselling tabloids *Daily Mirror* and *Sunday Mirror*, worked through Nicholas Davies, his editor for foreign affairs, and the Mossad, the Israeli intelligence agency, to ensnare and capture Mordechai Vanunu, a onetime worker in the Israeli nuclear bomb program whom Israel was seeking to put on trial on charges of treason and espionage. Vanunu, a Jew who converted to Christianity, had gone public in a competing British newspaper with extensive details about the Israeli bomb program—the exposé created an international sensation—and then disappeared. Maxwell, who was Jewish, was not a spy for Israel but someone who supported the country and was willing to do what he could for it. I had cited Davies as a sometime arms dealer and a key figure in the seizure of Vanunu. The allegation led to a tabloid frenzy of accusation and denial, with a banner headline in the *Daily Mirror* screaming "FORGERY" in huge type about one of the documents I had, and its main competitor responding with an equally bold headline, "YOU LIAR," when my document proved to be real.

The dispute generated even more headlines a few weeks after the Mirror Group sued me for libel when Maxwell was found dead—mysteriously dead—later in 1991 on his yacht in the waters off the Canary Islands. The Mirror Group's suit against me was dismissed in 1995, and a libel suit I had filed, at the urging of Michael Nussbaum, my attorney, was settled the next year when the newspaper issued a very abject apology to me and also paid me substantial damages that under the terms of the settlement I was not allowed to specify. The *Washington Post*, writing about the settlement, noted that the Mirror Group acknowledged that the allegations against me and Faber & Faber, my British publisher, "were completely without foundation and ought never to have been made." The Mirror Group statement added that I was "an author of excellent reputation and of the highest integrity who would never write anything which he did not believe to be true and that he was in this instance fully justified in writing what he did." The next sentence in the *Post* left me very puzzled: "The paper's lawyers seemed to be saying yesterday Hersh was right." I would guess so.

There were high hopes in the American market for the book, whose disclosures about the extent of the Israeli nuclear arsenal became a lead story in the *Times* just as the book was officially published in the fall of 1991. It soon became clear, however, that the book was far from a celebration of Israeli might, but a critical look at America's role, from the presidency of Dwight D. Eisenhower forward, in avoiding a confrontation with Israel over its secret nuclear weapons work. An early flurry of hot sales on New York's West Side, the home to many Jews, quickly diminished as the book's message became known. It was a message that very few, Jewish or not, wanted to hear. I had been inundated in the days after publication by invitations from synagogues and various Jewish groups, and it was disappointing, but no great shock, when all but one canceled. The one venue that did not, a synagogue in suburban Cleveland, became a scene of chaos when many in the audience tried to shout me down as I foolishly described how one president after another looked away as Israel began producing warheads. My point was not that Israel should not have a bomb but that the sub-rosa American support for it was known throughout the Middle East and made a mockery of American efforts to stop the proliferation of nuclear weapons in Pakistan and other nations with undeclared nuclear ambitions. The protests from the congregation grew stronger as I kept on talking, and eventually I was forced, only partly in jest, to ask the presiding rabbi if I could have a two-minute head start at the end of my talk to get to my rental car in the parking lot.

The reviews of the book, not surprisingly, were favorable or not depending on the reviewer's personal feelings about Israel and its relationship with its Arab neighbors. Those who supported Israel invariably cited my reliance on anonymous sources for refusing to believe the book's major revelations; they did so while ignoring the fact that day after day the *Times* and other mainstream media were citing unnamed officials and others on stories involving foreign policy. The book also gave me an insight into the disarray of the Arab world. *The Samson Option* was published a few days before the convening of the October 1991 Madrid Conference, an innovative effort sponsored by the United States and the Soviet Union aimed at renewing the Israel-Palestine peace talks. Syria, Jordan, and Lebanon also were to be involved in the process, with the approval of President George H. W. Bush. The book's arrival provided an immediate opportunity for those Arab nations who wanted to discuss the military and diplomatic implications of the Israeli nuclear arsenal, the proverbial elephant in the room when it came to any peace negotiations; Israel had a nuclear arsenal, and no one else in the region did. Thus I received numerous calls and messages from the Arab world asking me to visit and give a talk. My answer to all was that I would be delighted to speak about my book anywhere in the Middle East, but I did not have time to give the same talk in five or six different nations. I proposed instead that the nations that wanted to hear what I had to say work out a combined venue at which I could speak. It did not happen, despite the interest of many in the Middle East, and I did not make the trip. The lesson I learned was that there will be peace in the world between white and black, Russia and America, rich and poor, before there will be a settlement of the Arab-Israeli issue.

Both of the books "earned out," a publishing industry phrase for selling enough copies to offset the advance given, but appeared only briefly on bestseller lists. There were many foreign sales, reviews galore, and scores of newspaper and TV interviews with me, but hardback sales in the United States for neither book approached the number reached by *The Price of Power*.

I wondered whether it was time to forget about books, movies, and documentary television and return once again to daily journalism. I had been asked a few years earlier to rejoin the *Times* Washington bureau by Craig Whitney, the bureau chief, but I said no. Max Frankel, who had replaced Abe as executive editor in 1986, was more chary about allowing outsiders to break stories on the front pages of the newspaper, which was appropriate. (I was told that Rosenthal had explained my continued presence in the newspaper by saying that there was no need for him to buy the cow when he could get its milk through a fence. I hope he said that, or something like that, because the arrangement had worked for both of us.) So the daily *Times* was not available to me. The Sunday magazine was, however, and I was chafing to do a story on the failed Senate investigation into the Iran-contra scandal. I was immersed in the Korean shoot-down book when the story unfolded, and thought the daily press had failed to do what had been done in Watergate—focus on the role of President Reagan and Vice President George H. W. Bush. It was impossible to believe that Bush, as a former CIA director working for a muddled president, was not a key player in the mess. Bush and Reagan both escaped with their reputations intact and so, I believed, had the Senate investigators. I spent months on assignment for the magazine in 1990 and 1991 trying to figure out what had gone wrong. One finding was that there was no real stomach among the involved senators for going after Reagan.

The Senate investigation had been a flop, so I wrote: "More than three years of investigation and criminal proceedings have put no one in jail. Nor has the disclosure of Iran-Contra, the illicit selling of guns for profit by a renegade group in the White House, led to any constitutional or legal reforms." Ronald Reagan, the avuncular and weak-minded "Gipper," had been given a pass.

EIGHTEEN

A *New Yorker* Reprise

I was delighted when Tina Brown, who was named editor of *The New Yorker* in 1992, called and urged me to write again for the magazine. I knew that Harry Evans, her husband, had been a great supporter of investigative reporting when he ran the London *Sunday Times*, and there was every reason to think that Tina, as everyone seemed to call her, would do the same.

Tina's call came at a perfect time. I had struck out the year before after being given a dream assignment by Joe Lelyveld, Max Frankel's deputy. Joe had my respect—he was a first-rate reporter—and he wanted me to return to the paper on special assignment and take a stab at solving the lingering mystery of President Jimmy Carter's reelection defeat in 1980. The question was whether the Republicans had something to do with Iran's decision to release fifty-two American prisoners within a few minutes of the 1981 inauguration of President Ronald Reagan. The Americans, most of them diplomats, had been seized inside the U.S. embassy in Tehran in November 1979, nine months after the violent overthrow of the U.S.-supported regime of Shah Mohammad Reza Pahlavi. There were widespread rumors that William J. Casey, Reagan's campaign manager—and later his CIA director—had pulled off an October surprise by entreating the Iranian leadership to hold on to the prisoners until after the 1980 election, diminishing Carter's reelection prospects.

I spent months, and a lot of *Times* money, traveling back and forth to Europe without getting close to a visa to Tehran, and a possible answer. The fact that America had supported Saddam Hussein's Iraq with weapons and intelligence in its murderous eight-year war with Iran—it ended in 1988—did not help. I left the *Times* office in Washington after more than five months with three strikes against me: I had not broken the code, if there was one, of the October surprise; I had consistently forgotten the name of Maureen Dowd, its star columnist, whose office was next to mine; and the one substantial news story I wrote in those months for the paper, revealing that the Terex Corporation, an American company with a subdivision in Ireland, was manufacturing and selling trucks to Iraq that could easily be converted to Scud launchers, resulted in a lawsuit filed against me, though not the *Times*. There was much unpleasant back-and-forth before the *Times* legal office agreed to hire Michael Nussbaum to work with the excellent Washington firm that had been retained on the case. The suit, whose purpose I believed was to prevent me and others from writing more about the company's operations in Ireland, was eventually settled, over my objection, with a statement by the *Times* saying it had no evidence that Terex had supplied military equipment to Iraq. My key source for the story, an American businessman with long-standing ties to the Middle East and to the CIA, was kept from testifying because the Justice Department, citing the danger to American national security, invoked the States Secret Privilege, an often-relied-upon precedent to avoid the disclosure of highly classified information. It would be another decade before the real story became known—that more than one hundred Western business entities had been selling arms and military goods to Iraq, including sanctioned items that could be used for the manufacture of nuclear weapons. Such dealings became an embarrassment to the companies and nations involved after the first Gulf War against Iraq began in the late summer of 1990.* Michael's

---

* My story turned out to be a mere hint of the reality, in ways the *Times* editors (and I) could not have known. In 2003, the Scottish *Sunday Herald* reported that Terex was one of seventeen U.K. companies named by Iraq in a 12,000-page dossier as having supplied the government of Saddam Hussein with nuclear, chemical, rocket, and conventional weapons for many years, ending in 1991. The list of those nations doing such business included firms from all five permanent members of the United Nations Security Council—Britain, France, Russia, America, and China—and the Security Council, in obvious embarrass-

bill was minimal, but the newspaper's legal department had not paid it when in late December 1991 some genius there contacted Michael and offered what he called an end-of-the-year settlement of something like sixty cents on the dollar. The busy Nussbaum, whose clients included Lloyd's of London, ignored the cheesy offer. At his death two decades later, Michael still had made no effort to get paid.

Tina's call meant I would once again be working with Pat Crow, who had edited my My Lai excerpts so brilliantly, and also have the advantage of working again with *The New Yorker*'s solid fact-checkers. Crow and I had shared a very odd experience a year or so before when the esteemed Robert Gottlieb was editing the magazine. I had picked up a lot of inside information about turmoil inside the Pentagon over the planning for America's 1989 invasion of Panama that ousted Manuel Noriega but left hundreds dead and parts of Panama City, the capital, in ruins. I called Pat and the two of us met with Gottlieb, who was chatty and very informal—very un-Shawn-like. He told me how pleased he was that I was offering a story, heard me out carefully, and then said go for it. As Pat and I were walking out of his office, Gottlieb added these words: "Sy, I just want you to know that I don't like controversy."

We walked to the elevator in silence. I hit the down button, looked at Pat, and said, "I'll see you around." I assume he was as puzzled as I was, but that was that. I heard nothing more from Gottlieb.

The movie director Oliver Stone had been in the news at that time talking about wanting to do a film about the invasion of Panama, and I tossed my information into the lap of Esther Newberg, my irrepressible agent, whose advice I always followed.* The next step was a visit to Stone—I insisted on paying my own way—at his offices in Venice, California. I'd never met the guy, but was a fan of *Platoon*, his 1986 film that captured the intensity of the Vietnam War. (I had taken Daniel Ellsberg to see the movie, and Dan, who had repeatedly risked his life

---

ment, censored 8,000 pages of the dossier before its release. The deleted pages were later found to include details of the transactions of Western businesses that were aiding Iraq's nuclear program prior to 1989.

* I had needed a new agent years before. Esther and I met for the first time in 1985 over breakfast in Washington. After saying hello, I started yakking about some gossip I'd heard, and she interrupted me to say, "That's just bullshit." She became my agent for life at that moment.

in Vietnam, wept throughout the combat scenes.) I began telling Stone what I knew about the invasion of Panama, and its disconnects. After a few moments Stone waved a hand dismissively and said he'd been contacted by dozens of agents after announcing that he was thinking about doing a film about Panama. "I'm not interested in talking to you about that," he said. "What I want to know from you is whether you think the CIA is watching me." I'd been around Hollywood long enough to know Oliver was considered by many to be a bit off the wall, but this was truly nuts. I said as much and walked out of his office; tennis with my brother beckoned. I got to the door and Stone said, "Tell your agent to give me a call and we'll work out a deal." That actually happened. David Obst and I then spent weeks on U.S. military bases and in Panama City researching a script. Stone, to his credit, liked much of what we did and worked hard with us to find the right ending, and he also began lining up a cast. He insisted I join him and whichever actor he was interviewing—Jimmy Smits and Raul Julia were among those very interested—even if it meant a one-day trip for me to Los Angeles. I cannot fault Oliver's professionalism or his willingness to work. He flew into Washington one afternoon to have dinner at home with me and brood about how to get a stronger ending to the script. We did some work, but he was far more interested in expounding on his theory, which later became a movie, that President Kennedy's murder was a CIA conspiracy. We had a game-ending row the next morning when I told him that his idea was off the wall and he said in response that he always knew I was a CIA agent. The Panama project ended at that point, and I ended up telling what I had learned about Noriega in a cover piece for *Life* magazine. (It felt odd writing for a publication that had twice rejected the My Lai story, but the editors there, two decades later, were very supportive.)

Life at *The New Yorker* was rejuvenating, and far less complicated than at the *Times*. One of my first stories for Tina dealt with what had been a major nuclear crisis in 1990 between two perennial enemies, India and Pakistan. I can write now what I could not at the time, which was that the CIA had impeccable intelligence—conversations on nuclear issues in real time—from deep inside the Pakistan nuclear establishment. My disinterest in exposing the amazing work done by the CIA was a factor, I believe, in convincing two senior American officials who were monitoring the crisis, Robert Gates and Dick Kerr, to speak on the record with me. Gates had every reason to avoid any limelight; he had been a far too loyal deputy to Bill Casey in the 1980s as the Iran-contra scandal unfolded and withdrew his nomination to be Casey's replacement as CIA director after it became clear that the Senate would not confirm him. Once in office in 1989, President George H. W. Bush revived his career by naming him an assistant for national security affairs. (Gates was appointed CIA director two years later.) The low-key Kerr was a much-admired career CIA officer who was serving as deputy director of the Agency when the crisis arose.

The chronic hostility between India and Pakistan, abetted by inflammatory intelligence reporting on both sides, had risen once again in 1990 over disputed territory in Kashmir, and Pakistan feared that India was planning an invasion. There had been reports of nuclear tensions at the time, in London's *Sunday Times* and the *Los Angeles Times*, but inaccurate official denials by the Bush administration were taken at face value. The fear at the time inside the Bush administration was that India would cross the border in force and attack in Sindh province and Pakistan would cut off the advance with a nuclear weapon. I quoted an unnamed CIA operative as saying that the Pakistani air force had F-16s "prepositioned and armed for delivery—on full alert, with pilots in the aircraft."

Kerr would not talk about specifics on the record, but he did agree to be quoted as saying, "It was the most dangerous nuclear situation we have ever faced since I'd been in the government. It may be as close as we've come to a nuclear exchange. It was far more frightening than the Cuban missile crisis." Gates, meanwhile, had won much-needed respect inside the American intelligence community for his quiet back-and-forth mediation between New Delhi and Islamabad that helped defuse the crisis. I had told Gates what I knew about the extent of CIA penetration inside Pakistan, and made it clear that I was not interested in writing anything that would interfere with that vital flow of information. But there was a story that needed to be told. I'm pretty sure the fact that I was so open made Gates decide that we had to talk face-to-face, and so he came to my dingy hideaway office in downtown Washington in the early evening—my building was deserted by then—to answer some questions and make sure I did not inadvertently go too far in print. He told me that he understood at the time that a holocaust was a risk. "The analogy we kept making was to the summer of 1914," Gates said, when World War I broke out. "Pakistan and India seemed to be caught in a cycle that they couldn't break out of. I was convinced that if a war started it would be nuclear."

Crow edited, the fact-checkers did their job, and Tina let the story, titled "On the Nuclear Edge," run seventeen pages in the magazine. The story got attention, especially in South Asia, but there was little response from the mainstream media in America. I had hoped that the quotes from Gates and Kerr would spark follow-ups from my colleagues, but I also knew from my years at the *Times* those few journalists who had the knowledge and sources to report effectively on national security issues were uninterested in following stories written by others; they had stories of their own to pursue. I understood the process because when I was on the *Times*, there was no way I would deign to add to a story someone else had written.

I learned that reality anew in late November, when I challenged the facts and reasoning behind Bill Clinton's most applauded action in his first months as President—a Tomahawk missile attack he authorized on central Baghdad in June 1993 in response to an alleged plot, led by Iraq, to assassinate former president George H. W. Bush during an April visit to Kuwait. Clinton was the first American president since World War II to bomb a major Middle Eastern city, and three of the twenty-three missiles fired had gone off course and crashed into apartment buildings in central Baghdad, killing eight civilians, one of whom was a celebrated artist. Despite the deaths, it was the best day of Clinton's presidency; he was celebrated as a leader who was not afraid to use force in support of American values.

I was in the process then of researching what would become a searing report about Bush's April visit. The former president was seen by many Kuwaitis as a hero who had rescued Kuwait from imminent attack by authorizing the First Gulf War in August 1990 and vanquishing the regime of Saddam Hussein. The victory also was seen as America's most successful foreign war since Vietnam. Bush was invited to do a victory lap and flew to Kuwait in April on a special flight, paid for by Kuwait, that was crammed full of former aides, family members, and hangers-on, each of whom was greeted with a gold Rolex watch. There were bigger targets of sleaze: Kuwait's oil industry had been torn apart in the war, and James Baker, Bush's secretary of state, was on the hunt for rebuilding contracts potentially worth billions on behalf of the Enron Corporation, one of his consulting clients. Marvin Bush, the President's son, was lobbying on behalf of two Texas oil equipment firms that had been using the Bush name in prior bidding efforts. "I was embarrassed," an American banking official told me when I visited Kuwait after the President's visit. "Kuwaitis were snickering after dinner. We take such a self-righteous view in international business: 'We don't do family deals, and we don't take tips.' And then to have the President's children and the secretary of state come to Kuwait to get handouts . . ."

Clinton's lack of judgment in authorizing the bombing of Baghdad was offset by continuing mainstream press reporting on the assassination plot that allegedly had been ginned up by a revenge-driven Saddam Hussein. I learned while in Kuwait that there were many problems with the supposed plot, and followed up after my return. Tina Brown continued to be totally supportive. She called me one morning while I was chasing the story to say that at a dinner in New York the night before she had been told by army general Colin Powell, who was chairman of the Joint Chiefs of Staff, that I was a dishonest, lying reporter who invented stories. I laughed and told her that those were the nicest words an investigative reporter could hear—a badge of honor for someone who had never been invited to the White House or on a press junket, and never wanted to be. I was sure Powell said what Tina reported, and I was sure she did not like hearing it. But it did not give her pause. I, as all investigative reporters should be, was free to run.

The White House's public case against Saddam had been sanctified as rock solid by a major leak in early May to *The Washington Post*, which splashed a story on its front page accompanied by a banner headline declaring that the administration had much evidence of the Iraqi conspiracy to kill Bush. There were three unassailable elements in the White House's case, so the paper reported: the suspicious ease with which the hit team and its bomb gear had managed to cross the border from Iraq into Kuwait; the detonator of the bomb that was to be targeted on the limousine carrying Bush was of such sophistication that a state actor had to be involved; and the explosives to be used were capable of being "traced to the source." All three elements, as I was quickly able to learn from officials inside the Clinton administration—not in the White House—turned out to be false. A later leaker to the *Times* maintained that components of a car bomb that were to be used against Bush were "almost exactly the same," as the *Times* put it, as those found in Iraqi car bombs that had been recovered during the 1991 Iraqi war. That also turned out to be incorrect. The leaks to both papers made it easy for the administration, and the Washington press corps, to dismiss an inconvenient story published later by a *Boston Globe* reporter who had been given access to a classified CIA analysis that was skeptical of the Iraqi assassination attempt story. The study suggested that Kuwait might have "cooked the books" on the alleged plot in an effort to play up the continuing threat from Iraq. It did not fit the official version, and was essentially ignored.

Any hope I had, as a lifelong Democrat, that the Clinton White House would be more open to a different truth ended when I did an end-of-my-reporting interview in the White House with Sandy Berger, the deputy national security adviser. Berger was testy as I made my case, which I expected. My goal was to get him to authorize an on-the-record briefing for me by some of the analysts who had concluded that Iraq had to have been responsible. Sandy was not interested in doing so and at one point asked me why I had spent so much time on such a peripheral story. I replied that it wasn't peripheral to the eight people who were killed in the bombing. Sandy said, to my dismay, "C'mon, Sy. It was only eight." There was an intense exchange, and Sandy ended it by demanding I leave the White House . . . immediately. I did not include our exchange in the story that was published a month or so later.*

* The Kuwaiti government canceled its contract with Enron after my story appeared. Baker, who had refused to talk to me about the trip to Kuwait, ran into me on a flight from Washington to Houston a few months later. As he walked past me, he stopped, pointed a finger at me, and said, with much anger, "You didn't lay a glove on me. Not one finger." Years later, we sat side by side on a flight from Houston and had a pleasant chat. He was one of the few George W. Bush supporters who tried his best to mitigate the damage to America and the world that Bush and Dick Cheney had done after 9/11.

I broke off my reporting for *The New Yorker*, enjoyable as it had been, in late 1994 because James Silberman, the editor who whispered Kissinger to me, was now whispering Kennedy. There was still a story to be had, so Jim thought. I, too, was convinced there was much more to say about John F. Kennedy and the CIA—a hidden history. I began my research by focusing on Frank Church and the Senate committee he led—the one that had been set up after my 1974 article on domestic spying—that had investigated the CIA's activities in the 1960s and 1970s. The politician who cared the most about getting control of the U.S. intelligence community was Mike Mansfield of Montana, the quiet Senate majority leader who, as few appreciated at the time, had been brooding for decades about Congress's inability, and unwillingness, to provide effective oversight of the intelligence community. Mansfield had been elected to the Senate in 1952 after spending ten years in the House, and introduced legislation within a year to establish a permanent joint congressional committee to oversee the budget and activities of the CIA. It went nowhere, as did subsequent attempts to derail the quiet chats and whispering between a few Senate seniors and the CIA director that passed for congressional oversight since the Agency was created after World War II.

The domestic spying story had come at the right time for real change. America had slowly, but emphatically, turned against the Vietnam War, with its fifty-eight thousand combat deaths, horrific brutalities, and, most important, resounding defeat at the hands of an outgunned guerrilla force. The Watergate scandals had forced Nixon from office and put investigative reporting, albeit briefly, on a pedestal. Stories about illegal wiretapping of Washington officials, official lying as codified in the Pentagon Papers, and the CIA's covert activities in Chile and Africa had raised obvious questions about the integrity and competence of those who ran Washington. Even Congress had roused itself, once it was clear that the war was lost, and a coalition of Democrats and moderate Republicans had approved legislation in 1973 to end the war, and agreed on a joint resolution in an unsuccessful attempt to limit the President's powers to unilaterally declare a future war. Their efforts were unsuccessful.

Mansfield initially turned to Senator Philip Hart, a liberal Democrat from Michigan and World War II veteran who was highly respected by his peers in Congress, to be chairman of the Senate committee that would investigate CIA abuse. Hart demurred, explaining privately to Mansfield that he was being treated for cancer and would not have the stamina to serve as chairman, although he agreed to serve on the committee. Mansfield was being lobbied hard by Church, who had chaired a series of penetrating hearings on foreign bribery and corruption by American multinational corporations. Church's public persona was glowing, but he lacked Hart's standing among his peers. He was especially viewed with ambivalence by the senior staff members of the Senate Foreign Relations Committee, which had been dominated for decades by Democrat William Fulbright of Arkansas, whose skeptical hearings on the Vietnam War set a standard that Congress would not match in subsequent years. Church was seen as pompous and overly ambitious—even among senators famously known to be pompous and ambitious—and far too willing, despite his firm voice in public, to compromise in private on key legislative issues.

I wanted to get close to Church because he was chairman of a foreign relations subcommittee investigating the business practices of multinational corporations in the early 1970s. His staff quickly began unraveling illegal overseas payoffs by American firms seeking foreign contracts. The extent of the corruption, the subcommittee learned, was known to the Central Intelligence Agency. Jerry Levinson, the staff director of the subcommittee, would share inside information with me, with Church's approval, in the hope that I could verify it and get it published in the *Times*, with credit to Church and his subcommittee. One of Church's hearings stumbled into the CIA's covert operation to undermine the Allende government in Chile, and there was intense peer pressure on the senator to back off. Levinson, who became a good friend, urged me at one crucial point to telephone Church and tell him how important his work was and how I and the *Times* were totally behind him. I did so without hesitation; Church's subcommittee was going where Congress had not, in terms of oversight of the CIA. My role in all of this was unique, but I had information and access to information that the committee did not, and it was important that they know it. I made sure my editors understood what I was doing. What I did not comprehend at the time was the extent of Church's desperate desire to be President—an ambition that had perhaps led him to take the risks he did in exposing American political and financial corruption overseas.

Mansfield knew his man, however. Sometime in late January 1975—the committee was formally approved on January 27—Mansfield summoned Church for an interview about the chairmanship with a small leadership group that included Fulbright and Barry Goldwater, the conservative Republican senator from Arizona whose party would be in the minority on the committee. A senior Democratic staff aide was also in attendance, and decades later, with the involved senators deceased, he felt free to tell me over dinner about an extraordinary request Mansfield made. "If you take this job," the aide recalled Mansfield telling Church, "you must understand that you cannot run for President." Church immediately agreed and told Mansfield that he had discussed that possibility with his wife, Bethine—the two were known to make decisions together—and the Senate leaders understood that his presidential ambition would be put off.

Church got the job and was immediately invited on *Face the Nation*, a CBS television Sunday morning interview show. I was one of the interrogators, along with Daniel Schorr of CBS. Asked by me if he might run for the presidency, Church was categorical in his denial. "Let's scotch that right now," he said, explaining that he had told all who volunteered to work on a primary campaign that there would be no political activity on his behalf during the life of the committee. "I'm not going to mix presidential politics with anything so important."

Church was lying; there is no other word for it. More than a decade after his death in 1984, Kathryn Olmsted, a scholar researching a book about the CIA scandal, found a few letters among the Church collection at Boise State University suggesting that Church had remained in extensive contact with Joseph Napolitan, a sophisticated political operative who had worked in the presidential campaigns of Jack Kennedy, Lyndon Johnson, and Hubert Humphrey. The letters show that Church was committed to a run for the presidency in 1976 and, with Napolitan's advice, sought in the fall of 1975 to use a much-anticipated series of public hearings to rally popular support for his campaign by dramatically showing the extent of CIA and FBI abuses.

By late summer, however, Church's presidential ambitions were in big trouble. He had campaigned for the committee chairmanship early in the year in the belief it would focus on domestic spying and other outrages that had been promulgated in the Johnson and Nixon administrations, with their paranoia about anti–Vietnam War activists. By spring there was a new element—reporting suggesting that Jack Kennedy had teamed with his brother Bobby, then the attorney general, in repeated attempts to assassinate Cuba's Fidel Castro, perhaps as payback for Castro's outmaneuvering of the President at the Bay of Pigs.

Jack Kennedy had been a role model for Church, who was smitten by all things Kennedy. Church had delivered a passionate keynote at the 1960 Democratic convention that nominated Kennedy and, with his wife, had taken Teddy Kennedy on a safari to Africa in 1961, a year before the youngest Kennedy would win a Senate seat from Massachusetts. He had every reason to believe that his years of loyalty and friendship would be repaid by Kennedy family support in his race for the presidency.

It was a classic conflict of interest: An all-out inquiry into the Kennedy brothers' wrongdoing in the early 1960s would cost him vital Kennedy family financial and political support in 1976. So Frank Church trimmed. The CIA, he declared early in the assassination investigation, should be compared to a "rogue elephant on a rampage" that had spun out of presidential control. He went further that fall when he publicly confronted William Colby with an electronic gun that, so he claimed, was capable of firing a dart filled with a highly lethal toxin into an intended assassination victim. The Agency had been ordered a decade earlier to destroy such materials, Church claimed, but had chosen to defy the presidential order. The show-and-tell generated enormous headlines and television coverage, as Church knew it would, and left the impression that not even a president could stop assassination planning.

Church's posturing was too much for Gary Hart, who had been elected to the Senate as a Democrat from Colorado in 1974 and had been serving for less than a week when he was appointed by Mike Mansfield as the most junior member of the committee. He was a quick study and took the assignment seriously, especially after a Republican investigator named David Bushong and a colleague turned up evidence that Jack Kennedy, while in the White House, was having an affair with Judith Exner, a sometime Los Angeles model who was sleeping at the same time with Sam Giancana, a notorious Mafia leader. Hart later told me of his surprise, as a most junior senator, at being asked by Church to meet privately with Ted Kennedy to inform him about the game-changing new information. "I did so and Ted simply thanked me and said nothing else," Hart said. The link between Exner and Kennedy was known to J. Edgar Hoover's FBI, so the committee would learn, but had been kept from the Warren Commission during its investigation of Jack Kennedy's assassination.

Church's waffling as new details of Kennedy's recklessness poured forth ended any chance, slim as it was, of significant cooperation with the Republicans on the committee. Once again, my work on intelligence issues for the *Times,* and my continuing access to information, led to some special access inside the committee. I had a few private meetings at critical times with various members, Democrat and Republican, and with a few of the senior members of the staff. Goldwater had correctly come to believe by the spring of 1975 that Church, as chairman, was doing all he could to protect the Kennedy family and was using the hearings to run for the presidency. As the investigation neared its end, there was another private meeting of the lions of the Senate—Mansfield, Fulbright, Church, and Goldwater—to decide how to handle the issue of presidential responsibility. The Democratic staff aide also attended the session and told me years later what he had not told me at the time—that Goldwater flatly declared, at one point, "We know what the Presidents have done," referring to Eisenhower's and Kennedy's authorization of the assassination of foreign leaders. Goldwater then added, in language that the aide had not forgotten, "If there was presidential authorization for what the Agency was doing, we have the responsibility of deciding what is constitutional or not." The issue was whether the CIA was acting as if it were part of the king's personal staff, as Richard Helms had suggested at one point, or whether the men running the Agency were subject, like all citizens and all government entities, to the checks and balances of the Constitution.

In the end, the committee took a pass on the issue of presidential authority and noted it was unable to "make a finding that the assassination plots were authorized by the Presidents or other persons above the governmental agency or agencies involved." Its final report, titled "Alleged Assassination Plots Involving Foreign Leaders," was marked by language that can only be described as anodyne:

> The Committee finds that the system of executive command and control was so ambiguous that it is difficult to be certain at which levels assassination activity was known and authorized. This situation creates the disturbing prospect that Government officials might have undertaken the assassination plots without it having been incontrovertibly clear that there was explicit authorization from the President. It is also possible there might have been a successful "plausible denial" in which Presidential authorization was issued but is now obscured. . . . There is admittedly a tension among the findings.

Gary Hart would tell me years later that, in essence, the Democrats on the committee had blinked. "My role was to pursue matters that others didn't want to know about. What we could not find is anyone under either President [Eisenhower or Kennedy] who would say, 'He ordered it and he knew.' Lots of euphemisms—'who will rid me of this troublesome priest?' kind of stuff. It wasn't that witnesses told us the boss ordered it and we, the committee, covered it up. We simply could not get anyone to state that a president ordered an assassination. But it was clear they knew what was going on."

After talking to Hart, I tracked down David Bushong, the Republican investigator who had worked directly for Barry Goldwater, and he told me that Goldwater was convinced there was ample evidence to prove that the path to presidential authorization ran through Bobby Kennedy. "We never directly tagged Jack Kennedy with authorization—a direct order to assassinate Castro—but we did tag Bobby with participating as well as authorizing an assassination attempt during a secret meeting," Bushong said. "Bobby was coordinating covert operations in Cuba and separately participating in meetings that involved using Giancana's mob to get poison pills to Castro. And we had Hoover, who warned the President over a lunch about wiretaps showing that he was dealing with Judy Exner while she had ties to Giancana. Kennedy immediately cut off all contact with Exner. Six weeks later, Bobby authorized the passing of the poison pills to Cuba. All of this gets us to a strong case of presidential authorization to take to the senators."

The inevitable result was acute mistrust at the top of the CIA—even among those who knew mistakes had been made—because Helms and other senior Agency officials found it impossible to believe that Frank Church and the Democratic senators did not understand that when the issue was assassination, the CIA had been doing what the President wanted, without, of course, anything in writing. The full extent of the CIA's contempt for Church, justified or not, came through in the declassified history of Bill Colby's tenure as director that was written by Harold Ford. John Waller, who later became the CIA inspector general, insisted in an interview with Ford that Church "was not interested in the issues. In our humble opinion, he was running for President. . . . Putting it bluntly, he was a political prostitute, not a seeker of truth." Richard Lehman, a respected intelligence officer who later became chairman of the National Intelligence Council—the in-house group responsible for long-term strategic analysis—depicted Church as "a sanctimonious son of a bitch. Hypocrite, thy name is Frank Church. . . . I'm convinced that he leapt for the job, hoping that it would turn out to be a chariot that would carry him to the presidency."

Given my involvement with the Church Committee members and senior staff, it did not take long for me to renew old contacts and get what I needed. A large FedEx box arrived one morning at my office, with no return address, full of highly classified CIA documents that had not been made public by the committee. I knew who sent them, of course. The papers made it clear that the continuous pressure to assassinate Fidel Castro emanated from Jack Kennedy. They also revealed that Kennedy knew precisely what Nixon was planning that fall against Castro—an invasion by Cuban dissidents. The plotting for what became known as the Bay of Pigs was a grave state secret, but senior Agency officers—fellow Ivy League graduates who socialized with Kennedy—shared the information with candidate Kennedy in the early fall. Kennedy, tough-minded as always, enraged Nixon and undoubtedly won crucial votes in Florida by taking him to task during the latter stage of the 1960 campaign for not doing enough about Castro. Nixon kept the secret and lost the election.

I took what I knew about the very tough Kennedy to Sam Halpern, a veteran of the *kill Castro* days in the Agency who had retired after years of working closely with Richard Helms. I could not understand, I told Halpern, why Kennedy would take the enormous risk, even in late 1963, to keep pressuring the CIA to do to Castro what it could not. Halpern's answer was startling: If you want to understand Kennedy's recklessness, go find his Secret Service agents. I did just that, and eventually ended up getting four retired Secret Service agents who were assigned to Kennedy's personal detail—men who were willing to take a bullet for him—to talk about his recklessness about sex. They also agreed to talk on the record, despite the knowledge that doing so would surely lead to censure and worse from their fellow retired agents.

The Secret Service agents were a major positive for the book. There was an equally significant negative, one that began innocuously. In my years as a reporter, I had repeatedly been approached by those with a story that, so they would insist, I had to investigate. I cannot recall any story I wrote based on a walk-in. In the process, though, I got to know some fascinating people. One of them was a likable businessman named Hal Kass from Annapolis, Maryland, who had been swindled in a business deal that I was not interested in writing about. Hal took no offense at my lack of interest, and we occasionally shared a sandwich when he was in Washington. He was a collector of historical documents and, knowing I was at work on a book about Kennedy, told me about what was purported to be a cache of previously unknown Kennedy notes and memos that had been offered to him and other wealthy collectors by a broker representing Lawrence Cusack. I checked around and learned that Cusack, known to his friends as Lex, was the son of a prominent New York lawyer whose clients included the Archdiocese of New York and Gladys Baker Eley, the mother of Marilyn Monroe. Cusack worked as a paralegal in his father's firm. The Cusack papers were said to be full of devastating stuff, in Kennedy's handwriting, about the Mafia and womanizing, including back-and-forth exchanges with Marilyn Monroe. I was assured that the papers had been analyzed and authenticated by one of America's foremost handwriting experts on such material; that, I learned, was true. I had no idea at the time what a shell game the business of handwriting documentation was, and was delighted when the businessman agreed to put me in touch with Cusack and his broker. The initial batch of documents I was permitted to photocopy—it took months to get Cusack to allow it—made sense to me.

I had no hesitation about immediately sharing them with Mark Obenhaus, the documentary filmmaker. I had approached Mark about working together on a Kennedy film as soon as I made contact with the Secret Service agents and learned that a few of them were willing to talk about Kennedy on camera. The Cusack documents were an added bonus, pending verification, of course. More than a year later, the verification was still uncertain. I believed the documents were real, and so did Mark, to a lesser degree, but we were troubled by the fact that Cusack and the broker for the sale of the documents would conveniently manage to come up with more of them in response to the frequent questions we raised. All of this was done in total secrecy.

I continued to research and write my revisionist book on the Kennedys as Mark and I and his production crew—we were under contract for a two-hour documentary with ABC—filmed interviews all over America. We knew we had a great story with or without the Cusack papers. The Secret Service agents had told what they saw, and we had gone deep into the Bay of Pigs story, as seen from the point of view of those CIA participants who felt that Kennedy had betrayed them.

The Kennedy book was set for publication in the fall of 1997 by Little, Brown, and the advance sales were running very high, enough to justify a first printing of at least 350,000 copies, without any public knowledge of the Cusack papers. Mark and his staff and I continued to brood about them. We wanted to go public with them of course, but we had come to distrust the so-called handwriting authenticators. Obenhaus spent tens of thousands of dollars within a year on handwriting experts who repeatedly assured us that the Cusack documents were the real thing. The always careful Mark kept on looking and eventually was led to a retired FBI document expert named Jerry Richards who found anomalies in a few documents—overwriting and the like—that raised serious questions. At the same time, in the late summer of 1997, Edward Gray, the producer of the documentary, broke through. Ed's assignment included being in charge of vetting the papers, and he realized that two of the alleged Kennedy letters, dated in 1961 and 1962, included zip codes that did not exist at the time. Ed, while in college, had spent the summer of 1969 working for the post office and somehow correctly remembered that America's uniform five-digit zip code system went into effect across the nation in mid-1963.

That was it. The papers were fraudulent. The next step was to tell the senior executives at ABC, arrange for the network to alert the FBI, and then make public the existence of the papers and the pending criminal investigation of Cusack. (He was eventually found guilty in a New York federal court of thirteen counts of forgery and sentenced to ten years in jail.) Without the documents, my book and the documentary were full of new information and new insights into the Kennedy presidency. I wanted to do what I had done before when working with Obenhaus: write a piece for the *Times* about the paper fraud and how we finally unraveled it, but was persuaded instead to break the story of Cusack and his papers in an interview for the ABC-TV news show *20/20*. How naive I was. The ABC interview, as edited, hung me out to dry. The network executives had invested $3.5 million in the two-hour documentary on Kennedy, which was to be broadcast in prime time at the end of the year, and, as I could not imagine, they were terrified that ABC would be accused of having been taken in by the fake Kennedy papers. I initially had been fooled, I admitted on air, but the notion that it was part of the reporting process and the fact that there always was great uncertainty about the papers—especially by Obenhaus and his team, but also by me—was left, as the cliché has it, on the cutting room floor. It was all about me, the reporter who broke My Lai, being duped.

The ensuing scandal over the fake JFK papers, as the tabloids put it, sold a lot of books but left me an easy target for the many in America who doted on all things Kennedy. I was in a war with Camelot I did not want and could not win. Needless to say, the documentary, when aired on ABC, was not called *The Dark Side of Camelot* but *Dangerous World*.

While doing research on my Kennedy book, I learned that I, as well as many other journalists, had wronged Edward Korry, who served as the U.S. ambassador to Chile from 1967 to 1971. He emerged as one of the most outspoken critics of the socialist government put in place by Allende after his election as president in 1970. In late 1974, after my initial articles about the CIA's dirty role in Chile were published, he had been publicly accused, along with Richard Helms and two other State Department officials, of providing misleading testimony to a Senate committee. Korry, who retired from government service after leaving Chile, insisted at the time that he had no knowledge of any coup plotting and focused in his complaints on my *Times* stories. He had befriended Abe Rosenthal at some point in his career and took his complaints to him. I explained to Abe that I had written a story about a routine report by a Senate committee, one of many stories I wrote about Chile, and there was no reason to believe Korry was not linked to the CIA's anti-Allende plotting. I was very surprised to learn six years later that Korry, indeed, had not been trusted by the CIA station chief and was excluded from any knowledge of what became known as the station's Track Two plotting to undermine the Allende government. I called Rosenthal and told him that I, and the paper, had screwed Korry. Abe told me to write a story about it for the front page of the paper.

The twenty-three-hundred-word piece I did was held for a few weeks—Abe wanted it on page 1 and needed a quiet day to get it there—and published in early February 1981. Abe and I both felt we had done right by Korry. The reaction from our peers, however, was cynicism, highlighted by a *Time* essay titled "The 2,300-Word Times Correction." The notion that Abe and I and the *Times* had righted a wrong in such prominent fashion—something rare in the newspaper world—was not acknowledged. The published dispatch was far more than a mere correction; it was an essay explaining how a newspaper, relying on a congressional report, can get stories wrong. After reading the *Time* piece, Abe told me, "I'm never going to show my ass to them again." I was especially pissed because the magazine had the gall to wrongly declare that the information I had learned from internal CIA documents—all of which were highly classified—"had been kicking around for years." There was also a widely shared suggestion in the media, pushed by Korry for reasons I could not fathom, that I had told him I would write a correction only if he provided me with adverse information about Kissinger. Such stuff was published repeatedly in the mainstream media without one reporter calling me. If one had, I might have produced letters to me from Korry, urging me to come talk to him about Kissinger. His easily refuted insinuation was published as fact again and again without any question raised about Korry's acknowledgment that if his allegations were correct, he had succumbed to my blackmail.

My book, *The Dark Side of Camelot*, when published, was an immediate bestseller—but for all the wrong reasons. The new material I dug up about Jack Kennedy's advance knowledge of the Bay of Pigs invasion and his political use of that information caused nary a stir; the initial news stories focused on the fake documents that were not in the book and the Secret Service sex stuff. After the furor died down, I did an interview with *The Atlantic* magazine in which I finally found something good to say about the falsified Kennedy documents: "In a funny way I'm glad the . . . papers scandal happened. Given the pretty much universally hostile reception to my book, thank God I had those papers, because otherwise I would have been accused of falsifying everything. . . . I've been criticized for a lot of things I've written—My Lai, CIA stuff—but this is the first time I've been criticized for what I thought. . . . The bottom line is that I didn't publish them. I don't understand what's so bad about chasing a story, finding out it's not real, and saying so."

There were a few journalists who got it. In a lead piece for the *Times*'s Sunday Book Review, Tom Powers criticized me for what he called my "far-too-long romance" with the forgeries, and then went on to note that since the fakery did not get into the book, "a lot of other stuff did, and the question on the table is what to make of it." He added,

The first thing to be said about "The Dark Side of Camelot" is that it is a reporter's book, not a historian's. What's in it is mainly Hersh's. Again and again we are told that so-and-so "said in an interview for this book" or "told me" thus-and-such or that certain documents were "obtained for this book" and are here "published for the first time." The first half-dozen times this seems boast-ful and aggrandizing, but we soon grow used to the litany, and it becomes clear that Hersh has done his legwork; he is not trying to smuggle things in from other books. He tells us what he's found up front, making judgment easier for reviewers and blood enemies alike. The source notes at the back can be a little cumbersome, but compared with investigative reporters who provide no source notes whatever, Hersh is standing in the choir with Edward Gibbon.

It was comforting to put the Kennedy book behind me and return, happily, to the sanity of *The New Yorker.* Pat Crow had retired, and Tina Brown had been replaced by David Remnick, a former *Washington Post* correspondent whom I did not know. Esther Newberg was a friend of David's, and years earlier she had sent me advance galleys of *Lenin's Tomb,* his Pulitzer Prize–winning 1993 book on the last days of the Soviet empire. It was nonfiction writing at its best, as I said in a jacket comment, and David's appointment as editor seemed like a perfect fit. He was as welcoming to me as anyone could be, and off we went.

My new editor was John Bennet, who, like all editors at the maga-zine at the time, saw his mission as understanding what the reporter was trying to say and helping him to say it. My first major article in the Remnick era was published in late 1998 and picked up where I had left off—challenging the public rationale for a Clinton administra-tion Tomahawk missile attack in the Middle East. The White House's target this time was an alleged pharmaceutical plant on the outskirts of Khartoum, the capital of Sudan, that the White House claimed had the capacity to manufacture chemical warfare agents as well as inexpensive generic medicines vitally needed by the local population. Clinton announced the bombing while on vacation in August 1998 in Martha's Vineyard. His decision came three days after he had finished testifying before a federal grand jury about his involvement with Mon-ica Lewinsky. He depicted the targeted plant as an "imminent threat" to American national security.

Nearly all of the senior military and intelligence officials I knew had stayed on the job during the four years I wrestled with the Kennedy myth, and to a man they were troubled by Clinton's decision to bomb. We use the word "sources" in the newspaper world to describe those who provide needed information, but it's a totally inadequate word. I shared 6:00 a.m. breakfasts in diners and other offbeat places with my sources, and many lunches and dinners with them when they were on duty outside Washington. Some meetings took place overseas. These insiders quickly became more than sources; they were friends and stayed friends after they left government.

As in the 1993 bombing attack on Baghdad, there were many questions about the intelligence linking the pharmaceutical plant, one of very few in Sudan, to the production of chemical warfare agents. There also were equally serious questions about how the Clinton White House prepared for the mission. Most significant, four members of the Joint Chiefs of Staff had been excluded from the attack planning until the last moment. Only army general Hugh Shelton, the chairman of the Joint Chiefs, had been involved in the operation from its inception, and I learned he had been instructed by Sandy Berger, Clinton's national security adviser, not to brief the chiefs on the mission, nor was he to involve the Defense Intelligence Agency in the planning. The operation was directed by Berger, and Berger was dealing back channel throughout the process with a lower-ranking admiral who, to the surprise of few in the Pentagon, was awarded at the end of the Clinton years with a promotion and a choice assignment as an overseas commander in chief.

The process reeked, and many senior officers and officials in the military and intelligence community understood that the ambitious Berger, who was expected to be named Clinton's chief of staff before the President's second term came to an end, was doing in Khartoum exactly what the President wanted. It was a *Wag the Dog* scenario, and I ended my piece by quoting a former high-level State Department official as explaining that Clinton was preoccupied at the time by his personal and professional problems stemming from his sexual relationship with Lewinsky, which began when she was a White House intern. "Survival is his most important issue," I quoted the former official as saying of the President. "It's always on his mind. If Clinton was not in all this trouble, he wouldn't have done it"—authorized the

Tomahawk raid. "He's too smart." Berger refused to see me while I was reporting the story, despite many entreaties.

Remnick did what every good editor would do as the story worked its way through the bureaucracy. He consulted with the fact-checkers— who did their work totally isolated from me—and, much to his credit, asked a lot of questions on the proofs. If he got heat from the White House after the story was published, he did not share it with me.

I turned from Sudan to Israel and wrote a piece in early 1999 reflecting the negative view of the American intelligence community about Clinton's likely decision to accede to Israeli demands that Jonathan Pollard be pardoned. Pollard was a Jewish navy intelligence official who had been caught spying for Israel in 1985 and subsequently given a life sentence. Clinton's anticipated pardon triggered threats of wholesale high-level Pentagon and CIA resignations. The obvious question was, why such rancor from the men and women at the top of the intelligence food chain?

Soon after I began asking questions, I was invited by a senior intelligence official to come have a chat at CIA headquarters. I had done interviews there before, but always at my insistence. (George Tenet was then the CIA director, but the invitation did not come from him.) When I arrived, I was taken into a small conference room on the seventh floor, where Tenet had his office, by an official I knew only by reputation; we had never talked, not for my want of trying. I was asked how I liked my coffee and told to take a seat. My host returned with coffee and a bound volume, handed both to me, said the equivalent of "Have fun," and walked out.

The volume included material that had been given under seal to the federal judge during Pollard's trial. It was a summary of many of the documents that Pollard was known to have illegally obtained from various classified libraries in Washington and delivered—that is, presumably delivered—to his Israeli handlers. It was stunning to me, because the documents made clear that much of Pollard's thievery dealt with how America spied on its greatest adversary—the Soviet Union. Spying on America seemed to be little more than an afterthought, or footnote, to the assignments given Pollard by his Israeli handler. As I wrote, the thrust of the documents I was reading did not deal primarily with the product of American intelligence—assessments and estimates—but instead focused on how America learned what it did, the data known in the intelligence community as "sources and methods." One series of papers obtained by Pollard revealed how a U.S. Navy signals attachment unit undercover in the Middle East tracked Russian nuclear submarines as they moved underwater into the Mediterranean Sea through the Strait of Gibraltar. Another described the frequencies at which America picked up Russian signals. Another document depicted details about a ten-volume American manual known as RASIN, an acronym for radio-signal notation. The manual, which I had no idea existed, listed the physical parameters of every known signal of friend and foe. "It's the bible," I quoted one NSA veteran as explaining to me. "It tells how we collect signals anywhere in the world."

I knew the people to see in order to verify the gist of what I had been allowed to review, but I was very ambivalent about being in the unfamiliar position of carrying water for the American intelligence community. I, who had worked so hard in my career to learn the secrets, had been handed the secrets. The senior official who led me to the water never talked to me again, although I tried for years to get him to do so. I was able to verify the information that had been thrown at me, and I also took care, as I liked to believe those who gave me the material assumed I would, not to go too far in what I made public. I had been given an insight into the unique documents obtained by Pollard and passed on, in most cases, to the Israelis. Each page was lathered with markings depicting the extreme secrecy of the stuff I was reading.

The files I saw also made clear that the men and women running American intelligence believed that the Israeli government was trading Pollard's information to Moscow in exchange for the emigration of Soviet Jews with skills and expertise needed by Israel. That belief has never been confirmed, but it was spread throughout the top secret assessments I saw.

I went back to writing stories I wanted to write and told of American attempts to interfere with, and covertly take over, a series of highly productive intelligence operations conducted in the late 1990s by the UN's Special Commission for Iraq, known as UNSCOM. The UN team's mission was to determine whether any weapons of mass destruction, nuclear or chemical, remained in Saddam's arsenal. The contrary American goal was to pretend to share the UN's interest in any information about Saddam's weaponry while actually assembling data that would help facilitate the assassination of the Iraqi leader. The cover headline for the piece, approved by Remnick, was "Saddam's Best Friend: How the C.I.A. Made It a Lot Easier for the Iraqi Leader to Rearm." It felt good to be once again writing a story my government did not want known. I had the best job in the world. I was working for a wonderful magazine, with sophisticated and fearless editors with the highest of standards, and I was free to investigate whatever seemed worthy, with the support and approval of Remnick.

I had been told repeatedly by those who worked for him of the aberrant behavior of Barry McCaffrey, a hard-charging and photogenic general who had led an army division in the 1991 Gulf War and retired from the military in 1996 after being named director of the White House Office of National Drug Control Policy, a.k.a. the drug czar, by Bill Clinton. McCaffrey's mercurial behavior continued in the White House. In late 1999, I shared an early morning coffee with a four-star general—who was itching to start his five-mile morning run—and talked about looking into McCaffrey's conduct as a civilian official. My friend, who also served as a division commander in the 1991 war, told me that the real story had to do with McCaffrey's decision to authorize and carry out a murderous surprise attack on a retreating Iraqi tank battalion after that war had ended—after the Iraqis had been assured of safe passage from the front near Kuwait back to Baghdad.

It took months and hundreds of interviews, nearly all of them on the record, before I felt I had an unimpeachable story. I had transcripts of radio calls from one headquarters to another questioning the attack as it was ongoing, and I felt I had devastating comments from a dozen of McCaffrey's fellow generals. Remnick, who was closely involved in the six-month inquiry, urged me to get as many critics of McCaffrey on the record as possible, which reflected a solid editorial instinct. I spent weeks negotiating watered-down on-the-record statements from McCaffrey's peers and superiors in the army, and their criticisms, no matter how reserved, added to a smarmy portrait of a general determined to make his mark in the desert, just as one of McCaffrey's heroes, German general Erwin Rommel, had done in North Africa in 1942.

The twenty-four-thousand-word article, titled "Overwhelming Force," was in the final stage of fact-checking when McCaffrey, who had consistently refused to talk to me and discouraged all of his peers he could from doing so, launched a preemptory attack. He issued a statement, through a lawyer, personally attacking me and complaining that I was conducting "defamatory" interviews out of "personal malice." The tactic worked; many in the media wrote about his attacks, which came weeks before my article was published.

My piece got plenty of attention, but did not provoke an official review of the incident. The 1991 victory over Saddam Hussein was seen as an end to the stigma of defeat that had haunted the American military since the end of the Vietnam War, and there was no official incentive to mar that picture. McCaffrey did not sue, despite his vitriolic complaints, and I was left with the impression that America did not care about the unnecessary killing of Iraqi prisoners or Iraqi soldiers heading home on a path fixed by an end-of-the-war peace agreement. It was a reminder of the Vietnam War's MGR, for Mere Gook Rule: If it's a murdered or raped gook, there is no crime. (I had learned a domestic version of that rule decades earlier while covering a fire that killed at least five in Chicago's black ghetto for the City News Bureau.)

My last story for Remnick before 9/11 dealt with a series of corrupt activities by Mobil Oil, an American giant, after the collapse of communism in the Soviet Union. Oil was to be had at ridiculously low prices per barrel in those chaotic days, as long as major bribes were given to those former Soviet officials, many of whom had been intelligence operatives, who were in the process of seizing billions of dollars in assets. The complicated story took months to edit and brought on threatened lawsuits by many of the most prominent law firms in New York, all of whom had been retained by Mobil and other involved entities. I remember one meeting at which the newly appointed general counsel for the magazine declared, plaintively, that he found it difficult to believe that a major corporation such as Mobil could operate as far outside the law as I was alleging. I, in despair about such comments, walked over to him, patted him on the cheek, and said, "You're such a nice boy." (The lawyer turned out to be a strong advocate for getting difficult-to-report stories into the magazine.) Remnick held firm, though his worry was eased by a number of modifications I made to the story, pursuant to legal advice. The complicated piece, published in July 2001, was a bitch to read, full of unfamiliar business transactions and many foreign names, but it attracted the attention of the federal government, which immediately opened an inquiry into the wrongdoing outlined in the piece.

For all its difficulty, and its lack of pizzazz, the article, titled "The Price of Oil," brought me to the attention of many oil traders and energy experts in Europe and the Middle East and made what I had to do after 9/11 much easier.

· NINETEEN ·

America's War on Terror

I was at home on the morning of September 11, 2001, sharing the same fears and anxieties as most Americans, after the first tower was struck. The call came, as I sensed it would, even before the second tower was hit. I don't remember David's exact words, but the message was simple: "You are now permanently assigned to the biggest story of your career." He was not talking about New York City's response to the attacks—the next issue of the magazine would be devoted to that—but he was relying on me to try to answer the classic questions editors pose in such times: who, what, and why?

I had an anxious flashback to that moment in late 1972 at the *Times* when Abe Rosenthal insisted that I stop reporting on what I knew well, the Vietnam War, and delve into Watergate. Abe had the same confidence in me as did David, but this assignment was far more challenging. Watergate was an in-house Washington story, and I knew I had a chance to get to some of the players. The New York attack seemed far more challenging: I had never explicitly covered Islamic terrorism, nor had I traveled to Afghanistan, where Osama bin Laden had his headquarters. On the other hand, I had written about Pakistan for *The New Yorker* and understood that the Pakistani intelligence service, the ISI, for Inter-Services Intelligence, had a profound, if murky, role inside Afghanistan.

I also knew that 9/11 was going to be a once-in-a-lifetime story that would require my developing new sources in Washington and the Middle East. I had done it many times before, so I wasn't surprised to be told that some inside *The New York Times*, among them Tom Friedman, were suggesting that I be immediately rehired. I did get a telephone message from a senior editor at the paper who obviously was ambivalent about once again dealing with me. I did not return the call and heard no more. It did not matter, because I was Remnick's man.

I began my new assignment by reading as much as I could absorb about the region in a few weeks as well as talking to those I knew inside the U.S. State Department and intelligence community who had served in South Asia; my goal was to get a basic understanding about Afghanistan, Pakistan, and international terrorism. I tracked down the few scholars in America who understood the ways of the Taliban, whose members were Pashtuns, the largest ethnic group in Afghanistan. It was unnerving to learn that revenge in Pashtun culture did not call for an immediate response, but could come months, and even years, after a violent act against a family member. I was convinced that George W. Bush and Dick Cheney would respond violently in Afghanistan not only against bin Laden but also against his hosts, the Taliban, without having any idea of the long-term consequences of their decision.

My reporting on Jonathan Pollard and on the 1998 raid on the pharmaceutical plant in Khartoum led me to a number of senior FBI officials, and I risked an early morning call at home to one of them a few days after 9/11. I had always tried to be as open and straightforward with senior intelligence officials as possible, and the good ones—there are many good ones who deserved my respect—usually responded in kind. Things were hectic, of course, the official said, but one thing seemed clear to him and his colleagues: The nineteen suicide bombers, whether controlled by bin Laden or not, were not the leading edge, as many initially feared, of what would be a wave of terror inside America. They were the equivalent, he said, of a pickup basketball team that made it to the Final Four or a weekend soccer team that got to the World Cup. The American intelligence community might never be able to learn the whole story of the attack, he said, but he was con-

vinced that the terrorists had been aided by the chronic lack of cooperation among the various intelligence services.

I set up meetings with some of those in and out of the CIA who had
helped me on stories going back to the Vietnam War; former agents
have always been able to gather amazing information from their onetime colleagues. I was eventually invited to join a group of operatives
at a post-9/11 lunch at a Chinese restaurant in suburban Virginia. The
discord was stunning as complaint after complaint was made about the
Agency's increasingly timid and rigid bureaucracy, the lack of freedom
to maneuver, and budget restrictions. In their view, the CIA's failure
to detect the plot in advance was not the fault of the guys in the clandestine service but rather of the Agency's vacillating leadership. The
talk eventually turned to the CIA's long-standing belief that its agents
were superior to the others in the intelligence community. With that,
I turned to an old friend, who had been a station chief in the Middle
East and knew far more about terrorism than I did, and asked why,
even after 9/11, there was so much contempt for the FBI. His answer
stunned me. "Don't you get it, Sy? The FBI catches bank robbers. We
rob banks." My friend went on: "And the NSA? Do you really expect
me to talk to dweebs with protractors in their pockets who are always
looking down at their brown shoes?" I was both shocked and bemused
by his cynicism and could not help but laugh at his mention of NSA
brown shoes.

I left the lunch convinced that total sharing of intelligence was
never going to happen—even after 9/11. The nineteen suicide bombers
had succeeded perhaps because of a culture war inside the intelligence
community.

The New Yorker was eager for any story relevant to 9/11, and my
immediate goal was to publish a detailed story on what had gone
wrong—why America had missed the nineteen hijackers who, as we
were learning day by day, had been far from discreet as they prepared
for the 9/11 attack. I was hunting for any inside information and intelligence assessments I could get my hands on: My thought was to find
a way to let those on the inside know I could be trusted to verify and
accurately describe even the most highly classified information and not
leave a trail that could point to sources. A similar process had worked

for me at the AP and the *Times*, because insiders with differing points of view about the Vietnam War or CIA activities saw me as a conduit to have their say without any risk. So, in the first few months after 9/11, I was able to write about NSA intercepts that showed bitter infighting among the royal family in Saudi Arabia over money;* provided new intelligence about Pakistan's emerging nuclear arsenal and its continual breach with India; and told of American fears about Iran and the possible decision of the Shiite leadership there to go nuclear, in part as a counter to the Pakistani threat. My reportage did not deal directly with 9/11, but it delineated other risks that America was facing in the region. My pieces in those early post-9/11 days were checked to death; Remnick made sure the most obsessive of the obsessive *New Yorker* fact-checkers were on the case.

Bush and Cheney, as expected, went to war in Afghanistan in early October. In a piece a few weeks later I revealed that twelve members of the army's secretive Delta Force had been injured, some seriously, as a result of a stupid decision by General Tommy Franks, the American commander in charge of the war. The special ops soldiers, moving at night and sleeping in foxholes during the day, were assigned to capture or kill a major Taliban leader and were nearing his well-protected home when Franks ordered Army Rangers and helicopters to provide backup. The show of force tipped off the Taliban that a raid was imminent, and the Delta Force soldiers were discovered and ambushed. It was, as one member of the Joint Special Operations Command told me, "a total goat fuck." The easy-to-understand story made headlines, and the fact that many of the army's best had been injured, some seriously, was predictably denied and denounced on the Sunday morning news shows by General Franks, Secretary of Defense Donald Rumsfeld, and

---

* The NSA material I obtained depicted enormous hypocrisy among the royal family, with widespread sexual partying and much talk about financial corruption and arguments about which prince would get which percentage of bribery proceeds from the state's many billion-dollar purchases of arms. The mainstream media ignored the story, although I named names, but financier George Soros did not. He invited me to dinner at his apartment in New York to talk more about Saudi Arabia. When I declined, he offered to pay a huge contribution to a public interest group whose director, Morton Abramowitz, was a retired diplomat, if I changed my mind. In his career, Mort had directed the State Department's office of intelligence and also served as the U.S. ambassador to Thailand and Turkey. He was a longtime friend of mine, and I felt I had no choice but to go. Much of the talk dealt with future oil prices, about which I cared not a bit.

Condoleezza Rice, the national security adviser. That afternoon I was called at home by a four-star officer who offered to provide me with a highly classified satellite photo showing the boot and part of a severed leg of one of those wounded. I said no to his offer but assured him that I and many of my colleagues knew what a disaster General Franks was proving to be when it came to special operations. I was contacted later by a second official with direct ties to the Special Forces Command who was offended by the Bush administration's constant public lying. I stayed in touch, off and on, with those two men over the next fifteen years.

I was troubled still by the failure of the major media to follow up on my stories, often dealing with the misuse of intelligence, as the American War on Terror intensified. After one such piece was published, James Risen, one of the best investigative reporters in the Washington bureau of the *Times*, telephoned me at home one night to compliment me on the piece and say that he and a few other reporters had been summoned to the office to try to match it. They found no one in the Bush administration willing or knowledgeable enough to help them do so, Risen said, with a laugh, and everyone had been told to go home. There would be no mention of the *New Yorker* story in the paper the next morning. "We couldn't match it," Risen added, "and so we're going to ignore it." I could not understand such thinking. During Watergate, Bob Woodward and I, aware that the story transcended competitiveness, had happily fed off each other's work, as well as the reporting of the *Los Angeles Times* and others, and did our best to add to what had been published.

Ironically, the *Times*, while seemingly continuing to ignore my reporting, saw fit late in 2001 to publish a complimentary feature piece about what was described as the renewal of a rivalry between me and Woodward that began during Watergate. "Some of the most startling and controversial information to emerge from the crisis has appeared under their bylines," the newspaper wrote, adding that three decades "after they battled each other in the unraveling of the Watergate scandal . . . they are at it again." Woodward was depicted as "polished, smooth, punctilious." I was "scruffy, scrappy, stubborn, loud. . . . His charm is his lack of it." Lack of charm and being scruffy, it seems, were the key to success in Washington—lots of reading, lots of interview-ing, a few gutsy sources, not as much.

By early 2002, I was getting information from inside the White House and inside one of the major military commands, and protect-ing the sources of my information became more complex as Cheney's authority grew. As usual, I was learning things I could not write at the time, lest the source, no matter how well disguised, become known to some on the inside. I knew, for example, that a decision had been made in late 2001—driven by neoconservative Republicans in and out of the government—to pull many special operations troops from Afghani-stan, and from the hunt for bin Laden, in order to begin building up toward an all-out invasion of Iraq. The argument for doing so was that Saddam Hussein posed a more immediate threat because he had the capability to make the bomb. That was total nonsense. I knew from my earlier reporting on UNSCOM, the United Nations team whose mis-sion had been to root out any weapons of mass destruction in Iraq, that the 1991 American bombing in the First Gulf War had demolished the Iraqi nuclear weapons infrastructure, which had not been rebuilt. For the next fifteen months—until America began the Second Gulf War in March 2003—I wrote again and again about the distortion of intel-ligence and official lying about weapons of mass destruction (WMDs) in Iraq that paved the way for the war.

I began to comprehend that eight or nine neoconservatives who were political outsiders in the Clinton years had essentially overthrown the government of the United States—with ease. It was stunning to realize how fragile our Constitution was. The intellectual leaders of the group—Dick Cheney, Paul Wolfowitz, and Richard Perle—had not hidden their ideology and their belief in the power of the executive but depicted themselves in public with a great calmness and a self-assurance that masked their radicalism. I had spent many hours after 9/11 in conversations with Perle that, luckily for me, helped me under-stand what was coming. (Perle and I had been chatting about policy since the early 1980s, but he broke off relations in 2003 over an article I did for *The New Yorker* linking him, a fervent supporter of Israel, to a series of meetings with Saudi businessmen in an attempt to land a multibillion-dollar contract from Saudi Arabia. Perle responded by publicly threatening to sue me and characterizing me as a newspaper terrorist. He did not sue.)

Meanwhile, Cheney had emerged as a leader of the neocon pack. From 9/11 on he did all he could to undermine congressional oversight. I learned a great deal from the inside about his primacy in the White House, but once again I was limited in what I would write for fear of betraying my sources. It was a burden I felt keenly. It was far more difficult after 9/11 to communicate with my contacts on the inside who had access to many of the secrets and were not afraid to talk about those operations, planned or ongoing—and only those operations— that were contrary to American values, or what was left of them. I came to understand that Cheney's goal was to run his most important military and intelligence operations with as little congressional knowledge, and interference, as possible. It was fascinating and important to learn what I did about Cheney's constant accumulation of power and authority as vice president, but it was impossible to even begin to verify the information without running the risk that Cheney would learn of my questioning and have a good idea from whom I was getting the information.

I was learning in detail about what amounted to a massively cynical and perhaps unconstitutional enterprise emanating out of the White House, but could tell no one about it. Maybe there would be a book in another decade, I thought. In the short run, however, what I had been told, and what I believed, darkened my view of the Bush/Cheney White House and convinced me that, as in Watergate, the worst was yet to come.

There was some tension between Remnick and me in the months before the invasion of Iraq. David saw the threatened American invasion as providing the Bush administration with a chance, as he wrote in the magazine at the time, to press "the case for peace and political reform in the Middle East." I thought he was kidding himself; the prospects for future peace or political reform in Iraq, given the extreme politics of those running the war, were nil. I'm sure David also disagreed with my skepticism about the possibility of any weapons of mass destruction remaining in the Iraqi arsenal. To his credit, David did not stop me from writing what my inside sources were telling me—that the Bush administration was simply making up such intelligence—but David did insist that I note in each story that there remained a possibility that Saddam did indeed have weapons of mass destruction.

The war went badly, as those I knew on the inside were convinced it would—given the American lack of understanding about the power structure in Iraq—and within months the quick and easy American victory became a contested occupation, with resistance growing daily. The American response was more violence, including an escalation in assassination, imprisonment, and torture. I was told again and again in those early days by involved officials who insisted on not being named that there was a widespread understanding that those who died in interrogation were not to be buried—lest the bodies be disinterred later—but had to be destroyed by acid and other means. It would be years, given the possibility that Cheney would begin a witch hunt for my sources, before I felt comfortable writing as much in print.

Over the years, the extent of Cheney's contempt for congressional oversight also became known to a few senior Democratic members of the House Appropriations Committee, among them David Obey of Wisconsin, the committee chairman, and John Murtha of Pennsylvania, a longtime member who, as a former marine, was close to the Pentagon's military leadership. Obey and Murtha were members of a special four-man intelligence subcommittee—the other two members were Republicans who usually did Cheney's bidding—that was to be briefed on all CIA covert operations. The two Democrats did not get along, and they rarely talked. I decided to share what I had been learning about Cheney's off-the-books operations with Murtha and realized that he knew much more than I did about them and was equally alarmed. My talks with Murtha became known to Obey, and I thought it important to relay to him some of the inside information that Murtha was telling me. It also led the very taciturn Obey to develop trust in me. At a later point, Obey told me, he had gone to see Cheney and David Addington, the vice president's counsel, and told them they were violating the Constitution by conducting their off-the-books operations without any congressional authorization and funding. The answer was, in essence, that President Bush had the authority to do whatever he deemed necessary in wartime. The specific message he got from the two men, Obey told me, was "If you don't like what we're doing, go into federal court and sue us."

It was confidential information I could not share with anyone and could not put into the magazine because it would suggest, whether accurate or not, where I had been getting some of the information I published on covert CIA operations. (Murtha passed away in 2010, and Obey retired in 2011 after more than forty years in Congress.)

A few months after the invasion of Iraq, during an interview overseas with a general who was director of a foreign intelligence service, I was provided with a copy of a Republican neocon plan for American dominance in the Middle East. The general was an American ally, but one who was very rattled by the Bush/Cheney aggression. I was told that the document leaked to me initially had been obtained by someone in the local CIA station. There was reason to be rattled: The document declared that the war to reshape the Middle East had to begin "with the assault on Iraq. The fundamental reason for this . . . is that the war will start making the U.S. the hegemon of the Middle East. The correlative reason is to make the region feel in its bones, as it were, the seriousness of American intent and determination." Victory in Iraq would lead to an ultimatum to Damascus, the "defanging" of Iran, Hezbollah, Hamas, and Arafat's Palestine Liberation Organization, and other anti-Israeli groups. America's enemies must understand that "they are fighting for their life: *Pax Americana* is on its way, which implies their annihilation." I and the foreign general agreed that America's neocons were a menace to civilization.

Donald Rumsfeld also was infected with neocon fantasy. Turkey had refused to permit America's Fourth Division to join the attack of Iraq from its territory, and the division, with its twenty-five thousand men and women, did not arrive in force inside Iraq until mid-April, when the initial fighting was essentially over. I learned then that Rumsfeld had asked the American military command in Stuttgart, Germany, which had responsibility for monitoring Europe, including Syria and Lebanon, to begin drawing up an operational plan for an invasion of Syria. A young general assigned to the task refused to do so, thereby winning applause from my friends on the inside and risking his career. The plan was seen by those I knew as especially bizarre because Bashar

Assad, the ruler of secular Syria, had responded to 9/11 by sharing with the CIA hundreds of his country's most sensitive intelligence files on the Muslim Brotherhood in Hamburg, where much of the planning for 9/11 was carried out. (I had written about Assad's action in *The New Yorker* in July 2003.) Rumsfeld eventually came to his senses and backed down, I was told, but not before demanding that all military planning for Syria and Lebanon be transferred to America's Central Command, headquartered at MacDill Air Force Base in Tampa, Florida, and led by the more accommodating Tommy Franks.*

I knew nothing of Rumsfeld's retreat when I hurriedly flew to Damascus and arranged an interview with Muṣṭafa Tlass, Syria's defense minister, who had been on the job for nearly three decades. Tlass invited me to dinner at his spacious home and afterward walked me down to his basement to show me—bizarrely—his collection of pornography, much of it focused on Gina Lollobrigida, a voluptuous Italian actress. Then it was time for a serious talk. I told Tlass, whose English was fluent, that there was a possibility, as he surely knew, that Rumsfeld would order the Fourth Division, then encamped close to the Iraq-Syria border, to drive across the desert to Damascus. What would you do? I asked. He shrugged. I asked if Syria would unleash its chemical warfare arsenal against the Americans. "Those things?" he asked with obvious contempt. "If we used them, America would incinerate us [by responding with nuclear weapons] and they would be within their right to do so." Tlass added that Syria's chemical arsenal had been the brainchild of Hafez Assad, Bashar's father, who had died

---

* Rumsfeld was charming and likable and became a hero of sorts to the Pentagon press corps, and to much of America, in the early days of the war. He was having fun at press briefings with his laughing denials of my early, and negative, stories about the conduct of the war while privately sending messages to his staff, some of which I obtained, raising questions about the honesty of General Franks. Robert Gallucci, who had a long career as a government arms control expert before becoming director of the School of Foreign Service at Georgetown University, told me of a Pentagon meeting with Rumsfeld at the time of a Middle East crisis in 1983. The meeting was attended by the Joint Chiefs of Staff and senior State Department officials; Gallucci was there as a deputy to his boss at State. Rumsfeld, then serving as a special envoy, outlined a diplomatic approach he thought would resolve the problem, if it was backed up by a display of American military might. He asked for comment and none was forthcoming. Gallucci finally asked Rumsfeld why he thought his approach would work, since the same concept had not worked in an earlier, similar crisis. Rumsfeld stared at him and said, loudly, "Out." Gallucci was stunned and looked at his boss, who looked away. Rumsfeld again said, "Out." Gallucci got up and walked to the door. As he did, Rumsfeld added, "I will not tolerate anyone who is not a team player."

in 2000 and who had envisioned them as a deterrent against the growing Israeli nuclear arsenal. They were useless as a deterrent, expensive, and hard to maintain, Tlass said. Okay, I said, if you did not have a deterrent, what would you do? "Let them come to Damascus," Tlass said, "and we will see what happens." He was talking about protracted guerrilla war. I returned to Washington and told my American military friends about the different approach to war of a Middle Eastern defense minister whose nation had been in a state of perpetual struggle for decades.

I wrote a bit about my evening with Tlass for *The New Yorker* but did not mention the courageous young general. A public account of what took place might cost the general his career, and I knew that keeping an officer with his integrity on the job was more important than a few lines in an article.

The one story that broke through, in terms of widespread media coverage, was my reporting on the Abu Ghraib prison and the sexual abuse there of young male prisoners. I had been tracking America's increasingly violent behavior in what had become a war of occupation in which al-Qaeda, with the support of many disaffected former Iraqi military officers, was creating chaos with hit-and-run ambushes. The brutality of American military prisons was far from a secret in the spring of 2004, when the first of three articles I wrote about Abu Ghraib was published; Amnesty International and Human Rights Watch had put out devastating reports on prisons in Iraq that received little attention. I had learned all I needed to know about Abu Ghraib the previous Christmas when I spent three days in a hotel in Damascus with a former Iraqi air force major general.

The Iraqi army had been banned, as had the Baath Party, and most of the Iraqi generals who did not flee the country or join the resistance had been interrogated by the American command and, in some cases, jailed; others were recruited to work with U.S.-supported militias in the fight against the growing insurgency. The air force general had escaped that fate and was quietly minding his business in the first months after the American invasion, making a meager living selling vegetables and fruits from his garden. He was fluent in English and had been assigned while on active duty in the 1990s to monitor the operations of the UNSCOM team. He became trusted and respected by the UN inspectors for his integrity. When Baghdad fell, he reached out to former UN members, including Scott Ritter, a former marine major who had led many inspections of suspected WMD sites in the 1990s. Ritter, who created controversy after 9/11 by publicly insisting that Iraq had no nuclear weapons, introduced me to the general via Gmail—the internet was up and running in the first months after the American invasion—and we agreed to meet in Damascus, when it was safe for him to make the drive by taxi.

The general had sad tales, mostly secondhand, of the horrors of the American occupation, beginning with the American GIs who went on house raids and repeatedly stole money—many Iraqis kept their savings in hundred-dollar bills—and other valuables. He told of U.S. sergeants who made arrests and demanded cash to free those arrested, and senior American officers who were demanding kickbacks on the many contracts being awarded to local and foreign contractors. In his telling, Iraqi interpreters working for American combat units were constantly abusing prisoners and constantly extorting money from fellow citizens by threatening to tell Americans they were collaborating with the enemy. His most distressing comments, in terms of direct knowledge, were about the American-run prisons and the incessant torture and occasional murder that took place there. The worst was Abu Ghraib, he said, where women prisoners were spied on and assaulted by American and Iraqi guards to the point where they would write to their fathers and brothers and beg them to come kill them in jail because they had been dishonored by American and Iraqi prison guards.

Much of what he told me was impossible to confirm without being in Iraq and, in some cases, hard to credit. But the words about Abu Ghraib were reflected in those pretty much ignored reports by the various human rights groups; his account also smelled right. A few months later I learned that photos depicting some astonishing sexual abuse of male prisoners were floating around, and some were in the possession of *60 Minutes*, the CBS news show. I also learned that a few GIs who were assigned there as prison guards were being prosecuted. The photos were said to show naked young male prisoners being forced to masturbate as female prison guards watched. The American military and the CIA had become desperate for reliable inside intelligence about future plans, and one scheme, so I had been told, was to grant early release to a few carefully vetted young male prisoners with the understanding that they, in return, would join the resistance and become informants on future attack planning. I wondered if the idea of converting some male prisoners into intelligence assets had somehow morphed into the sexual depravation shown in the photos. Those prisoners who had refused to become spies for the U.S. military might think differently if the military had photos of their masturbation in front of women. Nothing would be more shameful to a male in the Middle East. While researching the Abu Ghraib story, I was told, but could not confirm, that sexual extortion had been tried by the Israelis in an effort to get Palestinian prisoners to agree to join Hamas and similar radical groups and to spy on them.

I eventually got the names of a few American prison guards who were in trouble, learned who their lawyers were, and went to work. I soon had copies of the photographs, including some not in the possession of 60 Minutes, but I had managed to obtain something far more important—an internal report of the criminal goings-on at the prison that had been written by an army major general named Antonio Taguba. The detailed report was as incendiary as the photos. I learned that the senior executives at CBS were extremely skittish about broadcasting the photos, after being urged by the Bush administration not to do so. I convinced a skeptical Remnick that there was no need for our magazine to scoop 60 Minutes on its own story; an airing of the photos by the network would provide millions of dollars of free publicity for The New Yorker once we published the Taguba report. I sensed it would be easy to resolve the executive anxiety at CBS. I telephoned Mary Mapes, the CBS producer on the story, at her home in Texas and told her I had both the photos they had and a report they did not have and if CBS did not run the photos the next week—60 Minutes aired Sundays and Thursdays in those days—I would have no choice but to write about the network's continuing censorship in The New Yorker. I knew Mapes hated the extensive censorship at CBS. The photos aired Thursday, and, to my amusement, Dan Rather, the anchor for the show, who I knew had also been fighting to get the story on the air, began his report by stating that CBS was showing the photos only after learning other media—he did not say *The New Yorker*—had the story. It wasn't hard to guess that he had been ordered to make such an asinine excuse for an important news story.

It worked out beautifully. There was no way the mainstream media could ignore the report Taguba had written. Of course my old newspaper tried to avoid having to quote and give credit to another publication; Jeff Gerth was told to give me a call when *The New Yorker* came out and ask if I would give a copy of the report to the *Times*. We both laughed at the silliness of the request.

The *New Yorker* story was major news, and I was flooded with interview requests, and did many—it was good for the magazine and good for me—but I knew there was more to do.* The contempt GIs had for prisoners, and the notion that they could do what they wished, stemmed from the top. I said as much in one national radio interview and added, totally spur of the moment, that if anyone listening knew more about the prison they could call me, and quickly rattled off my office telephone number. I had no idea why I went so far, and feared that I would be flooded with callers trying to sell me magazine subscriptions and the like. I instead got a call from the mother of one of the soldiers, a young woman, who had been involved in the abuse. I returned the call and went immediately to see her. She had telephoned me out of desperation. Her young, vibrant daughter, in the army reserve, had been assigned to a military police unit at Abu Ghraib and returned from the war zone totally changed. She was depressed and disconso-

---

* I had been unable to find General Taguba before writing the first Abu Ghraib dispatch, and I did not track him down for two years. Taguba told me then that Rumsfeld seemed convinced that he had leaked his report to me. The general said he was summoned to a meeting with the defense secretary a week after the report became public and was greeted with sarcasm and scorn. "Here . . . comes . . . that *famous* General Taguba—of the Taguba report," Rumsfeld said, mockingly, in front of the senior generals of the army. His fast-rising career was cut short after that meeting, Taguba said, and he was eventually forced to retire with no further promotion. He and I have talked many times since about war crimes and torture—we still share lunch every few months—and his honesty is breathtaking. He told me, with much bitterness, of a limousine ride he shared in the aftermath of Abu Ghraib with an anxious General John Abizaid, then commanding the floundering war in Iraq. Abizaid rolled up the glass separating the two of them from the driver and warned Taguba that he was going too far and too deep in his inquiry. "You and your report will be investigated." "I'd been in the army thirty-two years by then, and it was the first time I thought I was in the Mafia," Taguba said.

late; newly married before going overseas, she left her husband, moved away from the family, and took a night job. No one could figure what was going on. The mother read the Abu Ghraib story in a local newspaper and confronted her daughter with the story. The daughter took a look and slammed the door. At that point, the mother remembered she had given her daughter a portable computer before she deployed to Iraq; the goal was to make it easier for the two of them to stay in touch. The computer had been left at home. The mother decided after reading about Abu Ghraib to take the computer to her office as a backup computer and, before doing so, began to delete files. She opened a file marked Iraq and was flooded with dozens of digital photographs of naked prisoners. One stood out: a terrified young Iraqi standing in terror in front of a prison cell with both hands protecting his privates as two snarling Belgian shepherd dogs strain at their leashes a foot away. She heard my interview soon after and called me. She was hesitant at first about releasing the photos for use in *The New Yorker*, but in the end she agreed, and also agreed to get permission from her troubled daughter to do so. There was something else she wanted to tell me as I was about to leave. Every weekend after she returned from Iraq, her beautiful daughter would go to a tattoo parlor and darken her body with large black tattoos that eventually covered all that could be seen. It was as if, the mother said, she wanted to change her skin.

The Abu Ghraib exposé and my other work led to a book contract, and Amy Davidson, my editor at the magazine, was hired to weave new material I had and the stories I had done into *Chain of Command*, which was published in late 2004. It probably sold as many copies overseas as it did in America, which may not have been what the publisher had hoped for, but I sure liked the reviews. One, written by Michiko Kakutani, a daily reviewer for the *Times*, went straight to my heart: "And much of his post-9/11 reporting—which frequently provoked controversy and criticism when it first appeared—had since come to be accepted as conventional wisdom." I was pretty sure I would continue for the next few decades to provoke controversy and criticism, and it felt good to begin doing so with a clean slate, at least in her view. I always paid more attention to peer reviews, rather than sniping that invariably came from academics, and Jonathan Mirsky, a former editor for the London *Times*, complained, very nicely, in a review for *The Spectator*, "This is the only book I have reviewed that is impossible to summarize. It covers . . . much of which appeared in over 20 New Yorker stories. . . . All of this becomes a titanic—devastating is not a strong enough adjective—case against Washington and, by extension, London."

It would be wonderful to say that my reporting on Abu Ghraib changed the course of the war and ended torture, but of course nothing like that happened, just as the My Lai story had not ended the Vietnam War or its brutality. I stayed with the growing American-made mess in Iraq, the Middle East, and South Asia over the next few years, writing about

- a critically important change in American policy in the War on Terror, in which the Bush administration decided it would work with extremist Sunni groups in Saudi Arabia and elsewhere in the Middle East in an effort to add to the pressure on Shiite-dominated Iran, Hezbollah, and Alawite Syria. The March 2007 article, titled "The Redirection," was heavily reprinted for years;
- Dick Cheney's repeated but unfulfilled desire to attack Iran, which, as I insisted, to much incredulity from my colleagues in the media, was repeatedly found by the U.S. intelligence community not to have an ongoing nuclear weapons program;
- Pakistan's burgeoning nuclear weapons programs, which had Washington terrified to the extent that there were secret plans to take out its entire nuclear weapons complex in a crisis;
- Cheney and Bush's secret intelligence and arms support for the failed 2006 Israeli war against Hezbollah that was, as I wrote, a strategic setback for Israel, and one that diminished its ability to deter a future Arab attack;
- the September 2007 Israeli bombing attack on what it claimed was a nuclear reactor in Syria, and why the site might not have been what Israel said it was;
- similar American covert intelligence and arms support for the Israeli war against Hamas in the Gaza Strip in late 2008, just as Bush and Cheney were leaving office. That war ended on

January 19, 2009, after President-elect Obama privately warned Israel that if it was still under way at his inauguration the next day, he would publicly call for its end.

My reporting after 9/11 necessarily involved many trips to the Middle East and interviews with prominent leaders relatively unknown to most Americans, including President Bashar Assad of Syria and Sheik Hassan Nasrallah, the leader of Hezbollah, the Shiite militia invariably depicted in the U.S. media as the A-team of terrorist organizations.

My first interview with the tall, gangly Assad took place in 2003 in his downtown office in Damascus. He had been president for three years and clearly was uncertain about dealing with an American reporter. I asked my first question, and he responded by asking me, shyly, if it was all right if he gave me a detailed answer. I told him he was the president and it was his call, and then asked why he had raised the issue. He explained that he had been interviewed sometime earlier by Lally Weymouth, the journalist daughter of Katharine Graham, and she told him his answers were much too long. Because I was the first American journalist he had met with since, he wondered if there was some rule about the length of answers. I later asked Weymouth, who wrote often on foreign affairs for *The Washington Post*, about Assad's comment, and she vigorously denied telling the president, essentially, to shut up.

Assad had not supported the Bush/Cheney invasion of Iraq, as his father had done during the Bush family's far more successful first invasion in 1991, but the secular Syrian leader assured me that he supported America's war against al-Qaeda. He reminded me that he had issued a statement in support of America after 9/11, and further said he had supplied thousands of intelligence files on the Muslim Brotherhood in Hamburg to the American intelligence community, as well as operational details about a future al-Qaeda attack on the U.S. Fifth Fleet headquarters in Bahrain.

Once back in Washington, I confirmed that Assad's intelligence had been invaluable; I also learned that some in Washington were convinced the 9/11 attack had been planned in Hamburg. I further learned—Assad had not given me this detail—the planned attack on the Fifth Fleet called for a glider loaded with explosives to crash into a headquarters building at the base. It also turned out that a tip about Bahrain had come from an invaluable source inside al-Qaeda who was cooperating with Syrian intelligence. The CIA, which had been unable to develop any similar sources, began pressuring Assad, through the U.S. embassy in Damascus, to tell all there was to know about the source. Assad resisted for months but finally relented after being guaranteed that the CIA would make no effort to contact the source. Assad told me in a later interview that he was stunned to learn that the CIA had done precisely what it promised not to do—made a clumsy effort to recruit the source who responded by immediately breaking off all contact with Syrian intelligence. Assad urged me not to write about the double cross because, he explained, he hoped the Bush administration would come to realize that Syria, as a secular nation, could be an asset in the War on Terror.

One rarely discussed issue among journalists has to do with access; we of course tend to like those senior officials and leaders, such as Assad, who grant us interviews and speak openly with us. But access inevitably provokes ethical dilemmas. I met again with Assad in Damascus at eleven o'clock in the morning on February 14, 2005, and the immediate topic had to do with a dispute he was known to have had with Rafic Hariri, the prime minister of Lebanon. Syria then played a dominant role in Lebanon and controlled many aspects of its politics and military. Hariri, like all Lebanese prime ministers at the time, toed the line and followed Syria's demands, but Damascus was buzzing with gossip about the meeting. I began my talk with a much more comfortable and confident Assad by asking what was up with Hariri. The issue was money, Assad said. Syria was going into the cell phone business, an extremely high-profit activity, and everyone wanted in, including members of his family. Hariri's proposal was especially onerous, because he was insisting on controlling 70 percent of the profit. Even his greedy in-laws, Assad said, were offering a larger slice of the take. The issue had been resolved, he said, and Hariri had returned to Beirut. Corruption was of course endemic in the region. We moved on to the important geopolitical issues of the day.

An hour or so into our talk, an aide opened the door to Assad's office, but Assad waved him away before he said a word. A few moments later a ranking officer again opened the door, and Assad said he would be available soon. We talked another half an hour or so—Assad is fluent in English—and when I left, there was a huge array of senior government officials waiting outside the office. I did not learn for another hour that, as Assad and I continued to chat, Hariri had been assassinated by a bomb that killed twenty-one others near the Lebanese parliament building. Assad was an obvious suspect because of the public dispute with Hariri that immediately preceded the murder. I was convinced that there was no way Assad knew that Hariri was going to be killed, given his openness with me about the Hariri offer and why it was a nonstarter. I also knew that there was much I did not know, and it was possible that the timing of our interview, which had been scheduled weeks earlier, was deliberate. In other words, I might have been used to create an alibi for an assassination ordered by the Syrian president. I thought that was extremely unlikely, but despite some pressure from *The New Yorker,* I decided not to write about the interview. It was a tough call, and to my surprise the fact that I did not write about our meeting did not prevent me from having further interviews with Assad. He never raised the issue, and the Hariri assassination remains unsolved to this day.

My contact with the reclusive Nasrallah revolved around the American war in Iraq. The sheik was known to be close to the Shiite leadership in Iran, who were bitterly anti-American, and I had been urged in mid-2003 by August Hanning, the longtime head of Germany's federal intelligence service, the BND (for Bundesnachrichtendienst), to meet with him. Hanning told me during an interview at his home in Berlin that he had worked with Nasrallah and Ariel Sharon, Israel's hard-line prime minister, on a series of prisoner exchanges stemming from the chronic state of war between Hezbollah and Israel. I was stunned to learn of such contacts: Hezbollah was known to consider Israel an existential enemy and an illegal state, and Israel saw Hezbollah as a terrorist organization operating on its border. Of course the round, plump sheik was professional and affable when we first met, and I was flooded with tea and cookies and what seemed to be straight talk about Israel and the war. Nasrallah had an ironic sense of humor and constantly toyed with prayer beads as we talked, through an interpreter. I asked him at the outset what he would do if Palestinian authorities entered into a permanent peace agreement with Israel. His answer surprised me. "If there is a deal, let it happen," he said. "I would not say anything. I would say nothing. At the end of the road no one can go to war on behalf of the Palestinians, even if one is not in agreement with what the Palestinians agreed on."*

I interviewed the sheik three or four times over the next few years, and he was steadfast in his belief that there was no way America would win the war in Iraq. He also assured me that the Iraqi opposition would win control of the Iraqi parliament in the 2005 election there—all sides abused the process—two weeks before the disputed election results were made public. Predicting an election victory was one thing, but Nasrallah's prediction came within one-tenth of a point of the winning margin. I concluded there was much we Americans did not know about fixing elections. I also came away from my meetings with Assad and Nasrallah convinced that American presidents, driven by fear of criticism and worry about the unknown, were making a huge mistake in not dealing with both men.

Remnick was far more skeptical than I was of the integrity of Assad and Nasrallah, but he did not hesitate to publish the gist of my interviews. It was a vote of confidence in my judgment, and it made it easier for me to respect his. There was one story, after my Abu Ghraib series, that I wanted him to publish but he did not. I had been told in early 2005 by a senior CIA official of his distress at hearing a respected former CIA station chief brag to his colleagues over a drink about how he

* There was a moment, in one of my last interviews with Nasrallah, that stuck with me. The sheik was beloved by his English translator, a Hezbollah cadre who was always ecstatic to see me because it meant he would spend what he called "quality time" with the sheik. During the interview, which took place a few months after Hezbollah's 2006 war with Israel, Nasrallah told me of the financial support for rebuilding—Israeli bombing had turned Shiite areas of Beirut into a wasteland—that flowed from Iran and Qatar. Nasrallah then cited a figure of something like twelve million dollars in daily aid from Iran. At that point, the interpreter began a strident conversation with the sheik. Back and forth they went in Arabic. I finally interrupted to ask what in hell was going on. It turned out that the interpreter thought that Nasrallah had not been fully forthcoming in discussing the funds supplied by Iran, and without a hint of rancor Nasrallah gave me a shrug and a smile and then substantially upped the amount given. The interview came a few weeks after President Bush had ordered a high-level State Department official fired for daring to correct him during a national security meeting.

got a major high-value target in the War on Terror to talk. The target was an Indonesian-born terrorist, known to the U.S. intelligence community as Hambali, whose arrest in the late summer of 2003 had been publicly trumpeted by the Bush administration as a major success in the American War on Terror. Hambali's real name was Riduan Isamuddin, and he was said to be the al-Qaeda point man for research into biological warfare. CBS News and the *Chicago Tribune*, citing intelligence sources, eventually reported that when captured, he had been in the process of "implementing plans" for the spread of a biological weapon, perhaps anthrax.

The former station chief, who had been promoted to a key Agency position in Washington, explained that he had broken Hambali by placing a sackful of fire ants over his head. Within minutes, he said, "the whimpering and simpering" Hambali turned into "a vegetable." The distressed CIA official, in his account to me, said he had checked the most secret Agency files on Hambali and found no evidence for the allegations about biological warfare. He then reported the fire ant story to the Agency's top management. In response, he was insultingly ordered to take a lie detector test. He resigned immediately and said nothing about what he knew until a year later, when he sought me out. He could understand George W. Bush's political need to show success in the floundering War on Terror by exaggerating the importance of Hambali, but he could not understand why his peers and the top management had not been troubled, as he was, by the claimed use of fire ants in interrogation. (It was a torture that had been practiced by Apache, Comanche, and other Indian tribes in their nineteenth-century war with the U.S. Army for control of the West.)

It was an appalling story about a man who knew no limit. Remnick was as horrified as I was about the extent of American torture in the Iraqi war, but, as he told me, given the importance of the station chief, he was troubled by the fact that the main source did not want to be named, and more so by the fact that many of the station chief's peers had claimed, as I wrote, that the station chief was known as a chronic liar. I was convinced that the station chief's pals were rallying around him with a collective lie, and I later learned that was so from one of them, but I did not know it when David decided the story was too risky. This was not Abu Ghraib, where there was an abundance of on-the-record evidence, including photographs of Iraqi prisoners being subjected to sexual humiliation and General Taguba's internal report on the prison. David's concern was not solely about the magazine but about me—the reporter who had unraveled the Abu Ghraib mess. The fire ant story, which had been edited and put into galleys, did not run.

There was a later codicil. I had kept the CIA's office of public affairs aware of what I was planning to write, and learned that the Justice Department had chosen to declassify a 2002 legal memorandum on torture as we were editing the story. The memorandum authorized the use of insects during interrogation, as long as the prisoner was known to be afraid of insects and was informed "that the insects will not have a sting that would produce death or severe pain." The suggested insect was a caterpillar. Even that sleight of hand, alas, obviously meant to diminish my story, was not enough to justify publication. David was still right. There was a reason, I thought, God made editors.

One constant theme of my reporting dealt with the free rein that Bush, Cheney, and Rumsfeld had given the Joint Special Operations Commands in Iraq and elsewhere. I ran into a wave of anger when, during a Q and A with former vice president Walter Mondale of Minnesota, who had served on the Church Committee when in the Senate, I was quoted complaining about what I called an "executive assassination ring" that was in place during much of the Iraqi war. I usually tried to let what I publish speak for me on provocative issues such as assassination—most Americans chose to remain innocent about such a reality—but there was, as I explained to an appropriately annoyed Remnick, a special circumstance in this case. My talk with Mondale had been scheduled months in advance as part of a foreign policy series at the University of Minnesota, where Mondale taught. I arrived in Minneapolis midmorning for the evening event, just as snow began to fall. By early evening, Minneapolis had been clobbered by snow and was at a standstill, but the show went on—before fewer than a hundred of the many hundreds who subscribed to the series. Mondale had become radicalized about the U.S. intelligence community by the seamy stuff he learned on the Church Committee, and he urged all in the audience to gather close to the stage as we chatted. The former vice president was very outspoken and angry about the abuses that I had been writing about. It was in that spirit I mentioned the existence of an American assassination ring. I knew more than I could say, which turned out to be a good thing. Ten months after 9/11 I had obtained a package of classified internal documents that were responses from various Pentagon offices to an astonishing question that had been poised by Donald Rumsfeld: How could America organize itself more efficiently for what he called "Manhunts"—the assassination of enemies? One special operations group responded by urging that the American military end its requirement for "actionable intelligence"—that is, evidence that the victim was the right target—and be "willing to take greater risks." America's military, said the special ops group, "must accept that we may have to take action before every question can be answered . . . This denies us the ability and tactical surprise so necessary for manhunts, snatches, and retribution raids." Knowing of such thinking helped shape my reporting, but at the time I did not publish the documents I had, in fear of exposing the source. Sure enough, someone in the audience was recording my remarks on a cell phone and wrote a blog item about them on the internet. Not a big deal, I initially thought—Mondale had agreed with my choice of words—but the blog went viral, and there was an immediate outcry about my allegation of a murder ring, which was comical given the extensive and consistent reporting I had done on that issue in *The New Yorker*.

By 2005, the brilliant Amy Davidson had been my editor for more than a year, and she responded to the criticism with a long essay, "Close Read," for *The New Yorker*'s internet page. In the piece she summarized much of what I had written about murder in the War on Terror. Even I, who had done the reporting and writing, was amazed by the amount of specific detail that had been published.

Davidson reviewed the many articles in the magazine I had written between late 2001 and 2008 in which I told how cold-blooded murder had become standard practice in the combat zone. The first, published within weeks of 9/11, quoted what I called a "C.I.A. man" as espousing the need to consider tactics that "defy the American rule of law. . . . We need to do this—knock them down one by one." In late 2002, I exposed the targeted assassination of an al-Qaeda leader whose demise had been approved by President Bush, although such killings had been expressly barred by President Ford in the wake of the Church hearings of 1975. I ended the article by quoting an experienced Pentagon consultant: "We've created a culture in the Special Forces—twenty- and twenty-one-year-olds who need adult leadership. They're assuming you've got legal authority, and they'll do it"—eagerly eliminate any target assigned to them. Eventually, the intelligence will be bad, he said, and innocent people will be killed. "And then they'll get hung." In late 2003, I depicted assassination as a standard tactic in Iraq, as what seemed to be a quick U.S. victory over the insurgents, many of them former members of the disbanded Iraqi army, had become far less likely. I quoted a former intelligence official as saying that when American Special Forces target an insurgent for death, "it's technically not assassination—it's normal combat operations." In a third article on Abu Ghraib in 2004, depicting assassination as part of the backdrop of the prison scandal, I quoted an official as saying, "The rules are 'Grab whom you must. Do what you want.'" (I also revealed in that article the existence of what became known as "black sites," undeclared American torture prisons in Europe and Asia that were operating in stringent secrecy, with no congressional funding or knowledge.) By early 2005, with the Iraqi war going badly and violence on the rise, I revealed a high-level order that "specifically authorized the military 'to find and finish' terrorist targets. . . . It included a target list that cited Al Qaeda network members, Al Qaeda senior leadership, and other high-value targets. . . . [T]he order further quoted an official as asking, pointedly, "Do you remember the right-wing execution squads in El Salvador?" He added, "And we aren't going to tell Congress about it."

As the Bush administration finished its eight years in office, I quoted "a recently retired high-level C.I.A. official" who told of bitter disagreements between the White House and the Agency over the issue of targeted assassination. "The problem is what constituted approval," the former CIA man said. "My people fought about this all the time. Why should we put our people on the firing line somewhere down the road? If you want me to kill Joe Smith, just tell me to kill Joe Smith. If I was the Vice-President or the President, I'd say, 'This guy Smith is a bad guy and it's in the interest of the United States for this guy to be killed.' They don't say that. Instead, George"—George Tenet, the director of the CIA until mid-2004—"goes to the White House and is told, 'You guys are professionals. You know how important it is. We know you'll get the intelligence.' George would come back and say to us: 'Do what you gotta do.'"

BEING AN INVESTIGATIVE REPORTER became far more compli-cated after Israel's disastrous war with Hezbollah in 2006. The war had gone badly for Israel, I wrote, despite significant advance support and intelligence from the Bush administration, very little of which was known to the public. Bush and Cheney had hoped that the Israeli attack on Lebanon, with its targeting of Hezbollah's underground missile and command-and-control complexes, would serve as a model for a preemptive U.S. attack on what was believed to be Iran's under-ground nuclear installations. The disappointing Israeli attack was far more costly than the mainstream American press reported. My arti-cle quoted Richard Armitage, an experienced navy veteran who had served as deputy undersecretary of state in Bush's first term, as saying, "If the most dominant military force in the region—the Israel Defense Force—can't pacify a country like Lebanon, with a population of four million, you should think carefully about taking that template to Iran, with strategic depth and a population of seventy million. The only thing that the bombing [of Lebanon] has achieved so far is to unite the population against the Israelis."

A year later Israeli warplanes flew into Syrian airspace to attack and destroy what the Israeli government claimed was a nuclear reac-tor under construction. There was no official acknowledgment of the attack, although newspapers there were flooded with leaks insisting that the reactor was nearing completion—ready to start up—when struck. Israel also made no effort to produce photographic or other evidence that the target indeed was a reactor, as it had done after its successful bombing in 1981 of an Iraqi nuclear reactor under construc-tion at Osirik, twelve miles southeast of Baghdad.

I flew to Damascus a few weeks after the bombing in 2007 and interviewed President Bashar Assad, foreign minister Walid Muallam, and a senior Syrian intelligence official. I was told that Syria did not have the funds or expertise to invest in a nuclear weapons program and, if it had, a reactor would not have been located in the desert to the northwest, near a major archaeological dig and close to the borders of Turkey and Iraq, two hostile regimes, with the prevailing winds blowing toward Damascus. I also was told, with no proof offered, that the structure bombed by Israel was to be used for upgrading low-range rockets and missiles.

I had met often with Assad by late 2007 and found that his factual assertions, including off-the-record statements about the sharing of intelligence with the CIA, invariably checked out. Assad told me he was stunned when Bush's response to his intelligence help in the aftermath of 9/11 was to include Syria as an ally in the President's famed "axis of evil"—Iran, Iraq, North Korea. Despite that, Assad continued to hold out hope, he said, for a better relationship with Washington.

Before flying to Syria, I had learned from my sources in Washington that there was a dispute inside the American intelligence community over the validity of the Israeli target. Some thought the intent of the Israeli mission had nothing to do with the alleged reactor, but was meant to reestablish Israel's military credibility in the wake of its disappointing war against Hezbollah the year before. I also showed that many of the specific assertions in support of the Israeli claim, such as the freight ship allegedly used to bring nuclear materials to Syria, were not correct. (In the decade since the attack America and Israel have made repeated allegations about the existence of a chemical warfare capability in Syria, but have said nothing further about a Syrian nuclear weapons program.)

I was not surprised when my skeptical article, replete with specific points of conflict, led to no further reporting on the issue. But there was a new element in the media's indifference to a complicated contrary account. The Israeli version of the attack and its endorsement by the Bush administration had been accepted without question by the American cable news networks, whose around-the-clock unquestioning news coverage was more and more becoming a dominant point of view. There were many reasons to be skeptical of the Israeli and American certitude. Israel was a nation that was still denying the existence of a nuclear arsenal that all knew exists, and the Bush administration's credibility had been eviscerated after its prewar insistence that there were WMDs in Iraq. I had also researched the cargo ship that, so Israel later insisted, had delivered nuclear supplies to Syria and reported that the vessel could not have done what Israel claimed it had. I watched over the next years as the American media, overwhelmed by twenty-four-hour news, would increasingly rely in a crisis on the immediate claims of a White House and a politically compliant intelligence community. Skepticism, the instinct that drives much investigative reporting, would diminish even more after Barack Obama, full of hope and promise, took office in early 2009.

Obama came into the White House talking of changes domestically and, more important to me, in foreign policy. I had learned late in 2008 that Bashar Assad was engaged in serious talks with Ehud Olmert, the Israeli prime minister, over regaining Syria's Golan Heights, whose western two-thirds had been seized and occupied by Israel in the 1967 Six-Day War. At one point, in early December, I knew Olmert had flown to Ankara and held a five-hour discussion with Turkish prime minister Recep Tayyip Erdogan, who was often in telephone contact with Assad. Those secret talks blew apart when Olmert authorized the Israeli military attack on Gaza City a few weeks later.

I spent the next six weeks talking to senior officials in the Middle East, Europe, and Washington about prospects for a renewed peace agreement in the Middle East—one that would end the impasse over the Golan Heights and bring Syria back into the mainstream. Assad told me he was eager to meet with Obama and engage with the West. The implicit understanding was that Syria's supportive relationship with Iran and Hezbollah, as well as with Hamas, the political party that ruled in Gaza, would have to change. I was surprised to find that it was no easier to get senior officials of the incoming Obama administration to talk to me, although the President-elect and his men had no hesitation to deal with those reporters inclined to parrot what they were told. There was a lot of chatter about a new era in foreign policy, but it did not happen as the months rolled by and Obama agreed to a dramatic increase in the number of American troops in Afghanistan. It seemed clear to me that once in office Obama was unwilling to take the risks he needed to take to change America's foreign policy.

Despite his cautious start, the world was in a better place with Obama in office, and I was tired and in need of a change after nearly eight years of working against the Bush/Cheney combine. There was another consideration: As much as I liked and respected Remnick, I was troubled by what I saw as his closeness to Barack Obama during the 2008 presidential campaign and the fact that he was planning to write a biography of him. I had learned over the years never to trust the declared aspirations of any politician and was also enough of a prude to believe that editors should not make friends with a sitting president.

It wasn't fair to David, or to me, to have such doubts, and it was time to move on. I had a standing offer to do a book about the Cheney years, and through my agent I made an agreement with Sonny Mehta, the chairman and editor in chief of Knopf, to do so. Jonathan Segal would be the editor. David was gracious about it. Parting was easy; we'd had a great run together, and we agreed I would stay alert for a good story. As with Abe Rosenthal, it did not take long before I was back at work for the magazine. I wrote a very tough article late in 2009 dealing with America's continuing effort to prevent a renewed India-Pakistan dispute from turning ugly, and nuclear. I had spent weeks in Pakistan and India reporting on the story and learned of some serious disconnects in the U.S.-Pakistan relationship. There would be hell to pay, and a violent American response, if the Pakistani leadership began arming its nuclear weapons in a crisis.

The story was checked with senior officials in the State Department and the White House who, as usual, had no comment for the record but privately took issue, to put it mildly, with much of what I wrote. The usual official denial had come from the Pentagon, too, but on the day before the magazine was going to press, David called me to say that a senior military officer had contacted him and urged that the article not be published as initially edited. One of my findings, if made public, could create dangerous rioting in front of the American embassy in Islamabad, Pakistan's capital, and at consulates scattered throughout the nation. Unless we were willing to make some significant changes, David was told, the State Department was going to ask that all U.S. foreign service dependents leave Pakistan immediately. This was pretty strong stuff for a story that earlier had drawn nothing but official denials. Of course I agreed to alter the story; any reporter would.

I cite this incident because it had to be obvious to David that I had sources in Pakistan and inside Washington who were reliable on what was, and remains, a major security issue for the United States—what to do about the Pakistani nuclear arsenal. Flash forward two years and President Obama's dramatic announcement in the spring of 2011 that bin Laden had been killed while hiding out in a Pakistani village north of Islamabad. The killing was a huge boost for the President's reelection chances, and the administration, as would any administration, played it to the utmost. I heard within days from inside Pakistan that there was a far more complicated reality, which involved the Obama administration working closely on bin Laden's assassination with the Pakistani intelligence service, the ISI, which had kept bin Laden imprisoned for years. I took the information I had to an American source and doubled up on how much I learned. The administration had killed bin Laden, no question about that, but much of what the White House had been telling reporters after the fact was not true. I went to David with the information, and he surprised me by asking if I would work with another reporter on the story; he was a new hire who happened to be in Pakistan. It was a first, but I said sure. A few weeks went by; the other reporter was not coming up with much—I could not give him the name of my Pakistani sources—and David told me he did not think I had enough reliable data for a story. I had done more reporting than he knew and wrote him a long memo summarizing what I planned to research and write. I got an email back saying that he was worried about my reliance on "the same old tired source." I was astonished; the tired source in question, as David and other editors and many fact-checkers at the magazine knew, had helped put *The New Yorker*'s reportage on the War on Terror in the forefront for the past decade.

Okay, I thought, he doesn't want the story now, but there were many stories he did not initially want that were published eventually. I went on a ten-day hiking vacation in Europe with my wife and, on the way back, sent David a long email from Frankfurt outlining what I had and what I was going to write. When I returned to Washington, David called and, after ominously telling me not to get upset, told me that a long inside report on the raid, from the point of view of the SEALs who did the mission, and the killing, was going to be published in the next edition of the magazine. He added that I was not to worry, that the story would not impinge in any way on what I was planning to write. He did not offer to send the piece to me in advance of publication, nor did I ask to see it. I learned from inside the magazine that John Brennan, then Obama's counterintelligence adviser, and Denis McDonough, the deputy national security director, had spent much time on the telephone with the fact-checkers verifying the details in the piece.

I was enraged—perhaps more hurt than angry—and I immediately wrote David a letter of resignation, saying that he did not need me to spell out why I was leaving. David telephoned me within minutes to urge me not to be so rash, saying again that he did not think I "had" the story and he was open to publishing it when I did. The underlying implication, so I thought, was that I owed him that much respect, given our years together. What the hell, I thought. We had done much together, and it had been a good ride. I also knew from experience that investigative reporters wear out their welcome; it had happened to me at the AP and at the *Times*. Editors get tired of difficult stories and difficult reporters. I did not resign but returned to my book on Cheney, and did not read the alleged inside story of the raid, as published, for a year.

I put together the first section of the Cheney book, which was based on many hundreds of interviews with variously involved officials and former officials, none of them cited by name, and began running into serious source problems. Writing a magazine story here and there was one thing, but a book full of secrets that was based on interviews with players still involved inside the intelligence and military communities posed a high risk of legal action, especially because Obama was cracking down as no other recent president had done on leaks. It was also a fact that a book full of quotes from those who could not be named was more than a little problematical. And so I went back to the ineluctable bin Laden story. The story, as finally written, ran more than ten thousand words, and I sent it, as promised, to David. He responded quickly, and acknowledged that there was much that was compelling in the story, but told me that without having someone on the record, it would not hold up. I am convinced he believed what he said when he said it, but I could not help but recall the dozens of articles I had written for the magazine that were devoid of even one on-the-record source.

The fact we had captured bin Laden with the support of the generals who ran Pakistani intelligence and then betrayed them was too important to be left unsaid. And so I published my bin Laden story many months later in the *London Review of Books* (*LRB*), after another intensive round of fact-checking by two former checkers from *The New Yorker*. The story got a good deal of attention, but I was not surprised by the refusal, or the inability, of the press to follow up on the vital aspect of my story—the double cross of Pakistan. The media focused, as I feared would happen, not on what I wrote but on why it wasn't in *The New Yorker*. The possibility that two dozen navy SEALs could escape observation and get to bin Laden without some help from the Pakistani military and intelligence communities was nil, but the White House press corps bought the story. Twenty-four-hour cable news was devouring the news-reporting business, TV panelist by TV panelist.

While continuing to work on the suddenly problematical Cheney book, I wrote three more long articles between 2013 and 2015 for the *LRB*, focused on the burgeoning civil war in Syria and the Obama administration's continued support, in secret, for the jihadist opposition to the Bashar Assad government. I also raised serious questions about the Obama administration's public certitude that a 2013 sarin attack near Damascus was the work of the Assad government. What the American public had not been told, I wrote, was that the U.S. intelligence community had determined earlier—I had a copy of the highly secret report—that the radical jihadist opposition in Syria also had access to the nerve agent. There were two suspects for the use of sarin, but the American public was told only of one. It was not Obama's finest moment.*

In the last week of 2014, I did what I had resisted doing for more

---

* David Obey would not have been surprised by Obama's waffling. I stayed in touch with the former chairman of the House Appropriations Committee after his retirement in 2011, and he told me of a leadership meeting with the President in early 2009, a few months after Obama took office, dealing with the war in Afghanistan, which was continuing to go badly. The issue was whether the President should authorize a significant increase in the American military presence there. Obey and Vice President Biden were the only two to voice any skepticism. Obey recalled warning Obama that if he authorized the troop surge,

than four decades and made my first visit, *en famille*, to My Lai. After the war, I had been asked many times by the Vietnamese government to do so, and I wasn't sure I could handle it. I had traveled to Hanoi two times after the massacre and had rebuffed efforts then to get me to make a visit. The reason I usually cited was the notion that I had earned enough fame and profit from the massacre, but there was a darker reason: There were things that were done at that village that I did not write about and do not want to remember. But after forty-five years, amid a complete lack of interest in my return by the Communist government in power, I gave in to constant entreaties by my wife, children, dog, cat, gerbil, and pet mouse and returned, as a *New Yorker* title for the subsequently published piece put it, to "The Scene of the Crime." My political disagreements with Remnick paled against the knowledge that he is a superb editor who would make sure I did not get too mawkish or self-serving in writing about the visit.

There is an excellent museum on the site of the slaughter and its director, Pham Thanh Cong, now in his fifties, was a survivor of the massacre. He was eager to meet me, and I was just as eager to finally meet a survivor. He was full of stock phrases when first addressing our group, which included my family and a few close friends, explaining the Vietnamese were "a welcoming people" and "We forgive, but we do not forget." After a tour, he and I sat on a bench and I told him a few things I knew and had not written about the massacre and asked him to describe exactly what he remembered from the time when he was eleven years old. When the shooting started, he said, his mother and four siblings had huddled in terror inside a bunker in their thatch-roof

---

he would have "to face the fact that it would crowd out large portions of your domestic program—except perhaps health care." Obey remained after the meeting to have a private word with the President and asked him whether he had listened to the broadcasts of Lyndon Johnson's telephone conversations about the wisdom of expanding the Vietnam War, which had been made public in 2003, creating a sensation in Washington. Obama said he had. Did the President recall listening to Johnson's conversation with Richard Russell, the conservative chairman of the Armed Services Committee, in which both men acknowledged that adding more American troops there would not help the war effort and could lead to a disastrous war with China? Obama again said yes. Obey then asked, "Who's your George Ball?" Ball, a senior State Department official in the Kennedy administration, repeatedly argued against escalating the American presence in Vietnam; it was a stand that hurt his reputation among the men around Kennedy. "Either the President chose not to answer, or he didn't have one," Obey told me. "But I didn't hear anyone tell the President that he ought to put the brakes on in Afghanistan." Obama authorized the deployment of thirty thousand more American troops to the war over the next six months.

home. A group of GIs ordered them out—perhaps they were looking for military-age men—and then pushed them back inside. A hand grenade was thrown and Cong passed out. When he awoke, he was surrounded by corpses. I knew there was more, much more, and, ignoring his comment about passing out, I asked him what he had seen the soldiers do to his mother and his teenage sister. His suddenly hardened face told me I had gone too far. He did acknowledge, however, that he welcomed those Americans who participated in the attack and made the pilgrimage to the museum, but he had no interest in easing the pain of those few who claimed little memory of the event and expressed no remorse for what they had done. I do not know why I needed to make him drop his mask, if only for a few moments, but I was glad he did. There can be no forgiveness, in my view, for what took place at My Lai.

It eventually became clear that I had to give up the Cheney project, at least in the short term. The draft of the book contained much secret information, and I could not justify risking the careers of those who had helped me since 9/11 and earlier. It was time to write this memoir.

While doing so, I took time to challenge the widespread perception that Bashar Assad had used a nerve agent two months earlier against his own people in a contested province in opposition-held Syria. The article, which was taken by many to be an ad hoc defense of the hated Assad and the Russians who supported him, and not the truth as I found it, worried Mary-Kay Wilmers, the wonderful editor of the *LRB*, to the point where she delayed publication until I could produce a particular fact—one that was irrelevant, in my view, as well as far too secret to get. I decided not to wait and took my information to *Welt am Sonntag*, the popular Sunday edition of *Die Welt*, the German newspaper run by the sure-footed Stefan Aust, who had edited *Der Spiegel* for years, and was always receptive to my work. Aust sent a colleague to Washington to do some critical fact-checking and also had a team of editors go over the story line by line, as must be done, before publishing it in June 2017.

In an early 2018 news conference at the Pentagon, Defense Secretary James Mattis, when asked about newly revived reports of nerve gas use in Syria by the Assad government, diverted from the previously stated American position that such had happened and said, "We do not have evidence of it." Syria's earlier use of nerve gas, he said, without saying when, gave "us a lot of reason to suspect them." But, Mattis added, "I have not got the evidence, not specifically. . . . Fighters on the ground have said that sarin has been used, so we are looking for evidence . . . credible or uncredible." Mattis's careful statement was significant and little noticed.

I did not relish being the odd man out in terms of writing stories that conflicted with the accepted accounts, but it was a familiar experience. My initial reporting on My Lai, Watergate, Kissinger, Jack Kennedy, and the American murder of Osama bin Laden was challenged, sometimes very bitterly. I will happily permit history to be the judge of my recent work.

I grew up in a world where the incentive to learn came from within me, as did a sense of whom to trust and whom to believe. I was guided as a confused and uncertain eighteen-year-old by a professor who saw potential in me, as did Carroll Arimond at the Associated Press, William Shawn at *The New Yorker*, and Abe Rosenthal at *The New York Times*. They published what I wrote without censorship and reaffirmed my faith in trusting those in the military and intelligence world whose information, and friendship, I valued but whose names I could never utter. I found my way when it came to issues of life and death in war to those special people who had the integrity and intelligence to carefully distinguish between what they knew—from firsthand observation at the center—from what they believed. The trust went two ways: I often obtained documents I could not use for fear of inadvertently exposing the sources, and there were stories I dared not write for the same reason.

I never did an interview without learning all I could about the person with whom I was meeting, and I did all I could to let those I was criticizing or putting in professional jeopardy know just what I was planning to publish about them.

I will return to the Cheney book when the time is right, and when those who helped me learn what I did after 9/11 will not be in peril. Meanwhile, we have a Donald Trump presidency; allegations of Russian involvement in the 2016 election; a Middle East in its usual disarray, with the apparent end of ISIS. There will always be much to do, and some magical moments along the way.

One came in the mid-1990s, as I was gathering material for my book on Jack Kennedy. I wrote to Cardinal John J. O'Connor, the archbishop of New York, and asked to meet with him about his most famous and controversial predecessor, Cardinal Francis Spellman, a good friend of Kennedy's who served as archbishop from 1939 until his death in 1967. I got an appointment almost immediately.

O'Connor was a major player in the world of New York. He was hostile to abortion, contraception, and homosexuality while being a fierce critic of unjust war, human trafficking, and those who opposed labor unions. He had served for years as a navy chaplain during the Korean War and repeatedly risked his life on the battlefield to give last rites to mortally wounded American soldiers. He ended his clerical career in the military as a rear admiral and chief of navy chaplains. I wondered if he knew of my reporting on My Lai and, if so, whether he would hold it against me.

O'Connor's office at St. Patrick's Cathedral on Fifth Avenue was spare, but the Archbishop was a delight. We traded stories on background about Spellman, and at one point he gestured toward one of the steel filing cabinets in his office and said that when he'd first arrived in New York one of the cabinet drawers was sealed. "Well," O'Conner told me with a laugh, "the first thing I did was call in a workman and get it opened. Inside was a wrapped package, also sealed, with a rope around it and a note saying, 'Not to be opened by anyone. Cardinal Spellman.' So I opened it. Hersh, it was fascinating. Full of letters." He laughed again as I practically leaped off my chair in anticipation, and then he told me that the papers would never be seen: "I had them sent to the Vatican archives."

He asked about reporting, and I asked about running a huge enterprise like the Catholic Church in New York. His secretary interrupted after forty-five minutes and again after an hour. He ignored her until she opened the door to the office and made it clear he was being rude. I got up to leave, and O'Connor walked me outside. It was a sunny, warm, early spring day, and as we approached the front door he threw an arm around me, pulled me close, and said, "My son, God has put you on earth for a reason, and that is to do the kind of work you do, no matter how much it upsets others. It is your calling."

Of course he knew what I had done at My Lai, and he was telling me that he was okay with it. I walked down Fifth Avenue blinking away tears, thinking that a belief as powerful as his was a profound and wonderful gift. The cardinal was diagnosed with brain cancer a few years later and passed away in 2000, but we exchanged letters on and off until then. I saved his.

Another special moment came in 2004 after I had a chat about the White House's War on Terror over lunch in Berlin with Joschka Fischer, Germany's foreign minister. Fischer had studied Marxism as a radical student leader in the late 1960s and the 1970s and led many violent street protests, but later emerged as a leader of Germany's Green Party as it moved to the center of German politics. He was brilliant, full of himself, and willing to be extremely caustic about America and its politics as long as we were chatting—make that gossiping—on background. We agreed it would be okay if there was something I wanted to use in *The New Yorker* and did not cite him by name. We talked about the Bush administration's ambitions in the Middle East, and Fischer described Paul Wolfowitz, Don Rumsfeld's influential and very conservative deputy secretary of defense, as a "Trotskyite"—one who believes in permanent revolution. In a subsequent piece for *The New Yorker*, I quoted a senior foreign diplomat in Europe as depicting Wolfowitz as a Trotskyite. Fischer was called by a fact-checker and read the phrase, a routine check. He then insisted that I immediately call him in Berlin. I did and assured him there was no way the quote could be linked to him: It did not cite him by name, did not mention Germany, and did not say the phrase came from a foreign minister. "But I'm the only diplomat in Europe who would understand what a Trotskyite is," he said. When I stopped laughing, I assured him we would take out the line.

It's a wonderful business, this profession of mine. I've spent most of my career writing stories that challenge the official narrative, and have been rewarded mightily and suffered only slightly for it. I wouldn't have it any other way.

Acknowledgments

I was convinced that I would never write a memoir until I was too old and infirm to drive a car or hit a tennis ball, and perhaps not then. The flap about my Cheney project, mentioned briefly in these pages, changed that, and here we are. I am thankful to Sonny Mehta and Jonathan Segal of Knopf for their forbearance and to my very heady literary agent, Esther Newberg, who led me out of the morass into this book. Jon Segal's early years as a writer and an editor for *The New York Times* gave him invaluable insight and a point of view that kept me focused on what was important in the business of being a good reporter. He insisted, again and again, that I tell why, and not just how, I did what I did.

Doing it turned out to be fun—who doesn't like writing about him or herself?—and it also assuaged my guilt at not wanting to teach investigative journalism or accept an appointment or chair in such at a university. I've tried to be as open as possible in telling how I did it. I remain convinced that the key to being a good reporter and getting the story is, as I said in these pages, to read before you write, and especially before you do an interview.

I apologize for the fact that only a few of my sources over fifty years in the business are named, but that is a necessity when one is focused on secret operations and secret lies. Of course every senior journalist in the profession understands the dilemma.

I've been aided by a bunch of wonderful researchers who constantly went beyond what I needed and cared about getting things as right as possible. And so thank you Max Paul Friedman, Bill Arkin, Jay

Peterzell, Benjamin Frankel, Mark Feldstein, and Gil Shochat. I also thank Thomas Lannon, a curator at the New York Public Library, for his much-needed help in guiding me through the library's extensive collection of the Abe Rosenthal papers, which cover his fifty-six-year career at *The New York Times*. Jeffrey Roth of the *Times* provided more photos from days gone by than I could use, and the staff of the newspaper's licensing group, including Gregory Miller, Kymberli Wilner, and Phyllis Collazo, produced the many too many reprints of articles and magazine covers I requested. All of this was done gratis at the direction of Dean Baquet, the executive editor of the *Times*. I thank all.

My wife and children loved me, laughed with and at me, and always felt free to tell me I was full of it. Nothing is more important.

Index

ALLEN LANE
an imprint of
PENGUIN BOOKS

Also Published

Justin Marozzi, *Islamic Empires: Fifteen Cities that Define a Civilization*

Bruce Hood, *Possessed: Why We Want More Than We Need*

Frank Close, *Trinity: The Treachery and Pursuit of the Most Dangerous Spy in History*

Janet L. Nelson, *King and Emperor: A New Life of Charlemagne*

Richard M. Eaton, *India in the Persianate Age: 1000-1765*

Philip Mansel, *King of the World: The Life of Louis XIV*

James Lovelock, *Novacene: The Coming Age of Hyperintelligence*

Mark B. Smith, *The Russia Anxiety: And How History Can Resolve It*

Stella Tillyard, *George IV: King in Waiting*

Donald Sassoon, *The Anxious Triumph: A Global History of Capitalism, 1860-1914*

Elliot Ackerman, *Places and Names: On War, Revolution and Returning*

Johny Pits, *Afropean: Notes from Black Europe*

Jonathan Aldred, *Licence to be Bad: How Economics Corrupted Us*

Walt Odets, *Out of the Shadows: Reimagining Gay Men's Lives*

Jonathan Rée, *Witcraft: The Invention of Philosophy in English*

Jared Diamond, *Upheaval: How Nations Cope with Crisis and Change*

Emma Dabiri, *Don't Touch My Hair*

Srecko Horvat, *Poetry from the Future: Why a Global Liberation Movement Is Our Civilisation's Last Chance*

Paul Mason, *Clear Bright Future: A Radical Defence of the Human Being*